Understanding Homeowners 2000

Dearborn Career Development

The information contained herein is provided to assist you in your efforts to learn about the ISO 2000 edition of the Homeowners Policy. This program is designed to provide accurate and authoritative information in regard to the subject matter. It is sold with the understanding that the program is not engaged in rendering of legal, accounting or professional services. If professional advice is required, the services of a competent professional should be sought. Any names appearing in this publication are fictional and have no relationship to any person living or dead.

This text is updated periodically to reflect changes in laws and regulations. To verify that you have the most recent update, you may call Dearborn at 1-800-423-4723.

Library of Congress Cataloging-in-Publication Data

Understanding Homeowners 2000.
    p. cm.
 ISBN 0-7931-6054-5 (pbk.)
 1. Homeowner's insurance—United States.   2. Homeowner's
insurance—United States—Forms.   I. Dearborn Financial Publishing.   II.
Insurance Services Office (U.S.)   III. Title.
 HG9986.3.U533 2003
 368'.096'076—dc21   2003012505

••••• Table of Contents

▪▪▪▪▪ **Acknowledgements**

T he publisher would like to acknowledge the following individuals for their contributions to the development of this text:

- Kim Allen Baker, MBA, CPCU

- Denise Iona, Inkslinger Research and Writing Services, Inc.

Lynda Nordling,
Director of Property and Casualty

▪ ▪ ▪ ▪ ▪

■■■■■ Permissions

 his course includes copyrighted and proprietary material of Insurance Services Office, Inc., with its permission. Copyright, Insurance Services Office, Inc., 2000.

ISO does not guarantee the accuracy or timeliness of the ISO information provided. ISO shall not be liable for any loss or damage of any kind and howsoever caused resulting from your use of the ISO information.

■ ■ ■ ■ ■

■■■■■ Introduction

■ **COURSE OVERVIEW**

The purpose of this course is to provide an in-depth review of the new Insurance Services Office (ISO) Homeowners Policy, October 2000 edition.

This course will provide students with a comprehensive overview of the need for homeowners coverage and enhance their ability to apply this knowledge in sales, underwriting and claims decisions. Expertise on this subject will help insurance professionals provide better advice and service to their clients.

Throughout this course, we will use a number of real-life examples and key points to underscore the important coverages, exclusions and limitations of the Homeowners Policy. These examples will enhance the learning experience by providing practical illustrations of how to apply homeowners coverages in the marketplace.

■ **COURSE OBJECTIVES**

When you complete this course, you should be able to

- explain the situations that create property exposures for an insured;

- explain the situations that create liability exposures for an insured;

- describe the coverages the homeowners policy provides;

- describe homeowners policy exclusions;

- determine the appropriate use of the various homeowners policy forms;

- determine how the limits apply under the various homeowners policy forms; and

- explain the conditions and definitions the homeowners policy contains.

■ POLICY LEARNING VERIFICATION PROCESS

To make your study more effective, we have included a systematic learning verification process with these exclusive features.

ISO Form References

Dearborn has structured its P & C courses to teach student how to use policy forms to understand and verify coverages. This course examines the current Insurance Services Office, Inc. (ISO) forms for each line of insurance being explained.

- *ISO Form Excerpts*—These quotes from the forms show you policy language relevant to the content being explained. The excerpts are a good way to reinforce the concepts treated in the course by examining the exact language of the ISO forms as the course progresses.

- *Sample Forms*—The Appendix contains the complete text of any form quoted in the body of the course.

ISO Form Updates

Throughout the course, material that represents a significant change from the previous form edition is marked as an ISO Form Update using the icon at left. Simple differences from current and previous editions are handled in a sentence or two. More complex changes are handled through charts with policy comparisons, detailed explanations and clear examples.

Reference Charts/ISO Comparison Charts

This course also offers two comparison charts, a form comparison for Sections I and II and Endorsements for the HO 2000 Program and a comparison of the HO-3 1991 and 2000 forms. You will find the charts in the Appendix. They are an excellent reference tool.

■ COURSE FEATURES

To make your study effective, we have included the following distinctive features in this course.

Key Points

When a concept is important to the understanding of a process or principle, it is introduced with the icon at left.

Real Life Application

Real Life Applications and Questions

We use a number of scenarios to help you apply concepts to everyday issues. Many of these scenarios include questions that reinforce the course instruction discussed in the scenario. The icon shown on the left identifies a scenario as a Real-Life Application. Answers to any questions following the hypothetical appear in footnotes at the bottom of the same page. Question numbers are consecutive within a chapter.

Study Questions

Study Questions

There are questions at intervals in each of the chapters. These questions provide an immediate check of understanding of important concepts. In some instances, you will find *Additional Study Questions* at the end of a chapter. The icon shown at left identifies a Study Question. You will find the answers to in-line questions in footnotes at the bottom of the same page. Answers to *Additional Study Questions* appear on the last page of a chapter.

Review Test

The 25-Question Review Test supplied with this text provides non-CE and firm element learning verification. It helps you prepare for the state CE exam if you are taking this course for CE credit.

State Continuing Education Exam

If you have not already done so, you can obtain a 50-question exam by ordering from Dearborn Customer Service at 1-800-824-8742. Instructions about monitoring and proctoring the exam are available on the outside of the exam package.

1

Homeowners Policies:
An Overview

A person's house, furniture, clothing and other personal belongings represent substantial financial investments. Unfortunately, property owners are exposed to *risk* (the chance of financial loss) either because something may happen or may not happen.

Property owners face three basic types of risks that may cause financial loss:

- direct physical damage to property caused by perils such as fire, wind, water and smoke;

- property loss because of robbery, burglary, vandalism or arson; and

- liability risk or a legal responsibility for the financial cost of another person's injuries or damage to another's property.

The most common method of dealing with these risks is to transfer them to an insurance company by purchasing a homeowners policy. A property owner once had to buy separate insurance coverage for fire, theft and other risks, but the insurance industry has developed a series of homeowners insurance policies that package property and liability coverage together. Most dwellings are now covered under homeowners policies that combine several coverages into a single contract, often with a savings in premium.

After completing this chapter, you will be able to

- trace the early origins of homeowner insurance policies;

- identify who is an insured under the Homeowners 2000 Program;

- determine the risks that are eligible for a homeowners policy; and

- identify the main parts of the homeowners policy.

■ ■ ■ ■ ■

■ ORIGINS OF THE HOMEOWNERS PROGRAM

Insurance companies originally developed policies that covered only one peril or cause of loss—fire. When coverage for additional perils, such as theft or wind damage, was needed, the insured purchased supplemental contracts—often from another insurer.

In 1734, the Friendly Society for the Mutual Insurance of Houses Against Fire was created. Early insurers developed risk classification systems, basing insurance rates on the construction of the building. Because it was less likely to be damaged by fire, a brick house generally was less expensive to insure than a frame house of comparable value and quality. It remains so. A uniform fire insurance policy, the 165-line New York Standard Fire Policy of 1943, is the only insurance policy to have been standardized by law. The standard fire policy is no longer used, but its concepts can be found in almost all property insurance policies today.

Combining Property and Liability in One Contract

Although the standard fire policy offered basic property protection, insurers argued that the combination of property and liability coverages in one contract could provide better protection for the insured than could be obtained separately, eliminating coverage gaps as well as costly duplication between policies. The insured would benefit by obtaining a single policy from one insurance company that provided broader protection at a lower cost than by purchasing several policies with various expiration dates from different companies.

When an insured purchases a number of policies from different insurers, each policy must be underwritten and rated separately. Insureds must be treated as equitably as possible in order to create satisfied clients and maintain adequate business volume. Therefore, rates must be competitive in order for the insurer to obtain a respectable market position.

At the same time, an insurer's rates must generate enough premium income to cover the costs of operation, losses and adjustment expenses, as well as leave a margin for profit, surplus and contingencies. By packaging homeowners coverages, an insurer is able to reduce the total premium while maintaining a profit. The lower premium is due to reduced administration expenses, stricter underwriting and higher minimum insurance amounts because the package must be approved or rejected as a whole.

Study Questions

1. Packaging coverages under a single homeowners policy is a practice that serves insurers only.

   A. True
   B. False

Answer and Rationale

1. **B.** Package policies benefit both insurance companies and insureds. Insureds benefit from convenience, eliminating coverage gaps, and lower policy cost.

Homeowner Package Policies

During the late 1940s, when state insurance regulations finally permitted insurers to write both property and casualty insurance in one contract, insurance companies began to create various forms of homeowners package policies. Many insurers experimented with broadening the standard fire policy to include personal liability coverages by endorsement. Some insurers developed programs that combined several coverages in a single contract to provide for most of a homeowner's, tenant's or condominium unit owner's insurance needs.

In recent years, ISO, a national advisory rating organization that provides loss costs, manual rules, policy forms and statistical reporting services for a number of insurance lines, has introduced several dwelling forms to cover most owner-occupied dwellings. ISO also led the campaign for creating a uniform, packaged homeowners insurance policy with simplified, easy-to-read language. In 1976, ISO developed an experimental homeowners program that basically eliminated the need to use the 165-line Standard Fire Policy as part of the program because all pertinent provisions of that form were included within the *Homeowners 76 Policy Program.*

The *Homeowners 76 Policy Program* simplified the language of the fire contract, made it more readable and created a homeowners policy with five sections:

- definitions;

- coverages;

- perils insured against;

- exclusions; and

- conditions.

ISO revised the homeowners policy in 1982, 1984, 1991 and 2000. Our discussion is based on the 2000 homeowners form drafted by the ISO. Although the Homeowners 2000 (HO 2000) program has been filed in every state, you should check with your company to see if it has adopted the filing or adopted a modified version of it for your state.

■ POLICY FORM STRUCTURE

One of the challenges the insurance industry faces is keeping its products current to meet the consumers' needs. New coverages have been added, obsolete or seldom-used forms have been eliminated and the policy language has evolved to respond to changes in society. Currently, five different forms are available for homeowners and one each for tenants and condominium owners.

The homeowners forms are

- HO–1 Basic Form (withdrawn from use in most states in the early 1990s);

- HO–2 Broad Form;

- HO–3 Special Form;

- HO–5 Comprehensive Form (reintroduced by ISO in 2000); and

- HO–8 Modified Form for Special Risks (based on value or construction).

The coverage forms for tenants and condominium owners are

- HO–4; and

- HO–6 Unit Owner's Form (also includes townhomes).

Homeowners policies have two major coverage sections. Section I contains the property insurance and Section II provides coverage for personal liability and medical payments to others.

Eligibility Guidelines

In order to qualify for coverage under the HO 2000, the insured and/or the residence must meet the following six requirements:

- The dwelling must be owner-occupied.

- Not more than four family units are permitted, and not more than two families, roomers or boarders may occupy any individual family unit.

- The owner-occupant must purchase the full homeowners package.

- The dwelling must be used only for residential purposes.

- A homeowners policy may not be written on property to which farm forms or rates apply.

- A homeowners policy may not be written on a manufactured housing unit.

The HO–4 form for tenants and the HO–6 form for condominium units permit some exceptions to this rule.

Other exceptions are

- **An occupant who is purchasing the dwelling under a land sale contract.** A land sale is similar to an installment contract. The occupant makes regular payments, at the conclusion of which title to the property is transferred to the occupant.

- **A dwelling occupied by someone under a life estate.** A life estate grants a person the right to occupy the dwelling or unit for rest of his or her life, but someone else holds actual title to the property.

- **Dwellings titled in the name of a trust.** Trusts are sometimes used to avoid estate taxes.

Family Unit Limit. Not more than four family units are permitted, and not more than two families, roomers or boarders may occupy any individual family unit.

ISO Form Update The family unit eligibility requirement means that up to eight families could actually occupy a building that is eligible for a homeowners policy, which represents a significant increase from earlier rules.

Full Purchase Required. The owner-occupant must purchase the full homeowners package. An insured cannot select contents-only or dwelling-only coverage if the dwelling is eligible for homeowners coverage.

Residence Only. The dwelling must be used only for residential purposes.

Insureds may have an incidental business, such as an office or private school, but generally they need to add certain endorsements to adequately cover their additional loss exposures. There are special forms to cover farms and ranches.

Manufactured Housing. An ISO homeowners policy may not be written on manufactured housing. Some insurance companies who do not use ISO forms elect to write manufactured homes on mobile homeowners policies. The addition of form MH 04 01 to a homeowners policy provides coverage for manufactured housing units.

Study Questions

2. Generally speaking, a dwelling _____ to be eligible for an unendorsed homeowners policy. (Fill in the blank.)

   A. must be owner occupied
   B. may not be occupied by more than two families
   C. must be a single-family dwelling
   D. may contain business exposures

Eligibility for coverage under each form depends on the type of dwelling, the use to which it is put; and its age as outlined in the points below:

HO–2, HO–3, HO–5

- owner-occupied, one to four-family dwellings;

- intended owner-occupant of a dwelling in the course of construction;

- one co-owner when each distinct portion of a two-family dwelling is occupied by co-owners;

Answer and Rationale

2. **A.** The dwelling must be owner occupied. Not more than four family units permitted, not more than two families may occupy any individual family unit, and the dwelling must be used only for residential purposes.

- purchaser-occupant when the seller retains title under an installment contract; and

- occupant of a dwelling under a life-estate arrangement.

HO–4

- renters of a single-family home, a condominium, an apartment or a manufactured unit.

HO–6

- owners of condominium or cooperative units.

HO–8

- owner-occupied dwellings;

- older or unusual construction; and

- replacement cost exceeds market value.

Risks not eligible include

- farms (a farmowners policy can be used);

- manufactured housing (covered by endorsement to a homeowners policy, by mobile homeowners policy or dwelling form); and

- dwellings that are not owner-occupied.

Most insurance companies use the HO 2000 forms listed above or some version of them. Although some generalizations can be made about a particular ISO form, many insurers amend the forms in some way. Whether the carriers you represent use standard ISO forms or their own modified forms, a comprehensive understanding of the ISO forms used in your state will allow you to distinguish specific company policy features and compete more effectively.

Named Perils and Open Perils Policies

Key Point

Homeowners policies insure against either named perils and/or open perils.

- Named peril policies specify perils insured against.

- Open perils policies provide coverage against risks of direct loss unless specifically excluded in the policy.

Open perils policies were formerly referred to as all risk; however, the industry no longer uses that name because it has been misinterpreted to mean broader coverage than the policy actually provides. Open perils policies have specific exclusions and limitations listed in the policy. Chapter 3 covers perils insured against.

HO–2—Broad Form

The HO 00 02 (or HO–2) form is a broad form policy that covers two groups of perils commonly referred to as the Basic and Broad Form perils. Combined, these two groups provide coverage for 16 causes of loss. A popular form of coverage, it is still frequently issued in the United States.

HO–3—Special Form

The HO 00 03 (or HO–3) form is a special contract form that most homeowners buy. This policy is often referred to as an *open perils,* or *special form.* It insures the dwelling and other structures against risks of direct physical loss unless specifically excluded by the policy. There are a number of perils, such as earth movement and water damage, that are excluded. In addition, a number of exclusions and conditions limit the risks the policy covers. The contents of the house however, are only insured against 16 named perils, which are clearly spelled out in the policy.

HO–4—Contents Broad Form

The HO 00 04 (or HO–4) is available for tenants who wish to cover the contents of a residence they rent, loss of its use and their own personal liability. Coverage is provided for the same broad form named perils listed in the HO–2. However, unlike the HO–2, the HO–4 may be broadened to provide open perils coverage with the Special Personal Property Coverage endorsement, HO 05 24.

Study Questions

3. Which one of the following coverage forms is used to cover tenants or renters?

   A. HO–2
   B. HO–4
   C. HO–6
   D. HO–7

Answer and Rationale

3. **B.** HO–4 is the coverage form for tenants and renters. HO–2 is the broad form of homeowners insurance. HO–6 provides coverage for condominium owners and townhome owners. The HO–7 form is not used.

HO–5—Comprehensive Form

The HO 00 05 (or HO–5) provides the broadest property coverage of any of the homeowners forms. Both dwelling and personal property are protected against open perils or *all risks of direct loss, subject to exclusions and limitations.* ISO reintroduced this form in 2000, having withdrawn it once before, almost 20 years ago. Before ISO reintroduced the HO–5, insureds could have obtained comparable coverage by adding an endorsement, HO 00 15, to the Special Form, HO–3, policy. Of course, now that the HO–5 is back, the HO 00 15 endorsement is no longer needed and has been withdrawn.

HO–6—Unit Owners Form

The HO 00 06 (or HO–6) was designed for condominium and cooperative unit owners. The condominium or co-op association carries insurance on the building itself and other property commonly owned by the unit owners. The HO–6 covers the personal property of the insured for the named perils listed in the HO–2 form. Replacement cost coverage may be added by endorsement.

HO–8—Modified Coverage Form

The HO 00 08 (or HO–8) is designed for older homes in urban neighborhoods or homes of unusual construction where the replacement cost of a house may substantially exceed its market value. Market value is defined as the most probable price a property would bring in a competitive and open market. The HO–8 is a modified HO–2 form that pays for losses to the dwelling and other structures based on the actual cash value or repair cost incurred to repair or replace the property using common construction materials. It covers property under the Basic Form perils and also limits theft to $1,000 per loss and excludes off-premises theft losses, except for certain storage locations.

Study Questions

4. The HO–3, HO–5, and HO–8 policies provide coverage on an open perils basis.

    A. True
    B. False

Answer and Rationale

4. **B.** HO–3 and HO–5 provide coverage on an open perils basis. HO–8 is a named perils policy.

Homeowners Policy Format

Regardless of the policy form selected, each homeowners policy contains the following three preliminary sections:

- Declarations Page;

- Insuring Agreement; and

- Definitions.

Declarations Page

The Declarations Page contains

- the policy number;

- period of coverage

- the insured's name and address

- agent's name;

- location of insured premises;

- the mortgagee (if any);

- limits that apply to the coverage amounts;

- any applicable deductible; and

- the premium amount.

Many companies personalize a Declarations Page in various ways, adding company names, logos and other significant information.

Insuring Agreement

The insuring agreement acts as a preface to the policy as a whole and makes the insurer's obligations under the policy contingent upon the insured's payment of premium and compliance with the policy provisions.

Definitions Section

The definition section is divided into two distinct parts. The first part explains that throughout the policy, "you" and "your" refer to the named insured and his or her spouse, if he or she resides in the same household, and that "we," "us" and "our" refer to the insurance company. This clarification of terms makes the policy language easier for the insured to read and understand. The second part of the definitions section lists commonly used terms in alphabetical order and defines each term. Some of the defined terms include "bodily injury," "occurrence" and "residence premises." Each time you see a word in quotes in the policy, note that this word is included in the policy definitions section.

5. Which of the following types of information is found on a homeowners Declarations Page?

A. Definition of insured

B. Identity of the named insured

C. The insuring agreement

D. Exclusions

Section I

Section I of the policy relates to property coverages and has four parts.

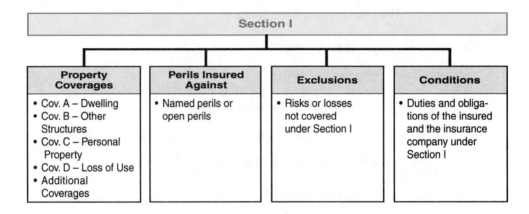

Section I			
Property Coverages	**Perils Insured Against**	**Exclusions**	**Conditions**
• Cov. A – Dwelling • Cov. B – Other Structures • Cov. C – Personal Property • Cov. D – Loss of Use • Additional Coverages	• Named perils or open perils	• Risks or losses not covered under Section I	• Duties and obligations of the insured and the insurance company under Section I

Section II

Section II of the homeowners policy relates to liability coverage and contains four parts.

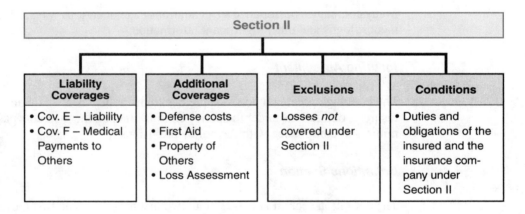

Section II			
Liability Coverages	**Additional Coverages**	**Exclusions**	**Conditions**
• Cov. E – Liability • Cov. F – Medical Payments to Others	• Defense costs • First Aid • Property of Others • Loss Assessment	• Losses *not* covered under Section II	• Duties and obligations of the insured and the insurance company under Section II

Answer and Rationale

5. **B.** The Declarations Page is the policy page containing the insured's name, address and other information.

Section I and II—Conditions

The final pages of the homeowners policy, called *Section I and II—Conditions,* outline certain additional conditions that apply to both the property and liability sections of the policy. These conditions primarily relate to

- policy period;

- concealment or fraud;

- changes in the policy's provisions; and

- cancellation or nonrenewal of the policy.

Homeowner Policy Structure Homeowner forms include the following parts:	
Policy Introductory Sections	
Declarations Page Insuring Agreement Definitions	
Section I: Property Coverages:	Section II: Liability Coverages:
*Coverage A — Dwelling Coverage B — Other Structures Coverage C — Personal Property Coverage D — Loss of Use Additional Coverages	Coverage E — Personal Liability Coverage F — Medical Liability Additional Coverages
Perils Insured Against: (named or open perils) Property Exclusions Property Conditions	N/A Personal Liability Exclusions Medical Exclusions Liability Conditions
Section I and II Conditions	

*The HO – 4 does not include coverage for the dwelling.

Property Coverages

We've just reviewed the structure that homeowners forms use. Next, we'll briefly look at the property coverages included in homeowners forms.

Section I–Property Coverages

The coverages that are part of most Homeowner forms
are illustrated below:

Coverage A – Dwelling

Coverage B – Other Structures

Coverage C –
Personal Property

Coverage D – Loss of Use

Coverage A and B

Coverages A and B insure the buildings and structures at a residence.

Coverage A includes the dwelling at the address shown on the declarations page and attached structures such as an attached garage.

Coverage B includes free-standing structures at the address shown on the declarations page that are separated from the dwelling by clear space. It includes structures attached to the dwelling only by a fence, or similar connection.

Examples of *other structures* covered under Coverage B are

- unattached garages or sheds;

- fences;

- free-standing guest houses; and

- swimming pools.

Coverage A and B Building Definition   The policy describes buildings to include the structure(s) and items that are permanently installed such as fixtures, machinery and equipment. This means permanently installed lights, cabinets, electrical and security systems etc. are all covered under Coverage A or B.

Examples of fixtures and permanently installed equipment that would be covered under Coverage A or B are

- kitchen cabinets;

- fireplaces;

- water softener;

- permanently installed air cleaning systems; and

- central air conditioning.

ISO forms are written so that coverages under one part of the policy exclude coverages within other parts. Therefore, anything covered under Coverage A will be excluded from Coverage B and vice versa. Together Coverage A and B cover the following:

- the dwelling (Coverage A);

- other structures at the address shown on the declarations page (Coverage B);

- construction materials at the residence premises for use in connection with the dwelling (Coverage A);

- construction materials at the residence premises for use in connection with the structures other than the dwelling (Coverage B);

- permanently installed fixtures, machinery and equipment in the dwelling (Coverage A); and

- permanently installed fixtures, machinery and equipment in other building structures (Coverage B).

Coverage C

Coverage C provides coverage for personal property owned or used by an insured person anywhere in the world. At the insured's option, personal property owned by a guest or residence employee while at the occupied insured's residence may also be covered.

6. What is the difference between fixtures and personal property?

It is important to help insureds understand the difference between building and personal property coverage so that proper limits of liability can be developed.

For example, an insured, John Smith, calls to ask you if his new wall-to-wall carpeting in his home and his study above his detached garage is covered under his homeowners personal property coverage. He wants to know if he should increase his coverage because of the sizeable investment of this improvement.

An increase in personal property coverage may not be needed because wall-to-wall carpeting is considered part of the building coverage as it is permanently installed. It would be covered under Coverage A if it is located in the dwelling and under Coverage B if it is located in any building that is separated from the dwelling by clear space or attached to the dwelling only with a fence or similar connection.

Coverage D

When an insured experiences a property loss, he or she is often unable to immediately return to the residence premises. When a loss by an insured peril forces the insured to move to temporary quarters, Coverage D pays reasonable excess expenses until the property is habitable. Examples of excess expenses will be explained in detail in Chapter 4: Section I—Property Coverages.

Coverage E

Coverage E provides personal liability coverage to pay for any bodily injury or property damage suffered on the insured's property, which the insured is legally obligated to pay.

Answer and Rationale

6. A fixture is a permanent part of the building or any equipment that is integral to the operation of the building like a furnace, air conditioner etc. Fixtures are covered under Coverage A and B. Personal property is mobile, which makes coverage anywhere in the world important.

Examples of situations covered under Coverage E are

- an insured's son breaks a neighbors window while playing soccer;

- a person falls and is injured on an insured's sidewalk; and

- an insured's dog bites a neighbor's child.

Coverage F

Coverage F provides coverage for the reasonable and necessary medical expenses of persons injured on the insured's premises with permission. For example, a guest slips and falls while at a party at the insured's residence. The insured may not have been negligent in any way. However, because it happened at the insured's residence, medical coverage will provide for reasonable and necessary medical expenses up to the policy limit.

It is important to distinguish what is covered under each of the Section I and II Coverages. In the next section of this chapter, you will learn that different limits apply to each coverage, and the limits vary by form type.

■ THE HOMEOWNERS PROGRAM (HO 2000)

The requirements that the homeowners and/or dwelling must meet in order to qualify for coverage are spelled out in an insurance company's *underwriting guide,* which states official company policy.

The underwriting guide lists

- the lines of insurance to be written;

- territories to be developed;

- forms and rating plans to be used;

- acceptable, borderline and prohibited business;

- amounts of insurance to be written;

- business that must be approved by a senior underwriter; and

- other underwriting details.

Rating Requirements

The underwriting guide also contains a rating manual with premium rates for various coverages. In order to meet certain regulatory and company objectives, the rates must

- be adequate to pay the insurance company's losses and expenses;

- not be excessive or so high that policyowners are paying more than the actual value of their protection; and

- not be unfairly discriminatory, which means that risks with similar loss exposures and expenses must be charged the same rates.

Reducing Frequency and Severity of Loss

Underwriters use these guides and rating manuals to select and price those risks that are sound from a physical, financial and moral standpoint. The underwriter also helps to determine appropriate coverages to indemnify the insured in the event of a loss. Almost every aspect of an insurance company's underwriting procedure is directed at ways to reduce its frequency and severity of loss by fire and other perils. Such factors as ownership, property valuation and occupancy are typical underwriting concerns when an underwriter looks at a risk.

Named Insured

The homeowners policy insures the named insured—the individual whose name is shown on the policy's Declarations Page (the policy page containing the insured's name, address and other information)—and his or her spouse, if a resident of the same household.

The following residents of the named insured's household are also covered as insureds under the policy:

- relatives of the named insured;

- other persons under age 21 who are in the care of any person named above; and

- full-time students away at school and under the age of 24 if a relative of the named insured; or

- under the age of 21 if in the care of the named insured or a relative, provided the student was living at home before leaving to attend school.

 ISO Form Update   The HO 2000 changes the definition of a named insured, which may create some issues for insureds who are students. For a coverage to apply, the student must be *full time* (which varies by school) and must be under a 24. To solve the problems, ISO developed the HO 05 27 Additional Insured—Student Away at School Endorsement.

The chart below has a comparison of the old and new policy language.

New Policy Form HO 00 03 00	Old Policy Form HO 00 03 04 91
3. "Insured" means you and residents of your household who are: a. Your relatives; or b. Other persons under the age of 21 and in the care of any person named above. Under Section II, "insured" also means:	5. "Insured" means: a. You and residents of your household who are: (1) Your relatives; or (2) Other persons under the age of 21 and in the care of any person named above; b. A student enrolled in school full time, as defined by the school, who was a resident of your household before moving out to attend school, provided the student is under the age of: (1) 24 and your relative; or (2) 21 and in your care or the care of a person described in a.(1) above; or

The homeowners policy broadens the definition of insured under the liability section of the policy to include certain other persons but only under specified conditions. For example, liability coverage is provided for persons or organizations who are legally responsible for watercraft that is owned by an insured.

Study Questions

7. Which of the following is an insured under a homeowners policy?

   A. Anybody on the insured premises
   B. The spouse of the named insured
   C. The named insured's employer
   D. A tenant of the named insured

■ MANDATORY COVERAGES

The amount of coverage for Other Structures, Personal Property and Loss of Use varies by the form selected. When the amount of insurance to carry on the dwelling is determined, the amounts for the other coverages have been selected automatically. In the HO–2, HO–3, HO–5, and HO–8 forms, the limits for Coverage B—Other Structures, Coverage C—Personal Property and Coverage D—Loss of Use are a specified percentage of the amount of insurance on the dwelling. Additional amounts of coverage are available by endorsement for an additional premium.

Because dwelling coverage is not provided for tenants, the amount for Coverage D—Loss of Use for the HO–4 (for tenants) is based on the amount of the selected for Coverage C—Personal Property.

Minimum Coverage Limits

The state pages of rate manuals specify the minimum amounts or limits that may be written for dwelling, personal property and liability coverages. The minimum limits may be amended by endorsement.

Minimum Policy Limits Determined From Coverage A Amount			
Coverage A	**Coverage B**	**Coverage C**	**Coverage D**
HO–2 Declared Amount*	1 or 2 family — 10% of Cov. A 3 or 4 family — 5% of Cov. A	1 or 2 family — 50% of Cov. A 3 family — 30% of Cov. A 4 family — 25% of Cov. A	30% of Cov. A
HO–3 Declared Amount*	Same as HO–2	Same as HO–2	Same as HO–2
HO–4 N/A	N/A	See State Pages	30% of Cov. C
HO–5 Declared Amount*	Same as HO–2	Same as HO–2	Same as HO–2
HO–6 Declared Amount*	N/A	See State Pages	50% of Cov. C
HO–8 Declared Amount*	Same as HO–2	Same as HO–2	10% of Cov. A

*Minimums determined by state rate manuals

Answer and Rationale

7. **B.** Insureds can be residing relatives of the named insured, persons under age 21 who are in the care of a named insured or residing relative, and certain full-time students away at school and under the age of 24. An employer or tenant of a named insured is not an insured.

The basic amount for Section II—Liability Coverage is typically $100,000 for all forms, but this may vary by company or state. In most cases, the limit can be increased for an additional premium.

The insuring agreements, exclusions and conditions for Section II are the same for all homeowners forms.

Study Questions

8. An HO–2 policy on a single-family dwelling provides _____ of additional insurance for personal property. (Fill in the blank.)

   A. 10 percent of the dwelling limit
   B. 20 percent of the dwelling limit
   C. 50 percent of the dwelling limit
   D. $50,000

■ UNDERWRITING CONSIDERATIONS

As an insurance professional, you will be asked to make recommendations about the amount and types of coverage that your clients should purchase. Dwellings or residences are grouped into categories by considering several factors, such as

- protection class;

- construction class; and

- type of policy selected.

These factors are applied to a basic or general rate for a given territory to determine the rate for the specific property being insured. This is termed **class rating.** You should be able to discuss how these various factors affect your clients' coverage and premiums.

Protection Class

Through inspections, engineering reports and study of loss experience in a given area, ISO has developed numbered rating classifications called protection classes that are rated on a scale of 1 to 10, with 1 being the most protected area in terms of fire-fighting ability.

The protection class is determined by two considerations:

- the loss experience of each designated territory; and

- the quality of the local fire department and available water supply.

Answer and Rationale

8. **C.** Under HO–2 (and HO–3, HO–5 and HO–8), one- or two-family units are automatically provided 50 percent of Coverage A for personal property.

Few losses and superior fire protection result in lower rates. An urban area with an extremely responsive fire department might be considered a protection class 2, while a rural area 30 miles from the closest town would be a protection class 10. Tinytown is a rural area. The risk of suffering a large property loss because of slower fire department response time is great. Are the rates for Tinytown's classification higher or lower than for an urban area? Tinytown's protection classification rating would be higher than that for an urban area.

Construction Classifications

Insurers also consider the materials used in the construction of the dwelling to be insured. Most companies describe a house in terms of the following construction classifications:

- *Frame*—dwellings with exterior wooden walls or metal-sheathed frame including dwellings with aluminum or plastic siding.

- *Masonry Veneer*—brick and stone or masonry veneer dwellings that contain a single thickness of brick or stone.

- *Masonry*—dwellings made of solid brick, stone or concrete block and floors and roof of combustible construction.

The fourth construction definition, *superior construction,* includes three subcategories:

- *Noncombustible*—exterior walls and floors constructed of and supported by metal, asbestos, gypsum or other noncombustible materials.

- *Masonry Noncombustible*—exterior walls constructed of masonry materials. Floors and roofs are constructed of metal or other noncombustible materials.

- *Fire Resistive*—dwellings in which the roof, walls and floors are made of fire-resistive materials, such as reinforced concrete or structural metal supports.

If the construction classification is *mixed,* classify it as frame when the exterior walls of the frame construction exceed one-third of the total exterior wall area; otherwise, classify the dwelling as masonry.

Indivisible Premium

Unlike the fire policy, in which a separate charge is made for each peril covered, the homeowners policy has an *indivisible premium*—a combined charge for all the perils covered under the policy. The premium is based on the entire package of property and liability coverages provided. The insurance company's rating manual contains premium charts that show the cost of the various forms based on varying amounts of coverage for the property and liability amounts.

The insured may select from a number of policy forms that fit his or her needs. Obviously, the broader the coverage afforded under the policy, the higher the premium.

For example, the HO–2 that provides broad form coverage on the dwelling and contents for owner-occupants is less expensive than the HO–5 that provides open perils coverage on the same property.

However, if the insured selects only basic coverage, he or she will have to bear the burden of any uninsured losses. The insured may be sacrificing valuable protection without saving a great deal of annual premium.

Study Questions

9. The HO–2 form is less expensive than the HO–5 form for coverage on the same property.

   A. True
   B. False

Deductible

A deductible requires the policyholder to contribute up to a specified sum per claim or per accident toward the total amount of the insured loss. Insurance is written on this basis to reduce the premium. Therefore, the higher the deductible, the lower the premium. Deductibles are an incentive for loss control for the insured. He or she must assume the risk of small losses that would be relatively time consuming for the insurance company to settle.

Homeowners policies currently apply a flat $250 deductible to all covered perils. Higher optional deductibles are available with a substantial savings in premium. Most agents advise insureds to select the largest deductible they can bear provided there is enough premium reduction to offset the extra burden in the event of a loss. For example, many companies offer the insured a savings of between 10 and 25 percent of the standard premium when a $500 deductible is selected.

The deductible does not apply to certain items such as

- fire department service charges;

- coverage for credit cards or fund-transfer cards, forgery or counterfeit money;

- scheduled personal property; and

- personal liability and medical coverages under Section II.

Assume the annual premium for an HO–3 form is $400 with a $250 deductible. The company offers a 10 percent discount for a $500 deductible.

Answer and Rationale

9. **A.** The HO–2 form that provides broad form coverage on the dwelling and contents for the owner occupants is less expensive than the HO–5 form that provides open perils coverage on the same property.

Study Questions

10. How much would the insured save annually by selecting a higher deductible?

Company Selected

Insurance premiums vary significantly among property insurance companies. Some of the factors contributing to this include

- loss experience;

- underwriting standards; and

- locations covered.

To help insurance consumers shop around for coverage, many state insurance departments have prepared shoppers' guides that compare homeowners premiums by company and city. These guides, however, seldom consider the financial strength and reputation of the insurer, its claim practices or its policy provisions or limitations. Insureds should investigate companies on their own or in conjunction with their insurance agent or broker.

Information about insurance companies can be obtain from *Best's Agents Guide or Best's Insurance Reports.* These guides provide ratings of insurer financial stability with classifications ranging from A++ (superior) to F (in liquidation or failed).

Loss Prevention or Reduction Devices

Insureds can reduce the total premium on a policy by qualifying for available discounts. Many companies offer discounts for loss prevention or loss reduction devices including

- smoke detectors;

- deadbolt locks;

- fire extinguishers; and

- fire and burglar alarm systems.

Insurers offer many of these discounts to encourage loss prevention activities that reduce both frequency and severity. This is important because loss prevention tends to keep insurance affordable for the insured and also stabilizes profits for the insurer. Preventing or reducing a loss helps both parties to the contract.

Answer and Rationale

10. The insured saves $40 annually by selecting a higher deductible. However, if a loss occurs, the insured is responsible for the first $500 of the loss rather than only $250 and must determine whether assuming the extra potential burden of $250 is worth the $40 savings in premium.

Some companies offer premium discounts if the insured fits into certain underwriting categories. For example, the company might discount the homeowners and automobile insurance premiums if the insured purchases both policies from the same company. Or, an insurer might also offer a discount for a new home or a discount if the insured is retired.

■ CHAPTER SUMMARY

Most individuals and families can retain some small property losses, but few can retain all the risks associated with owning property. People face damage to or destruction of the dwelling and its contents, loss of use of the home when property is damaged and potential liability when someone is injured on their property.

The most common method for handling risks associated with homeownership or rental is to transfer them to an insurance company by buying a homeowners policy. These policies combine property and liability coverages that protect the insured against the risk of financial loss.

In the next chapter, we will discuss the components of the homeowners policy.

■ **ADDITIONAL STUDY QUESTIONS**

1. Which homeowners form should be used to provide coverage for an owner-occupied one- or two-family dwelling?

   A. HO–2 or HO–3

   B. HO–4

   C. HO–6

   D. HO–8

2. Which homeowners form should be used to provide coverage for renters of single-family homes, apartments, condominiums or manufactured housing units?

   A. HO–2 or HO–3

   B. HO–4

   C. HO–6

   D. HO–8

3. Which homeowners form should be used to provide coverage for owners of dwellings who find it difficult to insure their properties on a replacement cost basis?

   A. HO–2 or HO–3

   B. HO–4

   C. HO–6

   D. HO–8

4. Which homeowners form should be used to provide coverage for owners of condominium or cooperative units?

   A. HO–2 or HO–3

   B. HO–4

   C. HO–6

   D. HO–8

5. An insurance company's loss experience will affect the premiums it charges for homeowners policies.

   A. True

   B. False

■ ANSWERS AND RATIONALES TO ADDITIONAL STUDY QUESTIONS

1. **A.** HO–2 and HO–3 provide coverage for one- or two-family, owner-occupied dwellings.

2. **B.** HO–4 is designed for renters.

3. **D.** The HO–8 Modified Form best insures properties that are older or are not eligible for an HO–2 or HO–3 because their replacement cost exceeds their market value.

4. **C.** HO–6 is specially designed for condo owners.

5. **A.** A company's loss experience, underwriting standards and locations covered are factors affecting premiums.

2
Policy Components

T he insurance contract or policy clearly spells out the rights and obligations of both the insured and the insurance company. Because an insurance policy can be an intimidating legal document, it is important for agents to help insureds fully understand the terms and conditions of coverage.

After completing this chapter, you will be able to

- identify the Declarations, Insuring Agreements, Perils Insured Against, Coverages, Conditions and Exclusions found in homeowners policies;

- determine who is an insured; and

- explain the purpose of exclusions and conditions.

■ ■ ■ ■ ■

■ THE POLICY

An insurance policy is a written contract between the insurance company and the insured. It transfers the risk of financial loss from the insured to the insurer in exchange for a premium. The insurance contract provides future benefits to the insured through its promise to pay the insured money in the event of a loss. The property owner who purchases homeowners insurance is unconcerned about having to bear the financial burden of a large potential loss, such as fire or windstorm, because the risk has been transferred to the insurance company.

The insured also benefits from a number of advisory services provided by his or her insurance agent. For example, the agent helps the insured learn about risk and how insurance can help to transfer risk, reduce financial losses and pay benefits in the event of a loss.

The law considers insureds bound by the terms of the written homeowners contract when they sign the application and pay the premium, regardless of whether they have read and understood the terms and conditions. It is important for the insured to know what is in the insurance contract by reading it, having it explained by an agent or both.

In this chapter, we'll begin our analysis of the first three components of the homeowner policy:

- Declarations;

- Definitions; and

- Insuring Agreement.

The last two components get just an introduction in this chapter. You'll study them in detail later:

- Conditions; and

- Exclusions.

Study Questions

1. The major components of the homeowners policy are

A. Definitions, Perils, Exclusions, Insuring Agreement and Coverages
B. Declarations, Coverages, Insuring Agreement, Perils, and Conditions
C. Declarations, Insuring Agreements, Conditions, Definitions and Exclusions
D. Insuring Agreement, Coverages, Conditions, Changes, and Exclusions.

The Declarations Page

The preliminary sections of each homeowners policy contain a Declarations Page (also called a dec page or the dec) that has pertinent information about the insured dwelling to show the basis upon which the policy was issued. The law expects the insurer, the maker of the insurance contract, to represent the intent and terms of the policy clearly.

The purpose of the Declarations Page is to eliminate ambiguity by providing information about

- who is covered—the named insured;

- what is covered—the property and perils listed in the policy;

- when it is covered—the effective dates of coverage;

Answer and Rationale

1. **C.** The major components of the homeowners policy are Declarations, Insuring Agreements, Conditions, Definitions and Exclusions.

- where it is covered—the described location; and

- why it is covered—a premium has been paid.

Specifically, the Declarations Page includes the

- policy number;

- insured's name and address;

- agent's name and address;

- location of the insured premises;

- name and address of the mortgagee, if any;

- limits that apply to the coverage amounts;

- any applicable deductible; and

- premium amount.

The Declarations Page also lists any modifications or endorsements that the insurer has included as part of the insurance contract.

Policy Jacket

The entire policy, including any endorsements or changes to the policy, is glued or stapled into a policy jacket that serves the same function as the covers of a book. The policy jacket keeps all the homeowners forms in one place, allowing the insured to easily find, read and review the insurance policy. Many insurance contracts have a policy jacket that contains the provisions common to several loss exposures.

Study Questions

2. All of the following information is found on the homeowners policy Declarations Page EXCEPT

A. agent's name and address
B. location of the insured premises
C. definitions
D. premium amount

Answer and Rationale

2. **C.** The agent's name and address, location of the insured premises, premium amount and other information are found on the policy's Declarations Page. Policy definitions are found in a separate section after the Insuring Agreement.

Property & Casualty Company

847 NORTH STATE STREET
JONESVILLE, MICHIGAN 49989

DECLARATIONS PAGE

POLICY PERIOD

POLCY NO.	ST. TERR. AGENT	FROM	TO	TERM
12345	12 33 0000	06-05-95	06-05-96	**ONE YEAR**

INSURED
 Tom & Judy Harrison
 2001 Stage Street
 Harvey, MI 49781

AGENT TELEPHONE: (906) 555-5555
 Benkin Insurance Company
 125 North Wilson
 Harvey, MI 49781

FIRST MORTGAGE
 First Savings Bank
 321 First Road
 Havey, MI 49781

SECOND MORTGAGE

THE DESCRIBED RESIDENCE PREMISES IS LOCATED AT THE ABOVE ADDRESS.	ZIP CODE 48781

PROPERTY COVERAGE				LIABILITY COVERAGE	
A. DWELLING	B. OTHER STRUCTURES	C.PERSONAL PROPERTY	D. LOSS OF USE	E. PERSONAL LIABILITY EACH OCCURRENCE	F. MEDICAL PAYMENT TO OTHERS EACH PERSON
$200,000	$20,000	$100,000	$40,000	$100,000	$1,000

BASIC PREMIUM	ADDITIONAL PREMIUM	SCHEDULED PROP. PREM.	TOTAL PREMIUM	
$350.00		$120.00	$470	

DEDUCTIBLE—PROPERTY COVERAGE, IN CASE OF LOSS WE COVER ONLY THAT PART OF THE LOSS OVER THE DEDUCTIBLE STATED.

$500 FLAT ALL PERILS

CURRENT EDITION OF FORMS WILL BE SUBSTITUTED AT EACH RENEWAL DATE FOR EARLIER EDITIONS IF REVISED DURING THE PREVIOUS POLICY TERM.

TERR	PREM GROUP	PROT CLASS	NO. OF FAMILIES	TOWN	YEAR CONST			
2	2	05	1	5306	1986	HO 00 05	0491	$350.00
CONSTRUCTION: BRICK			NEW HOME DISCOUNT: 05%			HO 04 61	0491	$120.00

COVERAGE A HAS BEEN INCREASED FROM $190,000 TO REFLECT THE CURRENT CONSTRUCTION COST IN YOUR AREA. PLEASE CONTACT YOUR AGENT IF YOU HAVE ANY QUESTIONS.

PLEASE REVIEW THE PERSONAL ARTICLES SCHEDULE ISSUED 06/05/92 FOR POSSIBLE INCREASES IN INSURABLE AMOUNT.

INSURANCE IS PROVIDED ONLY WITH RESPECT TO THE COVERAGE FOR WHICH A UNIT OF LIABILITY IS SPECIFIED. SUBJECT TO ALL CONDITIONS OF THE POLICY.

The Insuring Agreement

Every insurance policy contains a general statement of the promises the insurance company makes to the insured. The homeowners form calls this part of the policy the Insuring Agreement.

The specific obligation assumed by the insurance company is "We will provide the insurance described in this policy in return for the premium and compliance with all applicable provisions of this policy."

In other words, the insurance company agrees to repay, or indemnify, the named insured for losses covered under the policy in return for the insured's premium payment and his or her observance of certain conditions stated in the policy. To indemnify an insured means to restore him or her to the original financial condition before the loss. Under the indemnity rule, the insurance company agrees to repay the insured for destruction or damage to the property described in the contract after the insured has suffered a loss. The insurance company also agrees to pay for damage to other persons or their property if the insured is liable for damages within the scope of the contract.

Definitions

In response to complaints from insureds and the courts that the terms used in insurance policies were not clearly defined, the insurance industry developed a section called *Definitions* that is now contained in every homeowners policy. Although the section does not define every term used in the policy, it defines the most important, frequently used terms.

Definitions follows the Insuring Agreement paragraph. Paragraph **A** of the Definitions includes an explanation of the following words:

- *you* and *your* refer to the *named insured* in the Declarations and that person's spouse if a resident of the same household; and

- *we, us* and *our* refer to the insurance company.

Paragraph **B** of Definitions contains eleven subsections and many more clarifications within the definitions. All definitions apply to both Section I (Property) and Section II (Liability) coverages.

If you are looking at the form (See Appendix), you'll notice that the first definition—aircraft, hovercraft, vehicle and watercraft liability—applies specifically to Section II. Chapter 6, Section II—Liability Coverages, Exclusions and Conditions covers this definition in detail.

Bodily Injury

Bodily injury means bodily harm, sickness or disease, including

- required care;

- loss of services; and

- death that results.

Bodily injury is a liability term meaning any physical injury that results in bodily harm, sickness or disease, including the pain and suffering that may result. Any resulting care, loss of services or death caused by bodily injury are included in this definition. This definition does not include nonphysical injury to a person, such as damage caused by libel, slander, false imprisonment and so forth.

Business

Business is a term that includes

- any trade, profession or occupation engaged in on a full-time, part-time or occasional basis; or

- any other activity engaged in for money or other compensation.

Business does not include

- volunteer activities for which no money is received other than payment for expenses incurred to perform the activity;

- providing home day-care services for which no compensation is received, other than the mutual exchange of such services;

- the rendering of home day-care services to a relative of an insured; or

- one or more activities described above for which no insured receives more than $2,000 in total compensation for the 12 months before the beginning of the policy period.

 ISO Form Update   The Homeowners 2000 Program has redefined what business means. The following items are now exempted from the definition, which means they have coverage in the Homeowners Policy:

- business pursuits that generate less than $2,000 in compensation; and

- other activities for which the insured receives no compensation other than expense reimbursement or payment in kind, such as an exchange of day-care services.

Business activities and structures are generally excluded in personal lines, such as homeowners, coverages. The change in this definition exempts some small businesses from the business exclusion. The change in definition affects coverages under both Sections I and II of the policy.

Study Questions

3. Your insured, Sheila Marks, occasionally rents a room above her garage to college students in the summer. Is this activity a business under the terms of the definition?

    A. Yes

    B. No

■ SOME IMPORTANT TERMS

Employee

Employee means an employee of an insured, or an employee leased to an insured by a labor leasing firm under an agreement between an insured and the labor leasing firm and whose duties are other than those performed by a residence employee.

Insured

Insured usually means the named insured, the named insured's spouse, relatives and persons under the age of 21 in the care of any of the persons previously named, if they live in the insured's residence. As noted in Chapter 1, the HO 2000 Program clarifies the intent of the policy extending coverage to full-time students living away up to age 24, provided they live with the named insured before moving away to attend school.

Under Section II of the policy, the definition of an insured is expanded to include persons who, with permission, are responsible for watercraft or animals owned by an insured. However, there is no coverage if the watercraft or animals are used for business pursuits. The definition also applies to the insured's employees and other persons while they are operating vehicles covered under the policy on an insured location with the insured's permission.

> **■ ISO FORM**
>
> **5.** "Insured" means:
>   **a.** You and residents of your household who are:

Answer and Rationale

3. **B.** The insured only rents a portion of her residence on an occasional basis.

> **(1)** Your relatives; or
>
> **(2)** Other persons under the age of 21 and in the care of any person named above;
>
> **b.** A student enrolled in school full time, as defined by the school, who was a resident of your household before moving out to attend school, provided the student is under the age of:
>
> **(1)** 24 and your relative; or
>
> **(2)** 21 and in your care or the care of a person described in **a.(1)** above;

Insured Location

Insured location has eight subparts in the definition. The first four items refer to the dwelling that an insured may reside in

- the *residence premises* (defined later);

- any other residential premises listed on the Declarations Page;

- any residence premises acquired after the inception date of the policy; and

- any premises the insured does not own but where he or she is temporarily residing (such as a hotel room).

The definition of insured location includes four additional items:

- vacant land (other than farmland) owned or rented by the insured;

- land on which a one- or two-family residence is being built for the insured;

- individual or family cemetery plots or burial vaults owned by an insured; and

- any premises the insured occasionally rents for reasons other than business (such as a banquet hall for a wedding reception).

Motor Vehicle

Motor vehicle means

- a self-propelled land or amphibious vehicle; and

- any trailer or semi trailer that is being carried, towed by or hitched for towing by a self-propelled land or amphibious vehicle.

Occurrence

Occurrence is defined as an accident—an unintended, unforeseen and unexpected event, including continuous or repeated exposure to the same harmful condition, which generally results in bodily injury or property damage during the policy period. In other words, an occurrence may be a sudden event, a gradual series of events or a continuous condition, and coverage will apply as long as the occurrence is unanticipated and bodily injury or property damage occurs.

**Real Life
Application**

An insured's septic tank has been leaking over time, even though she has not been aware of it. The chronic leak has adversely affected a neighbor's water supply and the neighbor becomes ill.

4. Will the insured's homeowners policy respond to a liability claim presented by the neighbor?

Property Damage

Property damage means:

- physical injury to or destruction of tangible property; and

- any loss of use of tangible property.

For example, Section II of the homeowners policy would cover damage to a neighbor's roof that was inadvertently set on fire when the insured's residence premises burned. The policy would also cover costs related to loss of use, such as the costs a neighbor incurs to live elsewhere while his or her roof is being repaired as a result of the fire.

Residence Employee

Residence employees are those workers who perform household, domestic or maintenance duties at the residence premises or elsewhere, if the duties are similar.

---

4. **Yes.** Section II of the homeowners policy will respond. This occurrence is a continuous condition, and coverage will apply since the bodily injury was unanticipated.

Coverage does not apply to employees hired to perform any business of the insured. Coverage is excluded if the employee is eligible to receive workers' compensation.

■ **ISO FORM**

10. "Residence employee" means:

a. An employee of an "insured", or an employee leased to an "insured" by a labor leasing firm, under an agreement between an "insured" and the labor leasing firm, whose duties are related to the maintenance or use of the "residence premises", including household or domestic services; or

b. One who performs similar duties elsewhere not related to the "business" of an "insured".

A "residence employee" does not include a temporary employee who is furnished to an "insured" to substitute for a permanent "residence employee" on leave or to meet seasonal or short-term workload conditions.

Real Life Application

Marlene cooks and performs other household chores for the Baileys and watches their son, Junior, when he comes home from school. While playing with Junior in the park, Marlene sprains her ankle.

5. Would the Bailey's homeowner policy cover her medical expenses?

Residence Premises

A *residence premises* is the one- or two-family dwelling, unit or apartment where the insured lives, as well as other structures and grounds related to the residence. Regardless of the homeowners form chosen, the address of the residence premises must be shown in the Declarations Page.

Answer and Rationale

5. **Yes.** The family's homeowners policy would cover the medical expenses. Marlene is a residence employee and is covered while shopping for the family, performing household tasks or taking the children to the park. The injury does not have to take place on the residence premises if it occurs while she is performing her duties.

The definitions of residence premises and insured location clearly show the intention of the homeowners forms to cover only owner-occupied dwellings.

> ■ **ISO FORM**
>
> **11.** "Residence premises" means:
>
> **a.** The one family dwelling where you reside;
>
> **b.** The two, three or four family dwelling where you reside in at least one of the family units; or
>
> **c.** That part of any other building where you reside;
>
> and which is shown as the "residence premises" in the Declarations.
>
> "Residence premises" also includes other structures and grounds at that location.

Study Questions

6. All of the following are residence premises EXCEPT

    A. a single-family home

    B. a garage located at the address on the Declarations Page

    C. a tool shed located at the address on the Declarations Page

    D. an office the insured uses daily in a nearby town

Conditions

The homeowners policy is a *conditional contract*. If the insured does not comply with the conditions enumerated in the policy, the insurer may be released from its obligations to provide the coverage described in the policy. Therefore, it is important for the insured to read and understand his or her duties, especially after a loss. The conditions component describes the rights and duties of both parties to the insurance contract—the insurer and insured.

Answer and Rationale

    6. **D.** Dwellings used for business pursuits off premises are not included in the definition of residence premises.

Conditions in the homeowners policy apply to

- Section I only;

- Section II only; and

- Sections I and II together.

Conditions will vary slightly, depending on the homeowners form selected.

Section I—Property Conditions

Section I, the property portion of the homeowners policy, contains 16 conditions that limit coverages provided by the policy. These conditions describe

- the insured's duties after a loss;

- loss settlement duties and options (insured and company);

- when an insured can sue the company or abandon property to the company;

- how a loss becomes payable to a mortgageholder or person storing property for a fee;

- what happens in the event of a dispute between the insured and the insurer;

- policy period and other time periods for losses; and

- what happens if fraud occurs.

Section II—Liability Conditions

In addition to the 16 conditions that apply only to Section I, eight conditions apply only to Section II of the homeowners policy. These conditions, which also limit and clarify coverage, relate to:

- liability coverage limits;

- the number of insureds covered by the policy;

- the insured's duties after a loss;

- payment of claims;

- bankruptcy of the insured; and

- provisions that apply when other insurance is in force.

Conditions Applicable to Sections I and II

There are nine conditions that apply to the entire insurance contract. These conditions involve

- the length of time insurance coverage is provided;

- how intentional omissions by the insured affect the policy;

- how the coverage may be changed, canceled, nonrenewed or assigned;

- how the insurer is protected by subrogation; and

- how the death of an insured affects coverage.

Exclusions

The homeowners policy does not cover every risk that the insured faces. Policies generally have exclusions for these primary reasons:

- the peril is uninsurable, such as war-related events;

- the risk is best insured under a different form, such as vehicles under a Personal Auto Policy;

- there is a moral risk, such as arson for profit; and

- the premium involved doesn't contemplate every conceivable risk.

For example, many insurers will not provide coverage for perils such as earthquake or flood under unendorsed homeowner policies because of their catastrophic nature. Separate coverage with appropriate premiums are available in most situations.

Section I—Exclusions

Section I—Property and Section II—Liability have separate sets of exclusions that apply specifically to the coverages provided.

Section I—Exclusions contains nine property exclusions that apply to all homeowner policy forms, even when a concurrent cause or event isn't excluded. In other words, the policy does not pay for a loss caused directly or indirectly by the following:

- Ordinance or Law;

- Earth Movement;

- Water Damage;

- Power Failure;

- Neglect;

- War;

- Nuclear Hazard;

- Intentional Loss; and

- Governmental Action.

Next, in Section I—Exclusions, the following sources of loss are excluded because they are very general and almost impossible to underwrite:

- weather conditions;

- acts or decisions; and

- negligent work.

For example, insurance companies will not cover weather conditions but will cover the more specific perils of windstorm or lightning.

Section II—Coverages E and F

The next group of exclusions applies to Section II—Liability, Coverage E—Personal Liability and Coverage F—Medical Payments to Others.

Included in this group are exclusions for

- motor vehicle liability;

- watercraft liability;

- aircraft liability;

- hovercraft liability;

- expected or intended injury;

- business activities;

- professional services;

- other owned locations;

- war;

- communicable disease;

- sexual molestation, corporal punishment or physical or mental abuse; and

- controlled substances.

Coverage F—Medical Payments to Others

The last group of exclusions applies only to Coverage F—Medical Payments to Others:

- injuries to residence employees;

- claims for workers' compensation or similar benefits;

- nuclear energy claims; and

- injury to residents of the insured's household.

■ CHAPTER SUMMARY

You've studied the following parts of the policy in detail:

- Declarations;

- Insuring Agreement; and

- Definitions.

Although each homeowners policy follows this basic framework, some forms insure against loss by specific perils, while others insure against loss on an open perils basis.

In the next chapter, we'll look at the perils insured against within the various homeowner forms.

■ **ADDITIONAL STUDY QUESTIONS**

1. Your insured, Helen Anderson, watches her neighbor's child on Monday and Wednesday mornings. The neighbor watches Helen's child on Tuesday and Thursday mornings. This arrangement allows both women to work part time with peace of mind regarding day care. Is this activity a business under the homeowners policy for either person?

   A. Yes
   B. No

2. Your insured, David Brown, has a nephew named Alistair Fulton, who is 25. Alistair is renting a room at David's residence temporarily while he is on a short-term internship in David's city. Alistair's parents, the Fultons, have the same type of homeowners policy as David Brown does. Alistair is an insured under which policy (or policies)?

   A. Brown's homeowners
   B. Fulton's homeowners
   C. Both policies
   D. Neither policy

3. Tom and Mary are foster parents. William has been assigned by the court to live with them. William is considered an insured under Tom and Mary's homeowners policy until he reaches the age of

   A. 16
   B. 18
   C. 21
   D. 24

4. Your insured has badly worn carpet in the recreation room. Is this situation covered under the definition of occurrence?

   A. Yes
   B. No

■ ANSWERS AND RATIONALES TO ADDITIONAL STUDY QUESTIONS

1. **B.** Mutual exchange of home day-care services is not considered a business under the terms of the policy definition.

2. **A.** Alistair is an insured under Brown's policy because the definition of insured includes any resident relative of the insured's household. He is not covered under his parent's policy because he is more than 24 years old.

3. **C.** William is an insured until the age of 21 because he is in the care of the named insured and lives in the insured residence. William may be an insured until the age of 24 if he is a full-time student living away, provided he lived with Tom and Mary before going away to attend school.

4. **A.** Wear and tear and deterioration are not unforeseen or unexpected accidents. You will see later on that both wear and tear and deterioration are specifically excluded in the policy.

Perils Insured Against

T he various homeowners forms insure against perils that are, in a sense, natural perils—a building burns; a roof is damaged by wind or hail; pipes freeze and explode.

After completing this chapter, you will be able to

- describe the difference between named and open perils contracts;

- identify the perils covered in the different homeowners policies; and

- distinguish among the perils insured against in the HO–2, HO–3, HO–4, HO–5, HO–6 and HO–8 policies.

■ ■ ■ ■ ■

■ NAMED PERILS VS. OPEN PERILS COVERAGE

In insurance, a **loss** is an unintended, unforeseen reduction or destruction of financial or economic value. For example, the consumption of food or wearing out of clothing represents disappearance or decline in value, but these are not losses in insurance language because they are expected and intended. On the other hand, the destruction of a house by a tornado is unintended, unforeseen and a loss.

Named Perils

A number of perils, including fire, wind, smoke cause losses. For insurance purposes, a peril is the immediate, specific event causing loss. For example, when a structure burns, fire is the peril. A named perils homeowners policy specifically lists the perils it covers. If a loss is caused by a peril *not* named in the policy, the insured is not covered for the loss and may not collect from the insurer.

The following homeowners forms are named perils contracts.

Form Number	Covers
HO–2	owner-occupied dwellings
HO–3	open perils on dwelling and other structures, named perils on personal property
HO–4	renters' property and liability
HO–6	owner-occupied condominiums
HO–8	owner-occupied dwellings

Open Perils

The HO–3 form provides open perils coverage for

- the dwelling;

- other structures; and

- loss of use.

It provides personal property coverage on a named perils basis. The 2000 HO–5 form provides open perils coverage on *both* the dwelling and personal property. In other words, the exclusions define the coverage.

Open perils policies provide coverage against direct physical loss except as otherwise excluded or limited in the policy. An open perils policy generally covers unusual losses and those that the insured cannot reasonably anticipate. You may have heard the term *all risk* applied to open perils policies. Many insurance companies no longer endorse the use of that term because insureds and the courts often have interpreted it to mean that every loss would be covered—even if the policy clearly excludes some losses.

The following forms are open perils policies:

- HO–3 (Coverage A, B, and D); and

- HO–5 (Coverage A, B, C and D).

 ISO Form Update   The HO 2000 program allows insureds to endorse an HO–4 or HO–6 to provide open peril coverage for renters or condominium owners. One correct way of explaining an open perils policy to an insured is that it is subject to exclusions and limitations in coverage.

The homeowners policies differ in the number of perils each covers. Generally speaking, each form builds on the previous one and adds or broadens the coverage. To demonstrate how these forms differ, we'll briefly look at the perils covered under each form.

The Broad Form provides protection against 16 separate causes of loss. These causes of loss, or perils, fall into two groups: basic and broad perils. The policy does

Coverage Comparison			
Form	Named Perils	Open Perils	Open Perils by Endorsement
HO–2	X		
HO–3	X Coverage C	X Coverages A, B and D	
HO–4	X		X*
HO–5		X* Coverages A, B, C and D	
HO–6	X		X*
HO–8	X		

*New in the HO 2000 Program. Previously, inland marine policies provided open perils as requested or needed by insureds.

not provide a definition for many perils. However, a body of case law has developed that provides a set of commonly accepted definitions for the perils.

■ BASIC PERILS

The basic perils are the first line of defense in homeowners coverage, but this coverage is extremely limited. The following list represents the basic perils as originally stated in the now-withdrawn HO–1. The HO–2 Broad Form lists them in the same manner:

- fire or lightning;
- windstorm or hail;
- explosion;
- riot or civil commotion;
- aircraft;
- vehicles;
- smoke;
- vandalism or malicious mischief;
- theft; and
- volcanic eruption.

HO–2 BROAD FORM PERILS	
The HO–2 form includes the basic perils covered in the (withdrawn) HO–1 form *plus* the additional perils listed in the second column in the chart.	
Basic Perils	Broad Form Perils
• Fire or Lightning • Windstorm or Hail • Explosion • Riot or Civil Commotion • Aircraft • Vehicles • Smoke • Vandalism or Malicious Mischief • Theft • Volcanic Eruption	Additional Perils covered in the Broad Form: • Falling Objects • Weight of Ice, Snow or Sleet • Accidental Discharge or Overflow of Water or Steam • Sudden and Accidental Tearing Apart, Cracking, Burning or Bulging • Freezing • Sudden and Accidental Damage from Artificially Generated Electrical Current

Exclusions within Perils

As you learn about the perils, you'll see that many of them contain exclusions *within* the peril. The discussion of each peril includes a discussion of these exclusions. Keep in mind that a policy must always be read as a whole document when determining coverage. In other words, additional exclusions, conditions and limitations may apply to some of the broad form perils. When you've finished the Understanding HO 2000 course, you'll be able to read and interpret the HO–3 policy as a whole document, even though the chapters present the parts separately.

Fire or Lightning

The courts have defined *fire* as oxidation sufficiently rapid to cause a flame or glow. In other words, smoke is insufficient to establish the existence of a fire; there must be a spark or flame. The courts have also made a distinction between friendly fires and hostile fires. A *friendly fire* is one that burns within the confines for which it was intended. A *hostile fire* is one that has escaped from the confines for which it was intended. Homeowners policies generally cover hostile fires only.

Real Life Application

1. While the Smiths are sleeping, sparks from the logs burning in the fireplace leap from the fireplace and set fire to the carpet.

   • Is this a friendly or hostile fire?

   • Will the Smiths' homeowners policy provide coverage?

Answer and Rationale

1. The sparks were friendly while they were still in the fireplace but became hostile when they jumped to the carpet. Coverage will apply.

Lightning, generally defined as a flashing of light produced by a discharge of atmospheric electricity, may cause damage to property or it may start a fire that causes property damage. Because it is generally difficult to distinguish between damage caused by lightning or by fire, the policy specifically lists both fire and lightning as covered perils. Fire or lightning is peril number 1 in the HO–2 Broad Form list of perils.

Windstorm or Hail

Windstorm generally includes damage by the direct action of wind or by objects propelled by the wind. For example, if the wind blows a tree branch though an insured's window, the policy covers the resulting damage to the dwelling. Windstorm includes damage caused by tornadoes, cyclones and hurricanes. Most homeowners policies *exclude* interior damage to a building or its contents caused by wind-driven rain, snow, sleet and dust unless wind first damages the exterior walls or roof to cause an opening. This peril covers watercraft and equipment damage by windstorm only if they are inside a fully enclosed building.

Hail is precipitation in the form of small lumps of ice that can cause extensive damage to property. This peril is subject to the same conditions and exclusions as windstorm. Windstorm or hail is peril number 2 on the Broad Form list of perils.

Real Life Application

2. An insured leaves a window open during a storm and rain destroys some furniture.

   • Will coverage apply for the furniture?

   • Would coverage apply if the wind blows a branch through the windowpane, allowing rain to enter and damage the furniture?

Explosion

The policy covers any cause of loss that can be reasonably described as an *explosion.* This peril typically includes bursting of pipes or violent expansion of gas that causes damage to property. The Broad Form doesn't contain a definition or description of explosion, number 3 in the list of perils. As with many perils, it has gained definition by court interpretation and general usage in the industry.

Riot or Civil Commotion

A *riot* is generally considered to be an assembly of individuals (as few as two in some states) who commit a lawful or unlawful act in a violent or tumultuous manner, to the terror or disturbance of others. Damage caused by rioters or during *civil*

Answer and Rationale

2. If the insured leaves a window open during a storm and rain destroys furniture, there is no coverage because the policy excludes interior damage caused by wind-driven rain unless the exterior walls or roof are damaged by the wind that causes an opening for the rain to get in. If the wind blows a branch through a closed window and then rain enters and damages the furniture, coverage would apply.

*commotion—a*n uprising of people creating a prolonged disturbance—is broadly covered. Riot or civil commotion is peril number 4 on the Broad Form list.

Aircraft

The homeowners form provides coverage for damage that results from *aircraft,* missiles and spacecraft. This would include parts that fall from aircraft, causing damage to insured property. By extension, this peril covers damage from a sonic boom. Aircraft is number 5 on the Broad Form list.

Vehicles

Vehicles are mediums by which things are conveyed or transported. The peril provides coverage for losses as a result of vehicle damage to insured property. There is no coverage under the homeowners form for damage to the vehicle itself.

- The HO–8 form excludes all damage caused by a vehicle owned or operated by the insured or a resident of the property.

- HO–2 and HO–6 forms exclude damage to fences, driveways and walks caused by a vehicle owned or operated by a resident of the residence premises.

- HO–3, HO–4 and HO–5 forms cover loss caused by vehicles without any specific conditions.

Study Questions

3. The brakes fail on a neighbor's auto, and it crashes into our insured's garage. The neighbor is uninsured. Will the insured's HO–3 provide coverage for damage to the garage?

Smoke

The policy covers the peril of *smoke,* which includes gas from burning materials and puffback of smoke, soot, fumes or vapors from a boiler, furnace or related equipment. It does not include loss caused by smoke from agricultural smudging or industrial operations. Smoke is peril number 7.

Vandalism or Malicious Mischief

Vandalism or malicious mischief (V&MM) is intentional and spiteful damage to or destruction of the insured's property. If someone accidentally spills paint on the insured's carpeting, this is not considered V&MM. However, graffiti painted on the insured's garage door is V&MM and would be covered under this peril. When a dwelling is vacant, it is more susceptible to losses from certain perils, such as V&MM, theft and glass breakage. Therefore, most policies contain a provision that

---

Answer and Rationale

3. **Yes.** Coverage applies to damage to the garage. The HO–3 and HO–5 forms cover loss caused by vehicles without any specific conditions.

states that certain losses, such as V&MM, are not covered if the dwelling has been vacant for more than 60 consecutive days prior to the loss. Vandalism or malicious mischief is peril number 8.

The following terms applying to V&MM have gained definition by usage and court interpretation:

- *Vacant*—a dwelling empty of persons and contents

- *Unoccupied*—a dwelling empty of persons but containing furniture and being used

Generally, a dwelling can be unoccupied for 60 days or more for the V&MM coverage to apply. For example, sometimes people take extended vacations or have summer homes where the dwelling is unoccupied but not vacant. Obviously, they must continue to safeguard the house when people are not present but furnishings remain. Check with the companies you represent for their interpretations of V&MM coverage on vacant and/or unoccupied buildings.

Theft

All homeowners forms include *theft* as an insured peril. Theft is an act of taking or stealing property (including attempted theft) with the intent to deprive the owner of the property from a known place when it is likely that the property has been stolen. There are restrictions and limits on certain types of property, such as jewelry and furs, and certain types of theft are excluded under all homeowners forms. Note that theft, number 9 on the list, contains exclusions within the peril

- committed by an insured;

- of building materials until construction is complete and the dwelling is occupied

- from any part of the premises rented by an insured to a noninsured person; and

- off the residence premises for selected items

The selected items away from the residence premises include

- watercraft, including its furnishings, equipment and outboard motors;

- trailers and campers; and

- property on any premises owned by, rented to or occupied by an insured, other than on the premises described in the policy, unless the insured occupied the premises at the time of the theft.

For example, property in a summer home owned by the insured is covered for theft only while the insured is living there. However, the property of an insured who is a full-time student living away from home is covered if he or she has been at the school residence at any time during the 60 days immediately before the loss.

The HO 2000 program changes the provisions of the Theft peril.

 ISO Form Update In Chapter 2 you learned that the definition of residence premises contains some changes that apply to students away at school:

- a student must be under the age of 24 and the insured's relative; or

- under 21 and in the insured's care.

The student must be enrolled in school full time and have lived with his or her parents immediately before enrolling in school. The new HO forms also require that a student's residence be for the purpose of attending school. The older forms merely required that a student have lived there within a specified time period. If a student stops attending school, perhaps working for a semester, but continues to live in the school apartment, the insured must notify the company and secure an endorsement to continue coverage for personal property in the apartment.

Under previous forms, a student could be away from a school dorm or apartment for no more than 45 consecutive days. The new form provides a 60-day period for the student's residence to be unoccupied.

A disappearance of property without knowledge as to the place, time or manner of its loss is mysterious disappearance, not theft. Mysterious disappearance is not covered under named perils policies except by including the Scheduled Personal Property Endorsement, explained in Chapter 8.

 ISO Form Update Earlier homeowners policies contained an exclusion eliminating coverage for theft of property from an unattended motor vehicle, trailer, or watercraft. The HO 2000 program eliminates that exclusion.

Volcanic Eruption

A *volcanic eruption* occurs from an opening in the earth's crust from which molten rock and steam issue. The peril also provides coverage for airborne shock waves, volcanic ash and lava flow. Regardless of the number of eruptions that occur within a 72-hour period, they will be treated as one eruption or loss. Coverage is *not* provided for loss caused by earthquake, tremors or land shock waves under this peril. The HO–1 form listed this peril next after theft; therefore, we've listed it under Basic Perils. You'll remember that most states no longer offer the HO–1. Volcanic eruption is number 16 on the Broad Form list.

Broad Form Perils

Falling Objects

The policy does not define the term *falling objects,* but coverage generally applies to direct damage to the exterior of the dwelling or other structures, to fences, sidewalks, outdoor equipment and other personal property that is outdoors caused by objects dropped from taller structures, from an aircraft or from anywhere above the damaged property. Damage to property located inside a building is covered only if the falling object first damages the roof or an exterior wall.

HO–2 BROAD FORM PERILS	
The HO–2 form includes the basic perils covered in the (withdrawn) HO–1 form *plus* the additional perils listed in the second column in the chart.	
Basic Perils	**Broad Form Perils**
• Fire or Lightning • Windstorm or Hail • Explosion • Riot or Civil Commotion • Aircraft • Vehicles • Smoke • Vandalism or Malicious Mischief • Theft • Volcanic Eruption	Additional Perils covered in the Broad Form: • Falling Objects • Weight of Ice, Snow or Sleet • Accidental Discharge or Overflow of Water or Steam • Sudden and Accidental Tearing Apart, Cracking, Burning or Bulging • Freezing • Sudden and Accidental Damage from Artificially Generated Electrical Current

Real Life Application

4. If part of an airplane engine falls through an insured's roof and damages the living room furniture, would coverage apply to both the roof and the furniture?

Weight of Ice, Snow or Sleet

This peril covers damage caused by the *weight of ice, snow or sleet* to the dwelling, other structures and the property contained in these buildings. However, the policy excludes damage caused by this peril to awnings, fences, patios, pavements, swimming pools, foundations, retaining walls, bulkheads, piers, wharves or docks.

Accidental Discharge or Overflow of Water

Coverage applies for property lost because of the *accidental discharge or overflow* of water from within an appliance, such as a dishwasher, and from a heating, air conditioning, automatic sprinkler or plumbing system (other than a sump, sump pump or related equipment).

Since you'll see sump again later in the course, here is the definition. A *sump* is a reservoir into which liquid drains. The pump drains the reservoir, usually into the sewer.

In addition to the water damage to floors, carpets and other floor coverings, accidental discharge provides coverage for the cost to tear out and replace any part of

Answer and Rationale

4. **Yes.** Coverage applies to both the roof and the furniture. However, no coverage applies to the falling object itself (the engine part).

the building to repair the faulty pipe or appliance. However, the damage to the appliance or pipe itself is not covered.

As stated in the peril, three additional exclusions apply to accidental discharge:

- loss caused by the discharge or overflow of water that occurs off-premises, such as a broken water main;

- loss caused by freezing, which is covered under another peril; and

- loss to a building that has been vacant for 30 consecutive days immediately preceding the loss, except if the dwelling is under construction.

Sudden and Accidental Tearing Apart

The broad form perils includes coverage for damage to the air conditioning, water heating or other system or appliance itself caused by a *sudden and accidental tearing apart* of that system or appliance. When a system explodes, some of the damage may be covered under the explosion peril. However, the sudden and accidental tearing apart peril covers the system itself, as well as damage to or destruction of other property.

Freezing

The *freezing* peril covers damage due to a household appliance or plumbing, heating, sprinkler or air conditioning system that freezes—unless the dwelling is vacant or unoccupied. However, coverage *does* apply to a vacant or unoccupied dwelling if the insured

- has taken reasonable care to maintain heat in the building; or

- turns off the water supply and drains the system or appliance.

If the dwelling has an automatic fire protective sprinkler system the insured must use reasonable care to continue the water supply and maintain heat in the building for freezing coverage to continue to apply. Otherwise, the sprinkler system is inoperable. The peril excludes coverage for sumps, sump pumps, roof drains, gutters, downspouts or similar equipment. You can add the Water Back Up and Sump Overflow Endorsement (explained in Chapter 8) to the policy to cover $5,000 of these exposures. The endorsement adds coverage for water back up through sewer and drains and overflow of water from a sump to the policy.

**Real Life
Application**

5. Suppose the insureds winter in Florida but completely drain the water from the plumbing system in their upper peninsula Michigan home before they leave each fall. If the water pipes freeze and cause damage, will the loss be covered even though the house in Michigan is unoccupied?

Artificially Generated Electrical Current

Property—other than tubes, transistors or similar electronic components—is covered against the peril of *sudden and accidental damage from artificially generated electrical current.* In other words, any sudden surge of electrical current (other than lightning or naturally generated electrical current) that causes damage to wiring is covered. Lightning damage is covered under the lightning peril. Artificially generated electrical current completes our study of the 16 Broad Form perils.

■ CHAPTER SUMMARY

By examining the various homeowners polices, you will have a clear understanding of how most insurance companies will handle important coverage questions, even though the policy conditions can vary.

In the next chapter, we'll discuss how Section I—Property Coverages of the homeowners policy provides insurance protection against direct and indirect loss to buildings and/or personal property.

Answer and Rationale

5. **Yes.** The loss will be covered because the insureds take reasonable care to drain the water out of the pipes before they leave.

■ ADDITIONAL STUDY QUESTIONS

1. Which policy can be endorsed to ADD open perils coverage?

   A. HO–2

   B. HO–3

   C. HO–6

   D. HO–8

2. If an insured has open perils, the policy insures the dwelling and other structures against the risks of direct physical loss unless they are specifically excluded.

   A. True

   B. False

3. Which one of the following statements best describes the difference between an HO–2 policy and an HO–3 policy?

   A. The HO–2 policy provides a lower automatic limit of liability on personal property than the HO–3 policy.

   B. The HO–3 policy provides broader extensions of coverage than the HO–2 policy.

   C. The HO–2 policy provides named perils coverage while the HO–3 policy provides open perils coverage on the dwelling.

   D. The HO–3 policy contains more insuring agreements than the HO–2 policy.

■ ANSWERS AND RATIONALES TO ADDITIONAL STUDY QUESTIONS

1. **C.** HO–3 is already open perils for building coverage. If an insured wants open perils coverage for his or her dwelling and personal property he or she should purchase an HO–5 policy. The HO 2000 program allows you to endorse both the HO–4 and HO–6 to add open perils coverage.

2. **A.** Open perils coverage, as opposed to named perils coverage, insures against direct physical loss except as otherwise excluded or limited by the policy.

3. **C.** Both the HO–2 and HO–3 policy provide the same automatic limit of liability for other structures, personal property and loss of use. Both contain the same extensions of coverage, and both have the same number of insuring agreements. However, the HO–2 policy provides named perils coverage, while the HO–3 policy provides open perils coverage on the dwelling (both also provide named perils coverage on personal property).

4

Section I—Property Coverage

Many homeowners and tenants discover that their insurance coverage is inadequate only after they have experienced a loss. Although most people are able to retain small physical damage losses to property, few can retain all the risks associated with owning property.

In this chapter, we'll discuss Section I—Property Coverages of the homeowners policy. These coverages concern the insured's real property, such as the dwelling, and personal property (possessions owned or used by the insured), and the indirect losses that occur because of damage to real property. Because it is the most commonly used form and representative of the other homeowners forms, we'll examine the HO–3 form in detail.

After completing this chapter, you will be able to

- distinguish open perils coverage in the HO–3 for the dwelling and other structures from named perils coverage on personal property;

- describe and apply the five property coverages and exclusions in Section I of the homeowners policies: Coverage A—Dwelling, Coverage B—Other Structures, Coverage C—Personal Property, Coverage D—Loss of Use and Additional Coverages;

- explain how the HO–2, HO–4, HO–5, HO–6 and HO–8 Section I—Property Coverages differ from the HO–3 Section I—Property Coverages; and

- analyze a typical client's situation to determine coverage and limits of liability.

■ ■ ■ ■ ■

■ FORMS REFERENCED IN THIS CHAPTER

This and the following three chapters use the HO–3 policy form as a basis for discussion. If you have not already done so, you may want to locate the form in the Appendix.

At the end of the chapter you'll find a Policy Comparison heading that has a synopsis of how the remaining forms (HO–2, HO–4, HO–5, HO–6 and HO–8) differ from the HO–3. There is an HO Forms Comparison Chart in the Appendix that serves as an excellent reminder or job aid.

As mentioned in Chapter 3, a policy should be read and interpreted as a whole document. Because Section I of the policy contains exclusions within the coverage grants, we'll discuss those exclusions. The covered (and excluded) property may be subject to further conditions and limitations such as those discussed in Chapter 5.

■ UNDERWRITING CONSIDERATIONS FOR PROPERTY COVERAGE

The agent is responsible for obtaining full and accurate information necessary for analyzing the risk and the hazards involved in order to determine the prospect's needs accurately. Whenever possible, the agent should study the risk by physically inspecting the insured's property and gathering full and accurate information about it. This may involve taking photographs, making diagrams of the house and listing personal property. If the insured owns another residence, such as a vacation home, that property must be covered under a separate policy. However, if the same insurer provides homeowners coverage for both residences, the liability coverage for the second dwelling may be added to the homeowners policy covering the primary residence.

■ COVERAGE A—DWELLING

This section of the policy covers the residence and structures attached to it, such as an attached garage. Open perils, as mentioned in Chapters 1 and 3, apply to the dwelling under the HO–3 policy. Coverage A also protects the insured's interest in the materials and supplies located on or adjacent to the premises that are for use in the construction, alteration or repair of the dwelling or other structures on the premises.

This coverage grant offers coverage for materials used in the repair or alteration of an occupied and completed dwelling, or a new structure on the premises.

> ### ■ *ISO FORM*
>
> **A. Coverage A – Dwelling**
> 1. We cover:
>   a. The dwelling on the "residence premises" shown in the Declarations, including structures attached to the dwelling; and

> **b.** Materials and supplies located on or next to the "residence premises" used to construct, alter or repair the dwelling or other structures on the "residence premises".
>
> **2.** We do not cover land, including land on which the dwelling is located.

Building Materials Covered

In the Chapter 3 discussion of the theft peril, you learned that one of the exclusions within the peril includes theft "in or to a building under construction, or of materials and supplies for use in the construction *until the dwelling is finished and occupied* [emphasis ours]."

For theft of building materials

- in an occupied building, theft is *covered;* and

- in an unoccupied building, theft is *not covered*

> ■ *ISO FORM*
>
> **A. Coverage A – Dwelling**
> **1.** We cover:
> **a.** The dwelling on the "residence premises" shown in the Declarations, including structures attached to the dwelling; and
> **b.** Materials and supplies located on or next to the "residence premises" used to construct, alter or repair the dwelling or other structures on the "residence premises".
> **2.** We do not cover land, including land on which the dwelling is located.

This named peril theft exclusion doesn't negate the coverage grant in Coverage A. The HO–3 is not intended as a builder's risk policy for unoccupied dwellings where theft of building materials is concerned.

■ *ISO FORM*

9. Theft

a. This peril includes attempted theft and loss of property from a known place when it is likely that the property has been stolen.

b. This peril does not include loss caused by theft:

(1) Committed by an "insured";

(2) In or to a dwelling under construction, or of materials and supplies for use in the construction until the dwelling is finished and occupied;

Study Questions

1. If construction materials used to repair an attached garage damaged in a hail storm are stolen from behind the garage during the construction period, the loss would be covered under the homeowners policy.

A. True

B. False

Fixtures Covered

The coverage also includes fixtures, such as built-in appliances, plumbing, heating and electrical wiring attached to and considered part of the dwelling. The policy does not specifically define *fixtures*. This perception of the policy meaning, like many others mentioned in previous chapters, has come about through court interpretation and common usage. Fixtures are generally considered to be items that are permanently attached to the building.

The dwelling on the left has a built-in garage as an integral part of the dwelling. (See pictures on next page.) The dwelling on the right has a garage separated from the house by clear space. This garage is not a part of Coverage A—Dwelling.

Answer and Rationale

1. **A.** The materials and supplies that are for use in the construction and located on or adjacent to the premises are covered under Coverage A of the homeowners policy. Since the dwelling is occupied, the loss is not excluded under the theft peril.

What's Not Covered

Coverage A specifically excludes land, including the land on which the dwelling sits. When determining a limit of liability for an owner-occupied dwelling, remember that a selling price includes land. A full explanation of replacement cost and actual cash valuation of property appears in Chapter 5.

Physical Loss Required

The HO–3 form covers physical loss to the insured's dwelling and other structures stemming immediately from almost any peril or danger. The property must actually be damaged, not just threatened with damage. For example, a windstorm damages a tree on the insured's property to the point that there is a huge limb hanging over the insured's front porch. Will the policy pay to remove the limb? The form requires physical loss to the dwelling or other structures. Although it would seem that the best interest of the insurance company would be served by paying to remove the tree limb, the front porch (or the structure) must be damaged in order for limb removal to be covered.

■ COVERAGE B—OTHER STRUCTURES

The dwelling on the right has a built-in garage as an integral part of the dwelling. The built-in garage on the right is a part of Coverage A—Dwelling. The dwelling on the left has a garage separated from the house by clear space. This garage is a part of Coverage B—Other Structures.

Other structures on the premises include those set apart from the dwelling by clear space. Examples of other structures include

- detached garages;

- fences;

- gazebos;

- swimming pools; and

- storage sheds.

The coverage includes structures connected to the dwelling by only a fence or utility line. When the garage is separated from the residence premises or attached to it by only a fence, it is not part of Coverage A but is a part of Coverage B.

■ *ISO FORM*

B. Coverage B – Other Structures

1. We cover other structures on the "residence premises" set apart from the dwelling by clear space. This includes structures connected to the dwelling by only a fence, utility line, or similar connection.

What's Not Covered

Like Coverage A, Coverage B excludes land, including land on which the other structure sits. The following structures are also specifically excluded under Coverage B:

- structures rented or held for rental to any person not a tenant of the dwelling unless the structure is used solely as a private garage;

- buildings used in whole or in part for business purposes; and

- structures used by the insured or a tenant to store business property.

Stored business property cannot be gaseous or liquid fuel, other than what is in a vehicle's fuel tank.

■ *ISO FORM*

2. We do not cover:

a. Land, including land on which the other structures are located;

b. Other structures rented or held for rental to any person not a tenant of the dwelling, unless used solely as a private garage;

c. Other structures from which any "business" is conducted; or

> **d.** Other structures used to store "business" property. However, we do cover a structure that contains "business" property solely owned by an "insured" or a tenant of the dwelling provided that "business" property does not include gaseous or liquid fuel, other than fuel in a permanently installed fuel tank of a vehicle or craft parked or stored in the structure.

Study Questions

2. Fred owns a stationery store and keeps excess inventory in his garage. Is the garage covered under Coverage B?

Limit of liability

The minimum amount for Coverage B under the HO–3 is an automatic 10 percent of the Coverage A—Dwelling amount. This limit of liability is in addition to Coverage A, not a part of it. For example, a dwelling insured for $100,000 has an additional $10,000 (or 10 percent of $100,000) available automatically for other structures. If the insured needs more coverage, the policy may be endorsed to provide an additional amount of coverage on listed and described individual structures on the property.

■ COVERAGE C—PERSONAL PROPERTY

Personal property generally refers to portable property owned or used by an insured anywhere in the world. Covered personal property includes

- personal property the insured owns or uses that is located anywhere in the world;

- personal property of others, at the insured's request, while it is on the portion of the residence premises the insured occupies; and

- personal property of a guest or residence employee when it is located in any residence the insured occupies.

Answer and Rationale

2. The garage is covered under Coverage B because the inventory Fred owns falls outside the exclusion.

> ■ *ISO FORM*
>
> ### C. Coverage C – Personal Property
>
> **1.** Covered Property
>
> We cover personal property owned or used by an "insured" while it is anywhere in the world. After a loss and at your request, we will cover personal property owned by:
>
> **a.** Others while the property is on the part of the "residence premises" occupied by an "insured"; or
>
> **b.** A guest or a "residence employee", while the property is in any residence occupied by an "insured".

Property of Guests or Residence Employees

After a loss, and at the insured's request, the named insured may elect to provide insurance coverage for the personal property of a guest or residence employee while it is *in any residence owned by the insured.* For example, when a gardener leaves his or her coat and gloves on the residence premises each evening, this property can be covered at the request of the insured.

Secondary Residence

Personal property is afforded worldwide protection; however, there is a 10 percent limit on Coverage C on personal property usually situated at a secondary residence for the insured that is not shown in the Declarations Page of the policy.

For example, if the insured has a $50,000 limit under Coverage C, he or she has $5,000 under Coverage C at a vacation home.

> ■ *ISO FORM*
>
> **2.** Limit For Property At Other Residences
>
> Our limit of liability for personal property usually located at an "insured's" residence, other than the "residence premises", is 10% of the limit of liability for Coverage **C,** or $1,000, whichever is greater. However, this limitation does not apply to personal property:

> **a.** Moved from the "residence premises" because it is being repaired, renovated or rebuilt and is not fit to live in or store property in; or
>
> **b.** In a newly acquired principal residence for 30 days from the time you begin to move the property there.

Study Questions

3. Mary Grey's personal property is insured for $100,000 under her HO–3 Coverage C. How much coverage will Mary's policy provide for her son's personal property while he is living in the college dormitory?

   A. Nothing
   B. $5,000
   C. $10,000
   D. $50,000

What's Not Covered

In addition to listing certain special limits of liability that apply to personal property, the form also lists eleven categories of items that are specifically *not* covered.

Property Not Covered
a. articles described and insured separately elsewhere in this or another policy;
b. animals, birds and fish;
c. motor vehicles and their accessories, equipment or parts, or electronic apparatus powered by the vehicle's electrical system;
d. aircraft and parts, except model or hobby aircraft;
e. hovercraft and parts;
f. property of roomers, boarders or other tenants unrelated to the insured;
g. property in an apartment the insured rents to others (except as provided under Additional Coverages up to $2,500);
h. property rented or held for rental to others away from the residence premises;
i. business data, though the cost of blank recording, storage media and prerecorded computer programs is not covered;
j. credit cards, electronic fund transfer cards or access devices (except as provided under Additional Coverages up to $500); and
k. water or steam.

Answer and Rationale

3. **C.** $10,000 is 10% of Mary's personal property protection under Coverage C. Coverage is available provided her son meets the student eligibility requirements.

The Property Not Covered section eliminates duplication of insurance coverage for items that are better insured by another policy:

- motor vehicles by a *Personal Auto Policy;* and

- jewelry and furs under a *Scheduled Personal Property* endorsement.

The section also eliminates items that may be considered uninsurable by the company (for example, animals) because it is difficult or impossible to estimate the potential loss or replacement cost. Chapter 8 provides information on the Scheduled Personal Property Endorsement.

■ *ISO FORM*

4. Property Not Covered
We do not cover:
a. Articles separately described and specifically insured, regardless of the limit for which they are insured, in this or other insurance;

ISO Form Update   The Homeowners 2000 policies added two new categories of property not covered.

- *Hovercraft and parts.* Few people own hovercraft, but, since this type of vehicle was not previously excluded, it would have been possible for some hobbyists to have had a claim. The addition of this exclusion acts to preserve the intent of the policies, i.e., not to cover aircraft-type exposures that should be left to specialty insurers.

- *Water or steam.* At first glance, it might be difficult to think of a significant potential of loss to water. As an example, the cost of having to refill a swimming pool if it had to be drained because of an insured peril could run into the thousands of dollars.

■ *ISO FORM*

e. Hovercraft and parts. Hovercraft means a self-propelled motorized ground effect vehicle and includes, but is not limited to, flarecraft and air cushion vehicles;
k. Water or steam.

Limit of Liability

Coverage is automatically provided on a named peril basis for 25–50 percent of the dwelling coverage amount, depending on the number of family units in the building (up to four). For example, if a single family dwelling is insured for $100,000, personal property is automatically insured for $50,000.

Minimum Policy Limits Determined From Coverage A Amount			
Coverage A	**Coverage B**	**Coverage C**	**Coverage D**
HO–2 Declared Amount*	1 or 2 family — 10% of Cov. A 3 or 4 family — 5% of Cov. A	1 or 2 family — 50% of Cov. A 3 family — 30% of Cov. A 4 family — 25% of Cov. A	30% of Cov. A
HO–3 Declared Amount*	Same as HO–2	Same as HO–2	Same as HO–2
HO–4 N/A	N/A	See State Pages	30% of Cov. C
HO–5 Declared Amount*	Same as HO–2	Same as HO–2	Same as HO–2
HO–6 Declared Amount*	N/A	See State Pages	50% of Cov. C
HO–8 Declared Amount*	Same as HO–2	Same as HO–2	10% of Cov. A

*Minimums determined by state rate manuals

All homeowners policies place *special limits of liability* on certain types of personal property. Insurance companies reason that some insureds tend to be more careless about protecting certain property if it is insured and, therefore, the chance of loss is increased. Because of this moral hazard and the adjustment problems that the loss of certain valuable items creates, homeowners policies have maximum dollar limits on the amount that will be paid for loss of these items. Refer to Part II of the HO Comparison Chart for a synopsis of the special limits of liability.

> ■ *ISO FORM*
>
> ### 3. Special Limits Of Liability
> The special limit for each category shown below is the total limit for each loss for all property in that category. These special limits do not increase the Coverage **C** limit of liability.

Some personal property is limited because of the nature of the property. For example, the watercraft limit is $1,500. Boats and their equipment tend to carry high dollar values. The homeowners policy premium is based principally on the dwelling amount. The underwriting necessary to establish values for the exposure presented by expensive watercraft doesn't apply to the rate structure for dwellings. You may write a separate policy for watercraft valued at more than $1,500.

Some personal property, such as jewelry, furs and precious stones, is especially susceptible to theft. Loss by theft is limited to certain dollar amounts for these items. However, if any of these items is damaged or destroyed by a peril other than theft, coverage applies in the same manner as to other personal property. The special limits are *sublimits* and do not increase the amount of coverage for personal property.

ISO Form Update The HO 2000 program raises the sublimits of liability on the items shown below.

Personal Property	Limit In Form	Maximum Allowed
Jewelry, Watches and Furs	$1,500	$ 6,000
Money	$ 200	$ 1,000
Securities	$1,500	$ 3,000
Silverware, Goldware and Pewterware	$2,500	$10,000
Firearms	$2,500	$ 6,500
Electronic Apparatus		
• In or upon a motor vehicle or motorized land conveyance	$1,500	$ 6,000
• Not in or upon a motorized vehicle that is away from the residence premises and used for business	$1,500	$ 6,000

 ISO Form Update The Homeowners 2000 Program revises the limits for several of the categories as shown in the table above. Note that the limitations on electronic apparatus apply only if the electronic apparatus can be operated independently **or** from a vehicle's power source. If it operates only from the vehicle's electrical system, no coverage applies.

In the 2000 edition, ISO added *related equipment* to the category for firearms. As a result, items such as holsters, detached scopes and gun-cleaning equipment are now subject to the same $1,500 limit for theft as guns are.

■ *ISO FORM*

> **j.** $1,500 on electronic apparatus and accessories, while in or upon a "motor vehicle", but only if the apparatus is equipped to be operated by power from the "motor vehicle's" electrical system while still capable of being operated by other power sources.
>
> Accessories include antennas, tapes, wires, records, discs or other media that can be used with any apparatus described in this Category **j.**

> **k.** $1,500 on electronic apparatus and accessories used primarily for "business" while away from the "residence premises" and not in or upon a "motor vehicle". The apparatus must be equipped to be operated by power from the "motor vehicle's" electrical system while still capable of being operated by other power sources.
>
> Accessories include antennas, tapes, wires, records, discs or other media that can be used with any apparatus described in this Category **k.**

Study Questions

4. A gun valued at $3,000 is destroyed in a fire. How much will the loss settlement be?

Named Perils Coverage

You'll recall from Chapters 1 and 3 that the HO–3 provides protection for personal property against 16 named perils. The course presented the 16 broad form perils in detail in Chapter 3. Since it's sometimes easy to misinterpret how these perils apply to personal property, we'll review windstorm or hail and theft with examples that apply specifically to personal property.

Windstorm or Hail

Homeowners policies *exclude* interior damage to a building or its contents caused by wind-driven rain, snow, sleet and dust unless wind first damages the exterior walls or roof to cause an opening. For example, a severe windstorm blows large patches of shingles off an insured's roof. As a result, a leak occurs. Water warps the insured's dining room table, discolors the cloth and silk flowers. Because of the roof damage, the insured can recover for damage to the table, cloth and flowers. If rain had entered the house through an open window and caused the same damage, there would be no coverage for the damaged table, cloth and flowers.

Theft Peril

Theft of personal property is provided only *on the part of the residence premises occupied by an insured* and not to any part rented to people other than the insured. In other words, if a tenant in a duplex owned by the named insured invited a guest

---

Answer and Rationale

4. The loss will be settled at the gun's actual cash value (less any applicable deductible). If the gun had been stolen, the policy would pay only $2,000 for the loss because of the policy's special limits of liability.

to stay with him or her and the friend's luggage was stolen, the named insured's HO–3 policy would not provide coverage for the loss.

To review, here are the exclusions for theft. The peril does not include theft

- committed by an insured;

- of building materials until construction is complete and the dwelling is occupied; *

- from any part of the premises rented by an insured to a noninsured person; and

- off the residence premises for selected items.

  * Construction materials for unoccupied dwellings require Builders Risk coverage.

Study Questions

5. You may recognize a similar question from the discussion of Coverage A. Under Coverage C, if construction materials used to repair an attached garage due to a hailstorm are stolen from behind the garage during the construction period, is the loss covered under the theft peril?

   A. Yes
   B. No

The selected items not covered by theft away from the residence premises include

- watercraft, including its furnishings, equipment and outboard motors;

- trailers and campers; and

- property on any premises owned by, rented to or occupied by an insured, other than on the premises described in the policy, unless the insured is temporarily living there.*

  * Check with companies you represent to obtain a clarification of "temporarily living there". This generally does not mean the insured must occupy the dwelling at the time of loss; however, regular use must be established.

■ COVERAGE D—LOSS OF USE

When an insured experiences a property loss, he or she is often unable to immediately return to the residence premises. When a loss by an insured peril forces the insured to move to temporary quarters, Coverage D pays reasonable excess

---

Answer and Rationale

5. **A.** The materials and supplies that are for use in the construction and located on or adjacent to the premises are covered for theft under Coverage C of the homeowners policy as long as the dwelling is completed and occupied.

expenses until the property is habitable. Under Coverage D, the insured may elect to receive reimbursement under one of three types of protection:

- additional living expense;

- fair rental value; or

- prohibited use while the insured location is being repaired.

■ *ISO FORM*

D. Coverage D – Loss Of Use

The limit of liability for Coverage **D** is the total limit for the coverages in **1.** Additional Living Expense, **2.** Fair Rental Value and **3.** Civil Authority Prohibits Use below.

1. Additional Living Expense

If a loss covered under Section **I** makes that part of the "residence premises" where you reside not fit to live in, we cover any necessary increase in living expenses incurred by you so that your household can maintain its normal standard of living.

Additional Living Expense

Additional living expense pays any extra cost (over and above normal expenditures) the insured incurs in order to live elsewhere temporarily because of damage to the residence premises caused by a covered peril. The company usually asks the insured to provide receipts to prove the amount of loss. Coverage applies only to the time actually required to restore the home to habitable condition or for the named insured's household to become settled in other permanent quarters, whichever is less. The expiration date of the homeowners policy does not limit loss of use coverage. The coverage applies during

- the shortest time needed to repair or replace the damaged property; **or**

- the shortest time it takes the insured to permanently relocate to another premises.

Real Life Application

Assume that when Judy's apartment was severely damaged by fire, she temporarily moved to another apartment building while repairs were being made to her apartment. Before the loss, Judy paid $750 a month for rent. Because month-to-month leases are more expensive in the city where Judy lives, her rent rose to $1,000 for the temporary apartment.

Study Questions

6. How much additional living expense would be covered under her policy?

Fair Rental Value

Instead of additional living expense, the insured may choose to be reimbursed under the *fair rental value* provision. This provision provides cash reimbursement for loss of use—even if no additional costs are charged. After a covered loss, the insured may move in with friends or relatives during the time repairs are being made to the residence premises and actually incur no additional costs. In this case, the insured's fair rental value would be the cost that the insured *would have incurred* for renting comparable housing (less any noncontinuing expenses, such as utilities) for the time needed to restore the dwelling to the same habitable condition that existed before the loss.

■ *ISO FORM*

2. Fair Rental Value

If a loss covered under Section I makes that part of the "residence premises" rented to others or held for rental by you not fit to live in, we cover the fair rental value of such premises less any expenses that do not continue while it is not fit to live in.

Payment will be for the shortest time required to repair or replace such premises.

At some point prior to the covered loss, the named insured may have rented part of the residence premises to a boarder. At the time of the loss, coverage applies for the rental income (less any noncontinuing expenses, such as utilities) that the insured incurs because the tenant is unable to live in the rented space because of damage by a *covered peril.*

The table below represents the following facts about a rental value claim:

- the insured rents 6 percent of his or her 2,500-square-foot dwelling: one 10×15 bedroom (150 square feet);

- monthly rental received is $200, including telephone, electrical and cable TV;

Answer and Rationale

6. Coverage D would pay the $250 additional living expense Judy incurs until her original apartment is repaired.

- noncontinuing expenses are prorated at 6 percent of the total of each expense item for the month; and

- the contractor takes three months to make repairs after a fire loss.

Non-Continuing Expenses	Total	Loss As Determined	Total
Electrical $10 × 3	$30	Rental Income $200 × 3	$600
Telephone $40 × 3	$120	Less Noncontinuing Expenses	$180
Cable TV $10 × 3	$30		
TOTAL	$180	LOSS PAYABLE	$420

Civil Authority Prohibits Use

In some cases, the residence premises has not suffered a direct loss, but a neighbor's loss from a fire or other peril makes the other dwellings in the neighborhood inaccessible or uninhabitable. For example, the fire or police department may not permit residents to enter a subdivision if many homes were damaged by a natural disaster. If civil authority prohibits use of the insured premises because of damage to neighboring premises by a covered peril, any resulting loss for additional living expenses **or** fair rental value is covered for up to two weeks.

■ *ISO FORM*

3. Civil Authority Prohibits Use

If a civil authority prohibits you from use of the "residence premises" as a result of direct damage to neighboring premises by a Peril Insured Against, we cover the loss as provided in 1. Additional Living Expense and 2. Fair Rental Value above for no more than two weeks.

What's Not Covered

Loss of Use has no coverage for claims involving loss or expense due to *cancellation of a lease* or agreement, even if that cancellation resulted from a loss by a covered peril. The policy language is, "We do not cover loss or expense due to cancellation of a lease or agreement." For example, if an apartment building burns and the landlord decides not to rebuild and/or renew the current tenants' leases, Coverage D does not apply.

Study Questions

7. The purpose of Coverage D—Loss of Use is to

  A. cover the additional living expenses incurred following a loss
  B. cover the additional expenses needed to replace property following a loss
  C. cover the loss of wages incurred while replacing damaged property
  D. All of the above

■ ADDITIONAL COVERAGES

Under Section I, all homeowners forms contain certain supplemental benefits called *Additional Coverages*. The HO–3 form contains twelve additional coverages that either

- expand the coverage provided under the homeowners form; or

- add extra coverage.

As you review the twelve additional coverages in the ISO notice, notice the last paragraph in each. It will indicate whether the coverage is

- *in addition* to or

- *does not increase*

the limit of liability stated in the policy.

Debris Removal

There are two subparts to the Debris Removal coverage. Subpart **a.** applies to covered property damaged by a covered peril. When insured property is damaged by a covered peril, the insurer pays for reasonable expenses to remove the damaged property or debris, including the cost to remove the debris of shingles blown off by a windstorm. The expense is included in the limit of liability for the damaged property. The damaged property could be a building, other structures or personal property.

If the amount for the damaged property *plus* the cost for debris removal exceeds the limit under Coverage A, B or C (whichever one applies), there is an additional 5 percent increase in the liability limit.

Answer and Rationale

7. **A.** Coverage D pays reasonable excess expenses until the property is habitable.

■ *ISO FORM*

E. Additional Coverages

1. Debris Removal

a. We will pay your reasonable expense for the removal of:

(1) Debris of covered property if a Peril Insured Against that applies to the damaged property causes the loss; or

(2) Ash, dust or particles from a volcanic eruption that has caused direct loss to a building or property contained in a building.

This expense is included in the limit of liability that applies to the damaged property. If the amount to be paid for the actual damage to the property plus the debris removal expense is more than the limit of liability for the damaged property, an additional 5% of that limit is available for such expense.

Real Life Application

Sue has an HO–3 with a policy period from September 1, 2001, to September 1, 2002. On July 15, 2002, a fire causes $50,000 in damage to Sue's house. She is paid $49,000 after subtracting her $1,000 deductible. $5,000 of the settlement was earmarked for debris removal.

Debris removal can often be a substantial part of a loss settlement because of environmental considerations and restrictions on dumping in many states. In the event a direct loss plus debris removal expense exceeds the policy limit for the damaged property, the insurance company agrees to pay up to an additional 5 percent of the limit of the coverage involved for removing the debris. This statement means that the sum of the loss payable and basic amount payable for Debris Removal can exceed the limit of insurance in the Declarations by no more than 5 percent.

Real Life Application

Let's assume that Sue (from the previous Real Life Application) has a $100,000 limit of liability on the dwelling. She suffers a total fire loss. In the event that Sue's debris removal plus the dwelling loss exceeds $100,000, Sue will have an additional 5 percent of $100,000 available for this coverage, or $5,000, if needed.

Subpart **b.** of Debris Removal covers the reasonable expense of debris removal caused by wind or hail or weight of ice, snow or sleet. The company pays up to $1,000 per loss for the expense of removing the insured's trees that fall on the insured's premises after damage by windstorm, hail, weight of ice, snow or sleet.

Coverage up to $1,000 is also provided under Subpart **b.** if a neighbor's tree falls into the insured's yard. This coverage applies only if the tree damages a covered structure or blocks a ramp for a handicapped person. The $1,000 limit is per loss.

No more than $500 of the $1,000 limit applies per tree. The removal does not include the value of the debris.

■ **ISO FORM**

b. We will also pay your reasonable expense, up to $1,000, for the removal from the "residence premises" of:

(1) Your tree(s) felled by the peril of Windstorm or Hail or Weight of Ice, Snow or Sleet; or

(2) A neighbor's tree(s) felled by a Peril Insured Against under Coverage **C;**

provided the tree(s):

(3) Damage(s) a covered structure; or

(4) Does not damage a covered structure, but:

(a) Block(s) a driveway on the "residence premises" which prevent(s) a "motor vehicle", that is registered for use on public roads or property, from entering or leaving the "residence premises"; or

(b) Block(s) a ramp or other fixture designed to assist a handicapped person to enter or leave the dwelling building.

The $1,000 limit is the most we will pay in any one loss regardless of the number of fallen trees. No more than $500 of this limit will be paid for the removal of any one tree.

This coverage is additional insurance.

Reasonable Repairs

When the insured attempts to protect covered property from further damage, the insurance company will pay any reasonable costs the insured incurs. For example, to prevent further interior damage, the insured might rent a tarpaulin to cover a roof that has been damaged by fire. The policy pays for the tarp rental. If the insured repairs damaged property, the insurer will pay for the repairs only if the damage to that property was covered by a peril insured against by the policy. Any measures used to protect or repair the property are considered part of the limit of liability that applies to that property, not an additional amount of insurance protection.

> ■ *ISO FORM*
>
> ### 2. Reasonable Repairs
>
> **a.** We will pay the reasonable cost incurred by you for the necessary measures taken solely to protect covered property that is damaged by a Peril Insured Against from further damage.
>
> **b.** If the measures taken involve repair to other damaged property, we will only pay if that property is covered under this policy and the damage is caused by a Peril Insured Against. This coverage does not:
>
> **(1)** Increase the limit of liability that applies to the covered property; or
>
> **(2)** Relieve you of your duties, in case of a loss to covered property, described in **B.4.** under Section **I** – Conditions.

Trees, Shrubs and Other Plants

The policy provides coverage for the value of trees, shrubs, plants or lawns on the residence premises, but only for the following perils:

- fire or lightning;

- explosion;

- riot or civil commotion;

- aircraft;

- vehicles not owned or operated by a resident of the residence premises;

- vandalism or malicious mischief; or

- theft.

Up to 5 percent of Coverage A may be applied for covered damage to trees, shrubs, plants or lawns. This coverage is additional insurance. However, the policy pays no more than $500 for any one tree, shrub or plant and excludes property grown for business purposes.

■ *ISO FORM*

3. Trees, Shrubs And Other Plants

We cover trees, shrubs, plants or lawns, on the "residence premises", for loss caused by the following Perils Insured Against:

a. Fire or Lightning;

b. Explosion;

c. Riot or Civil Commotion;

d. Aircraft;

e. Vehicles not owned or operated by a resident of the "residence premises";

f. Vandalism or Malicious Mischief; or

g. Theft.

We will pay up to 5% of the limit of liability that applies to the dwelling for all trees, shrubs, plants or lawns. No more than $500 of this limit will be paid for any one tree, shrub or plant. We do not cover property grown for "business" purposes.

This coverage is additional insurance.

Study Questions

8. If the shrubs in front of a house burn when the house catches fire, how much is the insured entitled to recover for the shrubs under his homeowners policy?

A. Five percent of the limit on Coverage A with a maximum of $500 for any one shrub

B. $500

C. Replacement cost

D. Covered amount

Answer and Rationale

8. **A.** Trees, shrubs and other plants are covered to 5 percent of the limit on Coverage A, subject to a maximum of $500 for any one tree, shrub or plant.

Fire Department Service Charge

Some municipalities do not provide fire protection or limit protection to certain boundaries. People who are unprotected generally purchase fire fighting services from an area near where they live. The HO–3 policy pays up to $500 for liability the insured assumes *before a loss* by contract or agreement for fire department charges as a result of the fire department's future attempts to save or protect covered property from any peril insured against. The $500 is additional insurance. No deductible applies and coverage applies *only* if the property is located outside the city, municipality or protection district providing the fire fighting services.

Property Removed

If a loss occurs, the insured is required to protect personal property from further damage. Therefore, any property removed from the premises because it was threatened by a peril insured against, such as fire, wind or explosion, is covered for direct loss from *any cause* for 30 days. Property is covered while it is being removed and while it is stored at another location. This coverage does not change the limit of liability that applies to the property being removed. For example, if the policy provides a limit of $25,000 on Coverage C—Personal Property and $10,000 of personal property is removed, the coverage limit is not increased to $35,000; it remains at $25,000.

Credit Card, Forgery and Counterfeit Money

The insured may be held legally liable for certain losses resulting from

- acceptance of counterfeit money;

- check forgery; and

- theft or unauthorized use of credit or fund transfer cards.

The homeowners policy provides an additional amount of insurance—$500—without deductible for losses caused by or resulting from

- an insured's legal obligation to pay because of the theft or unauthorized use of credit cards in the insured's name;

- theft or unauthorized use of a fund transfer card registered in the insured's name;

- forgery or alteration of any check or negotiable instrument; and

- acceptance in good faith of counterfeit U.S. or Canadian paper currency.

■ *ISO FORM*

6. Credit Card, Electronic Fund Transfer Card Or Access Device, Forgery And Counterfeit Money

a. We will pay up to $500 for:

(1) The legal obligation of an "insured" to pay because of the theft or unauthorized use of credit cards issued to or registered in an "insured's" name;

(2) Loss resulting from theft or unauthorized use of an electronic fund transfer card or access device used for deposit, withdrawal or transfer of funds, issued to or registered in an "insured's" name;

(3) Loss to an "insured" caused by forgery or alteration of any check or negotiable instrument; and

All loss resulting from a series of acts committed by any one person or in which any one person is concerned or implicated is considered to be one loss.

(4) Loss to an "insured" through acceptance in good faith of counterfeit United States or Canadian paper currency.

This coverage is additional insurance. No deductible applies to this coverage.

Credit Card Losses

This additional coverage does not provide coverage for

- losses incurred by an insured because of a credit or fund transfer card used by a resident of the insured's household or anyone entrusted with the card; and

- loss arising out of business pursuits or dishonesty of an insured.

Coverage for stored-value cards and smart cards is limited to $200 under the Special Limits of Liability for Coverage C. The insurance company has the right to investigate and settle any claim or suit up to the limit of the policy's liability—$500. The insurer will defend the insured if he or she is named in a suit under the Credit Card or Fund Transfer Card coverage. At the insurance company's option, defense may also be provided for the insured or the insured's bank if either or both are named in a suit under the Forgery coverage.

**Study
Questions**

9. Credit card fraud, unless committed by a resident of the insured's household or a person entrusted with the card, is covered under a homeowners policy to a maximum of what amount?

    A. $100

    B. $500

    C. $1,000

    D. $2,000

Loss Assessment

Owners of homes in some subdivisions sometimes join associations of property owners that collectively own the common areas of the development, such as pools, playgrounds and some buildings. The owners pay monthly assessments for their proportionate share of the insurance costs and usual maintenance expenses for the property owned collectively. However, some expenses, such as inadequately insured or uninsured property losses, are not funded through regular maintenance charges. When association property is damaged and the loss is not fully covered by insurance, the association charges each insured a *loss assessment* for direct loss to property. The HO–3 policy provides up to $1,000 for the insured's share of that assessment. Even if a number of assessments are made for a single property loss, the policy will only pay up to $1,000. The coverage is additional insurance and can be increased by the Loss Assessment Coverage endorsement (HO 04 35 10 00).

■ *ISO FORM*

7. Loss Assessment

    a. We will pay up to $1,000 for your share of loss assessment charged during the policy period against you, as owner or tenant of the "residence premises", by a corporation or association of property owners. The assessment must be made as a result of direct loss to property, owned by all members collectively, of the type that would be covered by this policy if owned by you, caused by a Peril Insured Against under Coverage **A,** other than:

    (1) Earthquake; or

    (2) Land shock waves or tremors before, during or after a volcanic eruption.

Answer and Rationale

    9. **B.** Credit card fraud, unless committed by a resident of the insured's household or a person entrusted with the card, is covered to a maximum of $500.

> The limit of $1,000 is the most we will pay with respect to any one loss, regardless of the number of assessments. We will only apply one deductible, per unit, to the total amount of any one loss to the property described above, regardless of the number of assessments.
>
> **b.** We do not cover assessments charged against you or a corporation or association of property owners by any governmental body.

Collapse

Homeowners policies once treated collapse as a covered peril. However, collapse is seldom a *proximate cause*—an unbroken chain of events between the occurrence of an insured peril and the damage or destruction of property—of the loss.

ISO has added a definition of collapse which requires "an abrupt falling down or caving in" so that the property can no longer be occupied.

> ■ *ISO FORM*
>
> **8. Collapse**
>
> **a.** With respect to this Additional Coverage:
>
> **(1)** Collapse means an abrupt falling down or caving in of a building or any part of a building with the result that the building or part of the building cannot be occupied for its current intended purpose.
>
> **(2)** A building or any part of a building that is in danger of falling down or caving in is not considered to be in a state of collapse.
>
> **(3)** A part of a building that is standing is not considered to be in a state of collapse even if it has separated from another part of the building.
>
> **(4)** A building or any part of a building that is standing is not considered to be in a state of collapse even if it shows evidence of cracking, bulging, sagging, bending, leaning, settling, shrinkage or expansion.

What's Covered for Collapse

Collapse is usually the effect of some other cause, and the HO–3 policy now covers direct physical loss to covered property as a result of perils specifically listed. The policy provides for direct physical loss to property if all or part of an insured building collapses because of

- perils insured against under Coverage C—Property Damage;

- hidden decay, insect or vermin damage;

- weight of contents, equipment, animals, rain or people; and

- use of defective material or methods in construction, remodeling or renovation, if the collapse occurs during that process.

What's Not Covered for Collapse

Collapse coverage does not apply in some cases. There is no coverage for collapse of awnings, gutters, yard fixtures, outdoor swimming pools, piers, wharves, docks, beach or diving platforms, retaining walls, walks, roadways and other paved surfaces unless the building collapses. Losses such as a gutter falling off a building because of lack of maintenance are not covered. Collapse also does not include losses resulting from cracking, shrinkage, bulging or expansion, which have traditionally been excluded. This additional coverage does not increase the limits of insurance for the dwelling or personal property.

Study Questions

10. Under HO–3, collapse is not considered a cause of loss but an additional coverage.

    A. True
    B. False

Glass or Safety Glazing Material

As long as the building has not been vacant for more than 60 consecutive days prior to the loss, the policy covers breakage of glass as well as damage to covered property as a result of that glass breakage. If local building codes require that broken glass be replaced with safety glass or safety glazing materials, the policy provides for that replacement. This coverage does not increase the limit of liability applicable to the damaged property.

Answer and Rationale

10. **A.** By defining collapse as an additional coverage rather than a peril, losses involving collapse must be triggered by a named event. These events are similar to named peril property contracts but add additional perils such as weight of people, property or rain collecting on the roof and use of defective materials or methods in construction, renovation or remodeling.

> ### ■ *ISO FORM*
>
> **9. Glass Or Safety Glazing Material**
> **a.** We cover:
> **(1)** The breakage of glass or safety glazing material which is part of a covered building, storm door or storm window;
> **(2)** The breakage of glass or safety glazing material which is part of a covered building, storm door or storm window when caused directly by earth movement; and
> **(3)** The direct physical loss to covered property caused solely by the pieces, fragments or splinters of broken glass or safety glazing material which is part of a building, storm door or storm window.

■ LANDLORD'S FURNISHINGS

As anyone who has rented an apartment knows, landlords may require a substantial deposit against damage to the rented property. This additional coverage provides up to $2,500 for damage to *furnishings* supplied by the landlord (not for damage to the building itself). The damage must be caused by one of the Broad Form perils. This additional coverage does not increase the limit available to the insured for Coverage C—Personal Property. Therefore, an insured would be well advised to consider the value of any landlord's furnishings in determining how much coverage to purchase.

■ ORDINANCE OR LAW

Building codes sometimes require that damaged property comply with the existing code if and when the property is repaired or replaced. For some insureds, this may represent substantial additional costs. Remember, the policy covers the cost to repair or replace the existing property, not the cost of more expensive materials mandated by law. This additional coverage provides up to 10 percent of the Coverage A limit to pay for the additional costs incurred because of local building laws, including the cost to tear down all or part of the existing structure and the cost to remove construction debris.

This coverage is also in addition to the limit for Coverage A. For example, a dwelling insured for $100,000 will actually pay an additional $10,000 for Ordinance or Law coverage.

■ *ISO FORM*

11. Ordinance Or Law

a. You may use up to 10% of the limit of liability that applies to Coverage **A** for the increased costs you incur due to the enforcement of any ordinance or law which requires or regulates:

(1) The construction, demolition, remodeling, renovation or repair of that part of a covered building or other structure damaged by a Peril Insured Against;

(2) The demolition and reconstruction of the undamaged part of a covered building or other structure, when that building or other structure must be totally demolished because of damage by a Peril Insured Against to another part of that covered building or other structure; or

(3) The remodeling, removal or replacement of the portion of the undamaged part of a covered building or other structure necessary to complete the remodeling, repair or replacement of that part of the covered building or other structure damaged by a Peril Insured Against.

Real Life Application

Ruth's house suffers a major fire loss and is 60 percent destroyed. The city ordinance in effect where the house is located stipulates that Ruth has to tear down the undamaged part of the building as well in order to replace the roof structure with wind-resistant construction. The ordinance states that losses to buildings in excess of 51 percent of their value and of frame construction must be razed and rebuilt to code. This is not an unusual ordinance; many communities have similar ordinances.

Let's suppose that the losses incurred by Ruth in her fire loss are the same as in the graphic below. For the purposes of the example, disregard the deductible, mortgage clause and the personal property loss.

Item	Cost
New Building Cost	$125,000
Policy Limit	$100,000
Loss Amount – Old Building	$ 60,000
Increased Cost of Construction	$ 65,000

The next graphic shows Ruth's payment.

Covered Loss Payment	Amount	Ruth's Penalty	Cost
Loss to Old Building	$60,000	Loss Incurred by Ruth	$125,000
Ordinance of Law Additional Coverage	$10,000	Payment	$70,000
Payment to Ruth	$70,000	Total Uninsured Loss	$65,000

Ruth's agent could have offered her an Ordinance or Law Coverage endorsement (HO 0 77 10 00). The endorsement increases the limit of liability percentage from 10 to whatever percentage is needed to comply with a local ordinance. Ruth could have bought a 20 or 25 percent increase and reduced her uninsured loss substantially.

Grave Markers

ISO Form Update   The Homeowners 2000 Program added $5,000 coverage for damage to grave markers and mausoleums on or away from the residence premises for loss caused by a peril insured against.

This coverage does not increase the limits of liability that apply under Coverages A, B or C to the damaged property.

Insureds who own mausoleums can obtain higher limits, if desired, with a specific insurance policy. Additional limits on grave markers can be obtained with the HO 04 61—Scheduled Personal Property Endorsement.

■ POLICY COMPARISON

This part of the chapter provides information on the Section I coverages for the HO–2, HO–4, HO–5, HO–6 and HO–8 policies. We'll begin with the HO–2.

HO–2

The HO–2 and HO–3 policies are very similar. In fact, the following policy parts are identical:

- Coverage A—Dwelling;

- Coverage B—Other Structures;

- Coverage C—Personal Property;

- Coverage D—Loss of Use; and

- Additional Coverages.

For Section I—Perils Insured Against, the HO–2 provides named perils coverage for Coverages A, B and C. You learned in Chapter 1 that the HO–3 provides open perils coverage for Coverages A, B and D and named perils coverage for Coverage C.

■ *ISO FORM*

SECTION I – PERILS INSURED AGAINST
We insure for direct physical loss to the property described in Coverages **A, B** and **C** caused by any of the following perils unless the loss is excluded in Section I – Exclusions.

HO–4

Because a tenant does not own the premises where he or she lives, the HO–4 form does not provide coverage on the dwelling or other structures. Coverage is provided for the tenant's personal property for named perils as described under Coverage C of the HO–3 form. 1

The provisions of Coverages C and D are identical to those in the HO–3.

■ *ISO FORM*

A. Coverage C – Personal Property
   1. Covered Property
   We cover personal property owned or used by an "insured" while it is anywhere in the world. After a loss and at your request, we will cover personal property owned by:
   a. Others while the property is on the part of the "residence premises" occupied by an "insured"; or
   b. A guest or a "residence employee", while the property is in any residence occupied by an "insured".

 ISO Form Update   Adding an endorsement can broaden coverage to open perils. This provision is new to the HO 2000 program.

Building Additions and Alterations

The HO–3 has an additional coverage named Landlord's Furnishings. The HO–4 policy does not have this additional coverage. Instead, it provides an additional coverage named Building Additions and Alterations for an *additional amount of insurance,* up to 10 percent of the amount carried on personal property.

The coverage protects the insured from economic loss due to damage or destruction (by named perils) of any addition or alteration the **insured/tenant has made** to the building itself, such as wall-to-wall carpeting or kitchen cabinets paid for by the insured. There is no coverage for damage to the original walls, floors, ceilings or fixtures of the building.

The 10-percent limit may be increased for an additional premium by attaching the Building Additions and Alterations Increased Limit endorsement.

■ *ISO FORM*

10. Building Additions And Alterations

We cover under Coverage **C** the building improvements or installations, made or acquired at your expense, to that part of the "residence premises" used exclusively by you. The limit of liability for this coverage will not be more than 10% of the limit of liability that applies to Coverage **C.**

This coverage is additional insurance.

Glass or Safety Glazing Material

The additional coverage for glass or safety glazing material applies only for property covered as tenant's building additions or alterations. Glass installed by the landlord and for which the tenant is not responsible is not covered. This coverage is *not* additional insurance.

■ *ISO FORM*

9. Glass Or Safety Glazing Material

a. We cover:

(1) The breakage of glass or safety glazing material which is part of a building, storm door or storm window, and covered as Building Additions And Alterations;

(2) The breakage of glass or safety glazing material which is part of a building, storm door or storm window and covered as Building Additions And Alterations when caused directly by earth movement; and

> **(3)** The direct physical loss to covered property caused solely by the pieces, fragments or splinters of broken glass or safety glazing material which is part of a building, storm door or storm window.

Study Questions

11. The HO–4 policy has no coverage for kitchen cabinets or carpet installed by the tenant.

   A. True
   B. False

HO–5

As you learned in Chapter 1, the HO–5 provides open perils coverage for the dwelling, other structures, personal property and loss of use. The HO–5 is identical to the HO–3 for Coverages A, B, C and D, except for the perils insured against. The HO–3 has named perils coverage for personal property.

ISO Form Update Formerly, the insured had to purchase an endorsement to obtain open perils coverage for personal property. Endorsement HO–15 is no longer available since this change.

NEW POLICY FORM HO 00 05 10 00	OLD ENDORSEMENT HO 00 15 04 91
• Reintroduces the comprehensive HO–5 form withdrawn in 1984	• Formerly used with HO–03 form
• Provides open perils coverage under Coverages A, B, C, and D	• Provides open perils on personal property
• Cost to insured is 10% of the base premium	• Generally provides coverage for everything that is not specifically excluded
	• Replaced older HO–5 form which was withdrawn in '84 revision

HO–5

The perils insured against for Landlord's Furnishings in the HO–3 are all of the 16 named perils for Coverage C except theft. In the HO–5, named perils apply to landlord's furnishings, including all broad form named perils except theft and volcanic eruption.

Answer and Rationale

11. **B.** Building Additions and Alterations provides coverage for items installed at the tenant's expense in the building owned by the landlord.

HO–6

The HO–6 for Unit Owners differs significantly from the other forms in its approach to Coverage A. The form relies upon the definition of residence premises to define Coverage A. *Residence premises* means the unit where you reside, shown as the residence premises in the Declarations. Coverage for the residence premises as defined includes the following items under an HO–6:

- alterations, appliances, fixtures and improvements;

- items of real property;

- property that is the insured's responsibility under covenants adopted by an association of property owners; and

- structures owned solely by the insured.

■ *ISO FORM*

A. Coverage A – Dwelling
1. We cover:
   a. The alterations, appliances, fixtures and improvements which are part of the building contained within the "residence premises";
   b. Items of real property which pertain exclusively to the "residence premises";
   c. Property which is your insurance responsibility under a corporation or association of property owners agreement; or
   d. Structures owned solely by you, other than the "residence premises", at the location of the "residence premises".

There is no Coverage B in the HO–6. Note that the coverage grant, structures owned solely by the insured conveys coverage for other structures. Insurance professionals should assist insureds in estimating the value of other structures when determining the limit of liability for Coverage A.

■ HO–6 PROPERTY NOT COVERED

The following property is not covered under Coverage A of the HO–6:

- land;

- structures rented to any person not a tenant of the dwelling unless used as a private garage;

- structures from which a business is conducted; and

- structures used to store business property unless the property belongs to the insured.

■ *ISO FORM*

2. We do not cover:

a. Land, including land on which the "residence premises", real property or structures are located;

b. Structures rented or held for rental to any person not a tenant of the dwelling, unless used solely as a private garage;

c. Structures from which any "business" is conducted; or

d. Structures used to store "business" property. However, we do cover a structure that contains "business" property solely owned by an "insured" or a tenant of the dwelling provided that "business" property does not include gaseous or liquid fuel, other than fuel in a permanently installed fuel tank of a vehicle or craft parked or stored in the structure.

Debris Removal and Trees

Four additional coverages under the HO–6 contain slight differences in wording from the HO–3. The policy pays for tree removal as a result of windstorm, hail or weight of ice and snow if the insured *solely* owns the tree. A tree on common areas of the property is held in common, not solely owned. The policy provides named peril coverage for the value of trees, shrubs, plants and lawns that the insured *solely owns*. For example, the policy covers the insured's potted plants on the patio if they belong solely to him or her.

Glass

The perils insured against are identical to the HO–3. The scope of the coverage differs. The HO–3 covers glass breakage to material that is a part of a covered building, storm door or storm window. The HO–6 covers the same items **only if** they are covered under Coverage A.

You may recall that Coverage A of the HO–6 applies to the unit where the insured resides, shown as the residence premises in the Declarations. What this means is that glass breakage applies only to

- alterations, appliances, fixtures and improvements pertaining to the insured's unit;

- items of real property pertaining to the insured's unit;

- property that is the insured's responsibility under covenants adopted by an association of property owners; and

- structures owned solely by the insured.

Landlord's Furnishings

There is no additional coverage in the HO–6 for landlord's furnishings. There is an endorsement titled Landlord's Furnishings, but it is available only for an HO–2, HO–3 or HO–5 policy.

HO–6 Endorsements

A significant difference between the HO–4 and HO–6 forms is that various endorsements may be added to the HO–6 to meet the special needs of condominium unit owners. For example, endorsements can

- change the form to a special or open perils form;

- cover the insured's share of a loss to condominium common areas; and

- provide other additional coverages.

The most common endorsements are

- *Unit Owners Rental to Others*—provides protection for unit owners who rent the unit to someone else; and

- *Loss Assessment Coverage*—protects the insured for any assessment (up to a certain limit and subject to a deductible) that may be charged by the condominium association for losses not fully covered by the association's insurance or the Loss Assessment Additional Coverage.

■ HO–8 OVERVIEW

For Section I—Property Coverages, the HO–8 policy provides the same dwelling, other structures, personal property and loss of use coverage as the HO–3 does, but with limited named perils. You learned in Chapter 1 that the HO–8 policy covers older homes in urban neighborhoods where the replacement cost of a house may substantially exceed its market value. The form also limits theft to $1,000 per loss and excludes off-premises theft losses, except for certain storage locations.

Additional coverages under the HO–8 do not include the following:

- collapse;

- landlord's furnishings;

- ordinance or law; and

- grave markers.

■ HO–8 ADDITIONAL COVERAGES

Debris Removal—Unlike the HO–3, the HO–8 does not add an additional 5 percent of the limit of liability on the dwelling for the expenses of debris removal. The other provisions of the coverage are concurrent with those in the HO–3.

Glass or Safety Glazing Material—Although the HO–8 imposes a $100 limit on glass breakage, there is no such limit in the other forms.

■ CHAPTER SUMMARY

In this chapter, we discussed Section I—Coverages of the homeowners policy. You learned about the coverages for the insured's dwelling, other structures, loss of use and 12 additional coverages. The additional coverages either increase the limits of liability or are paid within the limits. In the next chapter, we will cover policy exclusions and conditions, describe the insured's duties following a loss and explain the procedure for resolving disagreements between the insurer and the insured.

■ **ADDITIONAL STUDY QUESTIONS**

The situations presented in the following questions evaluate your understanding of what is covered and not covered under Coverage B of the HO–3 policy. They also check your understanding of the definitions of *business* and *insured* included in the policy. (You may want to review the Definitions section of the HO–3 before you complete the exercise.)

Read the description of the coverage issue and then decide if the item is covered or not covered under Coverage B of the policy.

1. An apartment rented to the insured's nephew who is a student at a university sits over a detached garage next to the insured's dwelling. The nephew has lived there for three years, paying $300 per month rent. Is the apartment covered under Coverage B?

   A. Yes

   B. No

2. The insured has a cabana next to his swimming pool, located 100 feet away from the dwelling. Is the cabana covered under Coverage B?

   A. Yes

   B. No

3. The insured allows a neighbor to use a detached garage to repair automobiles for customers. The insured does not charge rent. Instead, the insured barters the rent for repair of owned automobiles. Is the detached garage covered under Coverage B?

   A. Yes

   B. No

4. The insured rents a detached garage to a neighbor for the purpose of storing an antique car. Is the rented garage a part of Coverage B?

   A. Yes

   B. No

The situations presented in the following questions evaluate your understanding of what is covered and not covered under Coverage C of the HO–3 policy. You can use Part II of the HO Comparison Chart and the HO–3 form to help you with the questions. Read the description of the coverage issue and then decide if the item is covered or not covered. Some of the questions evaluate your knowledge of the special limits of liability.

5. During a burglary at their home, Mrs. Alberta Thomas loses her $3,500 sable coat. How much will the HO–3 policy pay?

   A. Nothing, the policy does not cover animal fur.

   B. $1,500

   C. $2,500

   D. $3,500

6. While the Thomas's son Frank Jr. is visiting a friend, a thief breaks into the family auto and steals his CD player. Frank Jr. was very sad that he lost something that he had paid for himself. He had modified the player to operate from the car's battery and the batteries furnished with the player. Is the CD player covered?

   A. Yes

   B. No

7. During the same occurrence in the previous question, the thief steals the car's built-in telephone, CD player, tape player, radio and all antennas. Are these items covered?

   A. Yes

   B. No

The situations presented in the following questions evaluate your understanding of coverage and limits of liability under the Debris Removal Additional Coverage of the HO–3 policy. You may use Part I of the HO Forms Comparison Chart to help you with the questions on the following screens.

8. Debris Removal coverage requires only that property be damaged by a covered cause of loss.

   A. True

   B. False

9. Which of the following circumstances would be covered under the Debris Removal provision of the HO–3?

   A. Removing the insured's tree limbs from the backyard after a windstorm

   B. Removing the neighbors tree limbs from the insured's backyard after a windstorm

   C. Removing the insured's elm tree from the damaged house after a windstorm

10. The insured's elm tree falls during an ice storm and blocks the driveway. How much coverage is available?

    A. $500

    B. $1,000

11. This question reviews how to apply multiple coverages. Bill and Marge suffer the following losses as the result of a severe storm: $2,000 wind damage to their roof; $1,500 loss of income because a boarder in their house had to move; $5,000 loss to a grand piano destroyed by flood where it was temporarily stored; and $500 in medical expenses when Marge was hit by part of the falling roof. How much will their HO–3 policy pay for these losses? Disregard the deductible.

    A. $3,500

    B. $4,000

    C. $8,500

    D. $9,000

■ **ANSWERS AND RATIONALES TO ADDITIONAL STUDY QUESTIONS**

1. **B.** Part 2b of Coverage B excludes other structures rented or held for rental to any person not a tenant of the dwelling, unless used solely as a private garage.

2. **A.** The cabana falls within the definition of another structure as it is separated from the dwelling by clear space.

3. **B.** The neighbor conducts a business from the garage.

4. **A.** The garage is used solely as a private garage and is covered.

5. **B.** $1,500 of coverage is provided for loss by theft of jewelry, watches, furs and precious stones. Mrs. Thomas could have collected the actual cash value of the coat had it been destroyed by fire. The policy excludes animals, but not apparel items made from animal fur.

6. **A.** It is covered up to the limit of $1,500 provided in subparagraph **j.** of the HO–3 policy.

7. **B.** Motor vehicle equipment, accessories and parts are excluded if operated solely from the electrical system of the vehicle.

8. **B.** The property must be covered property damaged by a covered cause of loss. Damaged property not insured by the HO–3 would not be covered for debris removal.

9. **C.** As long as there is no damage to a structure or personal property, both A and B are not covered. Should the tree limbs damage a cabana or damage a swing set, then the policy would pay to remove them.

10. **A.** Only one tree fell. The limit per tree is $500.

11. **C.** All of the loss is covered except for the medical expenses. The loss of income from the boarder is covered under Loss of Use. The damage to the piano is covered under Property Removed, even though flood is not normally a covered peril. Medical expenses do not apply to injuries to an insured.

5

Section I—Exclusions and Conditions

H omeowners policies meet most of the insurance needs of the majority of property owners by using convenient and understandable forms. Homeowners policies give insureds the peace of mind that comes with knowing that money will be available if their homes or personal belongings are damaged or if someone is injured on their property. Standardized forms also minimize the insured's concern about the possibility of gaps in or duplication of coverage.

Whether a homeowners policy is named perils or open perils, the coverage it provides cannot be determined without considering the policy's exclusions and conditions. This is not always as easy as it may appear.

The HO–3 form limits or excludes certain perils that are either difficult or impossible to insure. It also contains certain conditions that apply to coverage, losses and loss payments. After completing this chapter, you will be able to

- explain the exclusions that apply to Section I—Property Coverages;

- describe the insured's duties following a property loss;

- apply the replacement cost formula to a partial loss settlement;

- describe the contractual procedure for resolving disagreements between the insured and insurance company;

- explain the purpose of the mortgage clause; and

- analyze a coverage situation involving a typical client.

■ ■ ■ ■ ■

■ INSURABLE RISKS

Insurance protection relies on proven principles supported by extensive statistical records that insurance companies have kept for decades. Information about the probability and severity of loss allows a company's actuaries to accurately predict the chance, nature and financial cost of a variety of losses.

Unearned Premium Reserves

According to law, property-casualty insurers must establish unearned premium reserves and loss reserves to assure that they will have the resources to meet future financial obligations. The *unearned premium reserve* is a debt to policyholders for protection not yet delivered. The full premium does not belong to the insurer until the policy expires. For example, if the annual policy premium is $730, the insurer earns two dollars as each day goes by (2×365). After 365 days, the entire premium is earned. However, until the premium is fully earned, it is accounted for in an unearned premium reserve. If either the insurer or the insured cancels the policy, the company returns the unearned premium to the policyholder.

Loss Reserves

Insurers also set up *loss reserves* for

- losses that have occurred but have not yet been reported to the company; and

- losses that have been reported but not yet paid.

Loss reserves include the expenses related to adjusting losses. Individual state laws prescribe the methods for determining the amounts to be held in reserve.

Pure Risks

Insurers provide coverage for pure risks only. Risks must also be accidental, unintentional and, therefore, insurable. Insurable risks share these characteristics:

- The potential loss from the risk must be large enough to cause an economic hardship to the insured, yet the cost of insuring the risk must be economically practical. Potential losses must be large enough to warrant the insurer's time, effort and expense.

- A risk should not be likely to incur repeated catastrophic losses, either to the same insured or to a significant number of similar insureds at the same time. Losses must be individually random; therefore, homeowners policies do not cover devastating losses such as floods and earthquakes.

- Losses must be fortuitous. Accidental and unintentional losses are uninsurable from the standpoint of the insured.

■ EXCLUSIONS WITHIN PERILS INSURED AGAINST

General Exclusions

As stated previously, the HO–3 is an open perils policy. Coverage is subject to named exclusions. Coverage A and B exclusions are found in *Coverages A and B—Perils Insured Against,* beginning on page 8 of 22 in the HO–3 2000 edition policy.

Note that the ISO Form below shows three subsections of Perils Insured Against for exclusions to property coverages.

- Part **2a.** of Section I—Perils Insured Against—references the nine exclusions that apply to all of Section I—Property Coverages. The next module contains an explanation of these exclusions.

- Part **2b.** of Section I—Perils Insured Against—involves collapse. It says that collapse isn't covered except as granted under the Additional Coverage Collapse. We discussed the Collapse Additional Coverage in Chapter 4.

- Part **2c.** of Section I—Perils Insured Against has six exclusions. We'll begin our study of these six exclusions next.

> ### ■ *ISO FORM*
>
> **SECTION I – PERILS INSURED AGAINST**
> **A. Coverage A – Dwelling And Coverage B – Other Structures**
> 1. We insure against risk of direct physical loss to property described in Coverages **A** and **B.**
> 2. We do not insure, however, for loss:
>   a. Excluded under Section I – Exclusions;
>   b. Involving collapse, except as provided in **E.8.** Collapse under Section I – Property Coverages; or
>   c. Caused by:

■ PART 2C.—EXCLUDED CAUSES OF LOSS

The first five exclusions within Part **2c.** include

1. freezing of a plumbing, heating, air conditioning or automatic fire-protective sprinkler system or household appliance;

2. freezing, thawing, pressure or weight of water or ice;

3. theft of materials from a building under construction;

4. vandalism and malicious mischief if the dwelling has been vacant; and

5. mold, fungus or wet rot.

There are eight additional exclusions within the sixth exclusion:

1. wear and tear;

2. mechanical breakdown;

3. smog, rust or corrosion, dry rot;

4. smoke from agricultural smudging;

5. discharge of pollutants;

6. settling, shrinking, bulging or expansion of foundations;

7. birds, vermin, rodents or insects; and

8. animals owned or kept by an insured.

We'll begin with freezing.

Freezing

When water freezes, it expands. If the water is in a pipe, expansion can cause the pipe to burst. Subsequently, when the ice melts, water can escape through the break in the pipe and cause substantial damage to the dwelling. If the insured uses reasonable care to maintain heat in the building, particularly if the building will be unoccupied for a time, the loss will be covered. What is reasonable can only be evaluated given the circumstances surrounding the loss. It might be unreasonable to expect the insured to have someone check on the heat in the dwelling if it is located in Florida and the insured is gone during the month of July.

If the dwelling is located in New York and it's February and the heating system has known problems, the same requirement might be reasonable.

■   *ISO FORM*

SECTION I – PERILS INSURED AGAINST
A. Coverage A – Dwelling And Coverage B – Other Structures
   1. We insure against risk of direct physical loss to property described in Coverages **A** and **B**.

> **2.** We do not insure, however, for loss:
> **a.** Excluded under Section I – Exclusions;
> **b.** Involving collapse, except as provided in **E.8.** Collapse under Section I – Property Coverages; or
> **c.** Caused by:

Study Questions

1. If an insured has open perils, the policy insures the dwelling and other structures against the risks of direct physical loss unless they are specifically excluded.

   A. True
   B. False

Freezing, Thawing, Pressure or Weight of Water or Ice

The next peril involves an exclusion for freezing, thawing, pressure or weight of water or ice, whether driven by wind or not, to a

- fence, pavement, patio or swimming pool;

- footing, foundation, bulkhead, wall or any other structure or device that supports all or part of a building or other structure;

- retaining wall or bulkhead that does not support all or part of a building or other structure; or

- pier, wharf or dock.

 ISO Form Update   While ISO revised the wording of this exclusion in the Homeowners 2000 program, the changes do not significantly alter the coverage provided.

Answer and Rationale

1. **A.** Open perils coverage, as opposed to named perils coverage, insures against direct physical loss except as otherwise excluded or limited by the policy.

The most significant part of the change is adding retaining walls to the list of property excluded for damage by this peril.

■ *ISO FORM*

(2) Freezing, thawing, pressure or weight of water or ice, whether driven by wind or not, to a:

(a) Fence, pavement, patio or swimming pool;

(b) Footing, foundation, bulkhead, wall, or any other structure or device that supports all or part of a building, or other structure;

(c) Retaining wall or bulkhead that does not support all or part of a building or other structure; or

(d) Pier, wharf or dock;

Theft of Building Materials

Theft of materials from a building under construction is excluded because such property is often difficult to protect. You'll remember that in Chapters 1 and 4 we talked about theft of building materials. The language here makes the coverage grant very clear because it takes away coverage only if the dwelling isn't completed and occupied. Theft coverage returns, however, as soon as the construction is finished and the dwelling is occupied, even if some materials have been left outside.

■ *ISO FORM*

(3) Theft in or to a dwelling under construction, or of materials and supplies for use in the construction until the dwelling is finished and occupied;

Vandalism and Malicious Mischief and Vacancy

This exclusion applies only if the dwelling has been vacant for more than 60 consecutive days before the loss. The exclusion includes vandalism or malicious mischief, and any ensuing loss caused by any intentional and wrongful act committed in the course of the vandalism or malicious mischief.

■ *ISO FORM*

(4) Vandalism and malicious mischief, and any ensuing loss caused by any intentional and wrongful act committed in the course of the vandalism or malicious mischief, if the dwelling has been vacant for more than 60 consecutive days immediately before the loss. A dwelling being constructed is not considered vacant;

 ISO Form Update   There were two changes to V&MM in the Homeowners 2000 Program:

- The number of days a building could be vacant and still retain coverage was increased from 30 days to 60 days.

- ISO now excludes "any ensuing loss caused by an intentional and wrongful act."

The practical impact of the exclusion of an ensuing loss remains to be seen since, presumably, a fire caused by a vandal would be covered under the fire peril, as would losses caused by other named perils. Nevertheless, the change does appear to represent a restriction on the scope of coverage for vandalism.

 Study Questions

2. The policy provides theft coverage for building materials if the dwelling has not been vacant for 60 consecutive days.

    A. True
    B. False

Mold, Fungus or Wet Rot

 ISO Form Update   Many insurance companies writing homeowners insurance have recently reported a significant increase in damage claims related to mold contamination and what is considered the toxicity of mold. An example of a mold recognized as toxic, and which is associated with the *sick building* cases discussed extensively in the media, is called *stachybotrys,* or *black mold.* The increased costs associated with mold claims are having an adverse effect on the availability and afford ability of homeowners insurance in a number of states.

Answer and Rationale

2. **B.** The 60-day limit for vacancy applies to vandalism or malicious mischief. Theft of building materials is excluded only if the dwelling isn't complete and occupied.

According to the Centers for Disease Control and Prevention (CDC), mold is everywhere. It grows all year and can be found both indoors and outdoors. Outdoors, mold is commonly found in shady, damp areas and in soil. Indoors, it can be found where humidity and moisture levels are high, such as in basements, kitchens, bathrooms and on ceilings and wall interiors where water from leaky pipes, roofs or windows can accumulate. While most molds pose no threat to humans, the CDC warns that certain molds can produce hay-fever-like allergic symptoms.

The Homeowners 2000 excludes coverage for "mold, fungus or wet rot." However, it gives back coverage if the mold condition is hidden within the walls, ceilings or beneath floors and if the loss resulted from the "accidental discharge or overflow of water or steam from within a plumbing, heating, air conditioning, sprinkler system or household appliance on the residence premises; or, a storm drain, or water, steam or sewer pipes, off the residence premises."

■ *ISO FORM*

(5) Mold, fungus or wet rot. However, we do insure for loss caused by mold, fungus or wet rot that is hidden within the walls or ceilings or beneath the floors or above the ceilings of a structure if such loss results from the accidental discharge or overflow of water or steam from within:

(a) A plumbing, heating, air conditioning or automatic fire protective sprinkler system, or a household appliance, on the "residence premises"; or

(b) A storm drain, or water, steam or sewer pipes, off the "residence premises".

> For purposes of this provision, a plumbing system or household appliance does not include a sump, sump pump or related equipment or a roof drain, gutter, downspout or similar fixtures or equipment; or

Mold, like rot and insect infestation, is generally not covered by a homeowners insurance policy. Standard homeowners policies provide coverage for disasters that are sudden and accidental. They are not designed to cover the cost of cleaning and maintaining a home. If, however, mold is caused as a direct result of a covered peril such as a burst pipe, there could be coverage for the cost of eliminating the mold.

As with prior versions of the homeowners policies, coverage for mold damage is provided when a loss is caused by a covered peril. For example, a windstorm might create an opening in the covered property that would allow moisture into the home; water from fighting a fire might create a moist area where mold could grow that is hidden from an insured. Coverage would exist because fire was the proximate cause of the loss.

Real Life Application

3. A hurricane blows the roof off a building and soaks the interior walls and floors. The repairs are done before the interior stud walls dry completely. After three months the insured notices a strong odor of mildew. Is this loss covered?

Eight Additional Exclusions

There are eight additional exclusions within number 6 on the list of exclusions within perils insured against:

1. wear and tear;

2. mechanical breakdown;

3. smog, rust or corrosion, dry rot;

4. smoke from agricultural smudging;

5. discharge of pollutants;

6. settling, shrinking, bulging or expansion of foundations;

7. birds, vermin, rodents or insects; and

8. animals owned or kept by an insured.

Answer and Rationale

3. The loss is most likely covered because of its proximate relationship to the initial damage done by the wind, a covered peril.

The characteristic that the first six of these perils have in common is that they are generally anticipated, ongoing, routine, or frequent occurrences. They also can be avoided with proper upkeep.

Wear and Tear   Losses that are not sudden or accidental but are the result of normal deterioration and degradation are typically excluded in many property forms; the same is true with the HO–3.

Mechanical Breakdown   The term *mechanical breakdown* implies that machinery would be involved in the loss. For example, the evaporator coil in a furnace/air conditioning unit may stop functioning. This type of mechanical breakdown is not covered.

If a fire loss causes smoke and soot to accumulate on the evaporator coil, causing it to need cleaning in order to return to functionality, the cleaning is covered.

Smog, Rust or Corrosion, Dry Rot   Smog damage in heavily industrialized areas is a type of loss that can be anticipated. Insurers often use the term *inherent vice* to refer to a characteristic in property itself that causes it to spoil, break, become defective, disintegrate or destroy itself. Rust and corrosion are innate characteristics of some materials, such as metal parts of machines. Dry rot is generally defined as being caused from fungi that cause wood to become brittle and crumble to powder.

Smoke from Agricultural Smudging   Before farmers used modern methods to control frost, many used smudge pots to keep the blooms and fruit already on trees from freezing. The smoke particles kept the temperature of the surfaces they coated from dropping below freezing. An offshoot of this process was that neighboring structures often became coated with a thick saltlike substance that was hard to remove. The exclusion arose from the frequency of this type of claim.

Discharge of Pollutants   This exclusion refers to damage to the insured's property. Coverage for pollution damage to someone else property may be available, if not specifically excluded, in Section II— Liability. For example, a bonfire that gets out of control causes severe damage to a tank in the back of Sue's house. The tank leaks a volatile and caustic chemical as a result of the fire, and an explosion ensues. The damage caused by the explosion is covered. The loss of the chemicals due to the fire is covered. The pollution cleanup is covered if it is a result of a peril not otherwise excluded. In this example, the proximate cause of the loss is a hostile fire.

Settling, Shrinking, Bulging or Expansion of Foundations   The policy excludes settling, shrinking, bulging or expansion, including resultant cracking, of bulkheads, pavements, patios, footings, foundations, walls, floors, roofs or ceilings. Once again, settlement cracks are a normal occurrence for all of the above structures.

Animals, Birds, Rodents   The two exclusions for damage done by various fauna include damage done by

- birds;

- vermin—pests such as cockroaches and ants;

- rodents—animals such as rats, mice and raccoons;

- insects; and

- animals owned or kept by an insured.

■ SECTION I—EXCLUSIONS

Section I—Exclusions has two distinct sets of exclusions—one listed after the letter **A** and one listed after the letter **B**. The first set of exclusions is standard to most homeowners policies:

- Ordinance or Law;

- Earth Movement;

- Water Damage

- Power Failure;

- Neglect;

- War;

- Nuclear Hazard;

- Intentional Loss; and

- Governmental Action.

> ### ■ *ISO FORM*
>
> **SECTION I – EXCLUSIONS**
> **A.** We do not insure for loss caused directly or indirectly by any of the following. Such loss is excluded regardless of any other cause or event contributing concurrently or in any sequence to the loss. These exclusions apply whether or not the loss event results in widespread damage or affects a substantial area.

The policy has a second set of exclusions under the letter **B:**

- weather conditions;

- acts or decisions; and

- faulty, inadequate or defective planning, design, materials or maintenance.

■ DOCTRINE OF CURRENT CAUSATION

Section I—Exclusions begins with a paragraph designed to break the concurrent causation theory, which holds that if two causes of loss happen at the same time or in conjunction with each other, only one cause of loss has to be covered for the loss itself to be covered.

> ### ■ *ISO FORM*
>
> **SECTION I – EXCLUSIONS**
> **A.** We do not insure for loss to property described in Coverages **A** and **B** caused by any of the following.

Concurrent causation is a judicial decision that previously allowed coverage even when an exclusion was present and was intended to exclude the loss regardless of other contributing causes. The first paragraph, which applies to the nine exclusions that follow it, is generally accepted by courts as being unambiguous and clear as to the company's intent *not* to pay losses that fall within the scope of concurrent causation's "Such loss is excluded regardless of any other cause or event contributing concurrently or in any sequence to the loss."

■ SECTION I—EXCLUSIONS, PART A

Ordinance or Law

The policy excludes any loss due to an ordinance or law that regulates the construction, repair or demolition of a building or other structure, unless specifically provided for under the policy.

For example, a city ordinance may require certain changes in a home's wiring in order to comply with the city's electrical codes. This is not covered under the policy; however, some states now permit coverage to be added by endorsement for an additional premium.

In Chapter 4, you saw an example that involved Ruth, a homeowner who suffered an underinsured loss. An ordinance obligated her to repair the roof structure of her fire-damaged home with wind-resistant construction. Her uninsured loss was $65,000. Ruth's agent could have offered her an Ordinance or Law Coverage endorsement. The endorsement increases the limit of liability percentage from 10 to whatever percentage is needed to comply with local ordinances.

Earth Movement

 ISO Form Update The HO 2000 program excludes any property damage caused by earth movement (earthquake, land shock waves due to a volcanic eruption, landslide, mine subsidence, mudflow, sinkholes, etc.), including loss stemming from the earth movement, such as fire.

In 1989, San Francisco was struck by a magnitude 7.1 earthquake. At least 27 fires were started across the Bay area. None of those fires would have been covered under the Homeowners 2000 policies. This represents a significant reduction in coverage (at least for people in earthquake zones) compared to earlier editions of the homeowners policies, which specifically included coverage for fire, explosion or breaking glass caused by earthquake. Coverage can be added back to the policy with the Earthquake Endorsement, (HO 04 54).

■ *ISO FORM*

2. Earth Movement

Earth Movement means:

a. Earthquake, including land shock waves or tremors before, during or after a volcanic eruption;

b. Landslide, mudslide or mudflow;

c. Subsidence or sinkhole; or

d. Any other earth movement including earth sinking, rising or shifting;

caused by or resulting from human or animal forces or any act of nature unless direct loss by fire or explosion ensues and then we will pay only for the ensuing loss.

This Exclusion **A.2.** does not apply to loss by theft

Earth Movement and Concurrent Causation

An insured's home is lost in a landslide because of faulty installation of a water drain by a contractor. Earth movement is specifically excluded as an insured peril. Considering the doctrine of current causation, would the homeowners policy provide coverage?

Yes, coverage would apply. The exclusion of earth movement in an HO–3 policy does not exclude coverage for damage done by a landslide since it was the faulty installation of a water drain by a third party that actually caused the earth to shift. Although earth movement is specifically excluded under the policy, insurance coverage would be granted because the concurrence of another peril (third-party negligence) that was not excluded.

Water Damage

Section I—Exclusions also specifically restrict coverage for certain types of water damage losses that are not entirely unexpected, such as flood damage to houses that are located near lakes, rivers or streams. Because these bodies of water typically overflow each spring, insurance companies consider the flood risk catastrophic and uninsurable.

Water that backs up through sewers or drains is also excluded because this type of loss is most often caused by improper maintenance or neglect. However, coverage may be purchased by endorsement—Water Back Up and Sump Discharge or Overflow (HO 04 95).

Direct loss by fire, explosion or theft resulting from water damage is covered under the policy. If water damages a fuel line that then causes a fire, property damaged by the water is not covered, but property damaged by the fire is covered.

Power Failure

The policy does not provide coverage for loss caused by the failure of power or other utility service if the failure takes place *off* the residence premises. For example, if electrical power fails because of a plant malfunction and the contents of a homeowner's freezer thaw and spoil, there is no coverage under the HO–3 form. However, if the power failure was a result of lightning striking the insured's dwelling, damaging the electrical connection to the freezer, the resulting food spoilage would be covered.

Neglect

The insured has a duty to make every rational effort to protect property. Loss to property is not covered if the insured fails to use all reasonable means to save and preserve the property during or after the loss or when it is endangered by an insured peril. The insurance company would not expect the insured to return to a burning building to retrieve property; however, it would expect that any property that was retrieved after a loss would be safely stored in another location to prevent further damage to it.

War and Nuclear Hazard

War   The homeowners policy specifically excludes property damage from war and warlike actions.

Nuclear Hazard   The policy excludes all nuclear hazard losses, including nuclear reaction, radiation or radioactive contamination. Any discharge of a nuclear weapon—even if accidental—is also excluded under these sections.

If a leak from a nuclear power plant contaminates the insured's property, the loss is not covered. These risks are potentially catastrophic and, therefore, uninsurable.

A further explanation of what is actually excluded is found in the Nuclear Hazard Condition.

■ *ISO FORM*

6. War

War includes the following and any consequence of any of the following:

a. Undeclared war, civil war, insurrection, rebellion or revolution;

b. Warlike act by a military force or military personnel; or

c. Destruction, seizure or use for a military purpose.

Discharge of a nuclear weapon will be deemed a warlike act even if accidental.

7. Nuclear Hazard

This Exclusion **A.7.** pertains to Nuclear Hazard to the extent set forth in **M.** Nuclear Hazard Clause under Section **I** – Conditions.

Intentional Loss

The homeowners policy excludes coverage for any *intentional loss* committed by or at the direction of an insured. For example, the policy doesn't cover fire if the insured intentionally burns down his or her house to collect the insurance. A more problematic situation is where a child intentionally starts a fire. Would the exclusion apply to prevent the parents from recovering their loss? The issue is whether the child had sufficient maturity to anticipate the consequences of the act. At common law and by statute in some states, a child under the age of 13 is presumed to be incapable of understanding the consequences of his or her acts and is incapable of forming the required intent.

Government Action

 ISO Form Update ISO added a new exclusion in 2000 that bars coverage for the destruction, confiscation or seizure of property insured under Coverages A, B or C.

The exclusion reflects public policy, which holds that people should not be protected for committing illegal acts. Thus, if police break into a house searching for drugs, the damage to the house would not be covered. Of course, the owner could still pursue a claim against the government in court if the break in turned out not to be justified. Governmental action means the destruction, confiscation or seizure of property described in Coverages A, B or C by order of any governmental or public authority. This exclusion does not apply to such acts ordered by any governmental or public authority that are taken at the time of a fire to prevent its spread, if the loss caused by fire would otherwise be covered under this policy.

■ EXCLUSIONS THAT DEFINE COVERAGE

These exclusions are specifically named in all open perils policies. They are not specifically listed in named perils policies. Because they are not listed as named perils, they are excluded. The three exclusions are included in the HO–3 to more clearly define coverage. Insureds have attempted to gain coverage in the homeowners and other open perils policies by claiming loss caused by ambiguous means (failure to plan, for example). These exclusions clarify that unless a specific covered cause of loss is identified, coverage will not be provided. Ensuing losses to structures insured under Coverages A and B are covered provided the ensuing loss is not excluded elsewhere in the policy.

> ### ■ ISO FORM
>
> **B.** We do not insure for loss to property described in Coverages **A** and **B** caused by any of the following. However, any ensuing loss to property described in Coverages **A** and **B** not precluded by any other provision in this policy is covered.

The following sources of loss are excluded because they are very general and almost impossible to underwrite:

- weather conditions;

- acts or decisions; and

- negligent work.

For example, insurance companies will not cover weather conditions but will cover the more specific perils of windstorm or lightning. The exclusions have been added to homeowners to clarify the coverages actually intended by the policy. However, ensuing losses that would otherwise be covered are not excluded.

Weather Conditions

Weather condition is too broad a term to be used as a peril and would include situations for which coverage is excluded. A windstorm is a weather condition and a covered peril; therefore, a loss by a windstorm would be covered. However, if a flood produced by a rainstorm causes a loss, the damage would not be covered because flood is an excluded peril. Both are examples of weather conditions, but only one is covered. However, the weather conditions exclusion applies only to the nine events excluded in Paragraph **A.**

Acts or Decisions

Acts or decisions, including the failure to act or decide by anyone, are not covered. For example, if the operator at a dam opens the floodgates in error and causes damage to an insured's house, no coverage would be provided. The resulting loss from an act or decision is not covered. The reasoning for this exclusion is identical to the reasoning for the weather exclusion. An insured may claim that it was not the flood, but the operator of the floodgates that caused the loss. Flood, of course, was never intended to be covered in the homeowners policy.

Origin of the Acts or Decisions Exclusions

This exclusion arose out of an actual California case in which the insured argued that although flood was not covered under the all risk policy in effect, the acts of the flood gate operator were, and coverage for the ensuing loss should be granted. The court agreed and thus the concept of concurrent causation was born, which we discussed earlier. This case also caused the industry to begin to move away from the term *all risk* because it is too broad a concept in property policies.

Negligent Work

For example, Mauricio discovers that the plumbing in his new house is inadequate. The cost to tear out and replace the defective material is not covered by his HO–3 policy. However, if a covered loss results from the bad plumbing, such as fire or water damage, the resulting loss is covered. Also excluded in the HO–3 are losses that result from faulty or inadequate work in the following areas:

- planning;

- zoning;

- design;

- workmanship;

- materials; and

- maintenance.

Ignoring the advice of his architect, the insured builds his house on the edge of a cliff because he likes the view.

Real Life Application

3. If the ground gives way causing the house to slide into the valley, will the insured be covered if he or she claims that the cause of the loss wasn't earth movement but was his own foolishness?

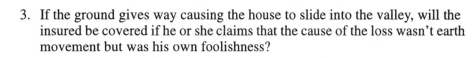

Answer and Rationale

3. **No.** Coverage will not apply. Earth movement was the cause of the damage, not the insured's foolishness. The insured cannot claim coverage under an open perils policy, because foolishness is not specifically excluded.

■ SECTION I—CONDITIONS

In addition to exclusions, homeowners policies have *conditions—certain situations or requirements that must be met in order for the insurance coverage to apply.*

There are 18 Section I—Conditions.

1. Insurable Interest and Limit of Liability;

2. Duties After Loss;

3. Loss Settlement;

4. Loss to a Pair or Set;

5. Appraisal;

6. Other Insurance and Service Agreement;

7. Suit Against Us;

8. Our Option; and

9. Loss Payment.

10. Abandonment of Property;

11. Mortgage Clause;

12. No Benefit to Bailee;

13. Nuclear Hazard Clause;

14. Recovered Property;

15. Volcanic Eruption Period;

16. Policy Period;

17. Concealment or Fraud; and

18. Loss Payable Clause.

Insurable Interest

Under the terms of the policy, the insurance company is liable for a loss only if the insured has an insurable interest in the property. The *principle of insurable interest* specifies that in order for an insurable interest to exist, the insured must suffer financially if a loss occurs or must incur some other kind of harm if the loss takes place.

For example, by the terms of their prenuptial agreement, Allan and Ashanti agree that Ashanti's interest in the marital domicile will be no more than 40 percent

Real Life Application

because Allan contributed 60 percent of the purchase price of the home. A fire and divorce ensue, in that order.

4. Applying the principle of insurable interest, how much of the coverage on the dwelling would go to Allan?

Duties After Loss

The Duties After Loss provision states that, after a loss, the insured must

- give immediate notice of the loss to the insurer or agent, to the police in case of theft and/or to the financial institution in case of the loss of a credit or fund transfer card;

- protect the property from further damage and make reasonable repairs to do so;

- keep accurate records of any repair expenses;

- prepare an inventory of damaged personal property showing the quantity, description, actual cash value and amount of loss;

- show the damaged property to the insurance company as reasonably required;

- in some cases, submit to an examination under oath;

- file a proof of loss statement within 60 days; and

Study Questions

- cooperate with the insurance company's investigation and settlement of a claim.

5. Which of the following is true about the insured's duties following a loss?

A. The insured must give prompt notice to the company or its agent of all covered losses.
B. The insured must give prompt notice to the police of all losses.
C. The insured must use all possible means to protect damaged property.
D. The insured must present receipts for all property covered by the policy.

Answers and Rationales

4. **60 percent.** Allan would receive no more than his insurable interest. Some states mandate the terms of loss settlements with State Amendatory Endorsements. Check your state's requirements for details.

5. **A.** The insured is required to provide notice to the police only in the case of theft; the insured must use *reasonable* means to protect damaged property; and the insured must present receipts only for damaged property.

Loss Settlement

Property insurance contracts usually follow one of two methods in settling losses:

- replacement cost (no depreciation in the event of a loss); or

- actual cash value (replacement cost less depreciation).

The type of HO form determines which method is to be used, based primarily on the type of property covered. In the HO–3, for example, replacement cost applies to Coverages A and B if the amount of insurance carried on the dwelling is equal to or greater than 80 percent of its replacement cost.

Actual cash value applies to these types of property:

- personal property;

- awnings, carpeting, household appliances, whether or not attached to buildings;

- structures that are not buildings; and

- grave markers, including mausoleums.

> ### ■ ISO FORM
>
> Covered property losses are settled as follows:
>
> **1.** Property of the following types:
>
> **a.** Personal property;
>
> **b.** Awnings, carpeting, household appliances, outdoor antennas and outdoor equipment, whether or not attached to buildings;
>
> **c.** Structures that are not buildings; and
>
> **d.** Grave markers, including mausoleums;
>
> at actual cash value at the time of loss but not more than the amount required to repair or replace.

ACV and RCV Defined

Actual cash value (ACV) is the sum of money required to pay for damage to or loss of property. This sum is the property's current replacement cost minus depreciation caused by obsolescence or wear and tear to the property. ACV also may be defined as the current fair market value (FMV) in some states.

Replacement cost (RCV) is the full amount necessary to replace or repair the damaged property to its condition before the loss. Replacement cost is generally more than the actual cash value because the insurer settles without a deduction for depreciation. Generally, however, the insured must in fact replace the property with like kind, quality and quantity before the full replacement cost is paid.

The Loss Settlement Condition states that the terms *cost to repair or replace* and *replacement cost* do not include the increased costs incurred to comply with the enforcement of any ordinance or law. The exception to this exclusion is the coverage provided under the Ordinance or Law Additional Coverage as discussed in Chapter 4.

Insured Meets the 80% Rule

Buildings insured under Coverage A or B at replacement cost without deduction for depreciation are subject to *insurance to value* conditions. Insurance to value is a policy condition that encourages insureds to adequately cover the value of property. It has been a vital part of property insurance contracts for many  years. Essentially, the policy states that to collect the full value of losses to buildings under Coverages A and B, the insured must carry an amount of insurance equal to or greater than 80 percent of the structure's replacement cost at the time the loss occurs. If the insured does not carry adequate coverage, he or she becomes a coinsurer and contributes to the loss. Simply stated, if the insured underinsures, the company underpays.

Here's how insurance to value works.

If the limit of insurance carried is equal to or greater than 80 percent of the full replacement cost of the property (either dwelling or other structures) at the time of the loss, the insured can collect the replacement cost of the damage less the applicable deductible. But if the insured carries less than 80 percent of the replacement cost, the company will pay the greater of the following amounts:

- the depreciated value (ACV) of the loss less the deductible; or

- the formula amount.

Next, we'll explain how to apply the formula.

Formula for Value Determination

1. Divide the amount of insurance carried by the amount required (80 percent of full replacement cost).

2. Multiply the result times the covered loss.

3. Subtract the deductible.

The entire formula for determining the amount of loss payable to the insured is:

$$\frac{\text{Amount of Insurance Carried}}{\text{Amount of Insurance Required}} \times \text{Loss} - \text{Deductible} = \text{Payment}$$

**Real Life
Application**

An insured owns a house worth $100,000 at replacement cost. The insurance policy requires 80 percent insurance to value.

$$\$100,000 \times 80\% = \$80,000$$

The amount of insurance required is $80,000.

The insurance to value provision of the homeowners policy rewards those policy-holders who carry adequate insurance with a replacement cost settlement. If, however, the amount of insurance carried is insufficient, the insured still receives at least the actual cash value of the loss or an amount between the ACV and replacement cost.

In the previous example we determined that the insured must carry $80,000 of insurance on the building to receive full payment for the loss without application of a penalty. Let's assume the insured carries only $40,000 of coverage on the building, the RCV loss is $10,000, and the deductible is $1,000.

If the insured is *underinsured* in a total loss, the insured participates in the loss without the application of the insurance to value penalty.

Applying the formula in the above scenario results in a payment of $4,000.

$$\frac{\$40,000}{\$80,000} \times \$40,000 - \$1,000 = \$4,000$$

But, we aren't finished applying the settlement provisions. The insured receives the *greater* of the following accounts:

- the ACV of the loss less the deductible; *or*

- the formula amount.

In the above example, the ACV of the loss was $8,000. By the terms of the policy, the payment to the insured would be $7,000 after subtracting the deductible.

The penalty for underinsurance is $2,000.

If the Insured Meets the 80% Rule

The insurer will pay the cost to repair or replace after any deductible and without deduction for depreciation, but not more than

- the limit of liability under the policy that applies to the building;

- the replacement cost of that part of the building damaged with material of like kind and quality; or

- the necessary amount actually spent to repair or replace the damaged building.

■ 80% RULE

 ISO Form Update   The 2000 form contains a new sentence in the replacement cost provision that does not appear in the 1991 form. The form states that if a building is rebuilt at a new premises, the cost is limited to the cost that would have been incurred had the building been built at the original premises.

Study Questions

6. Sue's home is a new building with a replacement cost of $500,000. Her homeowners policy insures the building for $400,000. How much would her policy pay on the building if she suffered a total loss?

   A. $200,000
   B. $320,000
   C. $400,000
   D. $500,000

Replacement Cost vs. Actual Cash Value

Typically, the only time an insured can collect the full replacement value of damaged property in a large loss is when the damage is actually replaced. An insurance company may pay the ACV shortly after the loss occurs and wait until all repairs have been made before paying the withheld depreciation. You should find out how your state mandates loss settlements regarding replacement cost. Some states require the loss to be paid at replacement cost even if the insured elects not to replace the damaged property. This information is provided in the required State Amendatory Endorsement attached to property policies sold in each state.

Answer and Rationale

6. **C.** Because Sue insures the building for 80 percent of its replacement value ($400,000), the policy would only cover that amount. Even though the building is worth $500,000, the homeowners policy cannot pay more than the limit of liability. Because Sue insures the building for the minimum 80 percent of its replacement value, she would not be penalized.

Small Loss Provision

The homeowners policy will pay a small loss of $2,500 or less at full replacement cost *and* without withholding depreciation until the insured makes repairs. However, to receive this benefit, the insured must carry a limit of insurance equal to at least 80 percent of the replacement cost of the damaged property.

Appraisal

The insurance company and policyholder may disagree in any loss situation on what amount should be paid. Either party may invoke the appraisal provision if this situation occurs. If appraisal is elected, each party selects an appraiser, and the two appraisers select an umpire. If the appraisers fail to agree on an amount of loss, the differences are submitted to the umpire. Agreement by any two of the three parties is binding. Both the insured and insurance company must pay their own appraisers and split any other costs involved. If the appraisers cannot agree upon an umpire within 15 days, a judge in a court of record will appoint one. The appraisers each set the amount of loss and, if they fail to agree on an amount, they submit their differences to the umpire. However, the existence of an appraisal does not always mean that the insurance company must pay the loss.

For instance, a fire loss may be a suspected arson, and the company is investigating the claim. If arson was the cause of loss and the named insured was responsible, the insurance company can still refuse payment (even if the appraisal process has been completed).

A growing trend in some states is to make the appraisal condition nonbinding. An Arkansas court reasoned that binding appraisal denies the insured his or her day in court, and other states are following this lead. If your state has changed the Appraisal condition, it is shown in the State Amendatory Endorsements, which are used to change various policy provisions to fit state laws.

Study Questions

7. The HO Appraisal provisions apply when the insurance company and policyholder disagree on whether coverage for the loss applies.

    A. True
    B. False

Other Insurance

In some cases, more than one insurance contract insures the property. Although this seldom occurs, an insured might purchase homeowners insurance from two different insurance companies. Regardless of the amount of insurance purchased, the Other Insurance provisions of each policy prevent the insured from collecting the full amount of a loss from each insurer. Each insurer's liability is limited to the

---

Answer and Rationale

7. **B.** The Appraisal provisions apply when the two parties disagree on the amount payable, not on the existence of coverage.

proportion that its insurance bears to the total amount of insurance on the property, whether collectible or not.

Real Life Application

In this example two companies share coverage on the same property. The building is insured for a total of $100,000. Both policies cover on the same basis. For ease of calculation, assume no deductible or replacement cost noncompliance penalty. The loss is prorated between the two policies.

Item	Amount	Loss as Determined	Pays
Fire Loss to Building	$10,000	Company A has ⅓ of coverage	$3,333
Company A's Policy	$33,333	Company B has ⅔ of coverage	6,667
Company B's Policy	$66,667	Amount Payable	$10,000

Suits Against Us

Under the terms of the policy, the insured may bring a lawsuit against the insurance company *only* if the conditions of the policy have been met *and* if the action is started within two years after the date of loss. Previous versions of the policies required that suit be brought within one year from the date of loss.

Our Option

The insurance company is *not* obligated to pay cash for any insured loss. Within 30 days after the insurance company receives the insured's signed, sworn statement about the insured loss, the insurer may elect to give the insured notice that the damaged property will be repaired or replaced with equivalent property in lieu of cash.

Loss Payment

Loss proceeds are payable within 60 days after the insurer receives proof of loss and reaches agreement with the insured, or within 60 days of the entry of a final judgment in the event that the insured and insurance company need to resolve a disagreement in court, or within 60 days of an agreed appraisal.

A loss payment is made to the named insured unless some other person is named in the policy. Because a homeowner is likely to have a mortgage on his or her property, a mortgagee may be named on the Declarations Page. It would also be named on any loss settlement check, along with the named insured. The check would have to be endorsed by both parties.

The *proof of loss,* a properly completed claim form, is a formal statement made by the insured to the insurance company regarding a loss. It is usually in the form of an affidavit. Its purpose is to give the insurer sufficient information about the loss to enable the insurer to determine its liability under the policy. The proof of loss contains such items as time and cause of loss, interest of the insured or other persons who may be partial owners of the property, identification of all liens on the property, other insurance, if any, and an inventory of damaged property.

Abandonment of Property

The insured may relinquish or surrender his or her rights or interests in the property (or the property itself) to the insurer, either expressly or by implication. However, under the terms of the contract, the insurer is under no obligation to accept the property.

Mortgage Clause

The Mortgage Clause is a provision noting that any loss payment will be payable to the mortgageholder or lienholder as its financial interest may appear (balance due on the loan). In addition, it states that the mortgageholder's right of recovery will not be defeated by any act or negligence of the insured.

The Mortgage Clause extends various rights to the mortgageholder because of its insurable interest in the property, including

- 10 days' written notice of cancellation;

- the ability to send its own proof of loss; and

- the ability to continue premium payments when the insured does not.

The mortgageholder may receive loss payments as its interest may appear, regardless of any violation of policy provisions by the owner and regardless of any change in occupancy or increase in hazard.

Study Questions

8. If an insured fails to pay his homeowners premium, the mortgageholder may pay the premium in order to protect its interest in the property.

  A. True
  B. False

No Benefit to Bailee

Homeowners policies are *personal contracts;* they insure against financial loss to a person, not to the property. In addition, homeowners policies do not apply to any bailee—a person or organization holding, storing or transporting property for a fee. Bailment contracts have traditionally included wording to the effect that the bailee is not liable for any loss covered by insurance, but insurance policies cannot be assigned without the permission of the insurance company.

Therefore, a furrier storing the insured's fur coat during the summer has no coverage under the insured's homeowners policy if the coat is stolen. This preserves the

---

Answer and Rationale

8. **A.** If the insured fails to pay the homeowners premium, the mortgagee may pay any premium due under the policy in order to keep coverage in force.

insurance company's rights to recover from a negligent furrier, which the insurance company would not be able to do if the furrier became an insured under the policy.

Nuclear Hazard Clause

Insurance polices define *nuclear hazard* to mean "any nuclear reaction, radiation, or radioactive contamination, all whether controlled or uncontrolled or however caused, or any consequence of any of these." Although the threat to residential property is generally limited to areas located near nuclear reactors, the nuclear hazard condition is included as protection for insurers who face potentially catastrophic losses if a nuclear accident should occur.

Recovered Property

In some cases, property is recovered after the claim has been settled. When this happens, the insured has the option of keeping the loss payment or the recovered property, but not both. Most commonly, the insured will have already replaced the property and will elect to keep the loss payment.

Volcanic Eruption

Although property in the continental United States is not particularly susceptible to volcanic eruptions, the damage done by the 1980 eruption of Mount St. Helens in Washington state gave evidence that such damage is possible. To protect the insured from having to submit a number of claims, each with separate deductibles, when several eruptions occur over a short period, the homeowners policy states that any eruptions that occur within a 72-hour period are considered one eruption and, therefore, one claim.

Policy Period

The policy applies only to loss that occurs during the policy period, as stated on the Declarations Page.

Concealment or Fraud

The insurance company provides no coverage to insureds under the policy if, either before or after a loss, an insured has

- intentionally concealed or misrepresented any material fact or circumstances;

- engaged in fraudulent conduct; or

- made false statements relating to the insurance.

Loss Payable Clause

If the Declarations show a loss payee for certain listed, insured personal property, the definition of *insured* is expanded to include the loss payee with respect to that property. If the insurance company decides to cancel or not renew the policy, the loss payee will be notified in writing. The Loss Payable Clause grants certain people the same rights as the insureds under the policy. However, this is not the same as the rights given to mortgagees, which are greater. Unlike the rights of mortgagees, the rights of loss payees are influenced by the acts of other insureds.

Real Life Application

9. Debbie purchases several rooms of furniture and adds the furniture store as Loss Payee to her homeowners policy. Following a fire, Debbie intentionally inflates the value of the damaged property to collect more than the property was worth.

As Loss Payee, will the furniture store collect on the policy?

■ POLICY COMPARISON

The table below summarizes the differences between the various forms and the HO–3 for Section I—Conditions and Exclusions. If the condition or exclusion isn't listed, there is no difference between the HO–3 policy language and the other forms. The HO–3 and HO–5 Section I—Conditions and Exclusions are identical.

Section I Property Conditions			
	HO–4	HO–6	HO–8
Loss Settlement	All Property at ACV	– Personal property and grave markers at ACV – Dwelling at actual cost to repair or replace	– Personal property at ACV – Buildings at amount actually spent for common construction materials
Mortgage Clause	Replaced by Loss Payable Clause	Same as HO–3	Same as HO–3
Other Insurance and Service Agreement	Same as HO–3	– HO–6 is excess to other coverage provided by the homeowners association – HO–6 shares loss with coverage on same property and on same terms as long as policy is not a homeowners association policy	Same as HO–3

Section I Property Exclusions				
	HO–2	HO–4	HO–6	HO–8
A.1. Ordinance or Law	Same as HO–3	Same as HO–3	Same as HO–3	No Ordinance or Law Additional Coverage and no exclusion regarding the Additional Coverage

---

Answer and Rationale

9. The furniture store as Loss Payee will collect nothing. The insured's fraudulent action extinguishes both her own and the Loss Payee's right to collect from the insurance company since the rights of loss payees are influenced by the acts of insureds.

HO–4

The HO–4 policy differs from the HO–3 policy with regard to the Loss Settlement and Mortgage Clause conditions.

The Mortgage Clause does not appear in the HO–4 because there is no dwelling coverage. Instead, the Loss Payable Clause gives the insured the opportunity to place a loss payee's name on the policy with respect to all or certain pieces of personal property. The definition of *insured* changes to include the loss payee. In the event of cancellation or nonrenewal, the company will notify the loss payee, as well as the insured.

The HO–4 Loss Settlement condition states that covered property losses are settled at actual cash value at the time of loss but not more than the amount required to repair or replace. We defined actual cash value in the first part of the lesson as replacement cost minus depreciation. The HO–4 adds a second condition, "but not more than the amount required to repair or replace."

Real Life Application

For example, Dana, who has no pets, lives alone on the top floor of an apartment building. A windstorm blows shingles off the roof of her building, allowing rain to damage most of her furniture. She is most concerned about her living room couch and loveseat—it's stained and completely wet and cannot be repaired or cleaned. Dana's on-site adjuster determines that the value of the set, which is approximately two years old, is $2,000 new. It is obvious to the adjuster that both items were in very good condition before the loss.

How will the adjuster determine the amount of payment for the loss?

The adjuster will start with the replacement cost—$2,000—and deduct an amount for depreciation. The insurance company may have depreciation guidelines for the adjuster, or he or she may be able to determine the deduction for the depreciation by observation and negotiation with Dana. The adjuster will take the following details into consideration:

- the average useful life of a similar sofa and loveseat;

- the condition of the furniture before the loss; and

- the cost of a similar, but used, sofa and loveseat.

Considering the above factors, a deduction between 10 percent and 20 percent may be agreeable to the insured and the adjuster.

HO–6

Losses to personal property and grave markers are payable at actual cash value. Losses to the dwelling are payable at "the actual cost to repair or replace." If the damage is not repaired within a reasonable time after the loss, the loss is payable at actual cash value (not to exceed the cost of repair or replacement of the damaged items).

The Loss Settlement condition in the HO–6 does not have an insurance to value provision.

The HO–6 modifies the Other Insurance and Service Agreement condition to take into account the possible existence of a master policy of insurance or service agreement on all condominium buildings collectively. Unit owners pay for this type of policy in their association dues or assessments, usually on a monthly or annual basis. The HO–6 specifically states that it is excess coverage over any amount payable under the master policy. The term *excess* means that the HO–6 will pay only if the claim uses up all of the other coverage available.

■ *ISO FORM*

F. Other Insurance And Service Agreement

1. If a loss covered by this policy is also covered by:

   a. Other insurance, except insurance in the name of a corporation or association of property owners, we will pay only the proportion of the loss that the limit of liability that applies under this policy bears to the total amount of insurance covering the loss; or

   b. A service agreement, except a service agreement in the name of a corporation or association of property owners, this insurance is excess over any amounts payable under any such agreement. Service agreement means a service plan, property restoration plan, home warranty or other similar service warranty agreement, even if it is characterized as insurance.

2. If, at the time of loss, there is other insurance or a service agreement in the name of a corporation or association of property owners covering the same property covered by this policy, this insurance will be excess over the amount recoverable under such other insurance or service agreement.

If another policy or service agreement covers the same property under the same terms as the HO–6, the HO–6 pays only its proportionate share of the loss. You saw a similar example of this type of settlement earlier in the chapter.

Study Questions

10. Policy A provides $40,000 of coverage and Policy B provides $60,000. The loss is $10,000. For ease of calculation, assume no deductible.

  • What is Policy A's share?

  • How about Policy B?

HO–8 Loss Settlement Condition

The first part of the Loss Settlement Condition in the HO–8 is similar to the Loss Setlement Condition in the HO–3. The property covered at actual cash value is the same with the exception of grave markers: the HO–8 does not include an Additional Coverage for grave markers. Therefore, it receives no mention in the first part of the Loss Settlement Condition.

The second part of the Loss Settlement Condition does not contain an insurance to value condition. It does, however, require the insured to repair or replace a damaged building, at the same site, within 180 days of the loss.

The HO–8 policy does not contain an Ordinance or Law Additional Coverage. The Loss Settlement Condition states, "the terms 'repair' or 'replace' do not include the increased costs incurred to comply with the enforcement of any ordinance or law."

In Chapter 1 you learned that the reason that an insured would purchase an HO–8 policy is that the HO–8 form provides packaged coverage for dwellings that do not meet the underwriting requirements of other forms, such as residences that have suffered extensive depreciation in value. In other words, *repair cost coverage* allows the contractor to use less costly materials than those originally used in the construction of the dwelling. This condition is especially important when the insured's house is an older, ornate home in a neighborhood where the market value of homes is below replacement cost and whose restoration to its preloss status would be cost prohibitive.

Loss Settlement Option 1

The insured has two options under the HO–8 policy. First, the insured may elect to repair or replace the loss to the building structure for the same occupancy and use at the same site within 180 days of the date of loss. In the event that the insured decides to make claim in this way, the policy pays the lesser of

  • the limit of liability that applies to the damaged building or structure; *or*

  • the amount actually spent to repair or replace the damage, but not more than the cost of common construction materials that restore functionality to damaged custom or antique construction methods.

Answer and Rationale

10. Policy A pays four-tenths of $10,000, or $4,000. Policy B pays six-thenths of $10,000, or $6,000.

Loss Settlement Option 2

Second, if the insured elects not to repair or replace the damage within 180 days of the date of loss, the policy pays the *least* of

- the limit of liability that applies to the damage building; *or*

- the market value of the damaged building (excluding land); *or*

- the cost of repair or replacement of the damaged part of the building with material of like kind and quality, less physical deterioration and depreciation.

In plainer words, the policy pays the *least* of

- the Coverage A or B limit on the Declarations Page; *or*

- the fair market value of the building; *or*

- the actual cash value of the repairs to or replacement of the building.

■ CHAPTER SUMMARY

As an insurance professional, your role is to help your clients select the homeowners policy and coverage limits that best meet their property and liability insurance needs. The types of policies your clients choose, the limits of liability they select and the endorsements they add will determine how well the policy will protect them should a loss occur.

In the next chapter, we'll continue our discussion of the homeowners policy by examining Section II—Liability Coverages. This important section of the homeowners policy covers personal liability and gives the insured financial protection when he or she is held responsible for injury to others or damage to their property. It also provides coverage for medical bills when a person is injured in an accident on the insured's property.

■ **ADDITIONAL STUDY QUESTIONS**

1. Which of the following losses is covered by the HO–3?

   A. Weather conditions

   B. Failure to act or decide

   C. A fire to your property set by an unidentified arsonist

   D. Inadequate zoning or planning

2. All of the following items are generally covered on a replacement cost basis EXCEPT

   A. damage to a building that is not repaired

   B. damage to a garage that has been repaired

   C. damage to an undercounter dishwasher and built-in oven—both have been repaired

   D. damage to a roof that has been repaired

■ **ANSWERS AND RATIONALES TO ADDITIONAL STUDY QUESTIONS**

1. **C.** Because a fire is a covered cause of loss, the action of an arsonist is covered. The actions or failure to act that are excluded do not apply to situations in which a covered cause of loss occurs. The damage by the covered cause of loss (fire) is covered.

2. **A.** Damage not repaired is most often settled on an ACV basis. All of the remaining items will be settled on a replacement cost basis as long as repair actually takes place.

6

Section II—Liability Coverages, Exclusions and Conditions

T he law requires that people behave as reasonable and prudent individuals, and, if they do not, this failure to do so can constitute negligence. If that negligence leads to the injury of another individual, the negligent party may be held liable for damages. In addition to being held liable for their own actions, people may be held liable for the actions of residents of their households, for animals they own or for the negligent operation of their vehicles that are used with their consent on the residence premises. Insureds should know how their homeowners policies protect them from economic loss in circumstances where they may be held legally liable.

Section II—Liability Coverages, provides protection for the insured against injuries to others resulting from the insured's acts or negligence.

In this chapter, we'll examine liability coverages, exclusions and conditions that apply under the homeowners policy. After completing this chapter, you will be able to

- explain the insuring agreements for Coverage E—Liability and Coverage F—Medical Payment To Others;

- describe the exclusions that are applicable to both insuring agreements;

- explain the additional coverages found in Section II of the homeowners policy; and

- explain the policy conditions applicable to Section II.

■ ■ ■ ■ ■

■ COVERAGE E—PERSONAL LIABILITY

The *Coverage E—Personal Liability* provision of the homeowners policy protects insureds (up to the policy limits) against claims and lawsuits brought against them and for damages for which they are held legally liable because of bodily injury or property damage to others.

- *Bodily injury* refers to bodily harm, sickness or disease, including injury that results in death. Coverage extends to the insured's legal liability for the required care and loss of services of anyone whose bodily injury is negligently caused by the insured.

- *Property damage* coverage applies to physical injury to or destruction of tangible property, including the loss of use of such property.

Coverage is *not* provided for libel, slander or invasion of privacy; however, coverage for these exposures may be added with a *personal injury* endorsement, discussed later, or by purchasing a Personal Umbrella Policy.

■ *ISO FORM*

A. Coverage E – Personal Liability

If a claim is made or a suit is brought against an "insured" for damages because of "bodily injury" or "property damage" caused by an "occurrence" to which this coverage applies, we will:

1. Pay up to our limit of liability for the damages for which an "insured" is legally liable. Damages include prejudgment interest awarded against an "insured"; and

2. Provide a defense at our expense by counsel of our choice, even if the suit is groundless, false or fraudulent. We may investigate and settle any claim or suit that we decide is appropriate. Our duty to settle or defend ends when our limit of liability for the "occurrence" has been exhausted by payment of a judgment or settlement.

Protection for the Insured

Coverage E protects the insured in two ways.

- If a claim is made for damages because of bodily injury or property damage caused by an occurrence, the policy will pay for damages for which the insured is found legally liable, up to the policy's limit of liability.

- The insurance company must defend any claim or lawsuit that is brought against the insured for bodily injury or property damage, even if it is groundless.

In other words, the insurer agrees to pay on the insured's behalf all sums up to the limit of liability that the insured becomes legally obligated to pay as damages because of bodily injury or property damage. The insurer also agrees to defend the insured in a lawsuit, even if the suit is fraudulent. The insurer may investigate and settle any claim it deems appropriate. The minimum limit is $100,000, but it can be increased by endorsement and additional premium.

Defense Costs

The Coverage E limit applies only to damages for which the insured is liable, not to the cost to defend the insured. Defense costs are in addition to the coverage for liability and an important part of the reason for carrying liability insurance.

For example, if the insured has a $100,000 Coverage E limit, a judgement of $90,000 and defense costs of $30,000, the policy will pay $120,000.

Once the Coverage E limits are exhausted by payment for damages, the insurance company's obligation to defend ceases.

If a company is faced with the likelihood of losing a large lawsuit in defense of an insured with low limits, the company may simply settle with the claimant for the policy limits. That doesn't mean that the insured's liability ends just because the policy limits were low. The insured may still face a loss for judgments above the policy limits. Some jurisdictions limit the ability of an insurance company to walk away from an insured's defense, even if the policy limits have been exhausted.

Minimum Coverage

Real Life Application

Some insureds (especially renters) feel that they don't need liability coverage; however, you should ask them to consider the many circumstances for which a person can be held legally responsible for injuries or damages to others.

For example, if a child enters your insured's property and is attacked by the insured's dog, the child's family can sue for the child's injuries. If the child merely enters the insured's property and injures himself or herself, the insured can still be sued. Even if the suit is groundless, the insured will have to defend against it, and that can be expensive. Although some states limit damage awards, the settlements for many bodily injury cases can be staggering.

Others as Insureds

You have learned that the definition of *insured* includes

- the named insured and spouse;

- resident relatives and other residents under the age of 21; and

- full-time students up to the age of 21 living away if they are in the insured's care, or up to the age of 24 if they are a relative of the insured.

You also learned that the HO 2000 program changed and expanded coverage for students.

- The student age limit changed from 21 to 24.

- The student must be a full-time student (which varies by school).

- The student must have lived at home prior to enrolling in school.

See below for an extension of this definition of *insured* in Section II.

■ *ISO FORM*

(1) With respect to animals or watercraft to which this policy applies, any person or organization legally responsible for these animals or watercraft which are owned by you or any person included in a. or b. above.

"Insured" does not mean a person or organization using or having custody of these animals or watercraft in the course of any "business" or without consent of the owner; or

(2) With respect to a "motor vehicle" to which this policy applies:

(a) Persons while engaged in your employ or that of any person included in a. or b. above; or

(b) Other persons using the vehicle on an "insured location" with your consent.

Vicarious Liability

The homeowners policies provide a degree of vicarious liability coverage for people who are legally responsible for the insured's ownership or use of animals or watercraft. For example, assume that a kennel allows an insured to take a show dog home for stud purposes. If the insured negligently allows the dog to escape and the dog injures someone, the kennel may be sued because of the insured's negligence.

1. A boat dealership allows Rick to test drive a boat, and he injures someone. The injured party files suit against Rick. Will Rick's homeowners policy provide coverage?

Liability and Negligence

Common law classifies wrongs that an individual may commit into two categories.

- The first is a *public wrong,* or a criminal act. This is a wrong against society, such as murder or arson, that is punishable by the courts.

- The second type of wrong that an individual can commit is a *private or civil wrong,* which is an infringement by one person on the rights of another individual. This infringement is also called a tort.

For example, you have the privilege of riding on the street on your bicycle. You do not have the right to move at an excessive speed (civil wrong) and strike a pedestrian (tort), causing injury or damage.

■ COVERAGE F—MEDICAL PAYMENTS TO OTHERS

If a person is accidentally injured on the insured's property, he or she does not have to prove that the insured was legally liable for the injury in order to collect nominal medical expenses.

Under *Coverage F—Medical Payments to Others,* the homeowners form will cover medical expenses of a third party, even if the insured is under no legal obligation to pay for a bodily injury that occurs on his or her property.

> ### ■ *ISO FORM*
>
> **B.** Coverage F – Medical Payments To Others
> We will pay the necessary medical expenses that are incurred or medically ascertained within three years from the date of an accident causing "bodily injury". Medical expenses means reasonable charges for medical, surgical, x-ray, dental, ambulance, hospital, professional nursing, prosthetic devices and funeral services. This coverage does not apply to you or regular residents of your household except "residence employees".

Answer and Rationale

1. **Yes.** Rick's homeowners policy will provide coverage under the theory of vicarious liability, in which indirect legal responsibility applies.

Coverage F pays for necessary medical expenses, regardless of legal liability, incurred within three years of the date of an accident by guests and others and who may be injured on the insured's premises or as a result of

- the insured's personal activities or a condition of the insured's premises;

- activities of a residence employee in the course of employment; or

- injuries caused by animals owned by or in the care of an insured.

Medical Payments to Others coverage does not apply to

- the insured;

- members of the insured's household; or

- tenants of the insured.

Coverage Limits

Medical Payments to Others coverage, usually written with a $1,000 per person limit, encompasses expenses for

- medical and surgical care;

- dental services;

- ambulance, hospital and professional nursing services;

- prosthetic devices; and

- funeral services.

Higher limits for Medical Payments are available by endorsement.

Study Questions

2. Medical Payments covers medical expenses that are incurred within how many year(s) from the date of the accident?

A. One
B. Two
C. Three
D. Four

Answer and Rationale

2. **C.** Coverage F pays for necessary medical expenses, regardless of legal liability, incurred within three years of the date of an accident by guests and others.

■ SECTION II—EXCLUSIONS

Insurance professionals must realize that reading only coverages or only exclusions on a given issue may be misleading and may miss the mark. Claims adjusters learn early that the insurance contract must be taken as a whole. Picking only the language or provision that supports one point without considering for the whole contract is counterproductive.

 ISO Form Update   New in the HO 2000 program, Section II of the homeowners policy contains four major categories of liability exclusions:

- motor vehicle liability;

- watercraft liability;

- aircraft liability; and

- hovercraft liability.

Motor Vehicle Liability

One of the more common reasons for an exclusion to be found in a policy is that another policy exists that is more appropriate for the exposure. In the case of motor vehicles, that policy is usually the Personal Auto Policy. The homeowners form excludes vehicles that are or are required to be registered for road use or that are engaged in certain high risk or business exposures such as racing or livery use. An exception is made for the use of golf carts while at the golf course.

■ *ISO FORM*

SECTION II – EXCLUSIONS

A. "Motor Vehicle Liability"

1. Coverages **E** and **F** do not apply to any "motor vehicle liability" if, at the time and place of an "occurrence", the involved "motor vehicle":

   a. Is registered for use on public roads or property;

   b. Is not registered for use on public roads or property, but such registration is required by a law, or regulation issued by a government agency, for it to be used at the place of the "occurrence"; or

c. Is being:

(1) Operated in, or practicing for, any prearranged or organized race, speed contest or other competition;

(2) Rented to others;

(3) Used to carry persons or cargo for a charge; or

(4) Used for any "business" purpose except for a motorized golf cart while on a golfing facility.

Registered Vehicles

There are some claims that might have been covered before HO 2000 but which are now excluded. For example, if a guest at the insured's house becomes intoxicated and drives off in his or her own car, the insured could face a host liquor liability claim. Under earlier language, the claim could be covered since the policy excluded automobile liability arising out of the ownership, maintenance or use of motor vehicles owned or operated by, rented to or loaned to an insured. None of those situations apply in our example. The HO 2000 forms do not provide coverage if the motor vehicle is registered (or is required to be).

■ *ISO FORM*

2. If Exclusion **A.1.** does not apply, there is still no coverage for "motor vehicle liability" unless the "motor vehicle" is:

a. In dead storage on an "insured location";

b. Used solely to service an "insured's" residence;

c. Designed to assist the handicapped and, at the time of an "occurrence", it is:

(1) Being used to assist a handicapped person; or

(2) Parked on an "insured location";

d. Designed for recreational use off public roads and:

(1) Not owned by an "insured"; or

(2) Owned by an "insured" provided the "occurrence" takes place on an "insured location" as defined in Definitions **B. 6.a., b., d., e.** or **h.;** or

Real Life Application

The homeowners policies carve out some exceptions to the motor vehicle exclusion. For example, the following occurrences are still covered.

- If a child is injured while playing in an auto in dead storage, not just parked, the occurrence is covered.

- If a guest is injured while using a pickup truck that is not registered and is used only to move equipment on the insured's premises, the occurrence is covered.

- If the insured's riding mower strikes a passerby, the occurrence is covered.

Golf Carts

ISO Form Update   The Homeowners 2000 edition added new language concerning the use of golf carts. Previously, liability arising out of the use of an owned golf cart was only covered if the cart was on the insured's premises or on a golf course for the purpose of playing golf. The newer forms extend coverage to include

- golf carts while stored at a golfing facility;

- other recreational use of a golf cart at a golfing facility;

- travel to and from parking areas;

- crossing public roads; and

- using a golf cart in a private residential community.

The following occurrences would be covered under the new forms.

Real Life Application

- The battery in a cart explodes while it is being charged, injuring the attendant and damaging other facility property.

- A third party is injured by a golf cart driven by the insured during a country club scavenger hunt.

- The insured fails to see an oncoming auto when crossing a public street between golf holes.

- A resident of a private community uses his golf cart to travel about the community and injures another resident.

Study Questions

3. Which of the following types of motor vehicles are not covered for liability in homeowners policies?

    A. Vehicles in dead storage on the insured's premises

    B. Automobiles while parked in the insured's driveway

    C. Golf carts used at a golfing facility

    D. A riding lawnmower used off of the insured's premises

Watercraft Liability

The first part of the Watercraft Liability exclusions tracks with the exclusion for Motor Vehicles. For example, it excludes liability arising out of racing contests, rental to others, livery exposures and business use.

■ *ISO FORM*

    B. "Watercraft Liability"

        a. Operated in, or practicing for, any prearranged or organized race, speed contest or other competition. This exclusion does not apply to a sailing vessel or a predicted log cruise;

        b. Rented to others;

        c. Used to carry persons or cargo for a charge; or

        d. Used for any "business" purpose.

The remainder of the exclusion defines *covered* watercraft liability.

- Coverage exists if the vehicle is stored on or off of the insured's premises.

- Owned sailboats under 26 feet and nonowned sailboats over 26 feet are covered, provided they are not also rented to an insured. For example, if an insured borrows a friend's 30-foot sailboat and runs into the marina dock with it, coverage would apply.

- Owned inboard or inboard/outboard motorboats under 50 horsepower if not owned by the insured, or over 50 horsepower if not owned by or rented to the insured are covered.

- Outboard motorboats under 25 horsepower, or over 25 horsepower if owned by the insured who acquired it before the policy period. There are specific reporting requirements for newly acquired outboards.

Answer and Rationale

3. **B.** Automobiles parked in the insured's driveway are not covered because this exposure is better insured under the Personal Auto Policy.

Outboard and Inboard

The difference between outboard, inboard and inboard/outboard watercraft is where the motor is located. Outboards have the motor located on the back or the transom of the boat. Inboards have the engine located inside the hull of the boat. Inboard/outboards have the engine located inside the hull of the boat but the power train goes through the back of the boat before entering the water.

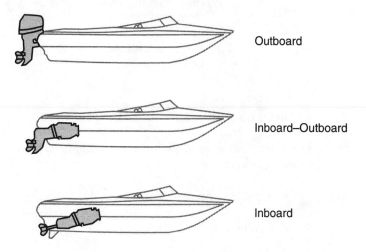

Outboard

Inboard–Outboard

Inboard

Study Questions

4. Which of the following types of watercraft are covered under Coverage E—Liability?

A. Jet boats over 50 horsepower owned by the insured

B. Sailboats over 26 feet in length owned by the insured

C. Outboard boats over 25 horsepower owned by the insured

D. Inboard boats over 100 horsepower stored on the insured's premises

Hovercraft Liability

 ISO Form Update *Aircraft Liability* and *Hovercraft Liability* are both defined at the start of the policy in the Definitions section. These exposures require specialized underwriting and pricing so they are excluded from the homeowners policies. ISO added the hovercraft exclusion with the introduction of Homeowners 2000.

Answer and Rationale

4. **D.** Inboard boats over 100 horsepower stored on the insured's premises are covered under Coverage E. The other watercraft named are excluded by the policy.

■ ISO FORM

(1) Aircraft means any contrivance used or designed for flight except model or hobby aircraft not used or designed to carry people or cargo;

(2) Hovercraft means a self-propelled motorized ground effect vehicle and includes, but is not limited to, flarecraft and air cushion vehicles;

Exclusions Applicable to Both Coverages E and F

The policy lists several exclusions that apply to both personal liability and medical payment coverages:

- expected or intended injury;
- business;
- professional services;
- rental of insured location;
- war;
- communicable disease;
- sexual molestation; and
- controlled substance.

Expected or Intentional Injury

Coverages E and F do not apply to expected or intended injury. Expected or intended bodily injury or property damage is excluded from Coverages E and F. Intentional bodily injury, however, is covered if it results from the use of reasonable force to protect people or property. This exclusion makes it clear that the intent to injure must be the insured's state of mind at the time. For example, after an insured had broken his neighbor's jaw in a fight, the insured tells an adjuster, "I meant to hit him; I didn't mean to hurt him." From the insured's standpoint, the punch was intentional but not the injury. The company and subsequently the courts, may view the actions differently.

Determining intent is difficult at best, but the policy clearly states that the intent of the insured at the time of the occurrence is the key to invoking either coverage and defense or denial of the claim.

ISO Form Update In homeowners 2000, ISO significantly modified the expected or intended injury exclusion in two respects:

- It broadened the exclusion to eliminate coverage for injuries that were not specifically intended by the insured.

- It included coverage for the use of *reasonable force.*

Real Life Application

1. William wakes to hear someone breaking into his house. He grabs his shotgun and sees an intruder entering through a window. Fearing for his life, William fires, wounding the intruder. Based only on these facts, William's actions are covered by the homeowners policy.

2. Max is concerned about burglary since there have been a number of incidents in his neighborhood. Max rigs a shotgun to a table, aimed at the door and set to go off if someone enters. While Max is on vacation, a burglar breaks in and is wounded by the shotgun. Based on only these facts, Max's actions are not covered by the homeowners policy.

The difference between numbers 1 and 2 is the *reasonableness* of the amount of force used by each insured. The general rule is that use of deadly force is only permitted to protect people, not property. In Situation number 2, no one was in danger, so the use of the shotgun was unreasonable.

Business

Bodily injury or property damage arising out of or in connection with a business conducted from an insured location or engaged in by an insured, whether or not the business is owned or operated by an insured or employs an insured, is excluded from coverage under both Coverages E and F.

This exclusion applies but is not limited to an act or omission, regardless of its nature or circumstance, involving a service or duty rendered, promised, owed or implied to be provided because of the nature of the business.

> ■ *ISO FORM*
>
> **2. "Business"**
>   **a.** "Bodily injury" or "property damage" arising out of or in connection with a "business" conducted from an "insured location" or engaged in by an "insured", whether or not the "business" is owned or operated by an "insured" or employs an "insured".

> This Exclusion **E.2.** applies but is not limited to an act or omission, regardless of its nature or circumstance, involving a service or duty rendered, promised, owed, or implied to be provided because of the nature of the "business".

Professional Services

The homeowners policies are intended to cover personal, nonbusiness exposures. This exclusion is an extension of the business pursuits exclusion described a few screens ago. Insureds with a professional liability exposure, such as lawyers and doctors, should obtain a professional liability policy.

Renting an Insured Location

Renting an insured location for use as a residence is permitted as long as there are no commercial occupancies other than

- an office;

- school;

- studio; or

- private garage.

Study Questions

5. All of the following may be an insured location for purposes of a homeowners policy EXCEPT

   A. nonowned premises that the insured sometimes rents for business use
   B. premises acquired by the insured's spouse during the policy term and used by the insured as a residence
   C. nonowned premises where the insured temporarily resides
   D. other premises described in the Declarations and used by the insured as a residence

War

As previously discussed, the catastrophic nature of war is such that it is frequently excluded. War exclusions are common to property and liability policies.

Answer and Rationale

5. **A.** A nonowned premises is an insured location only if the insured temporarily resides there or occasionally rents it to an insured for other-than-business use. In all other situations, a nonowned premises is not insurable under a homeowners policy.

Communicable Disease

Also excluded is bodily injury or property damage that arises out of the transmission of a communicable disease by an insured. Liability for the spread of diseases like AIDS may be established by showing that the insured knew or should have known that contagion was possible and that he or she did not act like a reasonable and prudent person would have acted to prevent transmitting the disease. Insurance companies may deny coverage in situations where insureds knowingly transmit communicable diseases.

Sexual Molestation

Bodily injury or property damage arising out of sexual molestation, corporal punishment or physical or mental abuse is excluded. Sadly, one can hardly open the newspaper or listen to news broadcasts without hearing of a molestation case. Insuring wrongdoers for such acts is against public policy.

Controlled Substance

People engaged in illegal acts do not have protection under the homeowners forms. Excluded is bodily injury or property damage arising out of the use, sale, manufacture, delivery, transfer or possession by any person of a controlled substance as defined by the Federal Food and Drug Law at 21 U.S.C.A. Sections 811 and 812. Controlled substances include but are not limited to cocaine, LSD, marijuana and all narcotic drugs. However, this exclusion does not apply to the legitimate use of prescription drugs by a person following the orders of a licensed physician.

Exclusions for Coverage E Only

Contractual Liability

These exclusions apply only to Coverage E:

- contractual liability;

- property damage to insured's own property; and

- bodily injury if workers' compensation should apply.

Contractual liability (that is, liability of others assumed by the insured under a contract) is excluded in most liability policies. Separate forms such as Contractual Liability Insurance or the Commercial Liability Policy are available to insureds that have this exposure. The homeowners policies do provide a form of personal contractual liability coverage.

One example would be if a lease requires that the insured tenant indemnify the landlord for any liability arising out of the rented premises, a common provision in leases. Another example is the rental agreement people sign when renting equipment for their residences, such as a posthole digger. The rental agreement usually requires that the lessee indemnify the rental company if someone is injured and sues the company.

Property Damage

Property damage to property owned by an insured is excluded because this is third party coverage, and a person cannot be liable to oneself. Property damage to property rented to, occupied or used by or in the care of an insured is also excluded. This, however, does not apply to property damage caused by fire, smoke or explosion.

This exception is important to anyone who rents an apartment or other property. If a tenant negligently starts a fire and damages the unit, the landlord or the landlord's insurance company will look to the tenant for reimbursement. The exception to the exclusion means that the insured would have coverage if the damage resulted from one of those perils.

Bodily Injury

This exclusion eliminates coverage if the insured provides or is required to provide workers' compensation benefits. Note that a workers' compensation policy doesn't have to be in force for the exclusion to be effective; the requirement for an in-force or voluntarily provided policy is enough to activate the exclusion.

> ■ **ISO FORM**
>
> **4.** "Bodily injury" to any person eligible to receive any benefits voluntarily provided or required to be provided by an "insured" under any:
> **a.** Workers' compensation law;
> **b.** Non-occupational disability law; or
> **c.** Occupational disease law;

Exclusions for Coverage F Only

Coverage F does not apply to bodily injury to a residence employee if the bodily injury

- occurs off the insured location; and

- does not arise out of or in the course of the residence employee's employment by an insured.

It does not apply to any person eligible to receive benefits voluntarily provided or required to be provided under any

- state workers' compensation laws;

- nonoccupational disability law; or

- occupational disease law.

Coverage F does not apply to bodily injury from any

- nuclear reaction;

- nuclear radiation; or

- radioactive contamination;

- all whether controlled or uncontrolled or howsoever caused; or

- any consequence of any of these.

Coverage F also does not apply to any person, other than a residence employee of an insured, regularly residing on any part of the insured location.

■ SECTION II—ADDITIONAL COVERAGES

In addition to personal liability and medical payments, Section II provides four other coverages under the provision called Additional Coverages:

- claim expenses;

- first-aid expenses;

- damage to the property of others; and

- loss assessment.

These coverages apply in addition to the policy's applicable limits of liability.

Claim Expenses

Coverage E—Personal Liability pays for claim expenses to encourage the insured to cooperate with the insurance company.

The claim expenses provision pays for

- expenses incurred by the insurance company to defend the insured in any suit, including any legal costs if the other party prevails;

- premiums on any bonds required in a lawsuit, up to the Coverage E liability limit; however, the insurance company is not obligated to apply for or furnish such bonds;

- reasonable expenses incurred by the insured at the insurer's request, including actual loss of earnings (but not loss of other income) up to $50 per day, for cooperating with the insurance company in investigating or defending claims or suits; and

- any interest that may accrue between the time the judgment is rendered and the time the insurance company tenders payment.

First-Aid Expenses

The insurance company will pay for *first-aid expenses* rendered to anyone other than an insured as a result of bodily injury that is otherwise covered under the policy.

This coverage differs from Medical Payments to Others in two ways:

- first aid covers only immediate medical care; and

- the insured may assume an obligation or make voluntary payment at the time first aid is given.

For example, if someone is injured on the insured's property and is taken to an emergency room for stitches, the insured may make payment directly to the hospital and then be reimbursed by the insurer for the costs.

Damage to Property of Others

Section I of the homeowners policy covers property of others on the insured premises at the option of the insured, but the loss must be caused by an insured peril.

Section II excludes liability coverage for damage to property in the insured's care, custody or control. The Additional Coverages in Section II give some of this coverage back. It also provides that the policy will pay up to $1,000 without regard to the insured's liability for damage to property of others.

For example, while visiting a friend's home, the insured accidentally spills a glass of red wine on the friend's white carpeting. The host prefers not to file a claim with his insurance company for the damage because the loss would be subject to a deductible. Instead, the insured places a claim with his own insurance company.

Study Questions

6. How much will the policy pay for the damaged carpeting?

Answer and Rationale

6. The policy will pay up to $1,000 for the damage to the carpet without regard to whether or not the insured was actually negligent in spilling the wine.

■ EXCLUSIONS FOR DAMAGE TO PROPERTY OF OTHERS

There are two exclusions:

- intentional damage caused by an insured over the age of 13; and

- damage to property owned by an insured or rented to a tenant of an insured or a resident of the insured's household

Any intentional acts by any insured, regardless of age, are excluded under personal liability. Under the Property Damage to Others provision, however, coverage could apply when a very young child, who may not be able to foresee the consequences of his or her actions, intentionally damages another's property.

For example, a 4-year-old might draw on a neighbor's walls or might set a fire without realizing the damage such actions could cause. The exclusion for intentional damage caused by those over the age of 13 most often applies to teenage vandalism, such as graffiti and other property damage, which would not be covered under the parents' homeowners policy.

The policy excludes damage to property owned by an insured or rented to a tenant of an insured or a resident of the insured's household. This exclusion applies for two reasons:

- coverage is better afforded under some other type of policy, such as property insurance; and

- the possibility of moral hazard, such as submitting false claims, could be increased if coverage were provided.

Note that coverage is *not* excluded for real and personal property rented to an insured. Therefore, if the insured rents a golf cart and damages it, coverage is provided up to $1,000.

Loss Assessment

The insurer will also pay part of a loss assessed by a homeowners association, up to $1,000 when the bodily injury or property damage isn't excluded under Section II. The limit of $1,000 is the most the policy will pay, regardless of how many assessments arise out of

- one accident, including continuous and repeated exposure to the same harmful condition; and

- a covered act of a director, officer or trustee.

> **■ ISO FORM**
>
> ### D. Loss Assessment
>
> 1. We will pay up to $1,000 for your share of loss assessment charged against you, as owner or tenant of the "residence premises", during the policy period by a corporation or association of property owners, when the assessment is made as a result of:
>
>   a. "Bodily injury" or "property damage" not excluded from coverage under Section II – Exclusions; or
>
>   b. Liability for an act of a director, officer or trustee in the capacity as a director, officer or trustee, provided such person:
>
>   (1) Is elected by the members of a corporation or association of property owners; and
>
>   (2) Serves without deriving any income from the exercise of duties which are solely on behalf of a corporation or association of property owners.

Loss Assessment Policy Period

The Policy Period condition says, "This policy applies only to 'bodily injury' or 'property damage' which occurs during the policy period."

The policy period under Section II—Conditions doesn't apply to this Additional Coverage. For example, homeowners associations often assess members long after an occurrence. The Loss Assessment Additional Coverage provides reimbursement up to $1,000 under the policy in effect when the homeowner receives notice of the assessment.

■ SECTION II—CONDITIONS

Limit of Liability

Under the terms of the policy, the insurance company agrees to pay up to its limit of liability under Coverage E for damages for which the insured is legally liable and up to its limit of liability for medical expenses for bodily injury. These limits are shown in the policy's Declarations Page. Coverage is further limited by the total amount applicable for damages resulting from one occurrence, regardless of the number of people injured, the number of claims made or the number of insureds covered under the policy.

Many insureds raise their limits of liability for an additional premium or purchase *personal umbrella liability insurance* that provides broad liability protection above a basic liability insurance program. Personal umbrella policies typically have limits of liability ranging from $1 to $5 million with *self-insured retentions (SIRs),* which are similar to deductibles, that vary from $250 to $10,000.

Severability

Homeowners insurance policies provide protection for each insured as if each has separate protection under the policy.

Assume that a husband and a wife own a house and purchase a homeowners policy naming them both as insureds. They host a party at which a guest is injured. The guest sues the husband and wife separately for different amounts. The policy will respond to both suits up to the policy limits. However, the policy will not pay more than its limits if the two suits add up to more than that amount.

Duties After Occurrence

Notify Insurer   Homeowners policies require that the insurance company or its agent be notified when an insured event, accident or loss occurs. According to the policy, written notice must be given "as soon as is practical," which usually means within days or weeks of the accident. Unfortunately, some insureds do not report accidents that seem inconsequential at the time (for example, a guest slips and falls on the property or the insured's cat scratches a neighbor).

If notice is not given to the insurer within a reasonable time after the loss or accident, the insurer is relieved of all responsibility under the homeowners contract. If the loss or accident is later found to be serious, the insurer may refuse to pay for the loss or defend the insured in a lawsuit. In that case, the insured could be held personally liable for all the expenses incurred.

Other Duties   The homeowners policy also includes the requirement that the insured may not, except at his or her own cost, voluntarily make any payment, assume any obligation or incur any expense other than first aid to others at the time of bodily injury. In addition, the insured is required to

- give the insurance company or its agent written notice of the loss;

- forward any notice, demand, summons or other process relating to the accident or occurrence to the insurer or its agent;

- assist the insurer when requested in any hearings, trials or settlements; and

- submit a proof of loss within 60 days after the loss and show the damaged property to the insurer, if possible.

In order to collect payments, the injured person must comply with certain conditions as explained on the next screen.

Duties of an Injured Person   If an injured person intends to make a claim for medical payments, he or she must provide written proof of loss to the insurer as soon as possible and authorize the company to obtain his or her medical records. He or she may also have to submit to a physical examination by a physician selected by the company whenever required by the company.

However, because the injured person is not a party to the insurance contract, it is unclear whether this condition is enforceable.

Payment of Claim to Others   If the insurance company reimburses the insured for the medical expenses of others or makes any medical payment to an injured party, such payments are not considered an admission of liability by any insured or the company.

Suits Against Us

Under the terms of the policy, neither the insured nor any person seeking coverage under Medical Payments to Others can take legal action against the insurer until the policy provisions have been met and the insurance company's obligation has been determined.

Bankruptcy of an Insured

The insurance company is not relieved of its responsibilities and obligations under the policy, even if the insured becomes insolvent or bankrupt. The insurer remains obliged to pay any responsible claim up to the policy's limits of liability.

For example, assume that 12 people are injured during a party at the residence premises. When each of the injured parties sues the insured for $50,000, the insured declares bankruptcy. If the homeowners policy has a liability limit of $100,000, the insurance company is still obligated to defend the suits up to $100,000. If the insured is found legally liable for the injuries, it is up to the court to determine whether the injured parties will be able to collect the remainder from the insured.

Other Insurance

Under the Other Insurance provision, coverage will not be paid for amounts reimbursed by other insurance companies or for which no reimbursement is legally required. Coverage will not apply if other insurance, such as a person's own health insurance, pays for bodily injury or an accident.

If an insured has a *personal umbrella policy* to protect him or her against liability losses that are unusual in their nature or size, such coverage is excess insurance over the homeowners liability limit.

Policy Period

It may seem obvious that coverage under a homeowners policy applies only to a loss that occurs during the *policy period* shown on the Declarations Page.

The policy period clearly shows the inception and expiration dates during which the homeowners contract provides protection, for example, June 1, 2002, to June 1,

2003. Problems may arise, however, when it is difficult to determine exactly when a loss occurred.

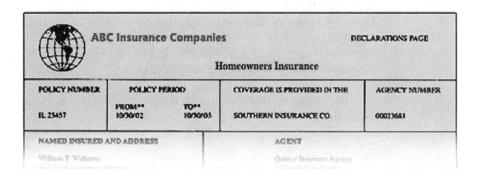

Study Questions

7. Bill had an H0–3 policy with Worldwide Insurance effective January 1, 2001 to January 1, 2002. Bill negligently repaired his roof with secondhand shingles and rusty nails in June. During a storm in November 2001, a shingle blew off Bill's roof, striking his neighbor Jerry in the head. Although Jerry had a few stitches in the emergency room, he did not mention the incident until he began to have severe headaches in February 2002. If Bill replaced his homeowners coverage with Statewide Insurance effective January 1, 2002, which of the two policies covers Jerry's bodily injury and medical payments?

A. Worldwide
B. Statewide
C. Both

Concealment or Fraud

Property insurance is a *personal contract* between the insurer and the insured. Strictly speaking, a property contract does not insure property but insures the owner of the property against loss. The owner is indemnified if the property is damaged or destroyed. Because the contract is personal and a contract of *utmost good faith,* the applicant for insurance must be acceptable to the company and meet certain underwriting standards regarding character, morals and credit. He or she must make a full and fair disclosure of information pertinent to the underwriting of the risk. If the insured intentionally conceals or misrepresents any *material* or important fact *with the intent and result* that the insurer relied upon it to issue coverage and was injured by doing so, the insurer may void the entire policy.

Answer and Rationale

7. **A.** Although the negligent act occurred in June, the neighbor's accident originally occurred in November and then escalated in February. Coverage is provided for bodily injury occurring during the policy period. Therefore, Worldwide's coverage would apply under its Medical Payments to Others for Jerry's emergency room visit. If it was determined that the headaches were a direct result of the November injury, coverage would also apply under the Worldwide policy since this policy was in effect at that time.

■ CHAPTER SUMMARY

Suits for damages based on liability are more common now and receive more publicity than in the past. From an economic point of view, the risk of financial loss due to bodily injury or damage to the property of others for which the insured is held legally liable can be more devastating than the risk of financial loss to his or her own property. Therefore, it is imperative that insureds purchase adequate homeowners insurance with an appropriate limit of liability.

In the next chapter, we will discuss the policy conditions that apply to both Sections I and II.

■ **ADDITIONAL STUDY QUESTIONS**

1. A guest in the home of an insured homeowner falls down the stairs during the course of an illegal gambling operation. Would the homeowners policy provide coverage for the guest's medical expenses?

   A. No

   B. Yes

2. The insured has a homeowners policy with personal liability coverage of $100,000 and suffers a covered loss in which four people are injured. If each person sues the insured for $50,000 and the court determines the insured is legally liable for the injuries, how much will the insurer pay under the policy?

   A. $50,000

   B. $100,000

   C. $400,000

   D. Cannot be determined

3. Michael breaks his arm playing touch football at a friend's house. Before Michael can bring a lawsuit to force the company to pay his medical expenses under the friend's Coverage F—Medical Payments to Others, he should do which of the following?

   A. Give the insurance company a written proof of his claim.

   B. Authorize the company to obtain copies of his medical records.

   C. Submit to a physical exam by a doctor chosen by the insurer.

   D. All of the above

■ ANSWERS AND RATIONALES TO ADDITIONAL STUDY QUESTIONS

1. **A.** No coverage will apply because the residence premises was being used in connection with an illegal act.

2. **B.** The insurer is responsible for only the limits of the policy, or $100,000. The insured is responsible for the remaining $100,000.

3. **D.** After Michael performs all of the duties described, the company will make a final determination about whether to cover the loss and, if so, how much to cover. Only then could Michael proceed with his lawsuit.

7

Conditions Applicable to Sections I and II

T he homeowners policy is the entire contract between the policyowner and the insurance company. If it isn't spelled out in the policy, it isn't covered. Unfortunately, many people learn most of what they know about their homeowners policy after a loss. Only then do they discover whether they are uninsured or underinsured. Neither the agent nor the insured can rewrite the insurance contract after a loss.

As an insurance professional, you should review homeowners policies with your clients to assure an understanding of coverages and exclusions. You should be certain they are aware of their rights and obligations under their contracts so they will have fewer problems should a loss occur.

In this chapter, we'll discuss the conditions that apply to both Sections I and II and explain how you can help your insureds to understand this important part of their coverage.

After completing this chapter, you will be able to describe each of the seven conditions that apply to both Section I and II of the homeowners policy:

- Liberalization Clause;

- Waiver or Change of Policy Provisions;

- Cancellation;

- Nonrenewal;

- Assignment;

- Subrogation; and

- Death.

■ CONDITIONS APPLICABLE TO THE ENTIRE POLICY

Insurance polices are *conditional contracts* that create a continuing relationship between the insured and the insurance company. Insureds know that they must pay premiums in order to keep their homeowners policies in force, but that isn't the only thing they have to do. Insurance policies usually enumerate the duties of the parties to the contract and, in some cases, define the terms used in sections of the homeowners policy called *conditions*.

Insureds should fully understand their obligations under their policies because they cannot expect the insurer to fulfill its part of the contract unless the insureds fulfill the policy's conditions. Failure to do so may release the insurer from its obligations. Many conditions apply only to certain sections of the contract; others apply to the entire contract. There are seven conditions that apply to both Section I—Property Coverages and Section II—Liability Coverages.

Liberalization Clause

Although the ISO homeowners forms are not completely revised on a frequent basis, some insurers may individually revise their forms to broaden the existing coverage without charge. If the coverage is substantially more comprehensive, insureds might be tempted to replace their homeowners insurance with the broader coverage. In order to prevent this, the Liberalization condition automatically amends the insured's current policy to match homeowners forms with the same edition date if the change takes place in the insured's state within 60 days prior to or during the policy period shown on the Declarations Page.

Waiver or Change of Policy Provisions

When a person applies for homeowners insurance, he or she may *think* that certain items are automatically covered under the policy. Some agents may even assure the applicant that a particular insurance company usually waives certain exclusions, such as water damage. However, the Waiver or Change of Policy Provisions condition clearly states that if any terms or conditions of the policy are changed, the changes must be made in writing by the insurer.

Study Questions

1. The Waiver or Change condition requires all changes to the policy to be made in writing.

   A. True
   B. False

Answer and Rationale

1. **A.** The Waiver or Change clause requires that any changes to the policy be in writing by the insurance company to be valid.

Cancellation by the Insured

The Cancellation condition has been amended in some states. As an agent or broker, it is important that you understand how the cancellation provision applies in the states where you write coverage. In most cases, the insured may cancel the policy by returning it to the company (or the agent) or by informing the company in writing of the date the policy is to be canceled.

Any unearned premium for the unexpired policy term is returned to the insured on a proportional or pro-rata basis. In other words, the portion of written premium applicable to the unexpired or unused part of the period for which the premium has been charged is returned to the insured.

Nonrenewal

In most cases, insurance companies automatically renew existing homeowners policies. The insured usually receives his or her renewal policy and annual invoice at least 30 days before the existing policy expires. In some cases, however, the company may choose not to renew the policy because of claim frequency or a number of other reasons. If the insurer decides not to renew the policy, it must provide written notice to the insured at least 30 days before the expiration date of the policy. Some states have additional provisions that apply to nonrenewal of coverage. As an agent or broker, you should be aware of the provisions that apply to the state(s) where you write business.

Return of Premium

When the insurance company cancels the policy, it must return any unearned premium on a pro-rata basis. Although the insurer is not required to return the unearned premium with the cancellation notice, it must do so within a reasonable period of time.

Cancellation and Nonrenewal

The table below contains the insurer's responsibilities for notice of cancellation and nonrenewal. Please note that state amendatory endorsements may change the policy provisions.

Policy Cancellation Provisions

Reason	# Days Policy In Effect	# Days Notice to Insured
Nonpayment of premium	N/A	10
Any reason, if policy isn't a renewal	Less than 60	10
Material misrepresentation or substantial change in risk	More than 60	30
Any reason	At Policy Renewal	30
Policy Nonrenewal Provisions		
Any reason	N/A	30 days before expiration date

Study Questions

2. How much notice must a company give before nonrenewing a homeowners policy?

    A. Notice is not required when nonrenewing a homeowners policy.

    B. 10 days' notice

    C. 30 days' notice

    D. 60 days' notice

Assignment

When an insured sells his or her house, the homeowners policy does not automatically transfer to the new homeowner. As stated earlier, a homeowners insurance contract is a personal contract between the insured and the insurer. Both the applicant for homeowners insurance and his or her property must meet certain underwriting standards imposed by the insurance company.

Because the policy is a personal contract between the two parties, the insured may not assign or transfer ownership of the policy to anyone without the written consent of the insurer. In a few cases, the insurer will assign the policy by endorsement, but it is more common to cancel the existing policy and issue a new policy to the new homeowner.

Subrogation

The right of subrogation is a common law right that the insurer has even without a contractual agreement. It is stated in the policy, however, so that the insured will be aware of it and refrain from releasing the party who is responsible for a loss. Subrogation gives the insurer whatever claim against third parties the insured might have as a result of a loss for which the insurer paid. It is basically the process of the insurer assuming the rights of the insured at the time of the loss.

Real Life Application

A negligent motorist drives his car through Lucia's front window, causing $3,000 damage to the house. If the homeowners policy pays for the loss, Lucia must assign her right to recover the $3,000 from the reckless driver to her insurance company.

3. Can the insurance company collect $3,000 from the responsible party?

Subrogation preserves the concept of indemnity and prevents the insured from collecting more than once for a loss. For example, an insured who is a landlord cannot collect from the tenant's liability insurer and the insured's first party carrier. For liability losses, the right to recover must be transferred to the insurance company. The insured cannot impair these rights. Subrogation does not apply to Coverage F—

Answers and Rationales

    2. **C.** If the insurer decides not to renew the policy, it must provide written notice to the insured at least 30 days before the expiration date of the policy.

    3. The insurance company can take action against the driver and seek to be reimbursed for the $3,000 paid to Lucia.

Medical Expense coverage or to Paragraph C. Damage to the Property of Others under Section II—Additional Coverage.

Real Life Application

Carol has an HO–3 policy, and her roof is damaged when a neighbor's tree branch falls on it during a storm. Damage to the roof is covered by Carol's policy but is limited by the loss settlement clause and deductible.

4. Upon payment to Carol for the loss, what right does the insurer have under the subrogation provision?

In the example above, the tree may have already been dead before the storm. The neighbor could be negligent if he or she failed to remove a dead tree before the approach of a storm. Any amount the insurer collects above the amount paid to the insured, such as the deductible, belongs to the insured.

Death

An important policy condition relates to the death of an insured. If the insured, or the spouse of a resident of the same household, should die, the policy covers the deceased's *legal representative,* such as an executor or administrator, but only with respect to the deceased's covered premises and property. In effect, the liability coverage is reduced to a *premises only* coverage, and any off-premises activities of the legal representative are *not* covered.

As part of the policy conditions, the definition of an *insured* includes

- any member of the household who is an insured at the time of the named insured's or spouse's death, but only while living at the residence premises; and

- the person who has proper temporary custody of the property until a legal representative is appointed.

If the executor of an estate accidentally damages someone's property while away from the residence premises, will coverage be provided under the deceased's homeowners policy?

Coverage is not provided under the deceased's homeowners policy. While it covers the deceased's legal representative, the executor, coverage applies only to the deceased's covered premises and property. Off-premises activities of the legal representative are not covered.

Answer and Rationale

4. Under the subrogation provision of the policy, the insurer, upon payment to Carol for the loss, has the right to recover damages from the neighbor, if the neighbor was negligent.

■ CHAPTER SUMMARY

As noted previously, insurance contracts contain certain conditions that qualify or place limitations on the insurer's promise to "provide the insurance described in this policy." In essence, the conditions sections impose certain duties on the insured if he or she wishes to receive payment for a covered loss. If the policy conditions are not met, the insurer can refuse to pay the claim. It is important, therefore, that you, as the agent, educate your client about the need to read and understand the entire homeowners policy.

In the next chapter, we'll discuss *endorsements*—written modifications to an insurance contract—that are commonly attached to homeowners policies to increase or decrease the coverage provided under a particular homeowners form, to change the premium, to correct a property description or to make a number of other changes.

8

■■■■■■

Homeowners Endorsements

T he property-liability insurance coverage provided by a homeowners policy is usually adequate to meet the average insured's needs. However, some insureds face unusual risks or may have special needs that they wish to cover. They may be willing to pay an additional premium to broaden coverage or delete certain exclusions and restrictions. On the other hand, some insureds may also wish to decrease their premiums by giving up coverages or by increasing their deductibles. Therefore, the insurance industry developed a way for insureds to make changes in their policies to better accommodate their individual needs by creating endorsements. When these endorsements are attached to the policy, they change the contract.

Endorsements may increase or decrease the insurance coverage, change the premium, correct the insured's name or make any number of other changes. We'll look at a number of ISO endorsements in this chapter. Like the homeowners policies, endorsements are easy-to-read forms, although even experienced insurance agents and adjusters may have to read an endorsement several times before being certain about the coverage provided or excluded. Endorsements may vary slightly by insurer; therefore, it is important to read each one carefully. Remember, when an endorsement's wording conflicts with the insurance contract, the endorsement takes precedence over the homeowners policy's wording.

After completing this chapter, you will be able to choose the correct endorsement, based on the insured's needs, from these often-used forms:

- Section I—Property Endorsements;

- Section II—Liability Endorsements; and

- Endorsements that apply to both Sections I and II of the policy.

■ ■ ■ ■ ■

■ PROPERTY EXPOSURES

The first group of common endorsements we'll discuss are those that apply to Section I—Property Coverages of the homeowners policy. You'll recall that this section covers the dwelling, other structures and personal property, as well as additional living expenses or fair rental value from a covered loss. However, because the homeowners form contains many exclusions or restrictions of coverage, insureds may wish to add endorsements to their policies.

Additional Insured—Residence Premises

It is possible for two or more people to own and insure a single residence, such as a two-family dwelling; however, only one can obtain a homeowners policy for coverage on the building. The other owner(s) must each purchase an HO–4 policy to cover their personal property and liability exposures and should be named as additional insureds on the HO–3 policy with the *Additional Insured—Residence Premises (HO 04 41)* endorsement.

The HO 04 41 endorsement may also be added to a homeowners policy to protect the interests of a nonoccupant co-owner of a property or to protect the seller when the house is being sold under a *land contract*—a contract for the sale of real estate whereby the purchase price is paid in periodic installments by the purchaser, who is in possession of the property even though the title is retained by the seller until a future date.

Building Additions and Alterations

Under the HO–4 policy, the tenant has up to 10 percent of the Coverage C—Personal Property limit to cover any additions, alterations, or fixtures made or acquired at the insured's own expense to that part of the residence in which the tenant exclusively resides. For example, the tenant may attach a ceiling fan or add built-in bookcases to his or her apartment. Tenants who have made significant improvements in their apartments might wish to add a *Building Additions and Alterations (HO 04 51)* endorsement to cover the exposure if they exceed the limits provided by the policy.

Study Questions

1. Thomas and Harold jointly own a two-family dwelling, but only Thomas resides in it. What endorsement should be added to Thomas's homeowners policy to protect Harold's interest in the property?

   A. Additional Insured—Residence Premises
   B. Other Structures—Increased Limits
   C. Special Loss Settlement
   D. Loss Payee

Answer and Rationale

1. **A.** Harold should be named as an additional insured on Thomas's HO–3 policy with the *Additional Insured—Residence Premises (HO 04 41)* endorsement.

Coverage B—Off Premises

Insureds with an HO–1, HO–2 or HO–3 form who want to cover a number of structures located away from the residence premises but used in connection with the residence may add a Coverage B—Off Premises (HO 04 91) endorsement to extend 10 percent of the Coverage A—Dwelling Coverage to these structures. With this endorsement, Coverage A is extended to include off-premises structures. It is an extension of coverage, not an addition to coverage. Coverage is provided only when the structures are used in connection with the residence premises. An example of such a structure is a shed located off the premises used to store lawn equipment.

Coverage is *not* provided for structures used as dwellings (or that could be used as dwellings), structures used in whole or in part as a business or those rented to someone who is not a tenant of the dwelling.

Study Questions

2. The insured owns an additional garage, which he parks his sports car in, located 200 feet from his premises. He wants to insure the garage under his homeowners policy. What should he do?

   A. No action is necessary because the garage is automatically covered.
   B. Add Building Additions and Alterations, HO 04 51.
   C. Add Other Structures—Increased Limits, HO 04 48.
   D. Add Coverage B—Off Premises, HO 04 91.

Specific Structures Away from Residence Premises

For those insureds who wish to specifically describe the locations to be covered, a *Specific Structures Away from the Residence Premises (HO 04 92)* endorsement is added to the homeowners form. This endorsement may be added when an insured is uncomfortable with blanket coverage and wants to specifically show *where* coverage is provided. When HO 04 92 is used, the coverage on the specific structures is additional insurance to the limit of liability automatically provided under Coverage B.

Coverage C—Increased Special Limits

Under Coverage C—Personal Property, specific dollar amounts apply to certain types of property, such as $2,500 for loss by theft of firearms or $200 for money. The special limits listed in the policy may be increased to varying amounts (depending on the state manual rules) with the addition of a *Coverage C—Increased Special Limits (HO 04 65)* or HO 04 66 with the HO–5 form. The special limits on certain property shown in the HO–3 or HO–5 may be increased up to the maximum shown on the endorsement.

Answer and Rationale

2. **D.** Because this garage is used in connection with the residence premises, the insured should add the Coverage B—Off Premises (HO 04 91) endorsement to cover this structure.

Credit Card and Counterfeit Money Coverage

As stated earlier, under Additional Coverages, the homeowners form provides up to $500 for the legal obligation of an insured that results because of lost or stolen credit or fund transfer cards or the acceptance in good faith of counterfeit U.S. or Canadian paper currency. The *Credit Card and Counterfeit Money Coverage—Increased Amounts (HO 04 53)* endorsement permits the insured to increase this limit up to the amounts specified in the state manuals.

Earthquake Coverage

Earthquake is specifically excluded under the homeowners forms, but coverage can be added with the *Earthquake (HO 04 54)* endorsement. Although quite expensive, it is usually a good idea to add this coverage if the homeowner lives in an area where earthquakes frequently occur, such as California. This endorsement covers any earthquakes, landslides, volcanic eruptions and earth movements that occur within a 72-hour period as if they were a single loss. Deductibles of 5 percent, 10 percent, 15 percent, 20 percent or 25 percent are available.

Coverage does *not* apply to loss or damage to brick veneer siding—unless an additional premium is paid. In addition, the HO 04 53 does *not* cover damage from a flood or tidal wave, even if caused by an earthquake, or the cost of filling land because of gaps or crevasses left by the earthquake.

Inflation Guard

It is important for the homeowner to have adequate insurance coverage on his or her home at the time of a loss, especially if the value of the house has substantially increased because of room additions or other improvements since the homeowners policy was originally purchased. Many homeowners may also be underinsured because of inflation. This means that if they have a loss, the replacement cost provision with respect to the 80-percent requirement may not be met. Fortunately, this problem can be reduced or solved with an *Inflation Guard (HO 04 46)* endorsement. Some companies automatically include this coverage; others add it only at the insured's request.

An *Inflation Guard* endorsement provides for an annual pro-rata increase in the limits of liability under Coverages A, B, C and D. The increase is usually between 4 and 6 percent. For example, if the insured selects a 4 percent Inflation Guard endorsement, the various policy limits are increased by 4 percent annually.

Some insurance companies pro rate the specified annual percent increase throughout the policy year; for example, a house insured for $100,000 would be covered for $102,000 at the end of six months. Other insurers increase the various limits by some specified percentage, such as at 1 percent every three months. Also, some inflation guard endorsements are based on a *construction cost index,* which is used to determine the correct amount of insurance needed to repair or replace the house.

Mine Subsidence Coverage

The *Mine Subsidence Coverage* (endorsement number varies) endorsement provides coverage for the dwelling and unscheduled other structures against *mine subsidence,* which means "lateral or vertical ground movement caused by a failure initiated at the mine level of man-made underground mines." These endorsements are state-specific and will vary. Loss settlement is usually made for either the Coverage A—Dwelling amount or up to a dollar amount (such as $350,000 in Illinois), whichever is less.

A deductible of $500 usually applies. Coverage is *not* provided for earthquake, landslide, volcanic eruption, soil conditions, soil erosion, soil freezing or thawing, improperly compacted soil, construction defects, roots of trees or shrubs or collapse of storm or sewer drains or rapid transit tunnels.

Mobilehome Endorsement

Mobilehomes present unusual risks, and some companies do not cover them with HO–2 or HO–3 forms. Homeowners forms may be endorsed to cover mobilehomes with a *Mobilehome* Endorsement (MH 04 01) amending the definition of "residence premises" to include the mobilehome listed in the Declarations. Section I is amended to cover the mobilehome and its attached structures, utility tanks and built-in appliances, dressers and cabinets on a replacement cost basis.

If the mobilehome is damaged by a covered peril while being moved, up to $500 of coverage applies. This coverage may be increased in increments of $250 up to a limit of $2,500.

The Mobilehome Endorsement amends Section I—Conditions as follows:

- Loss to panels or pieces of the mobilehome are treated under the *pair and set provision* and repaired or replaced to match the original material as closely as possible.

- Under the mortgagee clause, trustees and lienholders are treated as mortgagees.

Ordinance or Law Coverage

As discussed in Chapter 5, the homeowners form excludes any loss arising from an ordinance or law that regulates the construction, repair or demolition of property. If, for example, a local ordinance requires that damaged or destroyed frame houses must be replaced with more expensive brick construction, the homeowners form will not pay for the increased cost of construction. The *Ordinance or Law Coverage (HO 04 77)* endorsement removes this exclusion and provides coverage for the extra costs involved in complying with any ordinance or law to make the structure conform to code. The extra coverage is expressed as a specific percentage (5 percent, for example) of Coverage A.

Other Structures—Increased Limits

For an additional premium, an *Other Structures—Increased Limits (HO 04 48)* endorsement covers each structure on the residence premises described in the endorsement for an additional limit of liability in addition to the amount that is applicable under Coverage B-Other Structures.

For example, if the insured's house is covered for $100,000 under Coverage A—Dwelling, the detached garage is automatically covered for 10 percent of that amount, or $10,000, under Coverage B. If the insured needs an additional $10,000 in coverage to adequately insure the garage, an HO 04 48 form, which specifies the $10,000 increase, may be added to the policy.

Study Questions

3. What endorsement does the insured need to cover the higher cost to rebuild because of building codes?

A. Inflation Guard, HO 04 46

B. Building Ordinance or Laws, HO 04 77

C. Special Loss Settlement, HO 04 56

D. Other Structures—Increased Limits, HO 04 48

Water Back Up and Sump Discharge or Overflow

The *Water Back Up and Sump Discharge Overflow (HO 04 95)* endorsement provides $5,000 of coverage for loss caused by water or waterborne material that

- backs up through sewers or drains;

- overflows or is discharged from a sump, sump pump or related equipment.

The overflow or discharge may result from mechanical breakdown of the sump pump or related equipment. However, the coverage does not apply to direct physical loss of the pump caused by mechanical breakdown. Perils insured against are the same with this endorsement as with the underlying policy. The endorsement covers mechanical breakdown (as noted above) of sump pumps and related equipment that isn't provided in any of the other HO policies.

Any loss is subject to a $250 deductible, regardless of the deductible in the underlying policy. The HO 04 95 replaces the Water Damage exclusion in the HO–3 policy. The endorsement excludes coverage for sewer back up, overflow or discharge as a direct or indirect result of flood.

Answer and Rationale

3. **B.** The *Ordinance or Law Coverage* endorsement removes this exclusion from the policy, providing coverage for the costs of complying with any ordinance or law to make the structure conform to code.

Personal Property Replacement Cost

For an additional premium, the *Personal Property Replacement Cost (HO 04 90)* endorsement may be added to the homeowners policy to provide replacement costs for personal property at the time of loss. If the policy includes certain items, such as awnings, carpeting, household appliances, outdoor antennas and outdoor equipment, these items are also covered at replacement cost.

The endorsement lists several items that are *not* eligible for replacement cost coverage:

- antiques*;

- fine arts*;

- paintings*;

- articles of rarity or antiquity;

- memorabilia;

- souvenirs;

- collector's items;*

- articles not maintained in good condition; or

- outdated or obsolete items.

* These articles may be covered with a Scheduled Personal Property endorsement, discussed in this chapter.

Payment of replacement cost for some of these items would violate the *principle of indemnity,* which states that the insured should not profit from insurance. He or she should be returned to his or her financial position prior to the loss.

Limitations on Personal Property Replacement Cost

The insurer will pay no more than the *least* of the following:

- replacement cost at the time of loss without deduction for depreciation;

- the full cost of repair at the time of loss;

- the limit of Coverage C, if applicable;

- any applicable Special Limits of Liability stated in Coverage C; or

- the limit of liability that applies to any items separately described and insured under the policy, such as a jewelry item scheduled for $10,000.

When the replacement cost for the entire loss under this endorsement is more than $500, the insurer will pay no more than the ACV for the loss or damage *until* the item is repaired or replaced. The insured is permitted to make a claim on the ACV basis, then file for additional liability within 180 days after the loss.

Study Questions

4. The replacement cost endorsement covers all personal property, including jewelry, furs and antiques.

   A. True
   B. False

Refrigerated Property Coverage

Loss to refrigerated or frozen food caused by power failure that takes place off the residence premises is not covered *unless* the power failure was the result of a covered peril. The insured may add a *Refrigerated Property Coverage (HO 04 98) endorsement* that provides up to $500 of coverage for direct loss to property contained in a refrigerator or freezer if the unit experiences a mechanical failure or the power is interrupted.

Scheduled Personal Property

Homeowners policies impose limits on certain valuable items such as jewelry, furs and silverware. Insureds who own valuable personal property items should specifically schedule this property to provide full coverage. This can be accomplished by adding a *Scheduled Personal Property (HO 04 61)* endorsement to the homeowners policy. Each article is listed and described in detail on the form.

The endorsement lists the amount of insurance and premium for nine classes of scheduled property:

- jewelry;

- furs;

- cameras;

- musical instruments;

- firearms;

- silverware;

- golfer's equipment;

Answer and Rationale

4. **B.** Certain items, such as antiques, are not eligible for replacement cost coverage because of possible moral hazard and loss-adjustment problems.

- fine arts;

- postage stamps; and

- rare and current coins.

Open Perils Coverage for SPP

Scheduled personal property (SPP) is subject to the underlying policy's Definitions, Section I—Conditions, Sections I and II—Conditions and other provisions contained in the endorsement. The property described is covered worldwide, except fine arts, which are covered only in the United States and Canada. All direct physical loss to scheduled items are covered *except* for specifically excluded causes of loss. No deductible applies to the SPP.

Principal Coverage

You'll recall that the first item under "Property Not Covered" in the homeowners policy says that the policy doesn't cover "Articles separately described and specifically insured, regardless of the limit for which they are insured, in this or other insurance."

What this exclusion in the HO–3 means is that the items named in the SPP endorsement aren't covered under the homeowners policy. What this means to the insurance professional is that he or she should take care when determining the amount of liability for the items listed in the SPP. The homeowners policy will not pay any excess amount that the SPP limit of liability doesn't include.

Exclusions

The first two SPP exclusions are

- wear and tear, gradual deterioration or inherent vice; and

- insects or vermin.

Wear and Tear   Losses that are not sudden or accidental but are the result of normal deterioration and degradation are typically excluded in many property forms; the same is true with the Scheduled Personal Property endorsement.

Insects or Vermin   The exclusion for damage done by animals is limited to insects and vermin. You'll remember that the HO–3 excluded the following:

- birds;

- vermin—pests such as cockroaches and ants;

- rodents—animals such as rats, mice and raccoons;

- insects; and

- animals owned by the insured.

The Scheduled Personal Property endorsement gives back the coverage previously excluded for birds, rodents and animals owned by the insured.

Study Questions

5. Donna owns a diamond watch worth $25,000. Her Scheduled Personal Property endorsement lists the agreed value as $20,000. (Donna wanted to save money on the premium.) Her HO–3 covers personal property for $250,000. If the watch is stolen, what is the maximum Donna can receive under her HO–3 with the SPP endorsement added to it?

   A. $20,000 under the SPP and $5,000 under the HO–3
   B. $20,000 under the SPP and nothing under the HO–3
   C. $20,000 under the SPP and $1,500 under the HO–3
   D. Nothing since neither policy covers theft of jewelry

Warlike Acts   The next exclusion in the SPP includes the following warlike acts:

- undeclared war, civil war, insurrection, rebellion or revolution;

- warlike act by a military force or military personnel;

- destruction, seizure or use for a military purpose; and

- damage as a result of discharge of nuclear weapon, whether accidental or not.

Nuclear Hazard   The SPP refers to the Nuclear Hazard clause of Section I—Conditions in the homeowners policies. The HO–3 defines *nuclear hazard* to mean "any nuclear reaction, radiation, or radioactive contamination, all whether controlled or uncontrolled or however caused, or any consequence of any of these." Although the threat to residential property is probably limited to areas located near nuclear reactors, the nuclear hazard condition is included as protection for insurers who face potentially catastrophic losses if a nuclear accident should occur.

Fine Arts Exclusions   The policy excludes all loss caused by the repair, restoration or retouching processes. It provides named perils coverage for the following items:

- art glass windows;

- glassware;

- statuary;

Answer and Rationale

5. **B.** The SPP endorsement is the only coverage available because the HO–3 excludes property specifically described and insured elsewhere.

- marble,

- bric-a-brac;

- porcelains; and

- similar fragile articles.

The named perils coverage that applies to the above list includes fire or lightning, explosion, aircraft or collision, windstorm, earthquake or flood, malicious damage or theft, and derailment or overturn of a conveyance. The SPP does not cover property on exhibition from any cause unless the same SPP covers the exhibition premises and the item on exhibition.

Stamp and Coin Collections   The SPP does not cover the following types of losses to stamp and coin collections:

- fading, creasing, denting, scratching, tearing or thinning;

- transfer of colors, inherent defect, dampness, extremes of temperature or depreciation;

- being handled or worked on; and

- shipping by mail other than registered mail.

The final type of loss not covered involves the disappearance of individual stamps, coins or other articles unless the item is

- described and scheduled with a specific amount of insurance; or

- mounted in a volume and the page it is attached to is also lost.

Study Questions

6. All of the following losses to Scheduled Personal Property are covered EXCEPT

   A. the disappearance of a rare coin not mounted on a separate page in the volume of coins
   B. golfing equipment caught in floodwaters
   C. damage to a fur caused by a lice infestation
   D. theft of a painting from the insured's foyer

Sinkhole Collapse

Insureds in some states, such as Florida, are aware of the tremendous damage that can occur when the earth collapses because of water acting on limestone or similar

---

Answer and Rationale

6. **A.** The coin must be mounted on a page in a volume and specifically insured in the SPP.

rock, resulting in a situation known as a sinkhole. A *Sinkhole Collapse (HO 04 99)* endorsement provides coverage for damage to property caused by settlement or collapse of the earth under the insured property.

Special Loss Settlement

As explained in Chapter 5, unless a dwelling is insured for at least 80 percent of its replacement cost at the time of the loss, the loss cannot be settled on a replacement cost basis. This 80-percent requirement may create a moral hazard in an area where the *market value* (the most probable price a property should bring, according to guidelines published by federal lending institutions) of the home is far below its *replacement cost*—the cost of constructing a building with current materials and techniques. If insureds are unable to sell their houses for a reasonable profit, they might be tempted to intentionally damage or destroy their property in order to profit from their homeowners insurance.

To decrease this moral hazard, some insurers permit the addition of a *Special Loss Settlement (HO 04 56)* endorsement, which permits the insured to carry 50, 60 or 70 percent of the replacement cost of the dwelling without affecting the replacement cost loss payment provisions. As you would suspect, the rate for this coverage is significantly higher, although the decrease in the amount of insurance required may offset the increase. Obviously, if it didn't, the insured would be well advised not to add this endorsement.

Study Questions

7. The market value of a house is $40,000, but its replacement cost is $120,000. The insurance company permits insurance for 50 percent of replacement cost with the addition of the HO 04 56 form. If a total loss occurs, how much would the insurer pay?

Special Personal Property Coverage

Before the reintroduction of the HO–5 form, insureds who desired open perils coverage on their personal property could get it by adding the *Special Personal Property Coverage (HO 00 15)* endorsement to an HO–3 (only) policy. Now this endorsement has been withdrawn. Depending on when the HO–5 was filed in your state and adopted by your companies, there may or may not be some HO–3 policies with HO 00 15 attached up for renewal. Care should be taken to offer these insureds the option of converting to an HO–5 policy to maintain the same scope of coverage as before.

The Special Personal Property Coverage endorsement has been renumbered to *HO 05 24* and made available to HO–4 policyholders who wish to have open perils coverage on personal property.

Answer and Rationale

7. The house may be insured for $60,000, or 50 percent of its replacement cost. If a loss occurs, the insurer settles the loss on a replacement cost basis, not to exceed the policy limit.

■ SPECIAL COMPUTER COVERAGE

Except for the HO–5 policy, and HO–4 or HO–6 when endorsed to provide open perils coverage, personal computers are covered on a named perils basis. The *Special Computer Coverage (HO 04 14)* endorsement, which does not increase or modify the limit of liability or provisions that apply to Coverage C, provides *open perils* coverage for computer equipment including

- hardware;

- CRT screens;

- disc drives;

- printers;

- modems and other related equipment; and

- software media including tapes, wires, records, discs or other software.

The actual personal data or records kept on software is *not* covered because of the difficulty of assigning a value to that material.

Windstorm or Hail Exclusion

Many insureds feel that they should not pay for losses that are unlikely to occur. Therefore, insureds may add a *Windstorm or Hail Exclusion (HO 04 94)* that excludes the perils of windstorm and hail in return for a premium credit.

Coverage D—Loss of Use is not affected by the exclusion, nor does the endorsement eliminate coverage by fire or explosion resulting from windstorm or hail damage.

Study Questions

8. Insureds who live in areas not prone to windstorm or hail can endorse their policies to exclude this peril in order to save money.

   A. True
   B. False

■ RECREATIONAL ACTIVITY EXPOSURES

Millions of people own or operate snowmobiles and watercraft for pleasure and recreation. These are the only two types of recreational vehicles whose liability coverage can be broadened under the homeowners policy. Other recreational vehicles,

---

Answer and Rationale

8. **A.** In exchange for a premium credit, insureds may add a Windstorm or Hail Exclusion to their policies, which excludes the perils of windstorm and hail.

such as trail bikes and motorcycles, must be covered under separate recreational vehicles policies or, in some cases, by endorsing the personal auto policy.

Snowmobiles

The homeowners policy provides liability coverage for any vehicle (including snowmobiles) while being used by an insured, persons employed by an insured or others using the vehicle with the insured's consent on the insured location. In order to provide liability coverage away from the insured location, a *Snowmobiles (HO 24 64)* endorsement should be added to the policy. Each snowmobile to be insured must be listed on the endorsement.

Watercraft

The homeowners policy limits watercraft liability and medical payments to others to boats and motors within certain length or horsepower guidelines. Because boats and boating property are covered only against a limited number of named perils, broader protection should be provided by *outboard motor and boat insurance, a boat owners policy or personal yacht insurance.* For those boat owners who feel that such coverage is unnecessary and wish to add additional liability coverage for their watercraft to their homeowners policy, a *Watercraft (HO 24 75)* endorsement is available.

The Watercraft endorsement provides coverage for *vicarious parental liability* occurring when the watercraft is used by a child or a minor. The endorsement excludes coverage for bodily injury to any employee of the insured who is principally employed to operate the watercraft. It also *excludes* coverage if the watercraft is used to carry passengers for a fee or is rented to others.

Study Questions

9. All recreational vehicles can be covered under a homeowners policy with a recreational vehicle endorsement.

   A. True
   B. False

Answer and Rationale

9. **B.** Only snowmobiles and watercraft can be insured under a homeowners policy and by special endorsement. Other recreational vehicles, such as motorcycles and trail bikes, are better served by the personal auto policy.

■ SPECIAL LIABILITY EXPOSURES

Personal liability insurance pays on behalf of individuals, all sums that the insured becomes *legally obligated* to pay as a result of liability imposed upon him or her by law. A person whose negligence has caused bodily injury or property damage will not be held liable unless that negligence was the proximate cause of those damages. Generally, the injured party claiming damages must prove that the other party was negligent and that the negligence was the proximate cause of the bodily injury or property damage. Coverage may be added to the homeowners policy against certain liability exposures.

■ LIBEL, SLANDER, PRIVACY INVASION

The personal liability provided under the homeowners policy provides protection for bodily injury or property damage liability, but not *personal injury* that may include *any injury to another person's rights or reputation,* including torts such as libel, slander or invasion of privacy. The *Personal Injury (HO 24 82)* endorsement adds liability for this type of offense committed during the policy period.

The Personal Injury endorsement does *not* provide coverage for liability

- arising out of disputes between insureds;

- from contracts not related to the premises;

- from the injured person's employment by the insured;

- involving a violation of a penal law;

- arising out of business pursuits; or

- arising out of civic or public activities performed for pay.

 ISO Form Update In 2002, ISO modified this endorsement by adding a new exclusion eliminating coverage for liability arising out of the inhalation of fungi, wet or dry rot or bacteria. However, because the definition of *bodily injury* in the homeowners forms includes coverage for such claims, the effect of this exclusion is to eliminate the possibility of duplication of coverage between the basic form and this endorsement.

Loss Assessment Coverage

Many homeowners and condominium unit owners belong to an association of property owners. This association owns the condominium building(s) and other property, such as a swimming pool. When the association property is damaged, the homeowner may be liable for a share of the damage. You'll recall that the homeowners policy provides up to $1,000 of loss coverage for assessments that result from direct loss to collectively owned property by a peril insured against. Those insureds who wish additional coverage may add a *Loss Assessment Coverage (HO 04 35)* endorsement; however, the endorsement does not cover loss assessments due to earthquakes, land shock waves or tremors pertaining to a volcano.

Loss Assessment for Earthquake

If the insured wishes to cover loss assessments because of earthquake or land shock waves related to a volcano, he or she may request a *Loss Assessment for Earthquake (HO 04 36)* endorsement. This endorsement describes the deductible, which is a specified percentage of the limit stated in the endorsement but not less than $250 for any one assessment. Coverage does *not* apply for flood or tidal wave, even when caused by an earthquake.

■ BUSINESS EXPOSURES

Although the homeowners policy provides personal liability and medical payments to others as part of the Section II—Liability Coverages, any bodily injury or property damage that arises out of or in connection with a business engaged in by the insured is *not* covered. Fortunately, the insured may add a number of endorsements to the policy to broaden the liability coverage and to protect himself or herself in unusual situations.

Business Pursuits

The homeowners policy may be amended with a *Business Pursuits (HO 24 71)* endorsement that provides some liability coverage for insureds who use part of their dwelling for business activities such as tutorial services. Liability does not apply if the insured is the owner of the business or engages in professional activities such as architecture, medicine, dentistry or beauty shop operations. Teachers may add coverage for liability resulting from corporal punishment of pupils. Liability for teaching activities related to horses, motor vehicles, watercraft and aircraft are excluded.

Permitted Incidental Occupancies—Residence Premises

Many professionals, such as physicians, lawyers or accountants, have offices in their residences; however, coverage for bodily injury or property damage arising out of rendering or failing to render professional services is excluded under the homeowners form. The insured may protect himself or herself from various liability exposures by endorsing the homeowners policy. If the insured owns and operates a business in his or her home, a *Permitted Incidental Occupancies (HO 04 42)* endorsement may be added to cover business exposures.

Liability does not apply to

- bodily injury to an insured's employee, except to residence employees in the course of their employment; or

- bodily injury to a student as a result of corporal punishment administered by or at the direction of the insured.

Home Day Care Coverage

The unendorsed homeowners policy limits coverage for business property on the insured's premises to $2,500 and provides no coverage for other structures on the insured's premises used for business purposes. Those insureds providing day care services out of their homes can obtain this property coverage with the HO 04 97 endorsement. The endorsement maintains the Special Limit of Liability on business personal property but provides that the limit does not apply to property listed in the schedule contained in the endorsement. The insured is free to schedule any limit the insured desires and the underwriter is willing to accept.

The HO 04 97 provides personal liability and medical payments coverage arising out of a business *except*

- when aircraft, hovercraft, motor vehicles, watercraft or saddle animals are involved; or

- when an employee of the insured (except for a residence employee) is injured as a result of the day care operation.

The Home Day Care endorsement amends the dollar limit shown on the policy for Coverage E—Personal Liability to an annual *aggregate limit* for both personal liability and medical payments to others. The personal liability limit specified on the Declarations Page is the most that will be paid for all Section II day care liability coverage during the policy year.

Within this aggregate limit is a sublimit for Coverage F—Medical Payments to Others. No more than the stated limit will be paid to any one person for medical expenses during the policy year. Although the severability of insurance clause states that coverage applies separately to each insured, this is not true with respect to an aggregate limit. Therefore, when the Home Day Care endorsement is added, coverage does not apply separately to each insured. The aggregate limit is the total amount of insurance that is available to all insureds under the policy.

Incidental Farming

The homeowners policy may be endorsed to cover liability and medical payments to others as a result of farming on the residence premises. The *Incidental Farming Personal Liability (HO 24 72)* endorsement covers only inconsequential farming that is not done as a primary source of income. Coverage may also be added for incidental farming activities such as boarding and grazing animals that are conducted away from the residence premises.

Farmers Personal Liability

The intention of the ISO homeowners policies is not to provide liability coverage for farming activities; however, coverage may be added with the addition of a *Farmers Personal Liability (HO 24 73)* endorsement. This endorsement deletes the Section II—Liability Coverages and Section II—Exclusions and replaces them with liability sections tailored to the farm operation. The earlier revisions to the homeowners policies revised this form to add coverage for vehicles used on the insured location.

Structures Rented to Others

For an additional premium, coverage may be added for structures on the residence premises that are rented to someone as a private residence. The *Structures Rented to Others—Residence Premises (HO 04 40)* endorsement includes a description of the structure and the limit of liability that applies. The endorsement also deletes Exclusion **1.c.** under Section II—Exclusions, which excludes Coverage E—Personal Liability and Coverage F—Medical Payments to Others. The base policy excludes coverage for liability and medical payments "arising out of the rental or holding for rental any part of any premises by an insured." Therefore, coverage *is* provided. The structures listed on the form are also included in the definition of *insured location.*

■ UNIT OWNERS EXPOSURES

Ownership of a condominium unit may create some special risks. The absolute ownership of a *condominium unit* in a multiunit building is based on a legal description of the airspace the unit actually occupies plus an undivided interest in the ownership of the common elements, such as hallways and common grounds, which are owned jointly with other condominium unit owners.

Coverage A—Special Coverage

The HO–6 homeowners form includes named perils coverage on "alterations, appliances, fixtures and improvements which are part of the building contained within the residence premises" under Coverage A—Dwelling. However, the unit owner may add an endorsement, *Unit–Owners Coverage A—Special Coverage (HO 17 32),* to amend the coverage to open perils. The endorsement also broadens the Coverage D—Loss of Use to include protection when the premises cannot be used because of any insured loss caused by an open perils.

Coverage C—Special Coverage

Personal property is covered on a named perils basis under the HO–6 form; however, coverage may be amended to *open perils* with the addition of the *Unit–Owners Coverage C—Special Coverage (HO 17 31)* endorsement. Inclusion of this endorsement also broadens the perils to which Coverage D—Loss of Use applies to personal property.

Rental to Others Coverage

Some individuals purchase condominium units as investments and rent the units to others. These people should add *Unit–Owners Rental to Others Coverage (HO 17 33)* to the HO–6 form. This endorsement provides personal property coverage, theft coverage for most items (excluding some, such as money and securities, to which special limits would apply) and coverage for personal liability and medical payments to others.

■ CHAPTER SUMMARY

A homeowners policy offers more than just property and liability protection for your client's home. It covers loss or damage to other structures and personal property, loss of use and additional protection.

You should be thoroughly familiar with the homeowners policy and be able to explain policy terms, coverages, conditions and exclusions. Because most insurance companies use ISO forms, you should become comfortable with these forms. However, because some insurance companies use other forms, you should never make unqualified statements about what is and is not covered under a policy.

Some generalizations about coverages and exclusions can be made, but insurers handle situations differently. Examine as many forms as possible so that you will have a clear picture of how most companies will handle coverage questions. You'll become a more knowledgeable professional who can better assist clients in choosing the best homeowners insurance coverages to meet their needs.

■ ADDITIONAL STUDY QUESTIONS

1. Which endorsement provides coverage for libel and slander?

    A. Excess Liability endorsement
    B. Personal Liability Broad Form endorsement
    C. Personal Injury endorsement
    D. Extended Coverage E endorsement

2. Which of the following is true about the Home Day-Care endorsement?

    A. It provides increased coverage for personal property used in the day care business.
    B. It provides coverage for corporal punishment.
    C. It provides coverage for injury to day care employees.
    D. It changes the liability limits from an occurrence basis to an aggregate basis.

■ ANSWERS AND RATIONALES TO ADDITIONAL STUDY QUESTIONS

1. **C.** Injury to another's rights or reputation, including torts such as libel, slander or invasion of privacy, can be added to the homeowners policy with a Personal Injury endorsement.

2. **D.** The Home Day-Care Endorsement amends the Coverage E policy limit for personal liability to an annual aggregate limit for both personal liability and medical payments to others.

9

Case Studies

CASE STUDY 1: PREMIUM VARIABLES

Case Study

Jerry and Jeanette are discussing their homeowners premium with their neighbors. They don't understand why their premium is so much higher than some of their friends' premiums.

How would you explain to Jerry and Jeanette the way in which the following affect their premium?

1. The community's protection classification

2. Construction type

3. Policy form selected

4. Deductible

5. Insurance company selected

6. Discounts

CASE STUDY 2: NAME THAT PERIL

Case Study

The statements or questions that follow describe a few of the 16 perils you learned about in Chapter 3. In each one, you should try to name the peril.

Meet the Thomas family. They are your insureds and have an HO–3. They live in northern Minnesota; it's the first of January.

1. Francis Thomas, your insured, reports his 16-year-old son drove the family conveyance into the garage and damaged the siding. Disregarding any coverage issues, which property damage peril applies to the damaged siding?

_____

_____

_____

2. In a separate call, Mrs. Alberta Thomas reports that overnight, someone painted some unflattering words about her son Joseph on the damaged siding. Which peril applies?

_____

_____

_____

3. The string of terrible luck continues in the Thomas family. Joseph was cleaning the paint off of the siding with a pressure washer. He left the washer out while he went to get a burger and fries. The washer was gone when he returned. Which peril applies?

_____

_____

_____

4. One night while everyone was sleeping, the Thomas family heard a large crash. When they checked to see what had happened, they saw a propeller in the middle of the living room. Which two perils might apply to this loss?

_____

_____

_____

5. Mr. and Mrs. Thomas decided that their luck needed to change. In February, they took the family on a three-week vacation to Florida. Before leaving the house, Mr. Thomas drained the pipes and made sure that the furnace was on. Which peril did he prevent and break the string of bad luck?

_____

_____

_____

■ CASE STUDY 3: HOW MUCH INSURANCE?

Case Study An agent is meeting with a client for the first time. The client's initial question is, "How much insurance do I need?"

1. Are expensive jewelry and a gun collection covered and for how much?

_____

_____

_____

2. The homeowners policy specifies limits of liability for valuable property (jewelry, furs, firearms, silverware, etc.). The limit per occurrence for theft of jewelry, watches and furs is $1,500. The limit for firearms and related equipment is $2,500. If additional coverage is needed, a Scheduled Personal Property Endorsement can be added.

_____

_____

_____

■ CASE STUDY 4: INSURED'S DUTIES AFTER LOSS

Case Study The weight of ice during a long period of freezes and thaws has caused the Smiths' roof to collapse. Describe to the Smiths their duties to the insurance company after this loss by explaining the duties listed:

1. Give notice

_____

_____

_____

2. Protect the property

_____

_____

_____

3. Cooperate

_____

_____

_____

4. Prepare an inventory

_____

_____

_____

5. Provide proof of loss

_____

_____

_____

■ **CASE STUDY 5: LIABILITY INSURANCE**

Case Study The Wilsons have purchased their first home. Because they are on a tight budget, they ask their agent to explain the importance of liability insurance as part of their homeowners policy. Answer the Wilsons questions about liability coverage.

1. Can property insurance be purchased without the liability coverage?

_____

_____

_____

2. What is the purpose of the liability coverage?

_____

_____

_____

3. Who does liability coverage protect?

_____

_____

_____

4. What is the minimum amount of liability than can be purchased?

_____

_____

_____

5. Can additional liability coverage be purchased?

_____

_____

_____

■ **ANSWERS AND RATIONALES TO CASE STUDY 1**

1. The location of the dwelling is an important factor in determining the premium. The protection class is determined by

   – the loss experience of each designated territory, and

   – the quality of the local fire department and available water supply

   Few losses and a nearby fire department with excellent response will result in lower rates than an area where losses are greater because of the fire department's inability to respond quickly.

2. When people are talking about homeowners premiums, they're usually comparing apples and oranges. One house may be frame and the other brick. Or one's replacement cost may be $100,000 while the other's is $75,000.

   To accurately compare the premiums, the houses would have to be almost identical in the types of construction.

3. The insured may select from a number of policy forms that can be designed to fit his or her needs. However, the broader the coverage, the higher the premium. Consideration must be given to the premium savings compared to a potential loss.

4. Homeowners policies have a standard $250 deductible to all covered perils. Higher deductibles can result in significant premium savings.

5. Premiums vary based on an insurer's loss experience, underwriting standards and the locations covered. Insureds can compare insurer ratings from A. M. Best and premiums through their state insurance departments.

6. Many discounts are available to insureds based on age, occupancy, protection class and loss prevention or reduction devices.

■ **ANSWERS AND RATIONALES TO CASE STUDY 2**

1. *Vehicles* are mediums by which things are conveyed or transported. The peril provides coverage for losses as a result of vehicle damage to insured property. There is no coverage under the homeowners form for damage to the vehicle.

2. *Vandalism or malicious mischief (V&MM)* is intentional and spiteful damage to or destruction of the insured's property. If someone accidentally spills paint on the insured's carpeting, this is not considered V&MM. However, graffiti painted on the insured's garage door is V&MM and would be covered under this peril. When a dwelling is vacant, it is more susceptible to losses from certain perils, such as V&MM, theft and glass breakage. Therefore, most policies contain a provision that states that certain losses, such as V&MM, are not covered if the dwelling has been vacant for more than 60 consecutive days prior to the loss. Vandalism or malicious mischief is peril number 8.

3. All homeowners forms include *theft* as an insured peril. Theft is an act of taking or stealing property (including attempted theft) with the intent to deprive the owner of the property from a known place when it is likely that the property has been stolen. There are restrictions and limits on certain types of property, such as jewelry and furs, and certain types of theft are excluded under all homeowners forms.

4. The homeowners form provides coverage for damage that results from *aircraft,* missiles and spacecraft. This would include parts that fall from aircraft, causing damage to insured property. By extension, this peril covers damage from a sonic boom. Aircraft is number 5 on the Broad Form list. The second peril that might apply is *falling objects.*

5. The *freezing peril* covers damage due to a household appliance or plumbing, heating, sprinkler or air conditioning system that freezes—unless the dwelling is vacant or unoccupied. However, coverage *does* apply to a vacant or unoccupied dwelling if the insured:

   • has taken reasonable care to maintain heat in the building; or

   • turns off the water supply and drains the system or appliance.

■ **ANSWERS AND RATIONALES TO CASE STUDY 3**

1. What are the agent's responsibilities in determining the client's needs and recommending coverages?

2. The amount of coverage required and the amount of coverage needed may be very different. Under the terms of the homeowners policy, the insured must carry insurance equal to at least 80 percent of the replacement cost of the dwelling. An agent's responsibilities include obtaining full and accurate information necessary for analyzing the client's risk and the hazards involved so that the client's needs can be accurately determined. The agent must also see that the policy is written properly so that appropriate coverage applies.

■ **ANSWERS AND RATIONALES TO CASE STUDY 4**

1. The Smiths must give prompt notice of the loss to the insurer or agent. If the loss was due to theft, they must also notify the police. In the case of loss of a credit or fund transfer card, they must notify the appropriate financial institution.

2. The Smiths must protect the property from further damage. If repairs to the property are required, they must make the repairs and keep accurate records of repair expenses.

3. The Smiths must cooperate with the insurance company in the investigation of the claim.

4. The Smiths must prepare an inventory of damaged personal property showing the quantity, description, actual cash value and amount of loss. They must also include all receipts and related documents that justify the figures in the inventory.

5. Within 60 days after its request, the Smiths must provide the insurance company a signed, sworn proof of loss that sets forth the time and cause of loss; the interests of all insureds; other insurance, changes in title or occupancy of the property; specifications of damaged buildings and repair estimates; and receipts for additional living expenses.

■ ANSWERS AND RATIONALES TO CASE STUDY 5

1. The homeowners policy is a package policy. The property and liability sections of the policy cannot be purchased separately.

2. Liability coverage is designed to provide protection against a claim or lawsuit for bodily injury or property damage. Under Coverage E—Personal Liability, the insured must be found legally liable before a claim is paid. Under Coverage F—Medical Payments to Others, a claim may be paid without legal liability on the part of the insured.

3. The liability section of the homeowners policy protects the insured against claims for bodily injury or property damage of others.

4. The minimum liability limit for each homeowners policy form is $100,000. When determining if this is adequate coverage, insureds must consider how much they could afford to pay out of their own pocket for medical and legal expenses and damage to the property of others if someone is injured on their property.

5. Additional liability coverage may be purchased with an additional premium.

...... **Glossary**

A

Actual cash value   The sum of money required to pay for damage to or loss of property. This sum is the property's current replacement cost minus depreciation caused by obsolescence or wear and tear.

B

Bailee   A person who has care, custody or control of another's personal property, usually for repair, cleaning, processing, storage or service.

Bailment   A delivery of goods or personal property by one person to another in trust that the receiver of the goods will perform a certain service either stated in a contract or implied by the nature of the service.

C

Civil commotion   An uprising of people creating a prolonged disturbance.

Concurrent causation   If two causes of loss happen at the same time or in conjunction with each other, only one cause of loss has to be covered for the loss itself to be covered.

F

Fire   Oxidation sufficiently rapid to cause a flame or glow.

H

Hazards   Specific situations that increase the probability of a loss occurring from a peril.

I

Indemnify   To restore a person who has a loss to his or her original financial condition by making a payment, repair or replacement of the damaged items.

Indemnity   Payment of an amount to offset all or part of an insured loss.

Indirect losses   Refers to the financial losses incurred as a result of direct losses, such as fire or windstorm.

L

Lightning   A flashing of light produced by a discharge of atmospheric electricity.

Loss   An unintended, unforeseen reduction in value or destruction of financial value.

M

Mortgage clause   Homeowners policy provision noting that any loss payment will be payable to the mortgageholder or lienholder as its financial interest may appear (balance due on the loan).

N

Named perils   In the HO policies, 16 specifically named perils provide coverage for losses.

Nuclear Hazard   Any nuclear reaction, radiation, or contamination, all whether controlled or uncontrolled or however caused, or any consequence of these.

O

Occurrence   An unforeseen, unintended and unexpected event, including continuous and repeated exposure to the same harmful condition, which generally results in bodily injury or property damage.

P

Peril   An immediate, specific event causing a loss.

Personal property   In a broad and general sense, everything subject to ownership that does not come under the definition of real estate or real property. Refers to possessions of a personal and movable nature, as opposed to immovable objects, such as houses or land.

Proof of loss   A document by which an insured makes claim under Section I of the homeowners policy. Upon request of the company, the insured may be asked to submit a signed (and notarized) proof of loss that sets out the date and time of loss and such other details as the company may require.

Proximate Cause   The uninterrupted sequence of events that produces a loss. In other words, there is an unbroken chain of cause and effect between the occurrence of an insurance peril and the damage to property.

R

Riot   An assembly of individuals who commit a lawful or unlawful act in a violent or tumultuous manner to the terror and disturbance of others.

Real property   Land and generally whatever is erected or growing upon or affixed to the land. That which is not of a personal and movable nature.

Replacement cost   The cost to repair or replace property with like kind and quality materials without deduction for depreciation.

T

Theft   An act of taking or stealing property with the intent to deprive the owner of the property. Theft must occur from a known place at a time that it is likely that the property has been stolen.

U

Unoccupied   A dwelling empty of persons but containing furniture and being used.

V

Vacant   A dwelling empty of persons and contents.

····· **Appendix**

 e have made the following charts and ISO forms available for you.

·····

■ CHARTS

- HO Forms Comparison Chart
- HO–3 2000 vs. HO–3 0491

■ ISO FORMS

- Homeowners 2—Broad Form (ISO Edition HO 00 02 10 00)
- Homeowners 3—Special Form (ISO Edition HO 00 03 10 00)
- Homeowners 4—Contents Broad Form (ISO Edition HO 00 04 10 00)
- Homeowners 5—Comprehensive Form (ISO Edition HO 00 05 10 00)
- Homeowners 6—Unit Owner's Form (ISO Edition HO 00 06 10 00)
- Homeowners 8—Modified Coverage Form (ISO Edition HO 00 08 10 00)
- Additional Insured—Residence Premises (HO 04 41)
- Building Additions and Alterations (HO 04 51)
- Coverage B—Off Premises (HO 04 91)
- Coverage C—Increased Special Limits of Liability (HO 04 65)

- Credit Card and Counterfeit Money Coverage—Increased Amounts (HO 04 53)

- Earthquake Endorsement (HO 04 54)

- Inflation Guard (HO 04 46)

- Home Day-Care Coverage (HO 04 97)

- Mobilehome Endorsement (MH 04 01)

- Ordinance or Law Coverage (HO 04 77)

- Other Structures—Increased Limits (HO 04 48)

- Personal Property Replacement Cost (HO 04 90)

- Water Back Up and Sump Pump Overflow Endorsement (HO 04 95)

- Refrigerated Property Coverage (HO 04 98)

- Scheduled Personal Property Endorsement (HO 04 61)

- Sinkhole Collapse Endorsement (HO 04 99)

- Special Loss Settlement (HO 04 56)

- Special Personal Property Coverage Endorsement (HO 05 24)

- Special Computer Coverage (HO 04 14)

- Windstorm or Hail Exclusion (HO 04 94)

- Increased Limits on Business Property (HO 04 12)

- Unit Owners Coverage A—Special Coverage (HO 17 32)

- Unit Owners Coverage C—Special Coverage (HO 17 31)

- Unit Owners Rental to Others Coverage (HO 17 33)

HO Forms Comparison Chart
Part I: Section I—Property Coverages

Limits of Liability and Perils

	HO-2 Broad Form	HO-3 Special Form	HO-4 Contents Broad Form	HO-5 Comprehensive Form	HO-6 Unit Owners Form	HO-8 Modified Coverage Form
Cov. A—Dwelling	Refer to state rate pages for min. limits	Refer to state rate pages for min. limits	Refer to state rate pages for min. limits	Refer to state rate pages for min. limits	Refer to state rate pages for min. limits	Refer to state rate pages for min. limits
Cov. B—Other Structures						
1 or 2 family	10% of Cov. A	10% of Cov. A	N/A	10% of Cov. A	N/A	10% of Cov. A
3 or 4 family	5% of Cov. A	5% of Cov. A	N/A	5% of Cov. A	N/A	5% of Cov. A
Cov. C.—Personal Property						
1 or 2 family	50% of Cov. A	50% of Cov. A	Refer to Declarations Page	50% of Cov. A	Refer to Declarations Page	50% of Cov. A
3 family	30% of Cov. A	30% of Cov. A	N/A	30% of Cov. A	N/A	30% of Cov. A
4 family	25% of Cov. A	25% of Cov. A	N/A	25% of Cov. A	N/A	25% of Cov. A
Cov. D—Loss of Use	30% of Cov. A	30% of Cov. A	30 % of Cov. C	30% of Cov. A	50% of Cov. C	10% of Cov. A

Additional Coverages

	HO-2 Broad Form	HO-3 Special Form	HO-4 Contents Broad Form	HO-5 Comprehensive Form	HO-6 Unit Owners Form	HO-8 Modified Coverage Form
Debris Removal	Reasonable expense up to $500/$1,000 per tree/all trees	Reasonable expense up to $500/$1,000 per tree/all trees	Reasonable expense up to $500/$1,000 per tree/all trees	Reasonable expense up to $500/$1,000 per tree/all trees	Reasonable expense up to $500/$1,000 per tree/all trees	Reasonable expense up to $500/$1,000 per tree/all trees
Reasonable Repairs	All forms cover the reasonable cost incurred to protect property from further damage.					
Lawns, Trees, Shrubs, and Plants	$500 per tree 5% of Cov. A for all plants	$500 per tree 5% of Cov. A for all plants	$500 per tree 10% of Cov. C for all plants	$500 per tree 5% of Cov. A for all plants	$500 per tree 10% of Cov. C for all plants	$250 per tree 5% of Cov. A for all plants
Fire Dept. Service Charge	Up to $500	Up to $500	Up to $500	Up to $500	Up to $500	Up to $500
Property Removed	Open Perils up to 30 days	Open Perils up to 30 days	Open Perils up to 30 days	Open Perils up to 30 days	Open Perils up to 30 days	Open Perils up to 30 days
Credit Card, Fund Transfer, Forgery and Counterfeit Money	Up to $500	Up to $500	Up to $500	Up to $500	Up to $500	Up to $500
Loss Assessment	Up to $1,000	Up to $1,000	Up to $1,000	Up to $1,000	Up to $1,000	Up to $1,000
Collapse	All forms except HO-8 provide named perils coverage plus coverage for hidden decay, insect or vermin damage, weight of contents, weight of rain collected on a roof or use of defective construction material or methods.					Not Covered
Landlord's Furnishings	Up to $2,000	Up to $2,000	Not Covered	Up to $2,500 for named perils	N/A	Not Covered
Building Additions and Alterations	N/A	N/A	Up to 10% of Cov. C	N/A	Included under Cov. A	N/A
Ordinance or Law	10% of Cov. A	10% of Cov. A	10% of Bldg. Additions and Alterations	10% of Cov. A	10% of Cov. A	Not Covered
Grave Markers	Up to $5,000	Up to $5,000	Up to $5,000	Up to $5,000	Up to $5,000	Not Covered

HO Forms Comparison Chart

Section I—Property: Perils Insured Against

	HO-2 Cov A/B	Cov C	HO-3 Cov A/B	Cov C	HO-4 Cov A/B	Cov C	HO-5 Cov A/B	Cov C	HO-6 Cov A/B	Cov C	HO-8 Cov A/B	Cov C
Basic Form											X	X
Broad Form	X	X		X**	N/A	X*			X*	X*		
Open Perils			X				X	X				

*Can be endorsed to add open perils.
**Must use HO-5 to obtain open perils coverage.

Section I—Broad Form Perils and Exclusions

Basic Form Perils		Broad Form Perils (In Addition to Basic Perils)
Fire or Lightning	Smoke	Falling Objects
Windstorm or Hail	Vandalism or Malicious Mischief	Weight of Ice, Snow or Sleet
Explosion	Theft	Accidental Discharge or Overflow of Water or Steam
Riot or Civil Commotion	Volcanic Eruption	Sudden and Accidental Tearing Apart, Cracking, Burning or Bulging
Aircraft		Freezing
Vehicles		Sudden and Accidental Damage from Artificially Generated Electrical Current

Broad Form Named Perils	Standard Building and Personal Property Exclusions (All Forms)
Sudden and accidental direct physical loss caused by:	Loss caused directly or indirectly by:
1. Fire or Lightning	1. Ordinance or Law
2. Windstorm or Hail	2. Earth Movement
3. Explosion	3. Water Damage (including flood)
4. Riot or Civil Commotion	4. Power Failure
5. Aircraft	5. Neglect
6. Vehicles	6. War
7. Smoke	7. Nuclear Hazard
8. Vandalism or Malicious Mischief	8. Intentional Loss
9. Theft	9. Governmental Action
10. Falling Objects	
11. Weight of Ice, Snow or Sleet	
12. Accidental Discharge or Overflow of Water or Steam	
13. Sudden and Accidental Tearing Apart, Cracking, Burning or Bulging	
14. Freezing	
15. Sudden and Accidental Damage from Artificially Generated Electrical Current	
16. Volcanic Eruption	

Section I—Property Loss Settlement

	HO-2 Cov A/B	Cov C	HO-3 Cov A/B	Cov C	HO-4 Cov A/B	Cov C	HO-5 Cov A/B	Cov C	HO-6 Cov A/B	Cov C	HO-8 Cov A/B	Cov C
Replacement Cost	X		X				X		X			
Actual Cash Value		X		X	N/A	X		X		X		X
Cost of Repair with Current Material											X	

HO Forms Comparison Chart
Part IV: Endorsements

Endorsements that Apply to Section I	
Additional Insured—Residence Premises (HO 04 41)	Insures a single residence owned by two or more parties. One party insures the dwelling and names the other(s) as additional insured(s) with this endorsement. Additional insureds should use the HO-4 to cover any contents, loss of use and liability exposures.
Building Additions & Alterations (HO 04 51)	Covers improvements and alterations made by tenants in rented properties.
Coverage B—Off Premises (HO 04 91)	Covers structures located away from the residence premises but used in connected with the residence. Extends coverage to 10% of Coverage A.
Specific Structures Away from the Residence Premises (HO 04 92)	Covers specifically described locations to be insured. Coverage is additional insurance to what is automatically provided under Coverage B.
Coverage C Increased Special Limits of Liability (HO 04 65)	Increases coverage of certain categories of valuable property.
Credit Card and Counterfeit Money Coverage—Increased Amounts (HO 04 53)	Increases limits of loss due to lost or stolen credit or fund transfer cards or the acceptance of counterfeit paper currency.
Earthquake Endorsement (HO 04 54)	Covers earthquakes, landslides, volcanic eruptions and earth movements that occur within a 72-hour period as if they were a single loss.
Inflation Guard (HO 04 46)	Provides an annual pro-rata increase in the limits in Coverages A, B, C and D.
Mine Subsidence Coverage (Varies by State)	Covers against mine subsidence, which is lateral or vertical ground movement caused by a failure initiated at the mine level of man-made underground mines.
Mobilehome Endorsement (MH 04 01)	Amends the definition of "residence premises" to include the mobilehome listed in the Declarations. Also includes transportation coverage.
Ordinance or Law Coverage (HO 04 77)	Gives back the exclusion for loss arising from an ordinance or law that regulates the construction, repair or demolition of property.
Other Structures—Increased Limits (HO 04 48)	Alows an increase in the Coverage B limit beyond the 10% provided automatically.
Personal Property Replacement Cost (HO 04 90)	Without endorsement, losses to personal property are settled on an actual cash value basis. This endorsement changes the valuation basis for Coverage C to replacement cost, with few exceptions.
Refrigerated Property Coverage (HO 04 98)	Provides up to $500 of coverage for direct loss to property contained in a refrigerator or freezer if the unit experiences a mechanical failure or the power is interrupted.
Scheduled Personal Property Endorsement (HO 04 61)	Broader coverage for personal jewelry, furs, cameras, musical instruments, firearms, silverware, golf equipment, fine art and stamp and coin collections. Articles must be described and insured on a full value basis. Also covers mysterious disappearance, which can be an important coverage when the insured is uncertain as to whether an item was stolen.
Sinkhole Collapse Endorsement (HO 04 99)	Covers damage to property caused by settlement or collapse of the earth under the insured property.
Special Loss Settlement (HO 04 56)	Allows the insured to carry 50, 60 or 70%, instead of the customary 80%, of the replacement cost of the dwelling without affecting the replacement cost loss payment provisions.
Special Personal Property Coverage Endorsement (HO 05 24)	Available to HO-4 policyholders who wish to have open perils coverage on their personal property.
Special Computer Coverage (HO 04 14)	Provides open perils coverage for computer equipment including hardware; (CRT screens disc drives printers modems and other related equipment) and software media including tapes, wires, records, discs or other software. Data is not covered.
Windstorm or Hail Exclusion (HO 04 94)	Excludes windstorm or hail coverage for insureds who feel they do not need this coverage.
Unit Owners Coverage A—Special Coverage (HO 17 32)	Amends Coverage A of the HO-6 to open perils. Also broadens Coverage D to include protection when the premises cannot be used because of any insured loss caused by an open peril.
Unit Owners Coverage C—Special Coverage (HO 17 31)	Amends Coverage C of the HO-6 to open perils. Also broadens Coverage D to include protection when the premises cannot be used because of any insured loss caused by an open peril.
Water Backup and Sump Pump Overflow Endorsement (HO 04 95)	Pays for damage to a finished basement caused by sewer backup or sump pump overflow.

HO Forms Comparison Chart

Endorsements that Apply to Section II	
Snowmobile Endorsement (HO 24 64)	Provides coverage for snowmobiles away from the insured location.
Watercraft Endorsement (HO 24 75)	Covers vicarious parental liability. Bodily injury to an employee of an insured is excluded, as is coverage if the watercraft is used to carry passengers for a fee or is rented to others.
Personal Injury (HO 24 82)	Changes the definition of "bodily injury" to include false arrest, detention or imprisonment, malicious prosecution, libel, slander or defamation of character, invasion of privacy, wrongful eviction and wrongful entry.
Loss Assessment Coverage (HO 04 35)	Provides additional coverage for loss assessment to homeowners or condominium owners over the $1,000 covered by the standard policy.
Loss Assessment for Earthquake (HO 04 36)	Covers loss assessments due to earthquake or land shock waves related to a volcano.
Business Pursuits (HO 24 71)	Extends coverage to any of the insured's business pursuits listed in the endorsement. The endorsement does not apply to businesses the insured owns or controls, to professional liability or to injuries to fellow employees.
Incidental Farming Personal Liability Endorsement (HO 24 72)	Covers liability and medical payments to others as a result of farming on the residence premises. The endorsement covers only inconsequential farming that is not done as a primary source of income. Coverage may also be added for incidental farming activities that are conducted away from the residence premises, such as boarding and grazing animals.
Farmers Personal Liability Endorsement (HO 24 73)	Deletes the Section II—Liability Coverages and Exclusions and replaces them with liability sections tailored to the farm operation.

Endorsements that Apply to Both Sections I and II	
Permitted Incidental Occupancies–Residence Premises (HO 04 42)	Deletes or modifies the exclusions pertaining to a business under both the policy's property and liability sections. This endorsement eliminates the exclusion for other structures used in whole or in part for business, deletes the $2,500 limitation for business property under Coverage C and eliminates the exclusion for business pursuits under the policy's liability section.
Structures Rented to Others (HO 04 40)	Coverage B excludes coverage for structures rented to anyone other than a resident of the household. This endorsement deletes that exclusion and adds coverage under the liability section for property rented to others. This can be an important endorsement for someone with a garage or another outbuilding that has been converted to an apartment.
Home Day Care Coverage (HO 04 97)	Deletes the exclusion under Coverage B for business use, eliminates the $2,500 restriction on business property under Coverage C and extends the coverage under Section II to apply to day care operations. The endorsement also changes the limit for Coverage E Liability from an occurrence limit to an annual aggregate. Requests for this endorsement receive a great deal of underwriting scrutiny.
Unit Owners Rental to Others Coverage (HO 17 33)	Provides personal property coverage, theft for most items and coverage for personal liability and medical payments to others.

ISO Form Comparison Chart
HO 00 03 2000 vs. HO 00 03 04 91

NAMED INSURED

The HO 2000 changes the definition of a named insured, which may create some issues for insureds who are students. For coverage to apply, the student must be *full time* (which varies by school) and must be under a certain age. To solve the problems, ISO developed the HO 05 27 Additional Insured – Student Away At School endorsement.

NEW POLICY FORM HO 00 03 2000 PAGE 1 Of 23	OLD POLICY FORM HO 00 03 04 91 PAGE 1 OF 18

5. "Insured" means:
 	
  a. You and residents of your household who are:
 	
    (1) Your relatives; or
 	
    (2) Other persons under the age of 21 and in the care of any person named above;
 	
  b. A student enrolled in school full time, as defined by the school, who was a resident of your household before moving out to attend school, provided the student is under the age of:
 	
    (1) 24 and your relative; or
 	
    (2) 21 and in your care or the care of a person described in **a.(1)** above; or
	3. "Insured" means you and residents of your household who are:
	
	  a. Your relatives; or
	
	  b. Other persons under the age of 21 and in the care of any person named above.

MOTOR VEHICLE EXCLUSION

The HO 2000 Program changes the policy language to exclude *any person*, not just an insured, when a liability loss occurs involving a vehicle.

NEW POLICY FORM HO 00 03 20 00 PAGE 16 OF 23	OLD POLICY FROM HO-00 03 04 91 PAGE 18 OF 23
• Excludes coverage for a vehicle owned, maintained, occupied, operated, loaded or unloaded by any person • Newly excluded is entrustment of a vehicle, failure to supervise, and vicarious liability related to a motor vehicle	• No liability coverage if the vehicle involved in the claim was owned by, operated by, rented to, or loaned to an insured

VEHICLES USED TO SERVICE THE RESIDENCE

The HO 2000 revises the language of the policy to include coverage *only* if the vehicle is used *solely* to service the residence. The previous form permitted coverage if the vehicle was ever used to service the residence.

NEW POLICY FORM HO 00 03 10 00 PAGE 4 OF 23	OLD POLICY FORM HO 00 03 04 91 PAGE 3 OF 18
(2) We do cover "motor vehicles" not required to be registered for use on public roads or property which are: (a) Used solely to service an "insured's" residence; or (b) Designed to assist the handicapped;	We do cover vehicles or conveyances not subject to motor vehicle registration which are: a. Used to service an "insured's" residence; or b. Designed for assisting the handicapped;

COMPREHENSIVE PERSONAL PROPERTY COVERAGE

NEW POLICY FORM HO 00 05 10 00	OLD ENDORSEMENT HO 00 15 04 91
• Reintroduces the comprehensive HO-5 form withdrawn in 1984 • Provides open perils coverage under Coverages A, B, C, and D • Cost to insured is 10% of the base premium	• Formerly used with HO-03 form • Provides open perils on personal property • Generally provides coverage for everything that is not specifically excluded • Replaced older HO-5 form which was withdrawn in '84 revision

REPLACEMENT COST FOR OTHER STRUCTURES

The HO 2000 recognizes that many insureds have expensive structures, such a swimming pools or driveways, on their property that might not be adequately protected by the HO-3 policy. The HO 2000 program permits the addition of an HO 04 43 endorsement to provide replacement cost coverage rather than actual cash value.

NEW POLICY FORM HO 04 43 REPLACEMENT COST SETTLEMENT FOR CERTAIN NON-BUILDING STRUCTURES	OLD POLICY FORM HO 00 03 04 91 PAGE 10 OF 18
• Converts expensive structures to replacement cost loss settlement for a 2% premium surcharge • Construction must be reinforced masonry, metal, fiberglass, or plastic materials such as polyvinyl chloride • Wooden structures do not qualify for coverage	3. **Loss Settlement.** Covered property losses are settled as follows: a. Property of the following types: (1) Personal property; (2) Awnings, carpeting, household appliances, outdoor antennas and outdoor equipment, whether or not attached to buildings; and (3) Structures that are not buildings; at actual cash value at the time of loss but not more than the amount required to repair or replace.

MOLD IN YOUR INSURED'S HOUSE

According to the Centers for Disease Control and Prevention (CDC), mold is everywhere. It grows all year and can be found both indoors and outdoors. Outdoors, mold is commonly found in shady, damp areas and in soil. Indoors, it can be found where humidity and moisture levels are high, such as in basements, kitchens, bathrooms and on ceilings and wall interiors where water from leaky pipes, roofs or windows can accumulate. While most molds pose no threat to humans, the CDC warns that certain molds can produce hay fever-like allergic symptoms.

Mold, like rot and insect infestation, is generally not covered by a homeowners insurance policy. Standard homeowners policies provide coverage for disasters that are sudden and accidental. They are not designed to cover the cost of cleaning and maintaining a home. If, however, mold is caused as a direct result of a covered peril such as a burst pipe, there could be coverage for the cost of eliminating the mold.

HOMEOWNERS 2 – BROAD FORM

AGREEMENT

We will provide the insurance described in this policy in return for the premium and compliance with all applicable provisions of this policy.

DEFINITIONS

A. In this policy, "you" and "your" refer to the "named insured" shown in the Declarations and the spouse if a resident of the same household. "We", "us" and "our" refer to the Company providing this insurance.

B. In addition, certain words and phrases are defined as follows:

1. "Aircraft Liability", "Hovercraft Liability", "Motor Vehicle Liability" and "Watercraft Liability", subject to the provisions in **b.** below, mean the following:

   a. Liability for "bodily injury" or "property damage" arising out of the:

   (1) Ownership of such vehicle or craft by an "insured";

   (2) Maintenance, occupancy, operation, use, loading or unloading of such vehicle or craft by any person;

   (3) Entrustment of such vehicle or craft by an "insured" to any person;

   (4) Failure to supervise or negligent supervision of any person involving such vehicle or craft by an "insured"; or

   (5) Vicarious liability, whether or not imposed by law, for the actions of a child or minor involving such vehicle or craft.

   b. For the purpose of this definition:

   (1) Aircraft means any contrivance used or designed for flight, except model or hobby aircraft not used or designed to carry people or cargo;

   (2) Hovercraft means a self-propelled motorized ground effect vehicle and includes, but is not limited to, flarecraft and air cushion vehicles;

   (3) Watercraft means a craft principally designed to be propelled on or in water by wind, engine power or electric motor; and

   (4) Motor vehicle means a "motor vehicle" as defined in **7.** below.

2. "Bodily injury" means bodily harm, sickness or disease, including required care, loss of services and death that results.

3. "Business" means:

   a. A trade, profession or occupation engaged in on a full-time, part-time or occasional basis; or

   b. Any other activity engaged in for money or other compensation, except the following:

   (1) One or more activities, not described in **(2)** through **(4)** below, for which no "insured" receives more than $2,000 in total compensation for the 12 months before the beginning of the policy period;

   (2) Volunteer activities for which no money is received other than payment for expenses incurred to perform the activity;

   (3) Providing home day care services for which no compensation is received, other than the mutual exchange of such services; or

   (4) The rendering of home day care services to a relative of an "insured".

4. "Employee" means an employee of an "insured", or an employee leased to an "insured" by a labor leasing firm under an agreement between an "insured" and the labor leasing firm, whose duties are other than those performed by a "residence employee".

5. "Insured" means:

   a. You and residents of your household who are:

   (1) Your relatives; or

   (2) Other persons under the age of 21 and in the care of any person named above;

   b. A student enrolled in school full time, as defined by the school, who was a resident of your household before moving out to attend school, provided the student is under the age of:

   (1) 24 and your relative; or

   (2) 21 and in your care or the care of a person described in **a.(1)** above;

Copyright, Insurance Services Office, Inc., 1999 **Page 1 of 20**

c. Under Section **II:**

(1) With respect to animals or watercraft to which this policy applies, any person or organization legally responsible for these animals or watercraft which are owned by you or any person included in **a.** or **b.** above. "Insured" does not mean a person or organization using or having custody of these animals or watercraft in the course of any "business" or without consent of the owner; or

(2) With respect to a "motor vehicle" to which this policy applies:

(a) Persons while engaged in your employ or that of any person included in **a.** or **b.** above; or

(b) Other persons using the vehicle on an "insured location" with your consent.

Under both Sections **I** and **II,** when the word an immediately precedes the word "insured", the words an "insured" together mean one or more "insureds".

6. "Insured location" means:

a. The "residence premises";

b. The part of other premises, other structures and grounds used by you as a residence; and

(1) Which is shown in the Declarations; or

(2) Which is acquired by you during the policy period for your use as a residence;

c. Any premises used by you in connection with a premises described in **a.** and **b.** above;

d. Any part of a premises:

(1) Not owned by an "insured"; and

(2) Where an "insured" is temporarily residing;

e. Vacant land, other than farm land, owned by or rented to an "insured";

f. Land owned by or rented to an "insured" on which a one, two, three or four family dwelling is being built as a residence for an "insured";

g. Individual or family cemetery plots or burial vaults of an "insured"; or

h. Any part of a premises occasionally rented to an "insured" for other than "business" use.

7. "Motor vehicle" means:

a. A self-propelled land or amphibious vehicle; or

b. Any trailer or semitrailer which is being carried on, towed by or hitched for towing by a vehicle described in **a.** above.

8. "Occurrence" means an accident, including continuous or repeated exposure to substantially the same general harmful conditions, which results, during the policy period, in:

a. "Bodily injury"; or

b. "Property damage".

9. "Property damage" means physical injury to, destruction of, or loss of use of tangible property.

10. "Residence employee" means:

a. An employee of an "insured", or an employee leased to an "insured" by a labor leasing firm, under an agreement between an "insured" and the labor leasing firm, whose duties are related to the maintenance or use of the "residence premises", including household or domestic services; or

b. One who performs similar duties elsewhere not related to the "business" of an "insured".

A "residence employee" does not include a temporary employee who is furnished to an "insured" to substitute for a permanent "residence employee" on leave or to meet seasonal or short-term workload conditions.

11. "Residence premises" means:

a. The one family dwelling where you reside;

b. The two, three or four family dwelling where you reside in at least one of the family units; or

c. That part of any other building where you reside;

and which is shown as the "residence premises" in the Declarations.

"Residence premises" also includes other structures and grounds at that location.

DEDUCTIBLE

Unless otherwise noted in this policy, the following deductible provision applies:

Subject to the policy limits that apply, we will pay only that part of the total of all loss payable under Section **I** that exceeds the deductible amount shown in the Declarations.

SECTION I – PROPERTY COVERAGES

A. Coverage A – Dwelling

1. We cover:

a. The dwelling on the "residence premises" shown in the Declarations, including structures attached to the dwelling; and

b. Materials and supplies located on or next to the "residence premises" used to construct, alter or repair the dwelling or other structures on the "residence premises".

2. We do not cover land, including land on which the dwelling is located.

B. Coverage B – Other Structures

1. We cover other structures on the "residence premises" set apart from the dwelling by clear space. This includes structures connected to the dwelling by only a fence, utility line, or similar connection.

2. We do not cover:

a. Land, including land on which the other structures are located;

b. Other structures rented or held for rental to any person not a tenant of the dwelling, unless used solely as a private garage;

c. Other structures from which any "business" is conducted; or

d. Other structures used to store "business" property. However, we do cover a structure that contains "business" property solely owned by an "insured" or a tenant of the dwelling provided that "business" property does not include gaseous or liquid fuel, other than fuel in a permanently installed fuel tank of a vehicle or craft parked or stored in the structure.

3. The limit of liability for this coverage will not be more than 10% of the limit of liability that applies to Coverage **A.** Use of this coverage does not reduce the Coverage **A** limit of liability.

C. Coverage C – Personal Property

1. Covered Property

We cover personal property owned or used by an "insured" while it is anywhere in the world. After a loss and at your request, we will cover personal property owned by:

a. Others while the property is on the part of the "residence premises" occupied by an "insured"; or

b. A guest or a "residence employee", while the property is in any residence occupied by an "insured".

2. Limit For Property At Other Residences

Our limit of liability for personal property usually located at an "insured's" residence, other than the "residence premises", is 10% of the limit of liability for Coverage **C,** or $1,000, whichever is greater. However, this limitation does not apply to personal property:

a. Moved from the "residence premises" because it is being repaired, renovated or rebuilt and is not fit to live in or store property in; or

b. In a newly acquired principal residence for 30 days from the time you begin to move the property there.

3. Special Limits Of Liability

The special limit for each category shown below is the total limit for each loss for all property in that category. These special limits do not increase the Coverage **C** limit of liability.

a. $200 on money, bank notes, bullion, gold other than goldware, silver other than silverware, platinum other than platinumware, coins, medals, scrip, stored value cards and smart cards.

b. $1,500 on securities, accounts, deeds, evidences of debt, letters of credit, notes other than bank notes, manuscripts, personal records, passports, tickets and stamps. This dollar limit applies to these categories regardless of the medium (such as paper or computer software) on which the material exists.

This limit includes the cost to research, replace or restore the information from the lost or damaged material.

c. $1,500 on watercraft of all types, including their trailers, furnishings, equipment and outboard engines or motors.

d. $1,500 on trailers or semitrailers not used with watercraft of all types.

e. $1,500 for loss by theft of jewelry, watches, furs, precious and semiprecious stones.

f. $2,500 for loss by theft of firearms and related equipment.

g. $2,500 for loss by theft of silverware, silver-plated ware, goldware, gold-plated ware, platinumware, platinum-plated ware and pewterware. This includes flatware, hollowware, tea sets, trays and trophies made of or including silver, gold or pewter.

h. $2,500 on property, on the "residence premises", used primarily for "business" purposes.

i. $500 on property, away from the "residence premises", used primarily for "business" purposes. However, this limit does not apply to loss to electronic apparatus and other property described in Categories **j.** and **k.** below.

j. $1,500 on electronic apparatus and accessories, while in or upon a "motor vehicle", but only if the apparatus is equipped to be operated by power from the "motor vehicle's" electrical system while still capable of being operated by other power sources.

Accessories include antennas, tapes, wires, records, discs or other media that can be used with any apparatus described in this Category **j.**

k. $1,500 on electronic apparatus and accessories used primarily for "business" while away from the "residence premises" and not in or upon a "motor vehicle". The apparatus must be equipped to be operated by power from the "motor vehicle's" electrical system while still capable of being operated by other power sources.

Accessories include antennas, tapes, wires, records, discs or other media that can be used with any apparatus described in this Category **k.**

4. Property Not Covered

We do not cover:

a. Articles separately described and specifically insured, regardless of the limit for which they are insured, in this or other insurance;

b. Animals, birds or fish;

c. "Motor vehicles".

(1) This includes:

(a) Their accessories, equipment and parts; or

(b) Electronic apparatus and accessories designed to be operated solely by power from the electrical system of the "motor vehicle". Accessories include antennas, tapes, wires, records, discs or other media that can be used with any apparatus described above.

The exclusion of property described in **(a)** and **(b)** above applies only while such property is in or upon the "motor vehicle".

(2) We do cover "motor vehicles" not required to be registered for use on public roads or property which are:

(a) Used solely to service an "insured's" residence; or

(b) Designed to assist the handicapped;

d. Aircraft meaning any contrivance used or designed for flight including any parts whether or not attached to the aircraft.

We do cover model or hobby aircraft not used or designed to carry people or cargo;

e. Hovercraft and parts. Hovercraft means a self-propelled motorized ground effect vehicle and includes, but is not limited to, flarecraft and air cushion vehicles;

f. Property of roomers, boarders and other tenants, except property of roomers and boarders related to an "insured";

g. Property in an apartment regularly rented or held for rental to others by an "insured", except as provided under **E.10.** Landlord's Furnishings under Section I – Property Coverages;

h. Property rented or held for rental to others off the "residence premises";

i. "Business" data, including such data stored in:

(1) Books of account, drawings or other paper records; or

(2) Computers and related equipment.

We do cover the cost of blank recording or storage media, and of prerecorded computer programs available on the retail market;

j. Credit cards, electronic fund transfer cards or access devices used solely for deposit, withdrawal or transfer of funds except as provided in **E.6.** Credit Card, Electronic Fund Transfer Card Or Access Device, Forgery And Counterfeit Money under Section I – Property Coverages; or

k. Water or steam.

D. Coverage D – Loss Of Use

The limit of liability for Coverage **D** is the total limit for the coverages in **1.** Additional Living Expense, **2.** Fair Rental Value and **3.** Civil Authority Prohibits Use below.

1. Additional Living Expense

If a loss covered under Section I makes that part of the "residence premises" where you reside not fit to live in, we cover any necessary increase in living expenses incurred by you so that your household can maintain its normal standard of living.

Payment will be for the shortest time required to repair or replace the damage or, if you permanently relocate, the shortest time required for your household to settle elsewhere.

 HO 00 02 10 00

2. Fair Rental Value

If a loss covered under Section **I** makes that part of the "residence premises" rented to others or held for rental by you not fit to live in, we cover the fair rental value of such premises less any expenses that do not continue while it is not fit to live in.

Payment will be for the shortest time required to repair or replace such premises.

3. Civil Authority Prohibits Use

If a civil authority prohibits you from use of the "residence premises" as a result of direct damage to neighboring premises by a Peril Insured Against, we cover the loss as provided in **1.** Additional Living Expense and **2.** Fair Rental Value above for no more than two weeks.

4. Loss Or Expense Not Covered

We do not cover loss or expense due to cancellation of a lease or agreement.

The periods of time under **1.** Additional Living Expense, **2.** Fair Rental Value and **3.** Civil Authority Prohibits Use above are not limited by expiration of this policy.

E. Additional Coverages

1. Debris Removal

a. We will pay your reasonable expense for the removal of:

   (1) Debris of covered property if a Peril Insured Against that applies to the damaged property causes the loss; or

   (2) Ash, dust or particles from a volcanic eruption that has caused direct loss to a building or property contained in a building.

   This expense is included in the limit of liability that applies to the damaged property. If the amount to be paid for the actual damage to the property plus the debris removal expense is more than the limit of liability for the damaged property, an additional 5% of that limit is available for such expense.

b. We will also pay your reasonable expense, up to $1,000, for the removal from the "residence premises" of:

   (1) Your tree(s) felled by the peril of Windstorm or Hail or Weight of Ice, Snow or Sleet; or

   (2) A neighbor's tree(s) felled by a Peril Insured Against under Coverage **C**;

   provided the tree(s):

   (3) Damage(s) a covered structure; or

(4) Does not damage a covered structure, but:

   (a) Block(s) a driveway on the "residence premises" which prevent(s) a "motor vehicle", that is registered for use on public roads or property, from entering or leaving the "residence premises"; or

   (b) Block(s) a ramp or other fixture designed to assist a handicapped person to enter or leave the dwelling building.

The $1,000 limit is the most we will pay in any one loss regardless of the number of fallen trees. No more than $500 of this limit will be paid for the removal of any one tree.

This coverage is additional insurance.

2. Reasonable Repairs

a. We will pay the reasonable cost incurred by you for the necessary measures taken solely to protect covered property that is damaged by a Peril Insured Against from further damage.

b. If the measures taken involve repair to other damaged property, we will only pay if that property is covered under this policy and the damage is caused by a Peril Insured Against. This coverage does not:

   (1) Increase the limit of liability that applies to the covered property; or

   (2) Relieve you of your duties, in case of a loss to covered property, described in **B.4.** under Section **I** – Conditions.

3. Trees, Shrubs And Other Plants

We cover trees, shrubs, plants or lawns, on the "residence premises", for loss caused by the following Perils Insured Against:

a. Fire or Lightning;

b. Explosion;

c. Riot or Civil Commotion;

d. Aircraft;

e. Vehicles not owned or operated by a resident of the "residence premises";

f. Vandalism or Malicious Mischief; or

g. Theft.

We will pay up to 5% of the limit of liability that applies to the dwelling for all trees, shrubs, plants or lawns. No more than $500 of this limit will be paid for any one tree, shrub or plant. We do not cover property grown for "business" purposes.

This coverage is additional insurance.

4. Fire Department Service Charge

We will pay up to $500 for your liability assumed by contract or agreement for fire department charges incurred when the fire department is called to save or protect covered property from a Peril Insured Against. We do not cover fire department service charges if the property is located within the limits of the city, municipality or protection district furnishing the fire department response.

This coverage is additional insurance. No deductible applies to this coverage.

5. Property Removed

We insure covered property against direct loss from any cause while being removed from a premises endangered by a Peril Insured Against and for no more than 30 days while removed.

This coverage does not change the limit of liability that applies to the property being removed.

6. Credit Card, Electronic Fund Transfer Card Or Access Device, Forgery And Counterfeit Money

a. We will pay up to $500 for:

(1) The legal obligation of an "insured" to pay because of the theft or unauthorized use of credit cards issued to or registered in an "insured's" name;

(2) Loss resulting from theft or unauthorized use of an electronic fund transfer card or access device used for deposit, withdrawal or transfer of funds, issued to or registered in an "insured's" name;

(3) Loss to an "insured" caused by forgery or alteration of any check or negotiable instrument; and

(4) Loss to an "insured" through acceptance in good faith of counterfeit United States or Canadian paper currency.

All loss resulting from a series of acts committed by any one person or in which any one person is concerned or implicated is considered to be one loss.

This coverage is additional insurance. No deductible applies to this coverage.

b. We do not cover:

(1) Use of a credit card, electronic fund transfer card or access device:

(a) By a resident of your household;

(b) By a person who has been entrusted with either type of card or access device; or

(c) If an "insured" has not complied with all terms and conditions under which the cards are issued or the devices accessed; or

(2) Loss arising out of "business" use or dishonesty of an "insured".

c. If the coverage in **a.** applies, the following defense provisions also apply:

(1) We may investigate and settle any claim or suit that we decide is appropriate. Our duty to defend a claim or suit ends when the amount we pay for the loss equals our limit of liability.

(2) If a suit is brought against an "insured" for liability under **a.(1)** or **(2)** above, we will provide a defense at our expense by counsel of our choice.

(3) We have the option to defend at our expense an "insured" or an "insured's" bank against any suit for the enforcement of payment under **a.(3)** above.

7. Loss Assessment

a. We will pay up to $1,000 for your share of loss assessment charged during the policy period against you, as owner or tenant of the "residence premises", by a corporation or association of property owners. The assessment must be made as a result of direct loss to property, owned by all members collectively, of the type that would be covered by this policy if owned by you, caused by a Peril Insured Against under Coverage **A,** other than:

(1) Earthquake; or

(2) Land shock waves or tremors before, during or after a volcanic eruption.

The limit of $1,000 is the most we will pay with respect to any one loss, regardless of the number of assessments. We will only apply one deductible, per unit, to the total amount of any one loss to the property described above, regardless of the number of assessments.

b. We do not cover assessments charged against you or a corporation or association of property owners by any governmental body.

c. Paragraph **P.** Policy Period under Section **I** – Conditions does not apply to this coverage.

This coverage is additional insurance.

8. Collapse

a. With respect to this Additional Coverage:

Copyright, Insurance Services Office, Inc., 1999

(1) Collapse means an abrupt falling down or caving in of a building or any part of a building with the result that the building or part of the building cannot be occupied for its current intended purpose.

(2) A building or any part of a building that is in danger of falling down or caving in is not considered to be in a state of collapse.

(3) A part of a building that is standing is not considered to be in a state of collapse even if it has separated from another part of the building.

(4) A building or any part of a building that is standing is not considered to be in a state of collapse even if it shows evidence of cracking, bulging, sagging, bending, leaning, settling, shrinkage or expansion.

b. We insure for direct physical loss to covered property involving collapse of a building or any part of a building if the collapse was caused by one or more of the following:

(1) The Perils Insured Against;

(2) Decay that is hidden from view, unless the presence of such decay is known to an "insured" prior to collapse;

(3) Insect or vermin damage that is hidden from view, unless the presence of such damage is known to an "insured" prior to collapse;

(4) Weight of contents, equipment, animals or people;

(5) Weight of rain which collects on a roof; or

(6) Use of defective material or methods in construction, remodeling or renovation if the collapse occurs during the course of the construction, remodeling or renovation.

c. Loss to an awning, fence, patio, deck, pavement, swimming pool, underground pipe, flue, drain, cesspool, septic tank, foundation, retaining wall, bulkhead, pier, wharf or dock is not included under **b.(2)** through **(6)** above, unless the loss is a direct result of the collapse of a building or any part of a building.

d. This coverage does not increase the limit of liability that applies to the damaged covered property.

9. Glass Or Safety Glazing Material

a. We cover:

(1) The breakage of glass or safety glazing material which is part of a covered building, storm door or storm window;

(2) The breakage of glass or safety glazing material which is part of a covered building, storm door or storm window when caused directly by earth movement; and

(3) The direct physical loss to covered property caused solely by the pieces, fragments or splinters of broken glass or safety glazing material which is part of a building, storm door or storm window.

b. This coverage does not include loss:

(1) To covered property which results because the glass or safety glazing material has been broken, except as provided in **a.(3)** above; or

(2) On the "residence premises" if the dwelling has been vacant for more than 60 consecutive days immediately before the loss, except when the breakage results directly from earth movement as provided in **a.(2)** above. A dwelling being constructed is not considered vacant.

c. This coverage does not increase the limit of liability that applies to the damaged property.

10. Landlord's Furnishings

We will pay up to $2,500 for your appliances, carpeting and other household furnishings, in each apartment on the "residence premises" regularly rented or held for rental to others by an "insured", for loss caused by a Peril Insured Against other than Theft.

This limit is the most we will pay in any one loss regardless of the number of appliances, carpeting or other household furnishings involved in the loss.

This coverage does not increase the limit of liability applying to the damaged property.

11. Ordinance Or Law

a. You may use up to 10% of the limit of liability that applies to Coverage **A** for the increased costs you incur due to the enforcement of any ordinance or law which requires or regulates:

(1) The construction, demolition, remodeling, renovation or repair of that part of a covered building or other structure damaged by a Peril Insured Against;

(2) The demolition and reconstruction of the undamaged part of a covered building or other structure, when that building or other structure must be totally demolished because of damage by a Peril Insured Against to another part of that covered building or other structure; or

(3) The remodeling, removal or replacement of the portion of the undamaged part of a covered building or other structure necessary to complete the remodeling, repair or replacement of that part of the covered building or other structure damaged by a Peril Insured Against.

b. You may use all or part of this ordinance or law coverage to pay for the increased costs you incur to remove debris resulting from the construction, demolition, remodeling, renovation, repair or replacement of property as stated in **a.** above.

c. We do not cover:

(1) The loss in value to any covered building or other structure due to the requirements of any ordinance or law; or

(2) The costs to comply with any ordinance or law which requires any "insured" or others, to test for, monitor, clean up, remove, contain, treat, detoxify or neutralize, or in any way respond to, or assess the effects of, pollutants in or on any covered building or other structure.

Pollutants means any solid, liquid, gaseous or thermal irritant or contaminant, including smoke, vapor, soot, fumes, acids, alkalis, chemicals and waste. Waste includes materials to be recycled, reconditioned or reclaimed.

This coverage is additional insurance.

12. Grave Markers

We will pay up to $5,000 for grave markers, including mausoleums, on or away from the "residence premises" for loss caused by a Peril Insured Against.

This coverage does not increase the limits of liability that apply to the damaged covered property.

SECTION I — PERILS INSURED AGAINST

We insure for direct physical loss to the property described in Coverages **A, B** and **C** caused by any of the following perils unless the loss is excluded under Section I — Exclusions.

1. Fire Or Lightning

2. Windstorm Or Hail

This peril includes loss to watercraft of all types and their trailers, furnishings, equipment, and outboard engines or motors, only while inside a fully enclosed building.

This peril does not include loss to the inside of a building or the property contained in a building caused by rain, snow, sleet, sand or dust unless the direct force of wind or hail damages the building causing an opening in a roof or wall and the rain, snow, sleet, sand or dust enters through this opening.

3. Explosion

4. Riot Or Civil Commotion

5. Aircraft

This peril includes self-propelled missiles and spacecraft.

6. Vehicles

This peril does not include loss to a fence, driveway or walk caused by a vehicle owned or operated by a resident of the "residence premises".

7. Smoke

This peril means sudden and accidental damage from smoke, including the emission or puffback of smoke, soot, fumes or vapors from a boiler, furnace or related equipment.

This peril does not include loss caused by smoke from agricultural smudging or industrial operations.

8. Vandalism Or Malicious Mischief

This peril does not include loss to property on the "residence premises", and any ensuing loss caused by any intentional and wrongful act committed in the course of the vandalism or malicious mischief, if the dwelling has been vacant for more than 60 consecutive days immediately before the loss. A dwelling being constructed is not considered vacant.

9. Theft

a. This peril includes attempted theft and loss of property from a known place when it is likely that the property has been stolen.

b. This peril does not include loss caused by theft:

(1) Committed by an "insured";

(2) In or to a dwelling under construction, or of materials and supplies for use in the construction until the dwelling is finished and occupied;

(3) From that part of a "residence premises" rented by an "insured" to someone other than another "insured"; or

Copyright, Insurance Services Office, Inc., 1999 **HO 00 02 10 00**

(4) That occurs off the "residence premises" of:

(a) Trailers, semitrailers and campers;

(b) Watercraft of all types, and their furnishings, equipment and outboard engines or motors; or

(c) Property while at any other residence owned by, rented to, or occupied by an "insured", except while an "insured" is temporarily living there. Property of an "insured" who is a student is covered while at the residence the student occupies to attend school as long as the student has been there at any time during the 60 days immediately before the loss.

10. Falling Objects

This peril does not include loss to the inside of a building or property contained in the building unless the roof or an outside wall of the building is first damaged by a falling object. Damage to the falling object itself is not included.

11. Weight Of Ice, Snow Or Sleet

This peril means weight of ice, snow or sleet which causes damage to a building or property contained in a building.

This peril does not include loss to an awning, fence, patio, pavement, swimming pool, foundation, retaining wall, bulkhead, pier, wharf, or dock.

12. Accidental Discharge Or Overflow Of Water Or Steam

a. This peril means accidental discharge or overflow of water or steam from within a plumbing, heating, air conditioning or automatic fire protective sprinkler system or from within a household appliance. We also pay to tear out and replace any part of the building, or other structure, on the "residence premises", but only when necessary to repair the system or appliance from which the water or steam escaped. However, such tear out and replacement coverage only applies to other structures if the water or steam causes actual damage to a building on the "residence premises".

b. This peril does not include loss:

(1) On the "residence premises", if the dwelling has been vacant for more than 60 consecutive days immediately before the loss. A dwelling being constructed is not considered vacant;

(2) To the system or appliance from which the water or steam escaped;

(3) Caused by or resulting from freezing except as provided in Peril Insured Against **14. Freezing;**

(4) On the "residence premises" caused by accidental discharge or overflow which occurs off the "residence premises"; or

(5) Caused by mold, fungus or wet rot unless hidden within the walls or ceilings or beneath the floors or above the ceilings of a structure.

c. In this peril, a plumbing system or household appliance does not include a sump, sump pump or related equipment or a roof drain, gutter, downspout or similar fixtures or equipment.

d. Section I – Exclusion **3.** Water Damage, Paragraphs **a.** and **c.** that apply to surface water and water below the surface of the ground do not apply to loss by water covered under this peril.

13. Sudden And Accidental Tearing Apart, Cracking, Burning Or Bulging

This peril means sudden and accidental tearing apart, cracking, burning or bulging of a steam or hot water heating system, an air conditioning or automatic fire protective sprinkler system, or an appliance for heating water.

This peril does not include loss caused by or resulting from freezing except as provided in Peril Insured Against **14.** Freezing below.

14. Freezing

a. This peril means freezing of a plumbing, heating, air conditioning or automatic fire protective sprinkler system or of a household appliance but only if you have used reasonable care to:

(1) Maintain heat in the building; or

(2) Shut off the water supply and drain all systems and appliances of water.

However, if the building is protected by an automatic fire protective sprinkler system, you must use reasonable care to continue the water supply and maintain heat in the building for coverage to apply.

b. In this peril, a plumbing system or household appliance does not include a sump, sump pump or related equipment or a roof drain, gutter, downspout or similar fixtures or equipment.

15. Sudden And Accidental Damage From Artificially Generated Electrical Current

This peril does not include loss to tubes, transistors, electronic components or circuitry that are a part of appliances, fixtures, computers, home entertainment units or other types of electronic apparatus.

16. Volcanic Eruption

This peril does not include loss caused by earthquake, land shock waves or tremors.

SECTION I – EXCLUSIONS

We do not insure for loss caused directly or indirectly by any of the following. Such loss is excluded regardless of any other cause or event contributing concurrently or in any sequence to the loss. These exclusions apply whether or not the loss event results in widespread damage or affects a substantial area.

1. **Ordinance Or Law**

   Ordinance or Law means any ordinance or law:

   a. Requiring or regulating the construction, demolition, remodeling, renovation or repair of property, including removal of any resulting debris. This Exclusion **1.a.** does not apply to the amount of coverage that may be provided for in **E.11.** Ordinance Or Law under Section **I** – Property Coverages;

   b. The requirements of which result in a loss in value to property; or

   c. Requiring any "insured" or others to test for, monitor, clean up, remove, contain, treat, detoxify or neutralize, or in any way respond to, or assess the effects of, pollutants.

      Pollutants means any solid, liquid, gaseous or thermal irritant or contaminant, including smoke, vapor, soot, fumes, acids, alkalis, chemicals and waste. Waste includes materials to be recycled, reconditioned or reclaimed.

   This Exclusion **1.** applies whether or not the property has been physically damaged.

2. **Earth Movement**

   Earth Movement means:

   a. Earthquake, including land shock waves or tremors before, during or after a volcanic eruption;

   b. Landslide, mudslide or mudflow;

   c. Subsidence or sinkhole; or

   d. Any other earth movement including earth sinking, rising or shifting;

   caused by or resulting from human or animal forces or any act of nature unless direct loss by fire or explosion ensues and then we will pay only for the ensuing loss.

   This Exclusion **2.** does not apply to loss by theft.

3. **Water Damage**

   Water Damage means:

   a. Flood, surface water, waves, tidal water, overflow of a body of water, or spray from any of these, whether or not driven by wind;

   b. Water or water-borne material which backs up through sewers or drains or which overflows or is discharged from a sump, sump pump or related equipment; or

   c. Water or water-borne material below the surface of the ground, including water which exerts pressure on or seeps or leaks through a building, sidewalk, driveway, foundation, swimming pool or other structure;

   caused by or resulting from human or animal forces or any act of nature.

   Direct loss by fire, explosion or theft resulting from water damage is covered.

4. **Power Failure**

   Power Failure means the failure of power or other utility service if the failure takes place off the "residence premises". But if the failure results in a loss, from a Peril Insured Against on the "residence premises", we will pay for the loss caused by that peril.

5. **Neglect**

   Neglect means neglect of an "insured" to use all reasonable means to save and preserve property at and after the time of a loss.

6. **War**

   War includes the following and any consequence of any of the following:

   a. Undeclared war, civil war, insurrection, rebellion or revolution;

   b. Warlike act by a military force or military personnel; or

   c. Destruction, seizure or use for a military purpose.

   Discharge of a nuclear weapon will be deemed a warlike act even if accidental.

7. **Nuclear Hazard**

   This Exclusion **7.** pertains to Nuclear Hazard to the extent set forth in **M.** Nuclear Hazard Clause under Section **I** – Conditions.

8. **Intentional Loss**

   Intentional Loss means any loss arising out of any act an "insured" commits or conspires to commit with the intent to cause a loss.

   In the event of such loss, no "insured" is entitled to coverage, even "insureds" who did not commit or conspire to commit the act causing the loss.

9. **Governmental Action**

   Governmental Action means the destruction, confiscation or seizure of property described in Coverage **A, B** or **C** by order of any governmental or public authority.

   This exclusion does not apply to such acts ordered by any governmental or public authority that are taken at the time of a fire to prevent its spread, if the loss caused by fire would be covered under this policy.

SECTION I – CONDITIONS

A. Insurable Interest And Limit Of Liability

Even if more than one person has an insurable interest in the property covered, we will not be liable in any one loss:

1. To an "insured" for more than the amount of such "insured's" interest at the time of loss; or

2. For more than the applicable limit of liability.

B. Duties After Loss

In case of a loss to covered property, we have no duty to provide coverage under this policy if the failure to comply with the following duties is prejudicial to us. These duties must be performed either by you, an "insured" seeking coverage, or a representative of either:

1. Give prompt notice to us or our agent;

2. Notify the police in case of loss by theft;

3. Notify the credit card or electronic fund transfer card or access device company in case of loss as provided for in **E.6.** Credit Card, Electronic Fund Transfer Card Or Access Device, Forgery And Counterfeit Money under Section I – Property Coverages;

4. Protect the property from further damage. If repairs to the property are required, you must:

   a. Make reasonable and necessary repairs to protect the property; and

   b. Keep an accurate record of repair expenses;

5. Cooperate with us in the investigation of a claim;

6. Prepare an inventory of damaged personal property showing the quantity, description, actual cash value and amount of loss. Attach all bills, receipts and related documents that justify the figures in the inventory;

7. As often as we reasonably require:

   a. Show the damaged property;

   b. Provide us with records and documents we request and permit us to make copies; and

   c. Submit to examination under oath, while not in the presence of another "insured", and sign the same;

8. Send to us, within 60 days after our request, your signed, sworn proof of loss which sets forth, to the best of your knowledge and belief:

   a. The time and cause of loss;

   b. The interests of all "insureds" and all others in the property involved and all liens on the property;

   c. Other insurance which may cover the loss;

   d. Changes in title or occupancy of the property during the term of the policy;

   e. Specifications of damaged buildings and detailed repair estimates;

   f. The inventory of damaged personal property described in **6.** above;

   g. Receipts for additional living expenses incurred and records that support the fair rental value loss; and

   h. Evidence or affidavit that supports a claim under **E.6.** Credit Card, Electronic Fund Transfer Card Or Access Device, Forgery And Counterfeit Money under Section I – Property Coverages, stating the amount and cause of loss.

C. Loss Settlement

In this Condition **C.**, the terms "cost to repair or replace" and "replacement cost" do not include the increased costs incurred to comply with the enforcement of any ordinance or law, except to the extent that coverage for these increased costs is provided in **E.11.** Ordinance Or Law under Section I – Property Coverages. Covered property losses are settled as follows:

1. Property of the following types:

   a. Personal property;

   b. Awnings, carpeting, household appliances, outdoor antennas and outdoor equipment, whether or not attached to buildings;

   c. Structures that are not buildings; and

   d. Grave markers, including mausoleums;

   at actual cash value at the time of loss but not more than the amount required to repair or replace.

2. Buildings covered under Coverage **A** or **B** at replacement cost without deduction for depreciation, subject to the following:

   a. If, at the time of loss, the amount of insurance in this policy on the damaged building is 80% or more of the full replacement cost of the building immediately before the loss, we will pay the cost to repair or replace, after application of any deductible and without deduction for depreciation, but not more than the least of the following amounts:

   (1) The limit of liability under this policy that applies to the building;

   (2) The replacement cost of that part of the building damaged with material of like kind and quality and for like use; or

   (3) The necessary amount actually spent to repair or replace the damaged building.

If the building is rebuilt at a new premises, the cost described in **(2)** above is limited to the cost which would have been incurred if the building had been built at the original premises.

b. If, at the time of loss, the amount of insurance in this policy on the damaged building is less than 80% of the full replacement cost of the building immediately before the loss, we will pay the greater of the following amounts, but not more than the limit of liability under this policy that applies to the building:

(1) The actual cash value of that part of the building damaged; or

(2) That proportion of the cost to repair or replace, after application of any deductible and without deduction for depreciation, that part of the building damaged, which the total amount of insurance in this policy on the damaged building bears to 80% of the replacement cost of the building.

c. To determine the amount of insurance required to equal 80% of the full replacement cost of the building immediately before the loss, do not include the value of:

(1) Excavations, footings, foundations, piers, or any other structures or devices that support all or part of the building, which are below the undersurface of the lowest basement floor;

(2) Those supports described in **(1)** above which are below the surface of the ground inside the foundation walls, if there is no basement; and

(3) Underground flues, pipes, wiring and drains.

d. We will pay no more than the actual cash value of the damage until actual repair or replacement is complete. Once actual repair or replacement is complete, we will settle the loss as noted in **2.a.** and **b.** above.

However, if the cost to repair or replace the damage is both:

(1) Less than 5% of the amount of insurance in this policy on the building; and

(2) Less than $2,500;

we will settle the loss as noted in **2.a.** and **b.** above whether or not actual repair or replacement is complete.

e. You may disregard the replacement cost loss settlement provisions and make claim under this policy for loss to buildings on an actual cash value basis. You may then make claim for any additional liability according to the provisions of this Condition **C.** Loss Settlement, provided you notify us of your intent to do so within 180 days after the date of loss.

D. Loss To A Pair Or Set

In case of loss to a pair or set we may elect to:

1. Repair or replace any part to restore the pair or set to its value before the loss; or

2. Pay the difference between actual cash value of the property before and after the loss.

E. Appraisal

If you and we fail to agree on the amount of loss, either may demand an appraisal of the loss. In this event, each party will choose a competent and impartial appraiser within 20 days after receiving a written request from the other. The two appraisers will choose an umpire. If they cannot agree upon an umpire within 15 days, you or we may request that the choice be made by a judge of a court of record in the state where the "residence premises" is located. The appraisers will separately set the amount of loss. If the appraisers submit a written report of an agreement to us, the amount agreed upon will be the amount of loss. If they fail to agree, they will submit their differences to the umpire. A decision agreed to by any two will set the amount of loss.

Each party will:

1. Pay its own appraiser; and

2. Bear the other expenses of the appraisal and umpire equally.

F. Other Insurance And Service Agreement

If a loss covered by this policy is also covered by:

1. Other insurance, we will pay only the proportion of the loss that the limit of liability that applies under this policy bears to the total amount of insurance covering the loss; or

2. A service agreement, this insurance is excess over any amounts payable under any such agreement. Service agreement means a service plan, property restoration plan, home warranty or other similar service warranty agreement, even if it is characterized as insurance.

G. Suit Against Us

No action can be brought against us unless there has been full compliance with all of the terms under Section **I** of this policy and the action is started within two years after the date of loss.

H. Our Option

If we give you written notice within 30 days after we receive your signed, sworn proof of loss, we may repair or replace any part of the damaged property with material or property of like kind and quality.

I. Loss Payment

We will adjust all losses with you. We will pay you unless some other person is named in the policy or is legally entitled to receive payment. Loss will be payable 60 days after we receive your proof of loss and:

1. Reach an agreement with you;

2. There is an entry of a final judgment; or

3. There is a filing of an appraisal award with us.

J. Abandonment Of Property

We need not accept any property abandoned by an "insured".

K. Mortgage Clause

1. If a mortgagee is named in this policy, any loss payable under Coverage **A** or **B** will be paid to the mortgagee and you, as interests appear. If more than one mortgagee is named, the order of payment will be the same as the order of precedence of the mortgages.

2. If we deny your claim, that denial will not apply to a valid claim of the mortgagee, if the mortgagee:

   a. Notifies us of any change in ownership, occupancy or substantial change in risk of which the mortgagee is aware;

   b. Pays any premium due under this policy on demand if you have neglected to pay the premium; and

   c. Submits a signed, sworn statement of loss within 60 days after receiving notice from us of your failure to do so. Paragraphs **E.** Appraisal, **G.** Suit Against Us and **I.** Loss Payment under Section I – Conditions also apply to the mortgagee.

3. If we decide to cancel or not to renew this policy, the mortgagee will be notified at least 10 days before the date cancellation or nonrenewal takes effect.

4. If we pay the mortgagee for any loss and deny payment to you:

   a. We are subrogated to all the rights of the mortgagee granted under the mortgage on the property; or

   b. At our option, we may pay to the mortgagee the whole principal on the mortgage plus any accrued interest. In this event, we will receive a full assignment and transfer of the mortgage and all securities held as collateral to the mortgage debt.

5. Subrogation will not impair the right of the mortgagee to recover the full amount of the mortgagee's claim.

L. No Benefit To Bailee

We will not recognize any assignment or grant any coverage that benefits a person or organization holding, storing or moving property for a fee regardless of any other provision of this policy.

M. Nuclear Hazard Clause

1. "Nuclear Hazard" means any nuclear reaction, radiation, or radioactive contamination, all whether controlled or uncontrolled or however caused, or any consequence of any of these.

2. Loss caused by the nuclear hazard will not be considered loss caused by fire, explosion, or smoke, whether these perils are specifically named in or otherwise included within the Perils Insured Against.

3. This policy does not apply under Section I to loss caused directly or indirectly by nuclear hazard, except that direct loss by fire resulting from the nuclear hazard is covered.

N. Recovered Property

If you or we recover any property for which we have made payment under this policy, you or we will notify the other of the recovery. At your option, the property will be returned to or retained by you or it will become our property. If the recovered property is returned to or retained by you, the loss payment will be adjusted based on the amount you received for the recovered property.

O. Volcanic Eruption Period

One or more volcanic eruptions that occur within a 72 hour period will be considered as one volcanic eruption.

P. Policy Period

This policy applies only to loss which occurs during the policy period.

Q. Concealment Or Fraud

We provide coverage to no "insureds" under this policy if, whether before or after a loss, an "insured" has:

1. Intentionally concealed or misrepresented any material fact or circumstance;

2. Engaged in fraudulent conduct; or

3. Made false statements;

relating to this insurance.

R. Loss Payable Clause

If the Declarations show a loss payee for certain listed insured personal property, the definition of "insured" is changed to include that loss payee with respect to that property.

If we decide to cancel or not renew this policy, that loss payee will be notified in writing.

SECTION II – LIABILITY COVERAGES

A. Coverage E – Personal Liability

If a claim is made or a suit is brought against an "insured" for damages because of "bodily injury" or "property damage" caused by an "occurrence" to which this coverage applies, we will:

1. Pay up to our limit of liability for the damages for which an "insured" is legally liable. Damages include prejudgment interest awarded against an "insured"; and

2. Provide a defense at our expense by counsel of our choice, even if the suit is groundless, false or fraudulent. We may investigate and settle any claim or suit that we decide is appropriate. Our duty to settle or defend ends when our limit of liability for the "occurrence" has been exhausted by payment of a judgment or settlement.

B. Coverage F – Medical Payments To Others

We will pay the necessary medical expenses that are incurred or medically ascertained within three years from the date of an accident causing "bodily injury". Medical expenses means reasonable charges for medical, surgical, x-ray, dental, ambulance, hospital, professional nursing, prosthetic devices and funeral services. This coverage does not apply to you or regular residents of your household except "residence employees". As to others, this coverage applies only:

1. To a person on the "insured location" with the permission of an "insured"; or

2. To a person off the "insured location", if the "bodily injury":

   a. Arises out of a condition on the "insured location" or the ways immediately adjoining;

   b. Is caused by the activities of an "insured";

   c. Is caused by a "residence employee" in the course of the "residence employee's" employment by an "insured"; or

   d. Is caused by an animal owned by or in the care of an "insured".

SECTION II – EXCLUSIONS

A. "Motor Vehicle Liability"

1. Coverages **E** and **F** do not apply to any "motor vehicle liability" if, at the time and place of an "occurrence", the involved "motor vehicle":

   a. Is registered for use on public roads or property;

   b. Is not registered for use on public roads or property, but such registration is required by a law, or regulation issued by a government agency, for it to be used at the place of the "occurrence"; or

   c. Is being:

      (1) Operated in, or practicing for, any prearranged or organized race, speed contest or other competition;

      (2) Rented to others;

      (3) Used to carry persons or cargo for a charge; or

      (4) Used for any "business" purpose except for a motorized golf cart while on a golfing facility.

2. If Exclusion **A.1.** does not apply, there is still no coverage for "motor vehicle liability" unless the "motor vehicle" is:

   a. In dead storage on an "insured location";

   b. Used solely to service an "insured's" residence;

   c. Designed to assist the handicapped and, at the time of an "occurrence", it is:

      (1) Being used to assist a handicapped person; or

      (2) Parked on an "insured location";

   d. Designed for recreational use off public roads and:

      (1) Not owned by an "insured"; or

      (2) Owned by an "insured" provided the "occurrence" takes place on an "insured location" as defined in Definitions **B. 6.a., b., d., e.** or **h.;** or

   e. A motorized golf cart that is owned by an "insured", designed to carry up to 4 persons, not built or modified after manufacture to exceed a speed of 25 miles per hour on level ground and, at the time of an "occurrence", is within the legal boundaries of:

      (1) A golfing facility and is parked or stored there, or being used by an "insured" to:

         (a) Play the game of golf or for other recreational or leisure activity allowed by the facility;

         (b) Travel to or from an area where "motor vehicles" or golf carts are parked or stored; or

         (c) Cross public roads at designated points to access other parts of the golfing facility; or

(2) A private residential community, including its public roads upon which a motorized golf cart can legally travel, which is subject to the authority of a property owners association and contains an "insured's" residence.

B. "Watercraft Liability"

1. Coverages **E** and **F** do not apply to any "watercraft liability" if, at the time of an "occurrence", the involved watercraft is being:

a. Operated in, or practicing for, any prearranged or organized race, speed contest or other competition. This exclusion does not apply to a sailing vessel or a predicted log cruise;

b. Rented to others;

c. Used to carry persons or cargo for a charge; or

d. Used for any "business" purpose.

2. If Exclusion **B.1.** does not apply, there is still no coverage for "watercraft liability" unless, at the time of the "occurrence", the watercraft:

a. Is stored;

b. Is a sailing vessel, with or without auxiliary power, that is:

(1) Less than 26 feet in overall length; or

(2) 26 feet or more in overall length and not owned by or rented to an "insured"; or

c. Is not a sailing vessel and is powered by:

(1) An inboard or inboard-outdrive engine or motor, including those that power a water jet pump, of:

(a) 50 horsepower or less and not owned by an "insured"; or

(b) More than 50 horsepower and not owned by or rented to an "insured"; or

(2) One or more outboard engines or motors with:

(a) 25 total horsepower or less;

(b) More than 25 horsepower if the outboard engine or motor is not owned by an "insured";

(c) More than 25 horsepower if the outboard engine or motor is owned by an "insured" who acquired it during the policy period; or

(d) More than 25 horsepower if the outboard engine or motor is owned by an "insured" who acquired it before the policy period, but only if:

(i) You declare them at policy inception; or

(ii) Your intent to insure them is reported to us in writing within 45 days after you acquire them.

The coverages in **(c)** and **(d)** above apply for the policy period.

Horsepower means the maximum power rating assigned to the engine or motor by the manufacturer.

C. "Aircraft Liability"

This policy does not cover "aircraft liability".

D. "Hovercraft Liability"

This policy does not cover "hovercraft liability".

E. Coverage E – Personal Liability And Coverage F – Medical Payments To Others

Coverages **E** and **F** do not apply to the following:

1. Expected Or Intended Injury

"Bodily injury" or "property damage" which is expected or intended by an "insured" even if the resulting "bodily injury" or "property damage":

a. Is of a different kind, quality or degree than initially expected or intended; or

b. Is sustained by a different person, entity, real or personal property, than initially expected or intended.

However, this Exclusion **E.1.** does not apply to "bodily injury" resulting from the use of reasonable force by an "insured" to protect persons or property;

2. "Business"

a. "Bodily injury" or "property damage" arising out of or in connection with a "business" conducted from an "insured location" or engaged in by an "insured", whether or not the "business" is owned or operated by an "insured" or employs an "insured".

This Exclusion **E.2.** applies but is not limited to an act or omission, regardless of its nature or circumstance, involving a service or duty rendered, promised, owed, or implied to be provided because of the nature of the "business".

b. This Exclusion **E.2.** does not apply to:

(1) The rental or holding for rental of an "insured location";

(a) On an occasional basis if used only as a residence;

(b) In part for use only as a residence, unless a single family unit is intended for use by the occupying family to lodge more than two roomers or boarders; or

     (c) In part, as an office, school, studio or private garage; and

    (2) An "insured" under the age of 21 years involved in a part-time or occasional, self-employed "business" with no employees;

3. Professional Services

"Bodily injury" or "property damage" arising out of the rendering of or failure to render professional services;

4. "Insured's" Premises Not An "Insured Location"

"Bodily injury" or "property damage" arising out of a premises:

  a. Owned by an "insured";

  b. Rented to an "insured"; or

  c. Rented to others by an "insured";

that is not an "insured location";

5. War

"Bodily injury" or "property damage" caused directly or indirectly by war, including the following and any consequence of any of the following:

  a. Undeclared war, civil war, insurrection, rebellion or revolution;

  b. Warlike act by a military force or military personnel; or

  c. Destruction, seizure or use for a military purpose.

Discharge of a nuclear weapon will be deemed a warlike act even if accidental;

6. Communicable Disease

"Bodily injury" or "property damage" which arises out of the transmission of a communicable disease by an "insured";

7. Sexual Molestation, Corporal Punishment Or Physical Or Mental Abuse

"Bodily injury" or "property damage" arising out of sexual molestation, corporal punishment or physical or mental abuse; or

8. Controlled Substance

"Bodily injury" or "property damage" arising out of the use, sale, manufacture, delivery, transfer or possession by any person of a Controlled Substance as defined by the Federal Food and Drug Law at 21 U.S.C.A. Sections 811 and 812. Controlled Substances include but are not limited to cocaine, LSD, marijuana and all narcotic drugs. However, this exclusion does not apply to the legitimate use of prescription drugs by a person following the orders of a licensed physician.

Exclusions **A.** "Motor Vehicle Liability", **B.** "Watercraft Liability", **C.** "Aircraft Liability", **D.** "Hovercraft Liability" and **E.4.** "Insured's" Premises Not An "Insured Location" do not apply to "bodily injury" to a "residence employee" arising out of and in the course of the "residence employee's" employment by an "insured".

F. Coverage E – Personal Liability

Coverage **E** does not apply to:

1. Liability:

  a. For any loss assessment charged against you as a member of an association, corporation or community of property owners, except as provided in **D.** Loss Assessment under Section **II** – Additional Coverages;

  b. Under any contract or agreement entered into by an "insured". However, this exclusion does not apply to written contracts:

    (1) That directly relate to the ownership, maintenance or use of an "insured location"; or

    (2) Where the liability of others is assumed by you prior to an "occurrence";

    unless excluded in **a.** above or elsewhere in this policy;

2. "Property damage" to property owned by an "insured". This includes costs or expenses incurred by an "insured" or others to repair, replace, enhance, restore or maintain such property to prevent injury to a person or damage to property of others, whether on or away from an "insured location";

3. "Property damage" to property rented to, occupied or used by or in the care of an "insured". This exclusion does not apply to "property damage" caused by fire, smoke or explosion;

4. "Bodily injury" to any person eligible to receive any benefits voluntarily provided or required to be provided by an "insured" under any:

  a. Workers' compensation law;

  b. Non-occupational disability law; or

  c. Occupational disease law;

5. "Bodily injury" or "property damage" for which an "insured" under this policy:

  a. Is also an insured under a nuclear energy liability policy issued by the:

    (1) Nuclear Energy Liability Insurance Association;

    (2) Mutual Atomic Energy Liability Underwriters;

    (3) Nuclear Insurance Association of Canada;

    or any of their successors; or

b. Would be an insured under such a policy but for the exhaustion of its limit of liability; or

6. "Bodily injury" to you or an "insured" as defined under Definitions **5.a.** or **b.**

This exclusion also applies to any claim made or suit brought against you or an "insured":

a. To repay; or

b. Share damages with;

another person who may be obligated to pay damages because of "bodily injury" to an "insured".

G. Coverage F – Medical Payments To Others

Coverage **F** does not apply to "bodily injury":

1. To a "residence employee" if the "bodily injury":

a. Occurs off the "insured location"; and

b. Does not arise out of or in the course of the "residence employee's" employment by an "insured";

2. To any person eligible to receive benefits voluntarily provided or required to be provided under any:

a. Workers' compensation law;

b. Non-occupational disability law; or

c. Occupational disease law;

3. From any:

a. Nuclear reaction;

b. Nuclear radiation; or

c. Radioactive contamination;

all whether controlled or uncontrolled or however caused; or

d. Any consequence of any of these; or

4. To any person, other than a "residence employee" of an "insured", regularly residing on any part of the "insured location".

SECTION II – ADDITIONAL COVERAGES

We cover the following in addition to the limits of liability:

A. Claim Expenses

We pay:

1. Expenses we incur and costs taxed against an "insured" in any suit we defend;

2. Premiums on bonds required in a suit we defend, but not for bond amounts more than the Coverage **E** limit of liability. We need not apply for or furnish any bond;

3. Reasonable expenses incurred by an "insured" at our request, including actual loss of earnings (but not loss of other income) up to $250 per day, for assisting us in the investigation or defense of a claim or suit; and

4. Interest on the entire judgment which accrues after entry of the judgment and before we pay or tender, or deposit in court that part of the judgment which does not exceed the limit of liability that applies.

B. First Aid Expenses

We will pay expenses for first aid to others incurred by an "insured" for "bodily injury" covered under this policy. We will not pay for first aid to an "insured".

C. Damage To Property Of Others

1. We will pay, at replacement cost, up to $1,000 per "occurrence" for "property damage" to property of others caused by an "insured".

2. We will not pay for "property damage":

a. To the extent of any amount recoverable under Section **I**;

b. Caused intentionally by an "insured" who is 13 years of age or older;

c. To property owned by an "insured";

d. To property owned by or rented to a tenant of an "insured" or a resident in your household; or

e. Arising out of:

(1) A "business" engaged in by an "insured";

(2) Any act or omission in connection with a premises owned, rented or controlled by an "insured", other than the "insured location"; or

(3) The ownership, maintenance, occupancy, operation, use, loading or unloading of aircraft, hovercraft, watercraft or "motor vehicles".

This exclusion **e.(3)** does not apply to a "motor vehicle" that:

(a) Is designed for recreational use off public roads;

(b) Is not owned by an "insured"; and

(c) At the time of the "occurrence", is not required by law, or regulation issued by a government agency, to have been registered for it to be used on public roads or property.

D. Loss Assessment

1. We will pay up to $1,000 for your share of loss assessment charged against you, as owner or tenant of the "residence premises", during the policy period by a corporation or association of property owners, when the assessment is made as a result of:

   a. "Bodily injury" or "property damage" not excluded from coverage under Section II – Exclusions; or

   b. Liability for an act of a director, officer or trustee in the capacity as a director, officer or trustee, provided such person:

      (1) Is elected by the members of a corporation or association of property owners; and

      (2) Serves without deriving any income from the exercise of duties which are solely on behalf of a corporation or association of property owners.

2. Paragraph I. Policy Period under Section II – Conditions does not apply to this Loss Assessment Coverage.

3. Regardless of the number of assessments, the limit of $1,000 is the most we will pay for loss arising out of:

   a. One accident, including continuous or repeated exposure to substantially the same general harmful condition; or

   b. A covered act of a director, officer or trustee. An act involving more than one director, officer or trustee is considered to be a single act.

4. We do not cover assessments charged against you or a corporation or association of property owners by any governmental body.

SECTION II – CONDITIONS

A. Limit Of Liability

Our total liability under Coverage E for all damages resulting from any one "occurrence" will not be more than the Coverage E limit of liability shown in the Declarations. This limit is the same regardless of the number of "insureds", claims made or persons injured. All "bodily injury" and "property damage" resulting from any one accident or from continuous or repeated exposure to substantially the same general harmful conditions shall be considered to be the result of one "occurrence".

Our total liability under Coverage F for all medical expense payable for "bodily injury" to one person as the result of one accident will not be more than the Coverage F limit of liability shown in the Declarations.

B. Severability Of Insurance

This insurance applies separately to each "insured". This condition will not increase our limit of liability for any one "occurrence".

C. Duties After "Occurrence"

In case of an "occurrence", you or another "insured" will perform the following duties that apply. We have no duty to provide coverage under this policy if your failure to comply with the following duties is prejudicial to us. You will help us by seeing that these duties are performed:

1. Give written notice to us or our agent as soon as is practical, which sets forth:

   a. The identity of the policy and the "named insured" shown in the Declarations;

   b. Reasonably available information on the time, place and circumstances of the "occurrence"; and

   c. Names and addresses of any claimants and witnesses;

2. Cooperate with us in the investigation, settlement or defense of any claim or suit;

3. Promptly forward to us every notice, demand, summons or other process relating to the "occurrence";

4. At our request, help us:

   a. To make settlement;

   b. To enforce any right of contribution or indemnity against any person or organization who may be liable to an "insured";

   c. With the conduct of suits and attend hearings and trials; and

   d. To secure and give evidence and obtain the attendance of witnesses;

5. With respect to C. Damage To Property Of Others under Section II – Additional Coverages, submit to us within 60 days after the loss, a sworn statement of loss and show the damaged property, if in an "insured's" control;

6. No "insured" shall, except at such "insured's" own cost, voluntarily make payment, assume obligation or incur expense other than for first aid to others at the time of the "bodily injury".

D. Duties Of An Injured Person – Coverage F – Medical Payments To Others

1. The injured person or someone acting for the injured person will:

   a. Give us written proof of claim, under oath if required, as soon as is practical; and

   b. Authorize us to obtain copies of medical reports and records.

HO 00 02 10 00

2. The injured person will submit to a physical exam by a doctor of our choice when and as often as we reasonably require.

E. Payment Of Claim – Coverage F – Medical Payments To Others

Payment under this coverage is not an admission of liability by an "insured" or us.

F. Suit Against Us

1. No action can be brought against us unless there has been full compliance with all of the terms under this Section **II.**

2. No one will have the right to join us as a party to any action against an "insured".

3. Also, no action with respect to Coverage **E** can be brought against us until the obligation of such "insured" has been determined by final judgment or agreement signed by us.

G. Bankruptcy Of An "Insured"

Bankruptcy or insolvency of an "insured" will not relieve us of our obligations under this policy.

H. Other Insurance

This insurance is excess over other valid and collectible insurance except insurance written specifically to cover as excess over the limits of liability that apply in this policy.

I. Policy Period

This policy applies only to "bodily injury" or "property damage" which occurs during the policy period.

J. Concealment Or Fraud

We do not provide coverage to an "insured" who, whether before or after a loss, has:

1. Intentionally concealed or misrepresented any material fact or circumstance;

2. Engaged in fraudulent conduct; or

3. Made false statements;

relating to this insurance.

SECTIONS I AND II – CONDITIONS

A. Liberalization Clause

If we make a change which broadens coverage under this edition of our policy without additional premium charge, that change will automatically apply to your insurance as of the date we implement the change in your state, provided that this implementation date falls within 60 days prior to or during the policy period stated in the Declarations.

This Liberalization Clause does not apply to changes implemented with a general program revision that includes both broadenings and restrictions in coverage, whether that general program revision is implemented through introduction of:

1. A subsequent edition of this policy; or

2. An amendatory endorsement.

B. Waiver Or Change Of Policy Provisions

A waiver or change of a provision of this policy must be in writing by us to be valid. Our request for an appraisal or examination will not waive any of our rights.

C. Cancellation

1. You may cancel this policy at any time by returning it to us or by letting us know in writing of the date cancellation is to take effect.

2. We may cancel this policy only for the reasons stated below by letting you know in writing of the date cancellation takes effect. This cancellation notice may be delivered to you, or mailed to you at your mailing address shown in the Declarations. Proof of mailing will be sufficient proof of notice.

a. When you have not paid the premium, we may cancel at any time by letting you know at least 10 days before the date cancellation takes effect.

b. When this policy has been in effect for less than 60 days and is not a renewal with us, we may cancel for any reason by letting you know at least 10 days before the date cancellation takes effect.

c. When this policy has been in effect for 60 days or more, or at any time if it is a renewal with us, we may cancel:

(1) If there has been a material misrepresentation of fact which if known to us would have caused us not to issue the policy; or

(2) If the risk has changed substantially since the policy was issued.

This can be done by letting you know at least 30 days before the date cancellation takes effect.

d. When this policy is written for a period of more than one year, we may cancel for any reason at anniversary by letting you know at least 30 days before the date cancellation takes effect.

3. When this policy is canceled, the premium for the period from the date of cancellation to the expiration date will be refunded pro rata.

4. If the return premium is not refunded with the notice of cancellation or when this policy is returned to us, we will refund it within a reasonable time after the date cancellation takes effect.

D. Nonrenewal

We may elect not to renew this policy. We may do so by delivering to you, or mailing to you at your mailing address shown in the Declarations, written notice at least 30 days before the expiration date of this policy. Proof of mailing will be sufficient proof of notice.

E. Assignment

Assignment of this policy will not be valid unless we give our written consent.

F. Subrogation

An "insured" may waive in writing before a loss all rights of recovery against any person. If not waived, we may require an assignment of rights of recovery for a loss to the extent that payment is made by us.

If an assignment is sought, an "insured" must sign and deliver all related papers and cooperate with us.

Subrogation does not apply to Coverage **F** or Paragraph **C.** Damage To Property Of Others under Section **II** – Additional Coverages.

G. Death

If any person named in the Declarations or the spouse, if a resident of the same household, dies, the following apply:

1. We insure the legal representative of the deceased but only with respect to the premises and property of the deceased covered under the policy at the time of death; and

2. "Insured" includes:

a. An "insured" who is a member of your household at the time of your death, but only while a resident of the "residence premises"; and

b. With respect to your property, the person having proper temporary custody of the property until appointment and qualification of a legal representative.

 HO 00 02 10 00

HOMEOWNERS 3 – SPECIAL FORM

AGREEMENT

We will provide the insurance described in this policy in return for the premium and compliance with all applicable provisions of this policy.

DEFINITIONS

A. In this policy, "you" and "your" refer to the "named insured" shown in the Declarations and the spouse if a resident of the same household. "We", "us" and "our" refer to the Company providing this insurance.

B. In addition, certain words and phrases are defined as follows:

1. "Aircraft Liability", "Hovercraft Liability", "Motor Vehicle Liability" and "Watercraft Liability", subject to the provisions in **b.** below, mean the following:

   a. Liability for "bodily injury" or "property damage" arising out of the:

   (1) Ownership of such vehicle or craft by an "insured";

   (2) Maintenance, occupancy, operation, use, loading or unloading of such vehicle or craft by any person;

   (3) Entrustment of such vehicle or craft by an "insured" to any person;

   (4) Failure to supervise or negligent supervision of any person involving such vehicle or craft by an "insured"; or

   (5) Vicarious liability, whether or not imposed by law, for the actions of a child or minor involving such vehicle or craft.

   b. For the purpose of this definition:

   (1) Aircraft means any contrivance used or designed for flight except model or hobby aircraft not used or designed to carry people or cargo;

   (2) Hovercraft means a self-propelled motorized ground effect vehicle and includes, but is not limited to, flarecraft and air cushion vehicles;

   (3) Watercraft means a craft principally designed to be propelled on or in water by wind, engine power or electric motor; and

   (4) Motor vehicle means a "motor vehicle" as defined in **7.** below.

2. "Bodily injury" means bodily harm, sickness or disease, including required care, loss of services and death that results.

3. "Business" means:

   a. A trade, profession or occupation engaged in on a full-time, part-time or occasional basis; or

   b. Any other activity engaged in for money or other compensation, except the following:

   (1) One or more activities, not described in **(2)** through **(4)** below, for which no "insured" receives more than $2,000 in total compensation for the 12 months before the beginning of the policy period;

   (2) Volunteer activities for which no money is received other than payment for expenses incurred to perform the activity;

   (3) Providing home day care services for which no compensation is received, other than the mutual exchange of such services; or

   (4) The rendering of home day care services to a relative of an "insured".

4. "Employee" means an employee of an "insured", or an employee leased to an "insured" by a labor leasing firm under an agreement between an "insured" and the labor leasing firm, whose duties are other than those performed by a "residence employee".

5. "Insured" means:

   a. You and residents of your household who are:

   (1) Your relatives; or

   (2) Other persons under the age of 21 and in the care of any person named above;

   b. A student enrolled in school full time, as defined by the school, who was a resident of your household before moving out to attend school, provided the student is under the age of:

   (1) 24 and your relative; or

   (2) 21 and in your care or the care of a person described in **a.(1)** above; or

c. Under Section **II:**

   (1) With respect to animals or watercraft to which this policy applies, any person or organization legally responsible for these animals or watercraft which are owned by you or any person included in **a.** or **b.** above. "Insured" does not mean a person or organization using or having custody of these animals or watercraft in the course of any "business" or without consent of the owner; or

   (2) With respect to a "motor vehicle" to which this policy applies:

     (a) Persons while engaged in your employ or that of any person included in **a.** or **b.** above; or

     (b) Other persons using the vehicle on an "insured location" with your consent.

Under both Sections **I** and **II,** when the word an immediately precedes the word "insured", the words an "insured" together mean one or more "insureds".

6. "Insured location" means:

  a. The "residence premises";

  b. The part of other premises, other structures and grounds used by you as a residence; and

   (1) Which is shown in the Declarations; or

   (2) Which is acquired by you during the policy period for your use as a residence;

  c. Any premises used by you in connection with a premises described in **a.** and **b.** above;

  d. Any part of a premises:

   (1) Not owned by an "insured"; and

   (2) Where an "insured" is temporarily residing;

  e. Vacant land, other than farm land, owned by or rented to an "insured";

  f. Land owned by or rented to an "insured" on which a one, two, three or four family dwelling is being built as a residence for an "insured";

  g. Individual or family cemetery plots or burial vaults of an "insured"; or

  h. Any part of a premises occasionally rented to an "insured" for other than "business" use.

7. "Motor vehicle" means:

  a. A self-propelled land or amphibious vehicle; or

  b. Any trailer or semitrailer which is being carried on, towed by or hitched for towing by a vehicle described in **a.** above.

8. "Occurrence" means an accident, including continuous or repeated exposure to substantially the same general harmful conditions, which results, during the policy period, in:

  a. "Bodily injury"; or

  b. "Property damage".

9. "Property damage" means physical injury to, destruction of, or loss of use of tangible property.

10. "Residence employee" means:

  a. An employee of an "insured", or an employee leased to an "insured" by a labor leasing firm, under an agreement between an "insured" and the labor leasing firm, whose duties are related to the maintenance or use of the "residence premises", including household or domestic services; or

  b. One who performs similar duties elsewhere not related to the "business" of an "insured".

A "residence employee" does not include a temporary employee who is furnished to an "insured" to substitute for a permanent "residence employee" on leave or to meet seasonal or short-term workload conditions.

11. "Residence premises" means:

  a. The one family dwelling where you reside;

  b. The two, three or four family dwelling where you reside in at least one of the family units; or

  c. That part of any other building where you reside;

and which is shown as the "residence premises" in the Declarations.

"Residence premises" also includes other structures and grounds at that location.

 HO 00 03 10 00

DEDUCTIBLE

Unless otherwise noted in this policy, the following deductible provision applies:

Subject to the policy limits that apply, we will pay only that part of the total of all loss payable under Section **I** that exceeds the deductible amount shown in the Declarations.

SECTION I – PROPERTY COVERAGES

A. Coverage A – Dwelling

1. We cover:

   a. The dwelling on the "residence premises" shown in the Declarations, including structures attached to the dwelling; and

   b. Materials and supplies located on or next to the "residence premises" used to construct, alter or repair the dwelling or other structures on the "residence premises".

2. We do not cover land, including land on which the dwelling is located.

B. Coverage B – Other Structures

1. We cover other structures on the "residence premises" set apart from the dwelling by clear space. This includes structures connected to the dwelling by only a fence, utility line, or similar connection.

2. We do not cover:

   a. Land, including land on which the other structures are located;

   b. Other structures rented or held for rental to any person not a tenant of the dwelling, unless used solely as a private garage;

   c. Other structures from which any "business" is conducted; or

   d. Other structures used to store "business" property. However, we do cover a structure that contains "business" property solely owned by an "insured" or a tenant of the dwelling provided that "business" property does not include gaseous or liquid fuel, other than fuel in a permanently installed fuel tank of a vehicle or craft parked or stored in the structure.

3. The limit of liability for this coverage will not be more than 10% of the limit of liability that applies to Coverage **A.** Use of this coverage does not reduce the Coverage **A** limit of liability.

C. Coverage C – Personal Property

1. **Covered Property**

   We cover personal property owned or used by an "insured" while it is anywhere in the world. After a loss and at your request, we will cover personal property owned by:

   a. Others while the property is on the part of the "residence premises" occupied by an "insured"; or

   b. A guest or a "residence employee", while the property is in any residence occupied by an "insured".

2. **Limit For Property At Other Residences**

   Our limit of liability for personal property usually located at an "insured's" residence, other than the "residence premises", is 10% of the limit of liability for Coverage **C,** or $1,000, whichever is greater. However, this limitation does not apply to personal property:

   a. Moved from the "residence premises" because it is being repaired, renovated or rebuilt and is not fit to live in or store property in; or

   b. In a newly acquired principal residence for 30 days from the time you begin to move the property there.

3. **Special Limits Of Liability**

   The special limit for each category shown below is the total limit for each loss for all property in that category. These special limits do not increase the Coverage **C** limit of liability.

   a. $200 on money, bank notes, bullion, gold other than goldware, silver other than silverware, platinum other than platinumware, coins, medals, scrip, stored value cards and smart cards.

   b. $1,500 on securities, accounts, deeds, evidences of debt, letters of credit, notes other than bank notes, manuscripts, personal records, passports, tickets and stamps. This dollar limit applies to these categories regardless of the medium (such as paper or computer software) on which the material exists.

   This limit includes the cost to research, replace or restore the information from the lost or damaged material.

c. $1,500 on watercraft of all types, including their trailers, furnishings, equipment and outboard engines or motors.

d. $1,500 on trailers or semitrailers not used with watercraft of all types.

e. $1,500 for loss by theft of jewelry, watches, furs, precious and semiprecious stones.

f. $2,500 for loss by theft of firearms and related equipment.

g. $2,500 for loss by theft of silverware, silver-plated ware, goldware, gold-plated ware, platinumware, platinum-plated ware and pewterware. This includes flatware, hollowware, tea sets, trays and trophies made of or including silver, gold or pewter.

h. $2,500 on property, on the "residence premises", used primarily for "business" purposes.

i. $500 on property, away from the "residence premises", used primarily for "business" purposes. However, this limit does not apply to loss to electronic apparatus and other property described in Categories **j.** and **k.** below.

j. $1,500 on electronic apparatus and accessories, while in or upon a "motor vehicle", but only if the apparatus is equipped to be operated by power from the "motor vehicle's" electrical system while still capable of being operated by other power sources.

Accessories include antennas, tapes, wires, records, discs or other media that can be used with any apparatus described in this Category **j.**

k. $1,500 on electronic apparatus and accessories used primarily for "business" while away from the "residence premises" and not in or upon a "motor vehicle". The apparatus must be equipped to be operated by power from the "motor vehicle's" electrical system while still capable of being operated by other power sources.

Accessories include antennas, tapes, wires, records, discs or other media that can be used with any apparatus described in this Category **k.**

4. Property Not Covered

We do not cover:

a. Articles separately described and specifically insured, regardless of the limit for which they are insured, in this or other insurance;

b. Animals, birds or fish;

c. "Motor vehicles".

(1) This includes:

(a) Their accessories, equipment and parts; or

(b) Electronic apparatus and accessories designed to be operated solely by power from the electrical system of the "motor vehicle". Accessories include antennas, tapes, wires, records, discs or other media that can be used with any apparatus described above.

The exclusion of property described in **(a)** and **(b)** above applies only while such property is in or upon the "motor vehicle".

(2) We do cover "motor vehicles" not required to be registered for use on public roads or property which are:

(a) Used solely to service an "insured's" residence; or

(b) Designed to assist the handicapped;

d. Aircraft meaning any contrivance used or designed for flight including any parts whether or not attached to the aircraft.

We do cover model or hobby aircraft not used or designed to carry people or cargo;

e. Hovercraft and parts. Hovercraft means a self-propelled motorized ground effect vehicle and includes, but is not limited to, flarecraft and air cushion vehicles;

f. Property of roomers, boarders and other tenants, except property of roomers and boarders related to an "insured";

g. Property in an apartment regularly rented or held for rental to others by an "insured", except as provided in **E.10.** Landlord's Furnishings under Section I – Property Coverages;

h. Property rented or held for rental to others off the "residence premises";

i. "Business" data, including such data stored in:

(1) Books of account, drawings or other paper records; or

(2) Computers and related equipment.

We do cover the cost of blank recording or storage media, and of prerecorded computer programs available on the retail market;

         HO 00 03 10 00

j. Credit cards, electronic fund transfer cards or access devices used solely for deposit, withdrawal or transfer of funds except as provided in **E.6.** Credit Card, Electronic Fund Transfer Card Or Access Device, Forgery And Counterfeit Money under Section **I** – Property Coverages; or

k. Water or steam.

D. Coverage D – Loss Of Use

The limit of liability for Coverage **D** is the total limit for the coverages in **1.** Additional Living Expense, **2.** Fair Rental Value and **3.** Civil Authority Prohibits Use below.

1. Additional Living Expense

If a loss covered under Section **I** makes that part of the "residence premises" where you reside not fit to live in, we cover any necessary increase in living expenses incurred by you so that your household can maintain its normal standard of living.

Payment will be for the shortest time required to repair or replace the damage or, if you permanently relocate, the shortest time required for your household to settle elsewhere.

2. Fair Rental Value

If a loss covered under Section **I** makes that part of the "residence premises" rented to others or held for rental by you not fit to live in, we cover the fair rental value of such premises less any expenses that do not continue while it is not fit to live in.

Payment will be for the shortest time required to repair or replace such premises.

3. Civil Authority Prohibits Use

If a civil authority prohibits you from use of the "residence premises" as a result of direct damage to neighboring premises by a Peril Insured Against, we cover the loss as provided in **1.** Additional Living Expense and **2.** Fair Rental Value above for no more than two weeks.

4. Loss Or Expense Not Covered

We do not cover loss or expense due to cancellation of a lease or agreement.

The periods of time under **1.** Additional Living Expense, **2.** Fair Rental Value and **3.** Civil Authority Prohibits Use above are not limited by expiration of this policy.

E. Additional Coverages

1. Debris Removal

a. We will pay your reasonable expense for the removal of:

(1) Debris of covered property if a Peril Insured Against that applies to the damaged property causes the loss; or

(2) Ash, dust or particles from a volcanic eruption that has caused direct loss to a building or property contained in a building.

This expense is included in the limit of liability that applies to the damaged property. If the amount to be paid for the actual damage to the property plus the debris removal expense is more than the limit of liability for the damaged property, an additional 5% of that limit is available for such expense.

b. We will also pay your reasonable expense, up to $1,000, for the removal from the "residence premises" of:

(1) Your tree(s) felled by the peril of Windstorm or Hail or Weight of Ice, Snow or Sleet; or

(2) A neighbor's tree(s) felled by a Peril Insured Against under Coverage **C**;

provided the tree(s):

(3) Damage(s) a covered structure; or

(4) Does not damage a covered structure, but:

(a) Block(s) a driveway on the "residence premises" which prevent(s) a "motor vehicle", that is registered for use on public roads or property, from entering or leaving the "residence premises"; or

(b) Block(s) a ramp or other fixture designed to assist a handicapped person to enter or leave the dwelling building.

The $1,000 limit is the most we will pay in any one loss regardless of the number of fallen trees. No more than $500 of this limit will be paid for the removal of any one tree.

This coverage is additional insurance.

2. Reasonable Repairs

a. We will pay the reasonable cost incurred by you for the necessary measures taken solely to protect covered property that is damaged by a Peril Insured Against from further damage.

b. If the measures taken involve repair to other damaged property, we will only pay if that property is covered under this policy and the damage is caused by a Peril Insured Against. This coverage does not:

(1) Increase the limit of liability that applies to the covered property; or

(2) Relieve you of your duties, in case of a loss to covered property, described in **B.4.** under Section I – Conditions.

3. Trees, Shrubs And Other Plants

We cover trees, shrubs, plants or lawns, on the "residence premises", for loss caused by the following Perils Insured Against:

a. Fire or Lightning;

b. Explosion;

c. Riot or Civil Commotion;

d. Aircraft;

e. Vehicles not owned or operated by a resident of the "residence premises";

f. Vandalism or Malicious Mischief; or

g. Theft.

We will pay up to 5% of the limit of liability that applies to the dwelling for all trees, shrubs, plants or lawns. No more than $500 of this limit will be paid for any one tree, shrub or plant. We do not cover property grown for "business" purposes.

This coverage is additional insurance.

4. Fire Department Service Charge

We will pay up to $500 for your liability assumed by contract or agreement for fire department charges incurred when the fire department is called to save or protect covered property from a Peril Insured Against. We do not cover fire department service charges if the property is located within the limits of the city, municipality or protection district furnishing the fire department response.

This coverage is additional insurance. No deductible applies to this coverage.

5. Property Removed

We insure covered property against direct loss from any cause while being removed from a premises endangered by a Peril Insured Against and for no more than 30 days while removed.

This coverage does not change the limit of liability that applies to the property being removed.

6. Credit Card, Electronic Fund Transfer Card Or Access Device, Forgery And Counterfeit Money

a. We will pay up to $500 for:

(1) The legal obligation of an "insured" to pay because of the theft or unauthorized use of credit cards issued to or registered in an "insured's" name;

(2) Loss resulting from theft or unauthorized use of an electronic fund transfer card or access device used for deposit, withdrawal or transfer of funds, issued to or registered in an "insured's" name;

(3) Loss to an "insured" caused by forgery or alteration of any check or negotiable instrument; and

(4) Loss to an "insured" through acceptance in good faith of counterfeit United States or Canadian paper currency.

All loss resulting from a series of acts committed by any one person or in which any one person is concerned or implicated is considered to be one loss.

This coverage is additional insurance. No deductible applies to this coverage.

b. We do not cover:

(1) Use of a credit card, electronic fund transfer card or access device:

(a) By a resident of your household;

(b) By a person who has been entrusted with either type of card or access device; or

(c) If an "insured" has not complied with all terms and conditions under which the cards are issued or the devices accessed; or

(2) Loss arising out of "business" use or dishonesty of an "insured".

c. If the coverage in **a.** above applies, the following defense provisions also apply:

(1) We may investigate and settle any claim or suit that we decide is appropriate. Our duty to defend a claim or suit ends when the amount we pay for the loss equals our limit of liability.

(2) If a suit is brought against an "insured" for liability under **a.(1)** or **(2)** above, we will provide a defense at our expense by counsel of our choice.

(3) We have the option to defend at our expense an "insured" or an "insured's" bank against any suit for the enforcement of payment under **a.(3)** above.

7. Loss Assessment

a. We will pay up to $1,000 for your share of loss assessment charged during the policy period against you, as owner or tenant of the "residence premises", by a corporation or association of property owners. The assessment must be made as a result of direct loss to property, owned by all members collectively, of the type that would be covered by this policy if owned by you, caused by a Peril Insured Against under Coverage **A,** other than:

(1) Earthquake; or

(2) Land shock waves or tremors before, during or after a volcanic eruption.

The limit of $1,000 is the most we will pay with respect to any one loss, regardless of the number of assessments. We will only apply one deductible, per unit, to the total amount of any one loss to the property described above, regardless of the number of assessments.

b. We do not cover assessments charged against you or a corporation or association of property owners by any governmental body.

c. Paragraph **P.** Policy Period under Section **I** – Conditions does not apply to this coverage.

This coverage is additional insurance.

8. Collapse

a. With respect to this Additional Coverage:

(1) Collapse means an abrupt falling down or caving in of a building or any part of a building with the result that the building or part of the building cannot be occupied for its current intended purpose.

(2) A building or any part of a building that is in danger of falling down or caving in is not considered to be in a state of collapse.

(3) A part of a building that is standing is not considered to be in a state of collapse even if it has separated from another part of the building.

(4) A building or any part of a building that is standing is not considered to be in a state of collapse even if it shows evidence of cracking, bulging, sagging, bending, leaning, settling, shrinkage or expansion.

b. We insure for direct physical loss to covered property involving collapse of a building or any part of a building if the collapse was caused by one or more of the following:

(1) The Perils Insured Against named under Coverage **C;**

(2) Decay that is hidden from view, unless the presence of such decay is known to an "insured" prior to collapse;

(3) Insect or vermin damage that is hidden from view, unless the presence of such damage is known to an "insured" prior to collapse;

(4) Weight of contents, equipment, animals or people;

(5) Weight of rain which collects on a roof; or

(6) Use of defective material or methods in construction, remodeling or renovation if the collapse occurs during the course of the construction, remodeling or renovation.

c. Loss to an awning, fence, patio, deck, pavement, swimming pool, underground pipe, flue, drain, cesspool, septic tank, foundation, retaining wall, bulkhead, pier, wharf or dock is not included under **b.(2)** through **(6)** above, unless the loss is a direct result of the collapse of a building or any part of a building.

d. This coverage does not increase the limit of liability that applies to the damaged covered property.

9. Glass Or Safety Glazing Material

a. We cover:

(1) The breakage of glass or safety glazing material which is part of a covered building, storm door or storm window;

(2) The breakage of glass or safety glazing material which is part of a covered building, storm door or storm window when caused directly by earth movement; and

(3) The direct physical loss to covered property caused solely by the pieces, fragments or splinters of broken glass or safety glazing material which is part of a building, storm door or storm window.

Copyright, Insurance Services Office, Inc., 1999

b. This coverage does not include loss:

(1) To covered property which results because the glass or safety glazing material has been broken, except as provided in **a.(3)** above; or

(2) On the "residence premises" if the dwelling has been vacant for more than 60 consecutive days immediately before the loss, except when the breakage results directly from earth movement as provided in **a.(2)** above. A dwelling being constructed is not considered vacant.

c. This coverage does not increase the limit of liability that applies to the damaged property.

10. Landlord's Furnishings

We will pay up to $2,500 for your appliances, carpeting and other household furnishings, in each apartment on the "residence premises" regularly rented or held for rental to others by an "insured", for loss caused by a Peril Insured Against in Coverage **C,** other than Theft.

This limit is the most we will pay in any one loss regardless of the number of appliances, carpeting or other household furnishings involved in the loss.

This coverage does not increase the limit of liability applying to the damaged property.

11. Ordinance Or Law

a. You may use up to 10% of the limit of liability that applies to Coverage **A** for the increased costs you incur due to the enforcement of any ordinance or law which requires or regulates:

(1) The construction, demolition, remodeling, renovation or repair of that part of a covered building or other structure damaged by a Peril Insured Against;

(2) The demolition and reconstruction of the undamaged part of a covered building or other structure, when that building or other structure must be totally demolished because of damage by a Peril Insured Against to another part of that covered building or other structure; or

(3) The remodeling, removal or replacement of the portion of the undamaged part of a covered building or other structure necessary to complete the remodeling, repair or replacement of that part of the covered building or other structure damaged by a Peril Insured Against.

b. You may use all or part of this ordinance or law coverage to pay for the increased costs you incur to remove debris resulting from the construction, demolition, remodeling, renovation, repair or replacement of property as stated in **a.** above.

c. We do not cover:

(1) The loss in value to any covered building or other structure due to the requirements of any ordinance or law; or

(2) The costs to comply with any ordinance or law which requires any "insured" or others to test for, monitor, clean up, remove, contain, treat, detoxify or neutralize, or in any way respond to, or assess the effects of, pollutants in or on any covered building or other structure.

Pollutants means any solid, liquid, gaseous or thermal irritant or contaminant, including smoke, vapor, soot, fumes, acids, alkalis, chemicals and waste. Waste includes materials to be recycled, reconditioned or reclaimed.

This coverage is additional insurance.

12. Grave Markers

We will pay up to $5,000 for grave markers, including mausoleums, on or away from the "residence premises" for loss caused by a Peril Insured Against under Coverage **C.**

This coverage does not increase the limits of liability that apply to the damaged covered property.

SECTION I – PERILS INSURED AGAINST

A. Coverage A – Dwelling And Coverage B – Other Structures

1. We insure against risk of direct physical loss to property described in Coverages **A** and **B.**

2. We do not insure, however, for loss:

a. Excluded under Section I – Exclusions;

b. Involving collapse, except as provided in **E.8.** Collapse under Section I – Property Coverages; or

c. Caused by:

(1) Freezing of a plumbing, heating, air conditioning or automatic fire protective sprinkler system or of a household appliance, or by discharge, leakage or overflow from within the system or appliance caused by freezing. This provision does not apply if you have used reasonable care to:

(a) Maintain heat in the building; or

Copyright, Insurance Services Office, Inc., 1999

HO 00 03 10 00

(b) Shut off the water supply and drain all systems and appliances of water.

However, if the building is protected by an automatic fire protective sprinkler system, you must use reasonable care to continue the water supply and maintain heat in the building for coverage to apply.

For purposes of this provision a plumbing system or household appliance does not include a sump, sump pump or related equipment or a roof drain, gutter, downspout or similar fixtures or equipment;

(2) Freezing, thawing, pressure or weight of water or ice, whether driven by wind or not, to a:

(a) Fence, pavement, patio or swimming pool;

(b) Footing, foundation, bulkhead, wall, or any other structure or device that supports all or part of a building, or other structure;

(c) Retaining wall or bulkhead that does not support all or part of a building or other structure; or

(d) Pier, wharf or dock;

(3) Theft in or to a dwelling under construction, or of materials and supplies for use in the construction until the dwelling is finished and occupied;

(4) Vandalism and malicious mischief, and any ensuing loss caused by any intentional and wrongful act committed in the course of the vandalism or malicious mischief, if the dwelling has been vacant for more than 60 consecutive days immediately before the loss. A dwelling being constructed is not considered vacant;

(5) Mold, fungus or wet rot. However, we do insure for loss caused by mold, fungus or wet rot that is hidden within the walls or ceilings or beneath the floors or above the ceilings of a structure if such loss results from the accidental discharge or overflow of water or steam from within:

(a) A plumbing, heating, air conditioning or automatic fire protective sprinkler system, or a household appliance, on the "residence premises"; or

(b) A storm drain, or water, steam or sewer pipes, off the "residence premises".

For purposes of this provision, a plumbing system or household appliance does not include a sump, sump pump or related equipment or a roof drain, gutter, downspout or similar fixtures or equipment; or

(6) Any of the following:

(a) Wear and tear, marring, deterioration;

(b) Mechanical breakdown, latent defect, inherent vice, or any quality in property that causes it to damage or destroy itself;

(c) Smog, rust or other corrosion, or dry rot;

(d) Smoke from agricultural smudging or industrial operations;

(e) Discharge, dispersal, seepage, migration, release or escape of pollutants unless the discharge, dispersal, seepage, migration, release or escape is itself caused by a Peril Insured Against named under Coverage **C**.

Pollutants means any solid, liquid, gaseous or thermal irritant or contaminant, including smoke, vapor, soot, fumes, acids, alkalis, chemicals and waste. Waste includes materials to be recycled, reconditioned or reclaimed;

(f) Settling, shrinking, bulging or expansion, including resultant cracking, of bulkheads, pavements, patios, footings, foundations, walls, floors, roofs or ceilings;

(g) Birds, vermin, rodents, or insects; or

(h) Animals owned or kept by an "insured".

Exception To c.(6)

Unless the loss is otherwise excluded, we cover loss to property covered under Coverage **A** or **B** resulting from an accidental discharge or overflow of water or steam from within a:

(i) Storm drain, or water, steam or sewer pipe, off the "residence premises"; or

(ii) Plumbing, heating, air conditioning or automatic fire protective sprinkler system or household appliance on the "residence premises". This includes the cost to tear out and replace any part of a building, or other structure, on the "residence premises", but only when necessary to repair the system or appliance. However, such tear out and replacement coverage only applies to other structures if the water or steam causes actual damage to a building on the "residence premises".

We do not cover loss to the system or appliance from which this water or steam escaped.

For purposes of this provision, a plumbing system or household appliance does not include a sump, sump pump or related equipment or a roof drain, gutter, down spout or similar fixtures or equipment.

Section I – Exclusion **A.3.** Water Damage, Paragraphs **a.** and **c.** that apply to surface water and water below the surface of the ground do not apply to loss by water covered under **c.(5)** and **(6)** above.

Under **2.b.** and **c.** above, any ensuing loss to property described in Coverages **A** and **B** not precluded by any other provision in this policy is covered.

B. Coverage C – Personal Property

We insure for direct physical loss to the property described in Coverage **C** caused by any of the following perils unless the loss is excluded in Section I – Exclusions.

1. Fire Or Lightning

2. Windstorm Or Hail

This peril includes loss to watercraft of all types and their trailers, furnishings, equipment, and outboard engines or motors, only while inside a fully enclosed building.

This peril does not include loss to the property contained in a building caused by rain, snow, sleet, sand or dust unless the direct force of wind or hail damages the building causing an opening in a roof or wall and the rain, snow, sleet, sand or dust enters through this opening.

3. Explosion

4. Riot Or Civil Commotion

5. Aircraft

This peril includes self-propelled missiles and spacecraft.

6. Vehicles

7. Smoke

This peril means sudden and accidental damage from smoke, including the emission or puffback of smoke, soot, fumes or vapors from a boiler, furnace or related equipment.

This peril does not include loss caused by smoke from agricultural smudging or industrial operations.

8. Vandalism Or Malicious Mischief

9. Theft

a. This peril includes attempted theft and loss of property from a known place when it is likely that the property has been stolen.

b. This peril does not include loss caused by theft:

(1) Committed by an "insured";

(2) In or to a dwelling under construction, or of materials and supplies for use in the construction until the dwelling is finished and occupied;

(3) From that part of a "residence premises" rented by an "insured" to someone other than another "insured"; or

(4) That occurs off the "residence premises" of:

(a) Trailers, semitrailers and campers;

(b) Watercraft of all types, and their furnishings, equipment and outboard engines or motors; or

(c) Property while at any other residence owned by, rented to, or occupied by an "insured", except while an "insured" is temporarily living there. Property of an "insured" who is a student is covered while at the residence the student occupies to attend school as long as the student has been there at any time during the 60 days immediately before the loss.

10. Falling Objects

This peril does not include loss to property contained in a building unless the roof or an outside wall of the building is first damaged by a falling object. Damage to the falling object itself is not included.

11. Weight Of Ice, Snow Or Sleet

This peril means weight of ice, snow or sleet which causes damage to property contained in a building.

12. **Accidental Discharge Or Overflow Of Water Or Steam**

   a. This peril means accidental discharge or overflow of water or steam from within a plumbing, heating, air conditioning or automatic fire protective sprinkler system or from within a household appliance.

   b. This peril does not include loss:

     (1) To the system or appliance from which the water or steam escaped;

     (2) Caused by or resulting from freezing except as provided in Peril Insured Against **14.** Freezing;

     (3) On the "residence premises" caused by accidental discharge or overflow which occurs off the "residence premises"; or

     (4) Caused by mold, fungus or wet rot unless hidden within the walls or ceilings or beneath the floors or above the ceilings of a structure.

   c. In this peril, a plumbing system or household appliance does not include a sump, sump pump or related equipment or a roof drain, gutter, downspout or similar fixtures or equipment.

   d. Section I – Exclusion **A.3.** Water Damage, Paragraphs **a.** and **c.** that apply to surface water and water below the surface of the ground do not apply to loss by water covered under this peril.

13. **Sudden And Accidental Tearing Apart, Cracking, Burning Or Bulging**

   This peril means sudden and accidental tearing apart, cracking, burning or bulging of a steam or hot water heating system, an air conditioning or automatic fire protective sprinkler system, or an appliance for heating water.

   We do not cover loss caused by or resulting from freezing under this peril.

14. **Freezing**

   a. This peril means freezing of a plumbing, heating, air conditioning or automatic fire protective sprinkler system or of a household appliance but only if you have used reasonable care to:

     (1) Maintain heat in the building; or

     (2) Shut off the water supply and drain all systems and appliances of water.

   However, if the building is protected by an automatic fire protective sprinkler system, you must use reasonable care to continue the water supply and maintain heat in the building for coverage to apply.

   b. In this peril, a plumbing system or household appliance does not include a sump, sump pump or related equipment or a roof drain, gutter, downspout or similar fixtures or equipment.

15. **Sudden And Accidental Damage From Artificially Generated Electrical Current**

   This peril does not include loss to tubes, transistors, electronic components or circuitry that are a part of appliances, fixtures, computers, home entertainment units or other types of electronic apparatus.

16. **Volcanic Eruption**

   This peril does not include loss caused by earthquake, land shock waves or tremors.

SECTION I – EXCLUSIONS

A. We do not insure for loss caused directly or indirectly by any of the following. Such loss is excluded regardless of any other cause or event contributing concurrently or in any sequence to the loss. These exclusions apply whether or not the loss event results in widespread damage or affects a substantial area.

  1. **Ordinance Or Law**

    Ordinance Or Law means any ordinance or law:

    a. Requiring or regulating the construction, demolition, remodeling, renovation or repair of property, including removal of any resulting debris. This Exclusion **A.1.a.** does not apply to the amount of coverage that may be provided for in **E.11.** Ordinance Or Law under Section I – Property Coverages;

    b. The requirements of which result in a loss in value to property; or

    c. Requiring any "insured" or others to test for, monitor, clean up, remove, contain, treat, detoxify or neutralize, or in any way respond to, or assess the effects of, pollutants.

    Pollutants means any solid, liquid, gaseous or thermal irritant or contaminant, including smoke, vapor, soot, fumes, acids, alkalis, chemicals and waste. Waste includes materials to be recycled, reconditioned or reclaimed.

    This Exclusion **A.1.** applies whether or not the property has been physically damaged.

  2. **Earth Movement**

    Earth Movement means:

    a. Earthquake, including land shock waves or tremors before, during or after a volcanic eruption;

b. Landslide, mudslide or mudflow;

c. Subsidence or sinkhole; or

d. Any other earth movement including earth sinking, rising or shifting;

caused by or resulting from human or animal forces or any act of nature unless direct loss by fire or explosion ensues and then we will pay only for the ensuing loss.

This Exclusion **A.2.** does not apply to loss by theft.

3. Water Damage

Water Damage means:

a. Flood, surface water, waves, tidal water, overflow of a body of water, or spray from any of these, whether or not driven by wind;

b. Water or water-borne material which backs up through sewers or drains or which overflows or is discharged from a sump, sump pump or related equipment; or

c. Water or water-borne material below the surface of the ground, including water which exerts pressure on or seeps or leaks through a building, sidewalk, driveway, foundation, swimming pool or other structure;

caused by or resulting from human or animal forces or any act of nature.

Direct loss by fire, explosion or theft resulting from water damage is covered.

4. Power Failure

Power Failure means the failure of power or other utility service if the failure takes place off the "residence premises". But if the failure results in a loss, from a Peril Insured Against on the "residence premises", we will pay for the loss caused by that peril.

5. Neglect

Neglect means neglect of an "insured" to use all reasonable means to save and preserve property at and after the time of a loss.

6. War

War includes the following and any consequence of any of the following:

a. Undeclared war, civil war, insurrection, rebellion or revolution;

b. Warlike act by a military force or military personnel; or

c. Destruction, seizure or use for a military purpose.

Discharge of a nuclear weapon will be deemed a warlike act even if accidental.

7. Nuclear Hazard

This Exclusion **A.7.** pertains to Nuclear Hazard to the extent set forth in **M.** Nuclear Hazard Clause under Section **I** – Conditions.

8. Intentional Loss

Intentional Loss means any loss arising out of any act an "insured" commits or conspires to commit with the intent to cause a loss.

In the event of such loss, no "insured" is entitled to coverage, even "insureds" who did not commit or conspire to commit the act causing the loss.

9. Governmental Action

Governmental Action means the destruction, confiscation or seizure of property described in Coverage **A**, **B** or **C** by order of any governmental or public authority.

This exclusion does not apply to such acts ordered by any governmental or public authority that are taken at the time of a fire to prevent its spread, if the loss caused by fire would be covered under this policy.

B. We do not insure for loss to property described in Coverages **A** and **B** caused by any of the following. However, any ensuing loss to property described in Coverages **A** and **B** not precluded by any other provision in this policy is covered.

1. Weather conditions. However, this exclusion only applies if weather conditions contribute in any way with a cause or event excluded in **A.** above to produce the loss.

2. Acts or decisions, including the failure to act or decide, of any person, group, organization or governmental body.

3. Faulty, inadequate or defective:

a. Planning, zoning, development, surveying, siting;

b. Design, specifications, workmanship, repair, construction, renovation, remodeling, grading, compaction;

c. Materials used in repair, construction, renovation or remodeling; or

d. Maintenance;

of part or all of any property whether on or off the "residence premises".

Copyright, Insurance Services Office, Inc., 1999 HO 00 03 10 00

SECTION I – CONDITIONS

A. Insurable Interest And Limit Of Liability

Even if more than one person has an insurable interest in the property covered, we will not be liable in any one loss:

1. To an "insured" for more than the amount of such "insured's" interest at the time of loss; or

2. For more than the applicable limit of liability.

B. Duties After Loss

In case of a loss to covered property, we have no duty to provide coverage under this policy if the failure to comply with the following duties is prejudicial to us. These duties must be performed either by you, an "insured" seeking coverage, or a representative of either:

1. Give prompt notice to us or our agent;

2. Notify the police in case of loss by theft;

3. Notify the credit card or electronic fund transfer card or access device company in case of loss as provided for in **E.6.** Credit Card, Electronic Fund Transfer Card Or Access Device, Forgery And Counterfeit Money under Section I – Property Coverages;

4. Protect the property from further damage. If repairs to the property are required, you must:

   a. Make reasonable and necessary repairs to protect the property; and

   b. Keep an accurate record of repair expenses;

5. Cooperate with us in the investigation of a claim;

6. Prepare an inventory of damaged personal property showing the quantity, description, actual cash value and amount of loss. Attach all bills, receipts and related documents that justify the figures in the inventory;

7. As often as we reasonably require:

   a. Show the damaged property;

   b. Provide us with records and documents we request and permit us to make copies; and

   c. Submit to examination under oath, while not in the presence of another "insured", and sign the same;

8. Send to us, within 60 days after our request, your signed, sworn proof of loss which sets forth, to the best of your knowledge and belief:

   a. The time and cause of loss;

   b. The interests of all "insureds" and all others in the property involved and all liens on the property;

   c. Other insurance which may cover the loss;

   d. Changes in title or occupancy of the property during the term of the policy;

   e. Specifications of damaged buildings and detailed repair estimates;

   f. The inventory of damaged personal property described in **6.** above;

   g. Receipts for additional living expenses incurred and records that support the fair rental value loss; and

   h. Evidence or affidavit that supports a claim under **E.6.** Credit Card, Electronic Fund Transfer Card Or Access Device, Forgery And Counterfeit Money under Section I – Property Coverages, stating the amount and cause of loss.

C. Loss Settlement

In this Condition **C.**, the terms "cost to repair or replace" and "replacement cost" do not include the increased costs incurred to comply with the enforcement of any ordinance or law, except to the extent that coverage for these increased costs is provided in **E.11.** Ordinance Or Law under Section I – Property Coverages. Covered property losses are settled as follows:

1. Property of the following types:

   a. Personal property;

   b. Awnings, carpeting, household appliances, outdoor antennas and outdoor equipment, whether or not attached to buildings;

   c. Structures that are not buildings; and

   d. Grave markers, including mausoleums;

   at actual cash value at the time of loss but not more than the amount required to repair or replace.

2. Buildings covered under Coverage **A** or **B** at replacement cost without deduction for depreciation, subject to the following:

   a. If, at the time of loss, the amount of insurance in this policy on the damaged building is 80% or more of the full replacement cost of the building immediately before the loss, we will pay the cost to repair or replace, after application of any deductible and without deduction for depreciation, but not more than the least of the following amounts:

      (1) The limit of liability under this policy that applies to the building;

      (2) The replacement cost of that part of the building damaged with material of like kind and quality and for like use; or

      (3) The necessary amount actually spent to repair or replace the damaged building.

If the building is rebuilt at a new premises, the cost described in **(2)** above is limited to the cost which would have been incurred if the building had been built at the original premises.

b. If, at the time of loss, the amount of insurance in this policy on the damaged building is less than 80% of the full replacement cost of the building immediately before the loss, we will pay the greater of the following amounts, but not more than the limit of liability under this policy that applies to the building:

(1) The actual cash value of that part of the building damaged; or

(2) That proportion of the cost to repair or replace, after application of any deductible and without deduction for depreciation, that part of the building damaged, which the total amount of insurance in this policy on the damaged building bears to 80% of the replacement cost of the building.

c. To determine the amount of insurance required to equal 80% of the full replacement cost of the building immediately before the loss, do not include the value of:

(1) Excavations, footings, foundations, piers, or any other structures or devices that support all or part of the building, which are below the undersurface of the lowest basement floor;

(2) Those supports described in **(1)** above which are below the surface of the ground inside the foundation walls, if there is no basement; and

(3) Underground flues, pipes, wiring and drains.

d. We will pay no more than the actual cash value of the damage until actual repair or replacement is complete. Once actual repair or replacement is complete, we will settle the loss as noted in **2.a.** and **b.** above.

However, if the cost to repair or replace the damage is both:

(1) Less than 5% of the amount of insurance in this policy on the building; and

(2) Less than $2,500;

we will settle the loss as noted in **2.a.** and **b.** above whether or not actual repair or replacement is complete.

e. You may disregard the replacement cost loss settlement provisions and make claim under this policy for loss to buildings on an actual cash value basis. You may then make claim for any additional liability according to the provisions of this Condition **C. Loss Settlement**, provided you notify us of your intent to do so within 180 days after the date of loss.

D. Loss To A Pair Or Set

In case of loss to a pair or set we may elect to:

1. Repair or replace any part to restore the pair or set to its value before the loss; or

2. Pay the difference between actual cash value of the property before and after the loss.

E. Appraisal

If you and we fail to agree on the amount of loss, either may demand an appraisal of the loss. In this event, each party will choose a competent and impartial appraiser within 20 days after receiving a written request from the other. The two appraisers will choose an umpire. If they cannot agree upon an umpire within 15 days, you or we may request that the choice be made by a judge of a court of record in the state where the "residence premises" is located. The appraisers will separately set the amount of loss. If the appraisers submit a written report of an agreement to us, the amount agreed upon will be the amount of loss. If they fail to agree, they will submit their differences to the umpire. A decision agreed to by any two will set the amount of loss.

Each party will:

1. Pay its own appraiser; and

2. Bear the other expenses of the appraisal and umpire equally.

F. Other Insurance And Service Agreement

If a loss covered by this policy is also covered by:

1. Other insurance, we will pay only the proportion of the loss that the limit of liability that applies under this policy bears to the total amount of insurance covering the loss; or

2. A service agreement, this insurance is excess over any amounts payable under any such agreement. Service agreement means a service plan, property restoration plan, home warranty or other similar service warranty agreement, even if it is characterized as insurance.

G. Suit Against Us

No action can be brought against us unless there has been full compliance with all of the terms under Section I of this policy and the action is started within two years after the date of loss.

H. Our Option

If we give you written notice within 30 days after we receive your signed, sworn proof of loss, we may repair or replace any part of the damaged property with material or property of like kind and quality.

I. Loss Payment

We will adjust all losses with you. We will pay you unless some other person is named in the policy or is legally entitled to receive payment. Loss will be payable 60 days after we receive your proof of loss and:

1. Reach an agreement with you;

2. There is an entry of a final judgment; or

3. There is a filing of an appraisal award with us.

J. Abandonment Of Property

We need not accept any property abandoned by an "insured".

K. Mortgage Clause

1. If a mortgagee is named in this policy, any loss payable under Coverage **A** or **B** will be paid to the mortgagee and you, as interests appear. If more than one mortgagee is named, the order of payment will be the same as the order of precedence of the mortgages.

2. If we deny your claim, that denial will not apply to a valid claim of the mortgagee, if the mortgagee:

   a. Notifies us of any change in ownership, occupancy or substantial change in risk of which the mortgagee is aware;

   b. Pays any premium due under this policy on demand if you have neglected to pay the premium; and

   c. Submits a signed, sworn statement of loss within 60 days after receiving notice from us of your failure to do so. Paragraphs **E.** Appraisal, **G.** Suit Against Us and **I.** Loss Payment under Section I – Conditions also apply to the mortgagee.

3. If we decide to cancel or not to renew this policy, the mortgagee will be notified at least 10 days before the date cancellation or nonrenewal takes effect.

4. If we pay the mortgagee for any loss and deny payment to you:

   a. We are subrogated to all the rights of the mortgagee granted under the mortgage on the property; or

   b. At our option, we may pay to the mortgagee the whole principal on the mortgage plus any accrued interest. In this event, we will receive a full assignment and transfer of the mortgage and all securities held as collateral to the mortgage debt.

5. Subrogation will not impair the right of the mortgagee to recover the full amount of the mortgagee's claim.

L. No Benefit To Bailee

We will not recognize any assignment or grant any coverage that benefits a person or organization holding, storing or moving property for a fee regardless of any other provision of this policy.

M. Nuclear Hazard Clause

1. "Nuclear Hazard" means any nuclear reaction, radiation, or radioactive contamination, all whether controlled or uncontrolled or however caused, or any consequence of any of these.

2. Loss caused by the nuclear hazard will not be considered loss caused by fire, explosion, or smoke, whether these perils are specifically named in or otherwise included within the Perils Insured Against.

3. This policy does not apply under Section I to loss caused directly or indirectly by nuclear hazard, except that direct loss by fire resulting from the nuclear hazard is covered.

N. Recovered Property

If you or we recover any property for which we have made payment under this policy, you or we will notify the other of the recovery. At your option, the property will be returned to or retained by you or it will become our property. If the recovered property is returned to or retained by you, the loss payment will be adjusted based on the amount you received for the recovered property.

O. Volcanic Eruption Period

One or more volcanic eruptions that occur within a 72 hour period will be considered as one volcanic eruption.

P. Policy Period

This policy applies only to loss which occurs during the policy period.

Q. Concealment Or Fraud

We provide coverage to no "insureds" under this policy if, whether before or after a loss, an "insured" has:

1. Intentionally concealed or misrepresented any material fact or circumstance;

2. Engaged in fraudulent conduct; or

3. Made false statements;

relating to this insurance.

R. Loss Payable Clause

If the Declarations show a loss payee for certain listed insured personal property, the definition of "insured" is changed to include that loss payee with respect to that property.

If we decide to cancel or not renew this policy, that loss payee will be notified in writing.

SECTION II – LIABILITY COVERAGES

A. Coverage E – Personal Liability

If a claim is made or a suit is brought against an "insured" for damages because of "bodily injury" or "property damage" caused by an "occurrence" to which this coverage applies, we will:

1. Pay up to our limit of liability for the damages for which an "insured" is legally liable. Damages include prejudgment interest awarded against an "insured"; and

2. Provide a defense at our expense by counsel of our choice, even if the suit is groundless, false or fraudulent. We may investigate and settle any claim or suit that we decide is appropriate. Our duty to settle or defend ends when our limit of liability for the "occurrence" has been exhausted by payment of a judgment or settlement.

B. Coverage F – Medical Payments To Others

We will pay the necessary medical expenses that are incurred or medically ascertained within three years from the date of an accident causing "bodily injury". Medical expenses means reasonable charges for medical, surgical, x-ray, dental, ambulance, hospital, professional nursing, prosthetic devices and funeral services. This coverage does not apply to you or regular residents of your household except "residence employees". As to others, this coverage applies only:

1. To a person on the "insured location" with the permission of an "insured"; or

2. To a person off the "insured location", if the "bodily injury":

    a. Arises out of a condition on the "insured location" or the ways immediately adjoining;

    b. Is caused by the activities of an "insured";

    c. Is caused by a "residence employee" in the course of the "residence employee's" employment by an "insured"; or

    d. Is caused by an animal owned by or in the care of an "insured".

SECTION II – EXCLUSIONS

A. "Motor Vehicle Liability"

1. Coverages **E** and **F** do not apply to any "motor vehicle liability" if, at the time and place of an "occurrence", the involved "motor vehicle":

    a. Is registered for use on public roads or property;

    b. Is not registered for use on public roads or property, but such registration is required by a law, or regulation issued by a government agency, for it to be used at the place of the "occurrence"; or

    c. Is being:

        (1) Operated in, or practicing for, any prearranged or organized race, speed contest or other competition;

        (2) Rented to others;

        (3) Used to carry persons or cargo for a charge; or

        (4) Used for any "business" purpose except for a motorized golf cart while on a golfing facility.

2. If Exclusion **A.1.** does not apply, there is still no coverage for "motor vehicle liability" unless the "motor vehicle" is:

    a. In dead storage on an "insured location";

    b. Used solely to service an "insured's" residence;

    c. Designed to assist the handicapped and, at the time of an "occurrence", it is:

        (1) Being used to assist a handicapped person; or

        (2) Parked on an "insured location";

    d. Designed for recreational use off public roads and:

        (1) Not owned by an "insured"; or

       (2) Owned by an "insured" provided the "occurrence" takes place on an "insured location" as defined in Definitions **B. 6.a., b., d., e.** or **h.;** or

    e. A motorized golf cart that is owned by an "insured", designed to carry up to 4 persons, not built or modified after manufacture to exceed a speed of 25 miles per hour on level ground and, at the time of an "occurrence", is within the legal boundaries of:

        (1) A golfing facility and is parked or stored there, or being used by an "insured" to:

           (a) Play the game of golf or for other recreational or leisure activity allowed by the facility;

(b) Travel to or from an area where "motor vehicles" or golf carts are parked or stored; or

(c) Cross public roads at designated points to access other parts of the golfing facility; or

(2) A private residential community, including its public roads upon which a motorized golf cart can legally travel, which is subject to the authority of a property owners association and contains an "insured's" residence.

B. "Watercraft Liability"

1. Coverages **E** and **F** do not apply to any "watercraft liability" if, at the time of an "occurrence", the involved watercraft is being:

a. Operated in, or practicing for, any prearranged or organized race, speed contest or other competition. This exclusion does not apply to a sailing vessel or a predicted log cruise;

b. Rented to others;

c. Used to carry persons or cargo for a charge; or

d. Used for any "business" purpose.

2. If Exclusion **B.1.** does not apply, there is still no coverage for "watercraft liability" unless, at the time of the "occurrence", the watercraft:

a. Is stored;

b. Is a sailing vessel, with or without auxiliary power, that is:

(1) Less than 26 feet in overall length; or

(2) 26 feet or more in overall length and not owned by or rented to an "insured"; or

c. Is not a sailing vessel and is powered by:

(1) An inboard or inboard-outdrive engine or motor, including those that power a water jet pump, of:

(a) 50 horsepower or less and not owned by an "insured"; or

(b) More than 50 horsepower and not owned by or rented to an "insured"; or

(2) One or more outboard engines or motors with:

(a) 25 total horsepower or less;

(b) More than 25 horsepower if the outboard engine or motor is not owned by an "insured";

(c) More than 25 horsepower if the outboard engine or motor is owned by an "insured" who acquired it during the policy period; or

(d) More than 25 horsepower if the outboard engine or motor is owned by an "insured" who acquired it before the policy period, but only if:

(i) You declare them at policy inception; or

(ii) Your intent to insure them is reported to us in writing within 45 days after you acquire them.

The coverages in **(c)** and **(d)** above apply for the policy period.

Horsepower means the maximum power rating assigned to the engine or motor by the manufacturer.

C. "Aircraft Liability"

This policy does not cover "aircraft liability".

D. "Hovercraft Liability"

This policy does not cover "hovercraft liability".

E. Coverage E – Personal Liability And Coverage F – Medical Payments To Others

Coverages **E** and **F** do not apply to the following:

1. Expected Or Intended Injury

"Bodily injury" or "property damage" which is expected or intended by an "insured" even if the resulting "bodily injury" or "property damage":

a. Is of a different kind, quality or degree than initially expected or intended; or

b. Is sustained by a different person, entity, real or personal property, than initially expected or intended.

However, this Exclusion **E.1.** does not apply to "bodily injury" resulting from the use of reasonable force by an "insured" to protect persons or property;

2. "Business"

a. "Bodily injury" or "property damage" arising out of or in connection with a "business" conducted from an "insured location" or engaged in by an "insured", whether or not the "business" is owned or operated by an "insured" or employs an "insured".

This Exclusion **E.2.** applies but is not limited to an act or omission, regardless of its nature or circumstance, involving a service or duty rendered, promised, owed, or implied to be provided because of the nature of the "business".

b. This Exclusion **E.2.** does not apply to:

(1) The rental or holding for rental of an "insured location";

(a) On an occasional basis if used only as a residence;

(b) In part for use only as a residence, unless a single family unit is intended for use by the occupying family to lodge more than two roomers or boarders; or

(c) In part, as an office, school, studio or private garage; and

(2) An "insured" under the age of 21 years involved in a part-time or occasional, self-employed "business" with no employees;

3. Professional Services

"Bodily injury" or "property damage" arising out of the rendering of or failure to render professional services;

4. "Insured's" Premises Not An "Insured Location"

"Bodily injury" or "property damage" arising out of a premises:

a. Owned by an "insured";

b. Rented to an "insured"; or

c. Rented to others by an "insured";

that is not an "insured location";

5. War

"Bodily injury" or "property damage" caused directly or indirectly by war, including the following and any consequence of any of the following:

a. Undeclared war, civil war, insurrection, rebellion or revolution;

b. Warlike act by a military force or military personnel; or

c. Destruction, seizure or use for a military purpose.

Discharge of a nuclear weapon will be deemed a warlike act even if accidental;

6. Communicable Disease

"Bodily injury" or "property damage" which arises out of the transmission of a communicable disease by an "insured";

7. Sexual Molestation, Corporal Punishment Or Physical Or Mental Abuse

"Bodily injury" or "property damage" arising out of sexual molestation, corporal punishment or physical or mental abuse; or

8. Controlled Substance

"Bodily injury" or "property damage" arising out of the use, sale, manufacture, delivery, transfer or possession by any person of a Controlled Substance as defined by the Federal Food and Drug Law at 21 U.S.C.A. Sections 811 and 812. Controlled Substances include but are not limited to cocaine, LSD, marijuana and all narcotic drugs. However, this exclusion does not apply to the legitimate use of prescription drugs by a person following the orders of a licensed physician.

Exclusions **A.** "Motor Vehicle Liability", **B.** "Watercraft Liability", **C.** "Aircraft Liability", **D.** "Hovercraft Liability" and **E.4.** "Insured's" Premises Not An "Insured Location" do not apply to "bodily injury" to a "residence employee" arising out of and in the course of the "residence employee's" employment by an "insured".

F. Coverage E – Personal Liability

Coverage **E** does not apply to:

1. Liability:

a. For any loss assessment charged against you as a member of an association, corporation or community of property owners, except as provided in **D.** Loss Assessment under Section II – Additional Coverages;

b. Under any contract or agreement entered into by an "insured". However, this exclusion does not apply to written contracts:

(1) That directly relate to the ownership, maintenance or use of an "insured location"; or

(2) Where the liability of others is assumed by you prior to an "occurrence";

unless excluded in **a.** above or elsewhere in this policy;

2. "Property damage" to property owned by an "insured". This includes costs or expenses incurred by an "insured" or others to repair, replace, enhance, restore or maintain such property to prevent injury to a person or damage to property of others, whether on or away from an "insured location";

3. "Property damage" to property rented to, occupied or used by or in the care of an "insured". This exclusion does not apply to "property damage" caused by fire, smoke or explosion;

4. "Bodily injury" to any person eligible to receive any benefits voluntarily provided or required to be provided by an "insured" under any:

a. Workers' compensation law;

 HO 00 03 10 00

b. Non-occupational disability law; or

c. Occupational disease law;

5. "Bodily injury" or "property damage" for which an "insured" under this policy:

a. Is also an insured under a nuclear energy liability policy issued by the:

(1) Nuclear Energy Liability Insurance Association;

(2) Mutual Atomic Energy Liability Underwriters;

(3) Nuclear Insurance Association of Canada;

or any of their successors; or

b. Would be an insured under such a policy but for the exhaustion of its limit of liability; or

6. "Bodily injury" to you or an "insured" as defined under Definitions **5.a.** or **b.**

This exclusion also applies to any claim made or suit brought against you or an "insured":

a. To repay; or

b. Share damages with;

another person who may be obligated to pay damages because of "bodily injury" to an "insured".

G. Coverage F – Medical Payments To Others

Coverage **F** does not apply to "bodily injury":

1. To a "residence employee" if the "bodily injury":

a. Occurs off the "insured location"; and

b. Does not arise out of or in the course of the "residence employee's" employment by an "insured";

2. To any person eligible to receive benefits voluntarily provided or required to be provided under any:

a. Workers' compensation law;

b. Non-occupational disability law; or

c. Occupational disease law;

3. From any:

a. Nuclear reaction;

b. Nuclear radiation; or

c. Radioactive contamination;

all whether controlled or uncontrolled or however caused; or

d. Any consequence of any of these; or

4. To any person, other than a "residence employee" of an "insured", regularly residing on any part of the "insured location".

SECTION II – ADDITIONAL COVERAGES

We cover the following in addition to the limits of liability:

A. Claim Expenses

We pay:

1. Expenses we incur and costs taxed against an "insured" in any suit we defend;

2. Premiums on bonds required in a suit we defend, but not for bond amounts more than the Coverage **E** limit of liability. We need not apply for or furnish any bond;

3. Reasonable expenses incurred by an "insured" at our request, including actual loss of earnings (but not loss of other income) up to $250 per day, for assisting us in the investigation or defense of a claim or suit; and

4. Interest on the entire judgment which accrues after entry of the judgment and before we pay or tender, or deposit in court that part of the judgment which does not exceed the limit of liability that applies.

B. First Aid Expenses

We will pay expenses for first aid to others incurred by an "insured" for "bodily injury" covered under this policy. We will not pay for first aid to an "insured".

C. Damage To Property Of Others

1. We will pay, at replacement cost, up to $1,000 per "occurrence" for "property damage" to property of others caused by an "insured".

2. We will not pay for "property damage":

a. To the extent of any amount recoverable under Section **I**;

b. Caused intentionally by an "insured" who is 13 years of age or older;

c. To property owned by an "insured";

d. To property owned by or rented to a tenant of an "insured" or a resident in your household; or

e. Arising out of:

(1) A "business" engaged in by an "insured";

(2) Any act or omission in connection with a premises owned, rented or controlled by an "insured", other than the "insured location"; or

(3) The ownership, maintenance, occupancy, operation, use, loading or unloading of aircraft, hovercraft, watercraft or "motor vehicles".

This exclusion **e.(3)** does not apply to a "motor vehicle" that:

- **(a)** Is designed for recreational use off public roads;

- **(b)** Is not owned by an "insured"; and

- **(c)** At the time of the "occurrence", is not required by law, or regulation issued by a government agency, to have been registered for it to be used on public roads or property.

D. Loss Assessment

1. We will pay up to $1,000 for your share of loss assessment charged against you, as owner or tenant of the "residence premises", during the policy period by a corporation or association of property owners, when the assessment is made as a result of:

    a. "Bodily injury" or "property damage" not excluded from coverage under Section II – Exclusions; or

    b. Liability for an act of a director, officer or trustee in the capacity as a director, officer or trustee, provided such person:

       (1) Is elected by the members of a corporation or association of property owners; and

       (2) Serves without deriving any income from the exercise of duties which are solely on behalf of a corporation or association of property owners.

2. Paragraph **I.** Policy Period under Section II – Conditions does not apply to this Loss Assessment Coverage.

3. Regardless of the number of assessments, the limit of $1,000 is the most we will pay for loss arising out of:

    a. One accident, including continuous or repeated exposure to substantially the same general harmful condition; or

    b. A covered act of a director, officer or trustee. An act involving more than one director, officer or trustee is considered to be a single act.

4. We do not cover assessments charged against you or a corporation or association of property owners by any governmental body.

SECTION II – CONDITIONS

A. Limit Of Liability

Our total liability under Coverage **E** for all damages resulting from any one "occurrence" will not be more than the Coverage **E** limit of liability shown in the Declarations. This limit is the same regardless of the number of "insureds", claims made or persons injured. All "bodily injury" and "property damage" resulting from any one accident or from continuous or repeated exposure to substantially the same general harmful conditions shall be considered to be the result of one "occurrence".

Our total liability under Coverage **F** for all medical expense payable for "bodily injury" to one person as the result of one accident will not be more than the Coverage **F** limit of liability shown in the Declarations.

B. Severability Of Insurance

This insurance applies separately to each "insured". This condition will not increase our limit of liability for any one "occurrence".

C. Duties After "Occurrence"

In case of an "occurrence", you or another "insured" will perform the following duties that apply. We have no duty to provide coverage under this policy if your failure to comply with the following duties is prejudicial to us. You will help us by seeing that these duties are performed:

1. Give written notice to us or our agent as soon as is practical, which sets forth:

    a. The identity of the policy and the "named insured" shown in the Declarations;

    b. Reasonably available information on the time, place and circumstances of the "occurrence"; and

    c. Names and addresses of any claimants and witnesses;

2. Cooperate with us in the investigation, settlement or defense of any claim or suit;

3. Promptly forward to us every notice, demand, summons or other process relating to the "occurrence";

4. At our request, help us:

    a. To make settlement;

    b. To enforce any right of contribution or indemnity against any person or organization who may be liable to an "insured";

 HO 00 03 10 00

c. With the conduct of suits and attend hearings and trials; and

d. To secure and give evidence and obtain the attendance of witnesses;

5. With respect to **C.** Damage To Property Of Others under Section **II** – Additional Coverages, submit to us within 60 days after the loss, a sworn statement of loss and show the damaged property, if in an "insured's" control;

6. No "insured" shall, except at such "insured's" own cost, voluntarily make payment, assume obligation or incur expense other than for first aid to others at the time of the "bodily injury".

D. Duties Of An Injured Person – Coverage F – Medical Payments To Others

1. The injured person or someone acting for the injured person will:

a. Give us written proof of claim, under oath if required, as soon as is practical; and

b. Authorize us to obtain copies of medical reports and records.

2. The injured person will submit to a physical exam by a doctor of our choice when and as often as we reasonably require.

E. Payment Of Claim – Coverage F – Medical Payments To Others

Payment under this coverage is not an admission of liability by an "insured" or us.

F. Suit Against Us

1. No action can be brought against us unless there has been full compliance with all of the terms under this Section **II.**

2. No one will have the right to join us as a party to any action against an "insured".

3. Also, no action with respect to Coverage **E** can be brought against us until the obligation of such "insured" has been determined by final judgment or agreement signed by us.

G. Bankruptcy Of An "Insured"

Bankruptcy or insolvency of an "insured" will not relieve us of our obligations under this policy.

H. Other Insurance

This insurance is excess over other valid and collectible insurance except insurance written specifically to cover as excess over the limits of liability that apply in this policy.

I. Policy Period

This policy applies only to "bodily injury" or "property damage" which occurs during the policy period.

J. Concealment Or Fraud

We do not provide coverage to an "insured" who, whether before or after a loss, has:

1. Intentionally concealed or misrepresented any material fact or circumstance;

2. Engaged in fraudulent conduct; or

3. Made false statements;

relating to this insurance.

SECTIONS I AND II – CONDITIONS

A. Liberalization Clause

If we make a change which broadens coverage under this edition of our policy without additional premium charge, that change will automatically apply to your insurance as of the date we implement the change in your state, provided that this implementation date falls within 60 days prior to or during the policy period stated in the Declarations.

This Liberalization Clause does not apply to changes implemented with a general program revision that includes both broadenings and restrictions in coverage, whether that general program revision is implemented through introduction of:

1. A subsequent edition of this policy; or

2. An amendatory endorsement.

B. Waiver Or Change Of Policy Provisions

A waiver or change of a provision of this policy must be in writing by us to be valid. Our request for an appraisal or examination will not waive any of our rights.

C. Cancellation

1. You may cancel this policy at any time by returning it to us or by letting us know in writing of the date cancellation is to take effect.

2. We may cancel this policy only for the reasons stated below by letting you know in writing of the date cancellation takes effect. This cancellation notice may be delivered to you, or mailed to you at your mailing address shown in the Declarations. Proof of mailing will be sufficient proof of notice.

a. When you have not paid the premium, we may cancel at any time by letting you know at least 10 days before the date cancellation takes effect.

b. When this policy has been in effect for less than 60 days and is not a renewal with us, we may cancel for any reason by letting you know at least 10 days before the date cancellation takes effect.

HO 00 03 10 00   Copyright, Insurance Services Office, Inc., 1999   **Page 21 of 22**

c. When this policy has been in effect for 60 days or more, or at any time if it is a renewal with us, we may cancel:

(1) If there has been a material misrepresentation of fact which if known to us would have caused us not to issue the policy; or

(2) If the risk has changed substantially since the policy was issued.

This can be done by letting you know at least 30 days before the date cancellation takes effect.

d. When this policy is written for a period of more than one year, we may cancel for any reason at anniversary by letting you know at least 30 days before the date cancellation takes effect.

3. When this policy is canceled, the premium for the period from the date of cancellation to the expiration date will be refunded pro rata.

4. If the return premium is not refunded with the notice of cancellation or when this policy is returned to us, we will refund it within a reasonable time after the date cancellation takes effect.

D. Nonrenewal

We may elect not to renew this policy. We may do so by delivering to you, or mailing to you at your mailing address shown in the Declarations, written notice at least 30 days before the expiration date of this policy. Proof of mailing will be sufficient proof of notice.

E. Assignment

Assignment of this policy will not be valid unless we give our written consent.

F. Subrogation

An "insured" may waive in writing before a loss all rights of recovery against any person. If not waived, we may require an assignment of rights of recovery for a loss to the extent that payment is made by us.

If an assignment is sought, an "insured" must sign and deliver all related papers and cooperate with us.

Subrogation does not apply to Coverage **F** or Paragraph **C.** Damage To Property Of Others under Section **II** – Additional Coverages.

G. Death

If any person named in the Declarations or the spouse, if a resident of the same household, dies, the following apply:

1. We insure the legal representative of the deceased but only with respect to the premises and property of the deceased covered under the policy at the time of death; and

2. "Insured" includes:

a. An "insured" who is a member of your household at the time of your death, but only while a resident of the "residence premises"; and

b. With respect to your property, the person having proper temporary custody of the property until appointment and qualification of a legal representative.

       HO 00 03 10 00

HOMEOWNERS 4 – CONTENTS BROAD FORM

AGREEMENT

We will provide the insurance described in this policy in return for the premium and compliance with all applicable provisions of this policy.

DEFINITIONS

A. In this policy, "you" and "your" refer to the "named insured" shown in the Declarations and the spouse if a resident of the same household. "We", "us" and "our" refer to the Company providing this insurance.

B. In addition, certain words and phrases are defined as follows:

1. "Aircraft Liability", "Hovercraft Liability", "Motor Vehicle Liability" and "Watercraft Liability", subject to the provisions in **b.** below, mean the following:

   a. Liability for "bodily injury" or "property damage" arising out of the:

   (1) Ownership of such vehicle or craft by an "insured";

   (2) Maintenance, occupancy, operation, use, loading or unloading of such vehicle or craft by any person;

   (3) Entrustment of such vehicle or craft by an "insured" to any person;

   (4) Failure to supervise or negligent supervision of any person involving such vehicle or craft by an "insured"; or

   (5) Vicarious liability, whether or not imposed by law, for the actions of a child or minor involving such vehicle or craft.

   b. For the purpose of this definition:

   (1) Aircraft means any contrivance used or designed for flight except model or hobby aircraft not used or designed to carry people or cargo;

   (2) Hovercraft means a self-propelled motorized ground effect vehicle and includes, but is not limited to, flarecraft and air cushion vehicles;

   (3) Watercraft means a craft principally designed to be propelled on or in water by wind, engine power or electric motor; and

   (4) Motor vehicle means a "motor vehicle" as defined in **7.** below.

2. "Bodily injury" means bodily harm, sickness or disease, including required care, loss of services and death that results.

3. "Business" means:

   a. A trade, profession or occupation engaged in on a full-time, part-time or occasional basis; or

   b. Any other activity engaged in for money or other compensation, except the following:

   (1) One or more activities, not described in **(2)** through **(4)** below, for which no "insured" receives more than $2,000 in total compensation for the 12 months before the beginning of the policy period;

   (2) Volunteer activities for which no money is received other than payment for expenses incurred to perform the activity;

   (3) Providing home day care services for which no compensation is received, other than the mutual exchange of such services; or

   (4) The rendering of home day care services to a relative of an "insured".

4. "Employee" means an employee of an "insured", or an employee leased to an "insured" by a labor leasing firm under an agreement between an "insured" and the labor leasing firm, whose duties are other than those performed by a "residence employee".

5. "Insured" means:

   a. You and residents of your household who are:

   (1) Your relatives; or

   (2) Other persons under the age of 21 and in the care of any person named above;

   b. A student enrolled in school full time, as defined by the school, who was a resident of your household before moving out to attend school, provided the student is under the age of:

   (1) 24 and your relative; or

   (2) 21 and in your care or the care of a person described in **a.(1)** above; or

c. Under Section **II:**

(1) With respect to animals or watercraft to which this policy applies, any person or organization legally responsible for these animals or watercraft which are owned by you or any person included in **a.** or **b.** above. "Insured" does not mean a person or organization using or having custody of these animals or watercraft in the course of any "business" or without consent of the owner; or

(2) With respect to a "motor vehicle" to which this policy applies:

(a) Persons while engaged in your employ or that of any person included in **a.** or **b.** above; or

(b) Other persons using the vehicle on an "insured location" with your consent.

Under both Sections **I** and **II,** when the word an immediately precedes the word "insured", the words an "insured" together mean one or more "insureds".

6. "Insured location" means:

a. The "residence premises";

b. The part of other premises, other structures and grounds used by you as a residence; and

(1) Which is shown in the Declarations; or

(2) Which is acquired by you during the policy period for your use as a residence;

c. Any premises used by you in connection with a premises described in **a.** and **b.** above;

d. Any part of a premises:

(1) Not owned by an "insured"; and

(2) Where an "insured" is temporarily residing;

e. Vacant land, other than farm land, owned by or rented to an "insured";

f. Land owned by or rented to an "insured" on which a one, two, three or four family dwelling is being built as a residence for an "insured";

g. Individual or family cemetery plots or burial vaults of an "insured"; or

h. Any part of a premises occasionally rented to an "insured" for other than "business" use.

7. "Motor vehicle" means:

a. A self-propelled land or amphibious vehicle; or

b. Any trailer or semitrailer which is being carried on, towed by or hitched for towing by a vehicle described in **a.** above.

8. "Occurrence" means an accident, including continuous or repeated exposure to substantially the same general harmful conditions, which results, during the policy period, in:

a. "Bodily injury"; or

b. "Property damage".

9. "Property damage" means physical injury to, destruction of, or loss of use of tangible property.

10. "Residence employee" means:

a. An employee of an "insured", or an employee leased to an "insured" by a labor leasing firm, under an agreement between an "insured" and the labor leasing firm, whose duties are related to the maintenance or use of the "residence premises", including household or domestic services; or

b. One who performs similar duties elsewhere not related to the "business" of an "insured".

A "residence employee" does not include a temporary employee who is furnished to an "insured" to substitute for a permanent "residence employee" on leave or to meet seasonal or short-term workload conditions.

11. "Residence premises" means:

a. The one family dwelling where you reside;

b. The two, three or four family dwelling where you reside in at least one of the family units; or

c. That part of any other building where you reside;

and which is shown as the "residence premises" in the Declarations.

"Residence premises" also includes other structures and grounds at that location.

DEDUCTIBLE

Unless otherwise noted in this policy, the following deductible provision applies:

Subject to the policy limits that apply, we will pay only that part of the total of all loss payable under Section **I** that exceeds the deductible amount shown in the Declarations.

 HO 00 04 10 00

SECTION I – PROPERTY COVERAGES

A. Coverage C – Personal Property

1. Covered Property

We cover personal property owned or used by an "insured" while it is anywhere in the world. After a loss and at your request, we will cover personal property owned by:

a. Others while the property is on the part of the "residence premises" occupied by an "insured"; or

b. A guest or a "residence employee", while the property is in any residence occupied by an "insured".

2. Limit For Property At Other Residences

Our limit of liability for personal property usually located at an "insured's" residence, other than the "residence premises", is 10% of the limit of liability for Coverage **C**, or $1,000, whichever is greater. However, this limitation does not apply to personal property:

a. Moved from the "residence premises" because it is being repaired, renovated or rebuilt and is not fit to live in or store property in; or

b. In a newly acquired principal residence for 30 days from the time you begin to move the property there.

3. Special Limits Of Liability

The special limit for each category shown below is the total limit for each loss for all property in that category. These special limits do not increase the Coverage **C** limit of liability.

a. $200 on money, bank notes, bullion, gold other than goldware, silver other than silverware, platinum other than platinumware, coins, medals, scrip, stored value cards and smart cards.

b. $1,500 on securities, accounts, deeds, evidences of debt, letters of credit, notes other than bank notes, manuscripts, personal records, passports, tickets and stamps. This dollar limit applies to these categories regardless of the medium (such as paper or computer software) on which the material exists.

This limit includes the cost to research, replace or restore the information from the lost or damaged material.

c. $1,500 on watercraft of all types, including their trailers, furnishings, equipment and outboard engines or motors.

d. $1,500 on trailers or semitrailers not used with watercraft of all types.

e. $1,500 for loss by theft of jewelry, watches, furs, precious and semiprecious stones.

f. $2,500 for loss by theft of firearms and related equipment.

g. $2,500 for loss by theft of silverware, silver-plated ware, goldware, gold-plated ware, platinumware, platinum-plated ware and pewterware. This includes flatware, hollowware, tea sets, trays and trophies made of or including silver, gold or pewter.

h. $2,500 on property, on the "residence premises", used primarily for "business" purposes.

i. $500 on property, away from the "residence premises", used primarily for "business" purposes. However, this limit does not apply to loss to electronic apparatus and other property described in Categories **j.** and **k.** below.

j. $1,500 on electronic apparatus and accessories, while in or upon a "motor vehicle", but only if the apparatus is equipped to be operated by power from the "motor vehicle's" electrical system while still capable of being operated by other power sources.

Accessories include antennas, tapes, wires, records, discs or other media that can be used with any apparatus described in this Category **j.**

k. $1,500 on electronic apparatus and accessories used primarily for "business" while away from the "residence premises" and not in or upon a "motor vehicle". The apparatus must be equipped to be operated by power from the "motor vehicle's" electrical system while still capable of being operated by other power sources.

Accessories include antennas, tapes, wires, records, discs or other media that can be used with any apparatus described in this Category **k.**

4. Property Not Covered

We do not cover:

a. Articles separately described and specifically insured, regardless of the limit for which they are insured, in this or other insurance;

b. Animals, birds or fish;

c. "Motor vehicles".

(1) This includes:

(a) Their accessories, equipment and parts; or

(b) Electronic apparatus and accessories designed to be operated solely by power from the electrical system of the "motor vehicle". Accessories include antennas, tapes, wires, records, discs or other media that can be used with any apparatus described above.

The exclusion of property described in **(a)** and **(b)** above applies only while such property is in or upon the "motor vehicle".

(2) We do cover "motor vehicles" not required to be registered for use on public roads or property which are:

(a) Used solely to service an "insured's" residence; or

(b) Designed to assist the handicapped;

d. Aircraft meaning any contrivance used or designed for flight including any parts whether or not attached to the aircraft.

We do cover model or hobby aircraft not used or designed to carry people or cargo;

e. Hovercraft and parts. Hovercraft means a self-propelled motorized ground effect vehicle and includes, but is not limited to, flarecraft and air cushion vehicles;

f. Property of roomers, boarders and other tenants, except property of roomers and boarders related to an "insured";

g. Property in an apartment regularly rented or held for rental to others by an "insured";

h. Property rented or held for rental to others off the "residence premises";

i. "Business" data, including such data stored in:

(1) Books of account, drawings or other paper records; or

(2) Computers and related equipment.

We do cover the cost of blank recording or storage media, and of prerecorded computer programs available on the retail market;

j. Credit cards, electronic fund transfer cards or access devices used solely for deposit, withdrawal or transfer of funds except as provided in **C.6.** Credit Card, Electronic Fund Transfer Card Or Access Device, Forgery And Counterfeit Money under Section **I** – Property Coverages; or

k. Water or steam.

B. Coverage D – Loss Of Use

The limit of liability for Coverage **D** is the total limit for the coverages in **1.** Additional Living Expense, **2.** Fair Rental Value and **3.** Civil Authority Prohibits Use below.

1. Additional Living Expense

If a loss by a Peril Insured Against under this policy to covered property or the building containing the property makes the "residence premises" not fit to live in, we cover any necessary increase in living expenses incurred by you so that your household can maintain its normal standard of living.

Payment will be for the shortest time required to repair or replace the damage or, if you permanently relocate, the shortest time required for your household to settle elsewhere.

2. Fair Rental Value

If a loss covered under Section **I** makes that part of the "residence premises" rented to others or held for rental by you not fit to live in, we cover the fair rental value of such premises less any expenses that do not continue while it is not fit to live in.

Payment will be for the shortest time required to repair or replace such premises.

3. Civil Authority Prohibits Use

If a civil authority prohibits you from use of the "residence premises" as a result of direct damage to neighboring premises by a Peril Insured Against, we cover the loss as provided in **1.** Additional Living Expense and **2.** Fair Rental Value above for no more than two weeks.

4. Loss Or Expense Not Covered

We do not cover loss or expense due to cancellation of a lease or agreement.

The periods of time under **1.** Additional Living Expense, **2.** Fair Rental Value and **3.** Civil Authority Prohibits Use above are not limited by expiration of this policy.

C. Additional Coverages

1. Debris Removal

a. We will pay your reasonable expense for the removal of:

(1) Debris of covered property if a Peril Insured Against that applies to the damaged property causes the loss; or

(2) Ash, dust or particles from a volcanic eruption that has caused direct loss to a building or property contained in a building.

Copyright, Insurance Services Office, Inc., 1999   HO 00 04 10 00

This expense is included in the limit of liability that applies to the damaged property. If the amount to be paid for the actual damage to the property plus the debris removal expense is more than the limit of liability for the damaged property, an additional 5% of that limit is available for such expense.

b. We will also pay your reasonable expense, up to $1,000, for the removal from the "residence premises" of:

(1) Your tree(s) felled by the peril of Windstorm or Hail or Weight of Ice, Snow or Sleet; or

(2) A neighbor's tree(s) felled by a Peril Insured Against under Coverage **C;**

provided the tree(s):

(3) Damage(s) a covered structure; or

(4) Does not damage a covered structure, but:

(a) Block(s) a driveway on the "residence premises" which prevent(s) a "motor vehicle", that is registered for use on public roads or property, from entering or leaving the "residence premises"; or

(b) Block(s) a ramp or other fixture designed to assist a handicapped person to enter or leave the dwelling building.

The $1,000 limit is the most we will pay in any one loss regardless of the number of fallen trees. No more than $500 of this limit will be paid for the removal of any one tree.

This coverage is additional insurance.

2. Reasonable Repairs

a. We will pay the reasonable cost incurred by you for the necessary measures taken solely to protect covered property that is damaged by a Peril Insured Against from further damage.

b. If the measures taken involve repair to other damaged property, we will only pay if that property is covered under this policy and the damage is caused by a Peril Insured Against. This coverage does not:

(1) Increase the limit of liability that applies to the covered property; or

(2) Relieve you of your duties, in case of a loss to covered property, described in **B.4.** under Section **I** – Conditions.

3. Trees, Shrubs And Other Plants

We cover trees, shrubs, plants or lawns, on the "residence premises", for loss caused by the following Perils Insured Against:

a. Fire or Lightning;

b. Explosion;

c. Riot or Civil Commotion;

d. Aircraft;

e. Vehicles not owned or operated by a resident of the "residence premises";

f. Vandalism or Malicious Mischief; or

g. Theft.

We will pay up to 10% of the limit of liability that applies to Coverage **C** for all trees, shrubs, plants or lawns. No more than $500 of this limit will be paid for any one tree, shrub or plant. We do not cover property grown for "business" purposes.

This coverage is additional insurance.

4. Fire Department Service Charge

We will pay up to $500 for your liability assumed by contract or agreement for fire department charges incurred when the fire department is called to save or protect covered property from a Peril Insured Against. We do not cover fire department service charges if the property is located within the limits of the city, municipality or protection district furnishing the fire department response.

This coverage is additional insurance. No deductible applies to this coverage.

5. Property Removed

We insure covered property against direct loss from any cause while being removed from a premises endangered by a Peril Insured Against and for no more than 30 days while removed.

This coverage does not change the limit of liability that applies to the property being removed.

6. Credit Card, Electronic Fund Transfer Card Or Access Device, Forgery And Counterfeit Money

a. We will pay up to $500 for:

(1) The legal obligation of an "insured" to pay because of the theft or unauthorized use of credit cards issued to or registered in an "insured's" name;

(2) Loss resulting from theft or unauthorized use of an electronic fund transfer card or access device used for deposit, withdrawal or transfer of funds, issued to or registered in an "insured's" name;

(3) Loss to an "insured" caused by forgery or alteration of any check or negotiable instrument; and

(4) Loss to an "insured" through acceptance in good faith of counterfeit United States or Canadian paper currency.

All loss resulting from a series of acts committed by any one person or in which any one person is concerned or implicated is considered to be one loss.

This coverage is additional insurance. No deductible applies to this coverage.

b. We do not cover:

(1) Use of a credit card, electronic fund transfer card or access device:

(a) By a resident of your household;

(b) By a person who has been entrusted with either type of card or access device; or

(c) If an "insured" has not complied with all terms and conditions under which the cards are issued or the devices accessed; or

(2) Loss arising out of "business" use or dishonesty of an "insured".

c. If the coverage in **a.** above applies, the following defense provisions also apply:

(1) We may investigate and settle any claim or suit that we decide is appropriate. Our duty to defend a claim or suit ends when the amount we pay for the loss equals our limit of liability.

(2) If a suit is brought against an "insured" for liability under **a.(1)** or **(2)** above, we will provide a defense at our expense by counsel of our choice.

(3) We have the option to defend at our expense an "insured" or an "insured's" bank against any suit for the enforcement of payment under **a.(3)** above.

7. Loss Assessment

a. We will pay up to $1,000 for your share of loss assessment charged during the policy period against you, as owner or tenant of the "residence premises", by a corporation or association of property owners. The assessment must be made as a result of direct loss to property, owned by all members collectively, of the type that would be covered by this policy if owned by you, caused by a Peril Insured Against under Coverage **C**, other than:

(1) Earthquake; or

(2) Land shock waves or tremors before, during or after a volcanic eruption.

The limit of $1,000 is the most we will pay with respect to any one loss, regardless of the number of assessments. We will only apply one deductible, per unit, to the total amount of any one loss to the property described above, regardless of the number of assessments.

b. We do not cover assessments charged against you or a corporation or association of property owners by any governmental body.

c. Paragraph **O.** Policy Period under Section I – Conditions does not apply to this coverage.

This coverage is additional insurance.

8. Collapse

a. With respect to this Additional Coverage:

(1) Collapse means an abrupt falling down or caving in of a building or any part of a building with the result that the building or part of the building cannot be occupied for its current intended purpose.

(2) A building or any part of a building that is in danger of falling down or caving in is not considered to be in a state of collapse.

(3) A part of a building that is standing is not considered to be in a state of collapse even if it has separated from another part of the building.

(4) A building or any part of a building that is standing is not considered to be in a state of collapse even if it shows evidence of cracking, bulging, sagging, bending, leaning, settling, shrinkage or expansion.

b. We insure for direct physical loss to covered property involving collapse of a building or any part of a building if the collapse was caused by one or more of the following:

(1) The Perils Insured Against;

(2) Decay that is hidden from view, unless the presence of such decay is known to an "insured" prior to collapse;

(3) Insect or vermin damage that is hidden from view, unless the presence of such damage is known to an "insured" prior to collapse;

(4) Weight of contents, equipment, animals or people;

HO 00 04 10 00

(5) Weight of rain which collects on a roof; or

(6) Use of defective material or methods in construction, remodeling or renovation if the collapse occurs during the course of the construction, remodeling or renovation.

c. Loss to an awning, fence, patio, deck, pavement, swimming pool, underground pipe, flue, drain, cesspool, septic tank, foundation, retaining wall, bulkhead, pier, wharf or dock is not included under **b.(2)** through **(6)** above, unless the loss is a direct result of the collapse of a building or any part of a building.

d. This coverage does not increase the limit of liability that applies to the damaged covered property.

9. Glass Or Safety Glazing Material

a. We cover:

(1) The breakage of glass or safety glazing material which is part of a building, storm door or storm window, and covered as Building Additions And Alterations;

(2) The breakage of glass or safety glazing material which is part of a building, storm door or storm window and covered as Building Additions And Alterations when caused directly by earth movement; and

(3) The direct physical loss to covered property caused solely by the pieces, fragments or splinters of broken glass or safety glazing material which is part of a building, storm door or storm window.

b. This coverage does not include loss:

(1) To covered property which results because the glass or safety glazing material has been broken, except as provided in **a.(3)** above; or

(2) On the "residence premises" if the dwelling has been vacant for more than 60 consecutive days immediately before the loss, except when the breakage results directly from earth movement as provided in **a.(2)** above. A dwelling being constructed is not considered vacant.

c. This coverage does not increase the limit of liability that applies to the damaged property.

10. Building Additions And Alterations

We cover under Coverage **C** the building improvements or installations, made or acquired at your expense, to that part of the "residence premises" used exclusively by you. The limit of liability for this coverage will not be more than 10% of the limit of liability that applies to Coverage **C**.

This coverage is additional insurance.

11. Ordinance Or Law

a. You may use up to 10% of the limit of liability that applies to Building Additions And Alterations for the increased costs you incur due to the enforcement of any ordinance or law which requires or regulates:

(1) The construction, demolition, remodeling, renovation or repair of that part of a covered building or other structure damaged by a Peril Insured Against;

(2) The demolition and reconstruction of the undamaged part of a covered building or other structure, when that building or other structure must be totally demolished because of damage by a Peril Insured Against to another part of that covered building or other structure; or

(3) The remodeling, removal or replacement of the portion of the undamaged part of a covered building or other structure necessary to complete the remodeling, repair or replacement of that part of the covered building or other structure damaged by a Peril Insured Against.

b. You may use all or part of this ordinance or law coverage to pay for the increased costs you incur to remove debris resulting from the construction, demolition, remodeling, renovation, repair or replacement of property as stated in **a.** above.

c. We do not cover:

(1) The loss in value to any covered building or other structure due to the requirements of any ordinance or law; or

(2) The costs to comply with any ordinance or law which requires any "insured" or others, to test for, monitor, clean up, remove, contain, treat, detoxify or neutralize, or in any way respond to, or assess the effects of, pollutants in or on any covered building or other structure.

Pollutants means any solid, liquid, gaseous or thermal irritant or contaminant, including smoke, vapor, soot, fumes, acids, alkalis, chemicals and waste. Waste includes materials to be recycled, reconditioned or reclaimed.

This coverage is additional insurance.

12. Grave Markers

We will pay up to $5,000 for grave markers, including mausoleums, on or away from the "residence premises" for loss caused by a Peril Insured Against.

This coverage does not increase the limits of liability that apply to the damaged covered property.

SECTION I – PERILS INSURED AGAINST

We insure for direct physical loss to the property described in Coverage **C** caused by any of the following perils unless the loss is excluded in Section **I** – Exclusions.

1. Fire Or Lightning

2. Windstorm Or Hail

This peril includes loss to watercraft of all types and their trailers, furnishings, equipment, and outboard engines or motors, only while inside a fully enclosed building.

This peril does not include loss to the property contained in a building caused by rain, snow, sleet, sand or dust unless the direct force of wind or hail damages the building causing an opening in a roof or wall and the rain, snow, sleet, sand or dust enters through this opening.

3. Explosion

4. Riot Or Civil Commotion

5. Aircraft

This peril includes self-propelled missiles and spacecraft.

6. Vehicles

7. Smoke

This peril means sudden and accidental damage from smoke, including the emission or puffback of smoke, soot, fumes or vapors from a boiler, furnace or related equipment.

This peril does not include loss caused by smoke from agricultural smudging or industrial operations.

8. Vandalism Or Malicious Mischief

This peril does not include loss to property on the "residence premises", and any ensuing loss caused by any intentional and wrongful act committed in the course of the vandalism or malicious mischief, if the dwelling has been vacant for more than 60 consecutive days immediately before the loss. A dwelling being constructed is not considered vacant.

9. Theft

a. This peril includes attempted theft and loss of property from a known place when it is likely that the property has been stolen.

b. This peril does not include loss caused by theft:

(1) Committed by an "insured";

(2) In or to a dwelling under construction, or of materials and supplies for use in the construction until the dwelling is finished and occupied;

(3) From that part of a "residence premises" rented by an "insured" to someone other than another "insured"; or

(4) That occurs off the "residence premises" of:

(a) Trailers, semitrailers and campers;

(b) Watercraft of all types, and their furnishings, equipment and outboard engines or motors; or

(c) Property while at any other residence owned by, rented to, or occupied by an "insured", except while an "insured" is temporarily living there. Property of an "insured" who is a student is covered while at the residence the student occupies to attend school as long as the student has been there at any time during the 60 days immediately before the loss.

10. Falling Objects

This peril does not include loss to the property contained in the building unless the roof or an outside wall of the building is first damaged by a falling object. Damage to the falling object itself is not included.

11. Weight Of Ice, Snow Or Sleet

This peril means weight of ice, snow or sleet which causes damage to the property contained in the building.

12. Accidental Discharge Or Overflow Of Water Or Steam

a. This peril means accidental discharge or overflow of water or steam from within a plumbing, heating, air conditioning or automatic fire protective sprinkler system or from within a household appliance.

b. This peril does not include loss:

(1) To the system or appliance from which the water or steam escaped;

(2) Caused by or resulting from freezing except as provided in Peril Insured Against **14.** Freezing;

(3) On the "residence premises" caused by accidental discharge or overflow which occurs away from the building where the "residence premises" is located; or

(4) Caused by mold, fungus or wet rot unless hidden within the walls or ceilings or beneath the floors or above the ceilings of a structure.

c. In this peril, a plumbing system or household appliance does not include a sump, sump pump or related equipment or a roof drain, gutter, downspout or similar fixtures or equipment.

d. Section I – Exclusion **3.** Water Damage, Paragraphs **a.** and **c.** that apply to surface water and water below the surface of the ground do not apply to loss by water covered under this peril.

13. Sudden And Accidental Tearing Apart, Cracking, Burning Or Bulging

This peril means sudden and accidental tearing apart, cracking, burning or bulging of a steam or hot water heating system, an air conditioning or automatic fire protective sprinkler system, or an appliance for heating water.

This peril does not include loss caused by or resulting from freezing except as provided in Peril Insured Against **14.** Freezing below.

14. Freezing

a. This peril means freezing of a plumbing, heating, air conditioning or automatic fire protective sprinkler system or of a household appliance but only if you have used reasonable care to:

(1) Maintain heat in the building; or

(2) Shut off the water supply and drain all systems and appliances of water.

However, if the building is protected by an automatic fire protective sprinkler system, you must use reasonable care to continue the water supply and maintain heat in the building for coverage to apply.

b. In this peril, a plumbing system or household appliance does not include a sump, sump pump or related equipment or a roof drain, gutter, downspout or similar fixtures or equipment.

15. Sudden And Accidental Damage From Artificially Generated Electrical Current

This peril does not include loss to tubes, transistors, electronic components or circuitry that are a part of appliances, fixtures, computers, home entertainment units or other types of electronic apparatus.

16. Volcanic Eruption

This peril does not include loss caused by earthquake, land shock waves or tremors.

SECTION I – EXCLUSIONS

We do not insure for loss caused directly or indirectly by any of the following. Such loss is excluded regardless of any other cause or event contributing concurrently or in any sequence to the loss. These exclusions apply whether or not the loss event results in widespread damage or affects a substantial area.

1. Ordinance Or Law

Ordinance Or Law means any ordinance or law:

a. Requiring or regulating the construction, demolition, remodeling, renovation or repair of property, including removal of any resulting debris. This Exclusion **1.a.** does not apply to the amount of coverage that may be provided for in **C.11.** Ordinance Or Law under Section I – Property Coverages;

b. The requirements of which result in a loss in value to property; or

c. Requiring any "insured" or others to test for, monitor, clean up, remove, contain, treat, detoxify or neutralize, or in any way respond to, or assess the effects of, pollutants.

Pollutants means any solid, liquid, gaseous or thermal irritant or contaminant, including smoke, vapor, soot, fumes, acids, alkalis, chemicals and waste. Waste includes materials to be recycled, reconditioned or reclaimed.

This Exclusion **1.** applies whether or not the property has been physically damaged.

2. Earth Movement

Earth Movement means:

a. Earthquake, including land shock waves or tremors before, during or after a volcanic eruption;

b. Landslide, mudslide or mudflow;

c. Subsidence or sinkhole; or

d. Any other earth movement including earth sinking, rising or shifting;

caused by or resulting from human or animal forces or any act of nature unless direct loss by fire or explosion ensues and then we will pay only for the ensuing loss.

This Exclusion **2.** does not apply to loss by theft.

3. Water Damage

Water Damage means:

a. Flood, surface water, waves, tidal water, overflow of a body of water, or spray from any of these, whether or not driven by wind;

b. Water or water-borne material which backs up through sewers or drains or which overflows or is discharged from a sump, sump pump or related equipment; or

c. Water or water-borne material below the surface of the ground, including water which exerts pressure on or seeps or leaks through a building, sidewalk, driveway, foundation, swimming pool or other structure;

caused by or resulting from human or animal forces or any act of nature.

Direct loss by fire, explosion or theft resulting from water damage is covered.

4. Power Failure

Power Failure means the failure of power or other utility service if the failure takes place off the "residence premises". But if the failure results in a loss, from a Peril Insured Against on the "residence premises", we will pay for the loss caused by that peril.

5. Neglect

Neglect means neglect of an "insured" to use all reasonable means to save and preserve property at and after the time of a loss.

6. War

War includes the following and any consequence of any of the following:

a. Undeclared war, civil war, insurrection, rebellion or revolution;

b. Warlike act by a military force or military personnel; or

c. Destruction, seizure or use for a military purpose.

Discharge of a nuclear weapon will be deemed a warlike act even if accidental.

7. Nuclear Hazard

This Exclusion **7.** pertains to Nuclear Hazard to the extent set forth in **L.** Nuclear Hazard Clause under Section I – Conditions.

8. Intentional Loss

Intentional Loss means any loss arising out of any act an "insured" commits or conspires to commit with the intent to cause a loss.

In the event of such loss, no "insured" is entitled to coverage, even "insureds" who did not commit or conspire to commit the act causing the loss.

9. Governmental Action

Governmental Action means the destruction, confiscation or seizure of property described in Coverage **C** by order of any governmental or public authority.

This exclusion does not apply to such acts ordered by any governmental or public authority that are taken at the time of a fire to prevent its spread, if the loss caused by fire would be covered under this policy.

SECTION I – CONDITIONS

A. Insurable Interest And Limit Of Liability

Even if more than one person has an insurable interest in the property covered, we will not be liable in any one loss:

1. To an "insured" for more than the amount of such "insured's" interest at the time of loss; or

2. For more than the applicable limit of liability.

B. Duties After Loss

In case of a loss to covered property, we have no duty to provide coverage under this policy if the failure to comply with the following duties is prejudicial to us. These duties must be performed either by you, an "insured" seeking coverage, or a representative of either:

1. Give prompt notice to us or our agent;

2. Notify the police in case of loss by theft;

3. Notify the credit card or electronic fund transfer card or access device company in case of loss as provided for in **C.6.** Credit Card, Electronic Fund Transfer Card Or Access Device, Forgery And Counterfeit Money under Section I – Property Coverages;

4. Protect the property from further damage. If repairs to the property are required, you must:

a. Make reasonable and necessary repairs to protect the property; and

b. Keep an accurate record of repair expenses;

5. Cooperate with us in the investigation of a claim;

Copyright, Insurance Services Office, Inc., 1999   HO 00 04 10 00

6. Prepare an inventory of damaged personal property showing the quantity, description, actual cash value and amount of loss. Attach all bills, receipts and related documents that justify the figures in the inventory;

7. As often as we reasonably require:

   a. Show the damaged property;

   b. Provide us with records and documents we request and permit us to make copies; and

   c. Submit to examination under oath, while not in the presence of another "insured", and sign the same;

8. Send to us, within 60 days after our request, your signed, sworn proof of loss which sets forth, to the best of your knowledge and belief:

   a. The time and cause of loss;

   b. The interests of all "insureds" and all others in the property involved and all liens on the property;

   c. Other insurance which may cover the loss;

   d. Changes in title or occupancy of the property during the term of the policy;

   e. Specifications of damaged buildings and detailed repair estimates;

   f. The inventory of damaged personal property described in **6.** above;

   g. Receipts for additional living expenses incurred and records that support the fair rental value loss; and

   h. Evidence or affidavit that supports a claim under **C.6.** Credit Card, Electronic Fund Transfer Card Or Access Device, Forgery And Counterfeit Money under Section I – Property Coverages, stating the amount and cause of loss.

C. Loss Settlement

Covered property losses are settled at actual cash value at the time of loss but not more than the amount required to repair or replace.

D. Loss To A Pair Or Set

In case of loss to a pair or set we may elect to:

1. Repair or replace any part to restore the pair or set to its value before the loss; or

2. Pay the difference between actual cash value of the property before and after the loss.

E. Appraisal

If you and we fail to agree on the amount of loss, either may demand an appraisal of the loss. In this event, each party will choose a competent and impartial appraiser within 20 days after receiving a written request from the other. The two appraisers will choose an umpire. If they cannot agree upon an umpire within 15 days, you or we may request that the choice be made by a judge of a court of record in the state where the "residence premises" is located. The appraisers will separately set the amount of loss. If the appraisers submit a written report of an agreement to us, the amount agreed upon will be the amount of loss. If they fail to agree, they will submit their differences to the umpire. A decision agreed to by any two will set the amount of loss.

Each party will:

1. Pay its own appraiser; and

2. Bear the other expenses of the appraisal and umpire equally.

F. Other Insurance And Service Agreement

If a loss covered by this policy is also covered by:

1. Other insurance, we will pay only the proportion of the loss that the limit of liability that applies under this policy bears to the total amount of insurance covering the loss; or

2. A service agreement, this insurance is excess over any amounts payable under any such agreement. Service agreement means a service plan, property restoration plan, home warranty or other similar service warranty agreement, even if it is characterized as insurance.

G. Suit Against Us

No action can be brought against us unless there has been full compliance with all of the terms under Section I of this policy and the action is started within two years after the date of loss.

H. Our Option

If we give you written notice within 30 days after we receive your signed, sworn proof of loss, we may repair or replace any part of the damaged property with material or property of like kind and quality.

I. Loss Payment

We will adjust all losses with you. We will pay you unless some other person is named in the policy or is legally entitled to receive payment. Loss will be payable 60 days after we receive your proof of loss and:

1. Reach an agreement with you;
2. There is an entry of a final judgment; or
3. There is a filing of an appraisal award with us.

J. Abandonment Of Property

We need not accept any property abandoned by an "insured".

K. No Benefit To Bailee

We will not recognize any assignment or grant any coverage that benefits a person or organization holding, storing or moving property for a fee regardless of any other provision of this policy.

L. Nuclear Hazard Clause

1. "Nuclear Hazard" means any nuclear reaction, radiation, or radioactive contamination, all whether controlled or uncontrolled or however caused, or any consequence of any of these.
2. Loss caused by the nuclear hazard will not be considered loss caused by fire, explosion, or smoke, whether these perils are specifically named in or otherwise included within the Perils Insured Against.
3. This policy does not apply under Section I to loss caused directly or indirectly by nuclear hazard, except that direct loss by fire resulting from the nuclear hazard is covered.

M. Recovered Property

If you or we recover any property for which we have made payment under this policy, you or we will notify the other of the recovery. At your option, the property will be returned to or retained by you or it will become our property. If the recovered property is returned to or retained by you, the loss payment will be adjusted based on the amount you received for the recovered property.

N. Volcanic Eruption Period

One or more volcanic eruptions that occur within a 72 hour period will be considered as one volcanic eruption.

O. Policy Period

This policy applies only to loss which occurs during the policy period.

P. Concealment Or Fraud

We provide coverage to no "insureds" under this policy if, whether before or after a loss, an "insured" has:

1. Intentionally concealed or misrepresented any material fact or circumstance;

2. Engaged in fraudulent conduct; or
3. Made false statements;

relating to this insurance.

Q. Loss Payable Clause

If the Declarations show a loss payee for certain listed insured personal property, the definition of "insured" is changed to include that loss payee with respect to that property.

If we decide to cancel or not renew this policy, that loss payee will be notified in writing.

SECTION II – LIABILITY COVERAGES

A. Coverage E – Personal Liability

If a claim is made or a suit is brought against an "insured" for damages because of "bodily injury" or "property damage" caused by an "occurrence" to which this coverage applies, we will:

1. Pay up to our limit of liability for the damages for which an "insured" is legally liable. Damages include prejudgment interest awarded against an "insured"; and
2. Provide a defense at our expense by counsel of our choice, even if the suit is groundless, false or fraudulent. We may investigate and settle any claim or suit that we decide is appropriate. Our duty to settle or defend ends when our limit of liability for the "occurrence" has been exhausted by payment of a judgment or settlement.

B. Coverage F – Medical Payments To Others

We will pay the necessary medical expenses that are incurred or medically ascertained within three years from the date of an accident causing "bodily injury". Medical expenses means reasonable charges for medical, surgical, x-ray, dental, ambulance, hospital, professional nursing, prosthetic devices and funeral services. This coverage does not apply to you or regular residents of your household except "residence employees". As to others, this coverage applies only:

1. To a person on the "insured location" with the permission of an "insured"; or
2. To a person off the "insured location", if the "bodily injury":
   a. Arises out of a condition on the "insured location" or the ways immediately adjoining;
   b. Is caused by the activities of an "insured";
   c. Is caused by a "residence employee" in the course of the "residence employee's" employment by an "insured"; or
   d. Is caused by an animal owned by or in the care of an "insured".

Page 12 of 19 Copyright, Insurance Services Office, Inc., 1999 HO 00 04 10 00

SECTION II – EXCLUSIONS

A. "Motor Vehicle Liability"

1. Coverages **E** and **F** do not apply to any "motor vehicle liability" if, at the time and place of an "occurrence", the involved "motor vehicle":

   a. Is registered for use on public roads or property;

   b. Is not registered for use on public roads or property, but such registration is required by a law, or regulation issued by a government agency, for it to be used at the place of the "occurrence"; or

   c. Is being:

      (1) Operated in, or practicing for, any prearranged or organized race, speed contest or other competition;

      (2) Rented to others;

      (3) Used to carry persons or cargo for a charge; or

      (4) Used for any "business" purpose except for a motorized golf cart while on a golfing facility.

2. If Exclusion **A.1.** does not apply, there is still no coverage for "motor vehicle liability" unless the "motor vehicle" is:

   a. In dead storage on an "insured location";

   b. Used solely to service an "insured's" residence;

   c. Designed to assist the handicapped and, at the time of an "occurrence", it is:

      (1) Being used to assist a handicapped person; or

      (2) Parked on an "insured location";

   d. Designed for recreational use off public roads and:

      (1) Not owned by an "insured"; or

      (2) Owned by an "insured" provided the "occurrence" takes place on an "insured location" as defined in Definitions **B. 6.a., b., d., e.** or **h.;** or

   e. A motorized golf cart that is owned by an "insured", designed to carry up to 4 persons, not built or modified after manufacture to exceed a speed of 25 miles per hour on level ground and, at the time of an "occurrence", is within the legal boundaries of:

      (1) A golfing facility and is parked or stored there, or being used by an "insured" to:

         (a) Play the game of golf or for other recreational or leisure activity allowed by the facility;

      (b) Travel to or from an area where "motor vehicles" or golf carts are parked or stored; or

      (c) Cross public roads at designated points to access other parts of the golfing facility; or

      (2) A private residential community, including its public roads upon which a motorized golf cart can legally travel, which is subject to the authority of a property owners association and contains an "insured's" residence.

B. "Watercraft Liability"

1. Coverages **E** and **F** do not apply to any "watercraft liability" if, at the time of an "occurrence", the involved watercraft is being:

   a. Operated in, or practicing for, any prearranged or organized race, speed contest or other competition. This exclusion does not apply to a sailing vessel or a predicted log cruise;

   b. Rented to others;

   c. Used to carry persons or cargo for a charge; or

   d. Used for any "business" purpose.

2. If Exclusion **B.1.** does not apply, there is still no coverage for "watercraft liability" unless, at the time of the "occurrence", the watercraft:

   a. Is stored;

   b. Is a sailing vessel, with or without auxiliary power, that is:

      (1) Less than 26 feet in overall length; or

      (2) 26 feet or more in overall length and not owned by or rented to an "insured"; or

   c. Is not a sailing vessel and is powered by:

      (1) An inboard or inboard-outdrive engine or motor, including those that power a water jet pump, of:

         (a) 50 horsepower or less and not owned by an "insured"; or

         (b) More than 50 horsepower and not owned by or rented to an "insured"; or

      (2) One or more outboard engines or motors with:

         (a) 25 total horsepower or less;

         (b) More than 25 horsepower if the outboard engine or motor is not owned by an "insured";

         (c) More than 25 horsepower if the outboard engine or motor is owned by an "insured" who acquired it during the policy period; or

---

HO 00 04 10 00   Copyright, Insurance Services Office, Inc., 1999   **Page 13 of 19**

(d) More than 25 horsepower if the outboard engine or motor is owned by an "insured" who acquired it before the policy period, but only if:

    (i) You declare them at policy inception; or

    (ii) Your intent to insure them is reported to us in writing within 45 days after you acquire them.

The coverages in **(c)** and **(d)** above apply for the policy period.

Horsepower means the maximum power rating assigned to the engine or motor by the manufacturer.

C. "Aircraft Liability"

This policy does not cover "aircraft liability".

D. "Hovercraft Liability"

This policy does not cover "hovercraft liability".

E. Coverage E – Personal Liability And Coverage F – Medical Payments To Others

Coverages **E** and **F** do not apply to the following:

1. Expected Or Intended Injury

"Bodily injury" or "property damage" which is expected or intended by an "insured" even if the resulting "bodily injury" or "property damage":

a. Is of a different kind, quality or degree than initially expected or intended; or

b. Is sustained by a different person, entity, real or personal property, than initially expected or intended.

However, this Exclusion **E.1.** does not apply to "bodily injury" resulting from the use of reasonable force by an "insured" to protect persons or property;

2. "Business"

a. "Bodily injury" or "property damage" arising out of or in connection with a "business" conducted from an "insured location" or engaged in by an "insured", whether or not the "business" is owned or operated by an "insured" or employs an "insured".

This Exclusion **E.2.** applies but is not limited to an act or omission, regardless of its nature or circumstance, involving a service or duty rendered, promised, owed, or implied to be provided because of the nature of the "business".

b. This Exclusion **E.2.** does not apply to:

(1) The rental or holding for rental of an "insured location";

(a) On an occasional basis if used only as a residence;

(b) In part for use only as a residence, unless a single family unit is intended for use by the occupying family to lodge more than two roomers or boarders; or

(c) In part, as an office, school, studio or private garage; and

(2) An "insured" under the age of 21 years involved in a part-time or occasional, self-employed "business" with no employees;

3. Professional Services

"Bodily injury" or "property damage" arising out of the rendering of or failure to render professional services;

4. "Insured's" Premises Not An "Insured Location"

"Bodily injury" or "property damage" arising out of a premises:

a. Owned by an "insured";

b. Rented to an "insured"; or

c. Rented to others by an "insured";

that is not an "insured location";

5. War

"Bodily injury" or "property damage" caused directly or indirectly by war, including the following and any consequence of any of the following:

a. Undeclared war, civil war, insurrection, rebellion or revolution;

b. Warlike act by a military force or military personnel; or

c. Destruction, seizure or use for a military purpose.

Discharge of a nuclear weapon will be deemed a warlike act even if accidental;

6. Communicable Disease

"Bodily injury" or "property damage" which arises out of the transmission of a communicable disease by an "insured";

7. Sexual Molestation, Corporal Punishment Or Physical Or Mental Abuse

"Bodily injury" or "property damage" arising out of sexual molestation, corporal punishment or physical or mental abuse; or

HO 00 04 10 00

8. Controlled Substance

"Bodily injury" or "property damage" arising out of the use, sale, manufacture, delivery, transfer or possession by any person of a Controlled Substance as defined by the Federal Food and Drug Law at 21 U.S.C.A. Sections 811 and 812. Controlled Substances include but are not limited to cocaine, LSD, marijuana and all narcotic drugs. However, this exclusion does not apply to the legitimate use of prescription drugs by a person following the orders of a licensed physician.

Exclusions **A.** "Motor Vehicle Liability", **B.** "Watercraft Liability", **C.** "Aircraft Liability", **D.** "Hovercraft Liability" and **E.4.** "Insured's" Premises Not An "Insured Location" do not apply to "bodily injury" to a "residence employee" arising out of and in the course of the "residence employee's" employment by an "insured".

F. Coverage E – Personal Liability

Coverage **E** does not apply to:

1. Liability:

    a. For any loss assessment charged against you as a member of an association, corporation or community of property owners, except as provided in **D.** Loss Assessment under Section **II** – Additional Coverages;

    b. Under any contract or agreement entered into by an "insured". However, this exclusion does not apply to written contracts:

        (1) That directly relate to the ownership, maintenance or use of an "insured location"; or

        (2) Where the liability of others is assumed by you prior to an "occurrence";

        unless excluded in **a.** above or elsewhere in this policy;

2. "Property damage" to property owned by an "insured". This includes costs or expenses incurred by an "insured" or others to repair, replace, enhance, restore or maintain such property to prevent injury to a person or damage to property of others, whether on or away from an "insured location";

3. "Property damage" to property rented to, occupied or used by or in the care of an "insured". This exclusion does not apply to "property damage" caused by fire, smoke or explosion;

4. "Bodily injury" to any person eligible to receive any benefits voluntarily provided or required to be provided by an "insured" under any:

    a. Workers' compensation law;

    b. Non-occupational disability law; or

    c. Occupational disease law;

5. "Bodily injury" or "property damage" for which an "insured" under this policy:

    a. Is also an insured under a nuclear energy liability policy issued by the:

        (1) Nuclear Energy Liability Insurance Association;

        (2) Mutual Atomic Energy Liability Underwriters;

        (3) Nuclear Insurance Association of Canada;

    or any of their successors; or

    b. Would be an insured under such a policy but for the exhaustion of its limit of liability; or

6. "Bodily injury" to you or an "insured" as defined under Definitions **5.a.** or **b.**

This exclusion also applies to any claim made or suit brought against you or an "insured":

    a. To repay; or

    b. Share damages with;

another person who may be obligated to pay damages because of "bodily injury" to an "insured".

G. Coverage F – Medical Payments To Others

Coverage **F** does not apply to "bodily injury":

1. To a "residence employee" if the "bodily injury":

    a. Occurs off the "insured location"; and

    b. Does not arise out of or in the course of the "residence employee's" employment by an "insured";

2. To any person eligible to receive benefits voluntarily provided or required to be provided under any:

    a. Workers' compensation law;

    b. Non-occupational disability law; or

    c. Occupational disease law;

3. From any:

    a. Nuclear reaction;

    b. Nuclear radiation; or

    c. Radioactive contamination;

all whether controlled or uncontrolled or however caused; or

    d. Any consequence of any of these; or

4. To any person, other than a "residence employee" of an "insured", regularly residing on any part of the "insured location".

SECTION II – ADDITIONAL COVERAGES

We cover the following in addition to the limits of liability:

A. Claim Expenses

We pay:

1. Expenses we incur and costs taxed against an "insured" in any suit we defend;

2. Premiums on bonds required in a suit we defend, but not for bond amounts more than the Coverage **E** limit of liability. We need not apply for or furnish any bond;

3. Reasonable expenses incurred by an "insured" at our request, including actual loss of earnings (but not loss of other income) up to $250 per day, for assisting us in the investigation or defense of a claim or suit; and

4. Interest on the entire judgment which accrues after entry of the judgment and before we pay or tender, or deposit in court that part of the judgment which does not exceed the limit of liability that applies.

B. First Aid Expenses

We will pay expenses for first aid to others incurred by an "insured" for "bodily injury" covered under this policy. We will not pay for first aid to an "insured".

C. Damage To Property Of Others

1. We will pay, at replacement cost, up to $1,000 per "occurrence" for "property damage" to property of others caused by an "insured".

2. We will not pay for "property damage":

   a. To the extent of any amount recoverable under Section **I**;

   b. Caused intentionally by an "insured" who is 13 years of age or older;

   c. To property owned by an "insured";

   d. To property owned by or rented to a tenant of an "insured" or a resident in your household; or

   e. Arising out of:

      (1) A "business" engaged in by an "insured";

      (2) Any act or omission in connection with a premises owned, rented or controlled by an "insured", other than the "insured location"; or

      (3) The ownership, maintenance, occupancy, operation, use, loading or unloading of aircraft, hovercraft, watercraft or "motor vehicles".

This exclusion **e.(3)** does not apply to a "motor vehicle" that:

(a) Is designed for recreational use off public roads;

(b) Is not owned by an "insured"; and

(c) At the time of the "occurrence", is not required by law, or regulation issued by a government agency, to have been registered for it to be used on public roads or property.

D. Loss Assessment

1. We will pay up to $1,000 for your share of loss assessment charged against you, as owner or tenant of the "residence premises", during the policy period by a corporation or association of property owners, when the assessment is made as a result of:

   a. "Bodily injury" or "property damage" not excluded from coverage under Section **II** – Exclusions; or

   b. Liability for an act of a director, officer or trustee in the capacity as a director, officer or trustee, provided such person:

      (1) Is elected by the members of a corporation or association of property owners; and

      (2) Serves without deriving any income from the exercise of duties which are solely on behalf of a corporation or association of property owners.

2. Paragraph **I.** Policy Period under Section **II** – Conditions does not apply to this Loss Assessment Coverage.

3. Regardless of the number of assessments, the limit of $1,000 is the most we will pay for loss arising out of:

   a. One accident, including continuous or repeated exposure to substantially the same general harmful condition; or

   b. A covered act of a director, officer or trustee. An act involving more than one director, officer or trustee is considered to be a single act.

4. We do not cover assessments charged against you or a corporation or association of property owners by any governmental body.

 HO 00 04 10 00

SECTION II – CONDITIONS

A. Limit Of Liability

Our total liability under Coverage **E** for all damages resulting from any one "occurrence" will not be more than the Coverage **E** limit of liability shown in the Declarations. This limit is the same regardless of the number of "insureds", claims made or persons injured. All "bodily injury" and "property damage" resulting from any one accident or from continuous or repeated exposure to substantially the same general harmful conditions shall be considered to be the result of one "occurrence".

Our total liability under Coverage **F** for all medical expense payable for "bodily injury" to one person as the result of one accident will not be more than the Coverage **F** limit of liability shown in the Declarations.

B. Severability Of Insurance

This insurance applies separately to each "insured". This condition will not increase our limit of liability for any one "occurrence".

C. Duties After "Occurrence"

In case of an "occurrence", you or another "insured" will perform the following duties that apply. We have no duty to provide coverage under this policy if your failure to comply with the following duties is prejudicial to us. You will help us by seeing that these duties are performed:

1. Give written notice to us or our agent as soon as is practical, which sets forth:

   a. The identity of the policy and the "named insured" shown in the Declarations;

   b. Reasonably available information on the time, place and circumstances of the "occurrence"; and

   c. Names and addresses of any claimants and witnesses;

2. Cooperate with us in the investigation, settlement or defense of any claim or suit;

3. Promptly forward to us every notice, demand, summons or other process relating to the "occurrence";

4. At our request, help us:

   a. To make settlement;

   b. To enforce any right of contribution or indemnity against any person or organization who may be liable to an "insured";

   c. With the conduct of suits and attend hearings and trials; and

   d. To secure and give evidence and obtain the attendance of witnesses;

5. With respect to **C.** Damage To Property Of Others under Section **II** – Additional Coverages, submit to us within 60 days after the loss, a sworn statement of loss and show the damaged property, if in an "insured's" control;

6. No "insured" shall, except at such "insured's" own cost, voluntarily make payment, assume obligation or incur expense other than for first aid to others at the time of the "bodily injury".

D. Duties Of An Injured Person – Coverage F – Medical Payments To Others

1. The injured person or someone acting for the injured person will:

   a. Give us written proof of claim, under oath if required, as soon as is practical; and

   b. Authorize us to obtain copies of medical reports and records.

2. The injured person will submit to a physical exam by a doctor of our choice when and as often as we reasonably require.

E. Payment Of Claim – Coverage F – Medical Payments To Others

Payment under this coverage is not an admission of liability by an "insured" or us.

F. Suit Against Us

1. No action can be brought against us unless there has been full compliance with all of the terms under this Section **II**.

2. No one will have the right to join us as a party to any action against an "insured".

3. Also, no action with respect to Coverage **E** can be brought against us until the obligation of such "insured" has been determined by final judgment or agreement signed by us.

G. Bankruptcy Of An "Insured"

Bankruptcy or insolvency of an "insured" will not relieve us of our obligations under this policy.

H. Other Insurance

This insurance is excess over other valid and collectible insurance except insurance written specifically to cover as excess over the limits of liability that apply in this policy.

I. Policy Period

This policy applies only to "bodily injury" or "property damage" which occurs during the policy period.

J. Concealment Or Fraud

We do not provide coverage to an "insured" who, whether before or after a loss, has:

1. Intentionally concealed or misrepresented any material fact or circumstance;

2. Engaged in fraudulent conduct; or

3. Made false statements;

relating to this insurance.

SECTIONS I AND II – CONDITIONS

A. Liberalization Clause

If we make a change which broadens coverage under this edition of our policy without additional premium charge, that change will automatically apply to your insurance as of the date we implement the change in your state, provided that this implementation date falls within 60 days prior to or during the policy period stated in the Declarations.

This Liberalization Clause does not apply to changes implemented with a general program revision that includes both broadenings and restrictions in coverage, whether that general program revision is implemented through introduction of:

1. A subsequent edition of this policy; or

2. An amendatory endorsement.

B. Waiver Or Change Of Policy Provisions

A waiver or change of a provision of this policy must be in writing by us to be valid. Our request for an appraisal or examination will not waive any of our rights.

C. Cancellation

1. You may cancel this policy at any time by returning it to us or by letting us know in writing of the date cancellation is to take effect.

2. We may cancel this policy only for the reasons stated below by letting you know in writing of the date cancellation takes effect. This cancellation notice may be delivered to you, or mailed to you at your mailing address shown in the Declarations. Proof of mailing will be sufficient proof of notice.

   a. When you have not paid the premium, we may cancel at any time by letting you know at least 10 days before the date cancellation takes effect.

   b. When this policy has been in effect for less than 60 days and is not a renewal with us, we may cancel for any reason by letting you know at least 10 days before the date cancellation takes effect.

c. When this policy has been in effect for 60 days or more, or at any time if it is a renewal with us, we may cancel:

   (1) If there has been a material misrepresentation of fact which if known to us would have caused us not to issue the policy; or

   (2) If the risk has changed substantially since the policy was issued.

   This can be done by letting you know at least 30 days before the date cancellation takes effect.

   d. When this policy is written for a period of more than one year, we may cancel for any reason at anniversary by letting you know at least 30 days before the date cancellation takes effect.

3. When this policy is canceled, the premium for the period from the date of cancellation to the expiration date will be refunded pro rata.

4. If the return premium is not refunded with the notice of cancellation or when this policy is returned to us, we will refund it within a reasonable time after the date cancellation takes effect.

D. Nonrenewal

We may elect not to renew this policy. We may do so by delivering to you, or mailing to you at your mailing address shown in the Declarations, written notice at least 30 days before the expiration date of this policy. Proof of mailing will be sufficient proof of notice.

E. Assignment

Assignment of this policy will not be valid unless we give our written consent.

F. Subrogation

An "insured" may waive in writing before a loss all rights of recovery against any person. If not waived, we may require an assignment of rights of recovery for a loss to the extent that payment is made by us.

If an assignment is sought, an "insured" must sign and deliver all related papers and cooperate with us.

Subrogation does not apply to Coverage **F** or Paragraph **C.** Damage To Property Of Others under Section **II** – Additional Coverages.

G. Death

If any person named in the Declarations or the spouse, if a resident of the same household, dies, the following apply:

1. We insure the legal representative of the deceased but only with respect to the premises and property of the deceased covered under the policy at the time of death; and

2. "Insured" includes:

   a. An "insured" who is a member of your household at the time of your death, but only while a resident of the "residence premises"; and

   b. With respect to your property, the person having proper temporary custody of the property until appointment and qualification of a legal representative.

HOMEOWNERS 5 – COMPREHENSIVE FORM

AGREEMENT

We will provide the insurance described in this policy in return for the premium and compliance with all applicable provisions of this policy.

DEFINITIONS

A. In this policy, "you" and "your" refer to the "named insured" shown in the Declarations and the spouse if a resident of the same household. "We", "us" and "our" refer to the Company providing this insurance.

B. In addition, certain words and phrases are defined as follows:

1. "Aircraft Liability", "Hovercraft Liability", "Motor Vehicle Liability" and "Watercraft Liability", subject to the provisions in **b.** below, mean the following:

   a. Liability for "bodily injury" or "property damage" arising out of the:

   (1) Ownership of such vehicle or craft by an "insured";

   (2) Maintenance, occupancy, operation, use, loading or unloading of such vehicle or craft by any person;

   (3) Entrustment of such vehicle or craft by an "insured" to any person;

   (4) Failure to supervise or negligent supervision of any person involving such vehicle or craft by an "insured"; or

   (5) Vicarious liability, whether or not imposed by law, for the actions of a child or minor involving such vehicle or craft.

   b. For the purpose of this definition:

   (1) Aircraft means any contrivance used or designed for flight except model or hobby aircraft not used or designed to carry people or cargo;

   (2) Hovercraft means a self-propelled motorized ground effect vehicle and includes, but is not limited to, flarecraft and air cushion vehicles;

   (3) Watercraft means a craft principally designed to be propelled on or in water by wind, engine power or electric motor; and

   (4) Motor vehicle means a "motor vehicle" as defined in **7.** below.

2. "Bodily injury" means bodily harm, sickness or disease, including required care, loss of services and death that results.

3. "Business" means:

   a. A trade, profession or occupation engaged in on a full-time, part-time or occasional basis; or

   b. Any other activity engaged in for money or other compensation, except the following:

   (1) One or more activities, not described in **(2)** through **(4)** below, for which no "insured" receives more than $2,000 in total compensation for the 12 months before the beginning of the policy period;

   (2) Volunteer activities for which no money is received other than payment for expenses incurred to perform the activity;

   (3) Providing home day care services for which no compensation is received, other than the mutual exchange of such services; or

   (4) The rendering of home day care services to a relative of an "insured".

4. "Employee" means an employee of an "insured", or an employee leased to an "insured" by a labor leasing firm under an agreement between an "insured" and the labor leasing firm, whose duties are other than those performed by a "residence employee".

5. "Insured" means:

   a. You and residents of your household who are:

   (1) Your relatives; or

   (2) Other persons under the age of 21 and in the care of any person named above;

   b. A student enrolled in school full time, as defined by the school, who was a resident of your household before moving out to attend school, provided the student is under the age of:

   (1) 24 and your relative; or

   (2) 21 and in your care or the care of a person described in **a.(1)** above; or

c. Under Section II:

(1) With respect to animals or watercraft to which this policy applies, any person or organization legally responsible for these animals or watercraft which are owned by you or any person included in **a.** or **b.** above. "Insured" does not mean a person or organization using or having custody of these animals or watercraft in the course of any "business" or without consent of the owner; or

(2) With respect to a "motor vehicle" to which this policy applies:

(a) Persons while engaged in your employ or that of any person included in **a.** or **b.** above; or

(b) Other persons using the vehicle on an "insured location" with your consent.

Under both Sections **I** and **II,** when the word an immediately precedes the word "insured", the words an "insured" together mean one or more "insureds".

6. "Insured location" means:

a. The "residence premises";

b. The part of other premises, other structures and grounds used by you as a residence; and

(1) Which is shown in the Declarations; or

(2) Which is acquired by you during the policy period for your use as a residence;

c. Any premises used by you in connection with a premises described in **a.** and **b.** above;

d. Any part of a premises:

(1) Not owned by an "insured"; and

(2) Where an "insured" is temporarily residing;

e. Vacant land, other than farm land, owned by or rented to an "insured";

f. Land owned by or rented to an "insured" on which a one, two, three or four family dwelling is being built as a residence for an "insured";

g. Individual or family cemetery plots or burial vaults of an "insured"; or

h. Any part of a premises occasionally rented to an "insured" for other than "business" use.

7. "Motor vehicle" means:

a. A self-propelled land or amphibious vehicle; or

b. Any trailer or semitrailer which is being carried on, towed by or hitched for towing by a vehicle described in **a.** above.

8. "Occurrence" means an accident, including continuous or repeated exposure to substantially the same general harmful conditions, which results, during the policy period, in:

a. "Bodily injury"; or

b. "Property damage".

9. "Property damage" means physical injury to, destruction of, or loss of use of tangible property.

10. "Residence employee" means:

a. An employee of an "insured", or an employee leased to an "insured" by a labor leasing firm, under an agreement between an "insured" and the labor leasing firm, whose duties are related to the maintenance or use of the "residence premises", including household or domestic services; or

b. One who performs similar duties elsewhere not related to the "business" of an "insured".

A "residence employee" does not include a temporary employee who is furnished to an "insured" to substitute for a permanent "residence employee" on leave or to meet seasonal or short-term workload conditions.

11. "Residence premises" means:

a. The one family dwelling where you reside;

b. The two, three or four family dwelling where you reside in at least one of the family units; or

c. That part of any other building where you reside;

and which is shown as the "residence premises" in the Declarations.

"Residence premises" also includes other structures and grounds at that location.

DEDUCTIBLE

Unless otherwise noted in this policy, the following deductible provision applies:

Subject to the policy limits that apply, we will pay only that part of the total of all loss payable under Section I that exceeds the deductible amount shown in the Declarations.

SECTION I – PROPERTY COVERAGES

A. Coverage A – Dwelling

1. We cover:

   a. The dwelling on the "residence premises" shown in the Declarations, including structures attached to the dwelling; and

   b. Materials and supplies located on or next to the "residence premises" used to construct, alter or repair the dwelling or other structures on the "residence premises".

2. We do not cover land, including land on which the dwelling is located.

B. Coverage B – Other Structures

1. We cover other structures on the "residence premises" set apart from the dwelling by clear space. This includes structures connected to the dwelling by only a fence, utility line, or similar connection.

2. We do not cover:

   a. Land, including land on which the other structures are located;

   b. Other structures rented or held for rental to any person not a tenant of the dwelling, unless used solely as a private garage;

   c. Other structures from which any "business" is conducted; or

   d. Other structures used to store "business" property. However, we do cover a structure that contains "business" property solely owned by an "insured" or a tenant of the dwelling provided that "business" property does not include gaseous or liquid fuel, other than fuel in a permanently installed fuel tank of a vehicle or craft parked or stored in the structure.

3. The limit of liability for this coverage will not be more than 10% of the limit of liability that applies to Coverage A. Use of this coverage does not reduce the Coverage A limit of liability.

C. Coverage C – Personal Property

1. **Covered Property**

   We cover personal property owned or used by an "insured" while it is anywhere in the world. After a loss and at your request, we will cover personal property owned by:

   a. Others while the property is on the part of the "residence premises" occupied by an "insured"; or

   b. A guest or a "residence employee", while the property is in any residence occupied by an "insured".

2. **Limit For Property At Other Residences**

   Our limit of liability for personal property usually located at an "insured's" residence, other than the "residence premises", is 10% of the limit of liability for Coverage C, or $1,000, whichever is greater. However, this limitation does not apply to personal property:

   a. Moved from the "residence premises" because it is being repaired, renovated or rebuilt and is not fit to live in or store property in; or

   b. In a newly acquired principal residence for 30 days from the time you begin to move the property there.

3. **Special Limits Of Liability**

   The special limit for each category shown below is the total limit for each loss for all property in that category. These special limits do not increase the Coverage C limit of liability.

   a. $200 on money, bank notes, bullion, gold other than goldware, silver other than silverware, platinum other than platinumware, coins, medals, scrip, stored value cards and smart cards.

   b. $1,500 on securities, accounts, deeds, evidences of debt, letters of credit, notes other than bank notes, manuscripts, personal records, passports, tickets and stamps. This dollar limit applies to these categories regardless of the medium (such as paper or computer software) on which the material exists.

   This limit includes the cost to research, replace or restore the information from the lost or damaged material.

c. $1,500 on watercraft of all types, including their trailers, furnishings, equipment and outboard engines or motors.

d. $1,500 on trailers or semitrailers not used with watercraft of all types.

e. $1,500 for loss by theft, misplacing or losing of jewelry, watches, furs, precious and semiprecious stones.

f. $2,500 for loss by theft, misplacing or losing of firearms and related equipment.

g. $2,500 for loss by theft, misplacing or losing of silverware, silver-plated ware, goldware, gold-plated ware, platinumware, platinum-plated ware and pewterware. This includes flatware, hollowware, tea sets, trays and trophies made of or including silver, gold or pewter.

h. $2,500 on property, on the "residence premises", used primarily for "business" purposes.

i. $500 on property, away from the "residence premises", used primarily for "business" purposes. However, this limit does not apply to loss to electronic apparatus and other property described in Categories **j.** and **k.** below.

j. $1,500 on electronic apparatus and accessories, while in or upon a "motor vehicle", but only if the apparatus is equipped to be operated by power from the "motor vehicle's" electrical system while still capable of being operated by other power sources.

Accessories include antennas, tapes, wires, records, discs or other media that can be used with any apparatus described in this Category **j.**

k. $1,500 on electronic apparatus and accessories used primarily for "business" while away from the "residence premises" and not in or upon a "motor vehicle". The apparatus must be equipped to be operated by power from the "motor vehicle's" electrical system while still capable of being operated by other power sources.

Accessories include antennas, tapes, wires, records, discs or other media that can be used with any apparatus described in this Category **k.**

4. Property Not Covered

We do not cover:

a. Articles separately described and specifically insured, regardless of the limit for which they are insured, in this or other insurance;

b. Animals, birds or fish;

c. "Motor vehicles".

(1) This includes:

  (a) Their accessories, equipment and parts; or

  (b) Electronic apparatus and accessories designed to be operated solely by power from the electrical system of the "motor vehicle". Accessories include antennas, tapes, wires, records, discs or other media that can be used with any apparatus described above.

The exclusion of property described in **(a)** and **(b)** above applies only while such property is in or upon the "motor vehicle".

(2) We do cover "motor vehicles" not required to be registered for use on public roads or property which are:

  (a) Used solely to service an "insured's" residence; or

  (b) Designed to assist the handicapped;

d. Aircraft meaning any contrivance used or designed for flight including any parts whether or not attached to the aircraft.

We do cover model or hobby aircraft not used or designed to carry people or cargo;

e. Hovercraft and parts. Hovercraft means a self-propelled motorized ground effect vehicle and includes, but is not limited to, flarecraft and air cushion vehicles;

f. Property of roomers, boarders and other tenants, except property of roomers and boarders related to an "insured";

g. Property in an apartment regularly rented or held for rental to others by an "insured", except as provided under **E.10.** Landlord's Furnishings under Section **I** – Property Coverages;

h. Property rented or held for rental to others off the "residence premises";

i. "Business" data, including such data stored in:

(1) Books of account, drawings or other paper records; or

(2) Computers and related equipment.

We do cover the cost of blank recording or storage media, and of prerecorded computer programs available on the retail market;

j. Credit cards, electronic fund transfer cards or access devices used solely for deposit, withdrawal or transfer of funds except as provided in **E.6.** Credit Card, Electronic Fund Transfer Card Or Access Device, Forgery And Counterfeit Money under Section **I** – Property Coverages; or

k. Water or steam.

D. Coverage D – Loss Of Use

The limit of liability for Coverage **D** is the total limit for the coverages in **1.** Additional Living Expense, **2.** Fair Rental Value and **3.** Civil Authority Prohibits Use below.

1. Additional Living Expense

If a loss covered under Section **I** makes that part of the "residence premises" where you reside not fit to live in, we cover any necessary increase in living expenses incurred by you so that your household can maintain its normal standard of living.

Payment will be for the shortest time required to repair or replace the damage or, if you permanently relocate, the shortest time required for your household to settle elsewhere.

2. Fair Rental Value

If a loss covered under Section **I** makes that part of the "residence premises" rented to others or held for rental by you not fit to live in, we cover the fair rental value of such premises less any expenses that do not continue while it is not fit to live in.

Payment will be for the shortest time required to repair or replace such premises.

3. Civil Authority Prohibits Use

If a civil authority prohibits you from use of the "residence premises" as a result of direct damage to neighboring premises by a Peril Insured Against, we cover the loss as provided in **1.** Additional Living Expense and **2.** Fair Rental Value above for no more than two weeks.

4. Loss Or Expense Not Covered

We do not cover loss or expense due to cancellation of a lease or agreement.

The periods of time under **1.** Additional Living Expense, **2.** Fair Rental Value and **3.** Civil Authority Prohibits Use above are not limited by expiration of this policy.

E. Additional Coverages

1. Debris Removal

a. We will pay your reasonable expense for the removal of:

(1) Debris of covered property if a Peril Insured Against that applies to the damaged property causes the loss; or

(2) Ash, dust or particles from a volcanic eruption that has caused direct loss to a building or property contained in a building.

This expense is included in the limit of liability that applies to the damaged property. If the amount to be paid for the actual damage to the property plus the debris removal expense is more than the limit of liability for the damaged property, an additional 5% of that limit is available for such expense.

b. We will also pay your reasonable expense, up to $1,000, for the removal from the "residence premises" of:

(1) Your tree(s) felled by the peril of Windstorm or Hail or Weight of Ice, Snow or Sleet; or

(2) A neighbor's tree(s) felled by a Peril Insured Against;

provided the tree(s):

(3) Damage(s) a covered structure; or

(4) Does not damage a covered structure, but:

(a) Block(s) a driveway on the "residence premises" which prevent(s) a "motor vehicle", that is registered for use on public roads or property, from entering or leaving the "residence premises"; or

(b) Block(s) a ramp or other fixture designed to assist a handicapped person to enter or leave the dwelling building.

The $1,000 limit is the most we will pay in any one loss regardless of the number of fallen trees. No more than $500 of this limit will be paid for the removal of any one tree.

This coverage is additional insurance.

2. Reasonable Repairs

a. We will pay the reasonable cost incurred by you for the necessary measures taken solely to protect covered property that is damaged by a Peril Insured Against from further damage.

b. If the measures taken involve repair to other damaged property, we will only pay if that property is covered under this policy and the damage is caused by a Peril Insured Against. This coverage does not:

(1) Increase the limit of liability that applies to the covered property; or

(2) Relieve you of your duties, in case of a loss to covered property, described in **B.4.** under Section **I** – Conditions.

3. Trees, Shrubs And Other Plants

We cover trees, shrubs, plants or lawns, on the "residence premises", for loss caused by the following Perils Insured Against:

a. Fire or Lightning;

b. Explosion;

c. Riot or Civil Commotion;

d. Aircraft;

e. Vehicles not owned or operated by a resident of the "residence premises";

f. Vandalism or Malicious Mischief; or

g. Theft.

We will pay up to 5% of the limit of liability that applies to the dwelling for all trees, shrubs, plants or lawns. No more than $500 of this limit will be paid for any one tree, shrub or plant. We do not cover property grown for "business" purposes.

This coverage is additional insurance.

4. Fire Department Service Charge

We will pay up to $500 for your liability assumed by contract or agreement for fire department charges incurred when the fire department is called to save or protect covered property from a Peril Insured Against. We do not cover fire department service charges if the property is located within the limits of the city, municipality or protection district furnishing the fire department response.

This coverage is additional insurance. No deductible applies to this coverage.

5. Property Removed

We insure covered property against direct loss from any cause while being removed from a premises endangered by a Peril Insured Against and for no more than 30 days while removed.

This coverage does not change the limit of liability that applies to the property being removed.

6. Credit Card, Electronic Fund Transfer Card Or Access Device, Forgery And Counterfeit Money

a. We will pay up to $500 for:

(1) The legal obligation of an "insured" to pay because of the theft or unauthorized use of credit cards issued to or registered in an "insured's" name;

(2) Loss resulting from theft or unauthorized use of an electronic fund transfer card or access device used for deposit, withdrawal or transfer of funds, issued to or registered in an "insured's" name;

(3) Loss to an "insured" caused by forgery or alteration of any check or negotiable instrument; and

(4) Loss to an "insured" through acceptance in good faith of counterfeit United States or Canadian paper currency.

All loss resulting from a series of acts committed by any one person or in which any one person is concerned or implicated is considered to be one loss.

This coverage is additional insurance. No deductible applies to this coverage.

b. We do not cover:

(1) Use of a credit card, electronic fund transfer card or access device:

(a) By a resident of your household;

(b) By a person who has been entrusted with either type of card or access device; or

(c) If an "insured" has not complied with all terms and conditions under which the cards are issued or the devices accessed; or

(2) Loss arising out of "business" use or dishonesty of an "insured".

c. If the coverage in **a.** above applies, the following defense provisions also apply:

(1) We may investigate and settle any claim or suit that we decide is appropriate. Our duty to defend a claim or suit ends when the amount we pay for the loss equals our limit of liability.

(2) If a suit is brought against an "insured" for liability under **a.(1)** or **(2)** above, we will provide a defense at our expense by counsel of our choice.

(3) We have the option to defend at our expense an "insured" or an "insured's" bank against any suit for the enforcement of payment under **a.(3)** above.

7. Loss Assessment

a. We will pay up to $1,000 for your share of loss assessment charged during the policy period against you, as owner or tenant of the "residence premises", by a corporation or association of property owners. The assessment must be made as a result of direct loss to property, owned by all members collectively, of the type that would be covered by this policy if owned by you, caused by a Peril Insured Against, other than:

(1) Earthquake; or

(2) Land shock waves or tremors before, during or after a volcanic eruption.

The limit of $1,000 is the most we will pay with respect to any one loss, regardless of the number of assessments. We will only apply one deductible, per unit, to the total amount of any one loss to the property described above, regardless of the number of assessments.

b. We do not cover assessments charged against you or a corporation or association of property owners by any governmental body.

c. Paragraph **P.** Policy Period under Section **I** – Conditions does not apply to this coverage.

This coverage is additional insurance.

8. Collapse

a. This Additional Coverage applies to property covered under Coverages **A** and **B**. With respect to this Additional Coverage:

(1) Collapse means an abrupt falling down or caving in of a building or any part of a building with the result that the building or part of the building cannot be occupied for its current intended purpose.

(2) A building or any part of a building that is in danger of falling down or caving in is not considered to be in a state of collapse.

(3) A part of a building that is standing is not considered to be in a state of collapse even if it has separated from another part of the building.

(4) A building or any part of a building that is standing is not considered to be in a state of collapse even if it shows evidence of cracking, bulging, sagging, bending, leaning, settling, shrinkage or expansion.

b. We insure for direct physical loss to covered property involving collapse of a building or any part of a building if the collapse was caused by one or more of the following:

(1) The Perils Insured Against under Coverages **A** and **B;**

(2) Decay that is hidden from view, unless the presence of such decay is known to an "insured" prior to collapse;

(3) Insect or vermin damage that is hidden from view, unless the presence of such damage is known to an "insured" prior to collapse;

(4) Weight of contents, equipment, animals or people;

(5) Weight of rain which collects on a roof; or

(6) Use of defective material or methods in construction, remodeling or renovation if the collapse occurs during the course of the construction, remodeling or renovation.

c. Loss to an awning, fence, patio, deck, pavement, swimming pool, underground pipe, flue, drain, cesspool, septic tank, foundation, retaining wall, bulkhead, pier, wharf or dock is not included under **b.(2)** through **(6)** above, unless the loss is a direct result of the collapse of a building or any part of a building.

d. This coverage does not increase the limit of liability that applies to the damaged covered property.

9. Glass Or Safety Glazing Material

a. We cover:

(1) The breakage of glass or safety glazing material which is part of a covered building, storm door or storm window;

(2) The breakage of glass or safety glazing material which is part of a covered building, storm door or storm window when caused directly by earth movement; and

(3) The direct physical loss to covered property caused solely by the pieces, fragments or splinters of broken glass or safety glazing material which is part of a building, storm door or storm window.

b. This coverage does not include loss:

(1) To covered property which results because the glass or safety glazing material has been broken, except as provided in **a.(3)** above; or

(2) On the "residence premises" if the dwelling has been vacant for more than 60 consecutive days immediately before the loss, except when the breakage results directly from earth movement as provided in **a.(2)** above. A dwelling being constructed is not considered vacant.

c. This coverage does not increase the limit of liability that applies to the damaged property.

10. Landlord's Furnishings

We will pay up to $2,500 for your appliances, carpeting and other household furnishings, in each apartment on the "residence premises" regularly rented or held for rental to others by an "insured", for loss caused only by the following Perils Insured Against:

a. Fire Or Lightning

b. Windstorm Or Hail

This peril includes loss to watercraft of all types and their trailers, furnishings, equipment, and outboard engines or motors, only while inside a fully enclosed building.

This peril does not include loss to the property contained in a building caused by rain, snow, sleet, sand or dust unless the direct force of wind or hail damages the building causing an opening in a roof or wall and the rain, snow, sleet, sand or dust enters through this opening.

c. Explosion

d. Riot Or Civil Commotion

e. Aircraft

This peril includes self-propelled missiles and spacecraft.

f. Vehicles

g. Smoke

This peril means sudden and accidental damage from smoke, including the emission or puffback of smoke, soot, fumes or vapors from a boiler, furnace or related equipment.

This peril does not include loss caused by smoke from agricultural smudging or industrial operations.

h. Vandalism Or Malicious Mischief

i. Falling Objects

This peril does not include loss to property contained in a building unless the roof or an outside wall of the building is first damaged by a falling object. Damage to the falling object itself is not included.

j. Weight Of Ice, Snow Or Sleet

This peril means weight of ice, snow or sleet which causes damage to property contained in a building.

k. Accidental Discharge Or Overflow Of Water Or Steam

(1) This peril means accidental discharge or overflow of water or steam from within a plumbing, heating, air conditioning or automatic fire protective sprinkler system or from within a household appliance.

(2) This peril does not include loss:

(a) To the system or appliance from which the water or steam escaped;

(b) Caused by or resulting from freezing except as provided in **m.** Freezing below;

(c) On the "residence premises" caused by accidental discharge or overflow which occurs off the "residence premises"; or

(d) Caused by mold, fungus or wet rot unless hidden within the walls or ceilings or beneath the floors or above the ceilings of a structure.

(3) In this peril, a plumbing system or household appliance does not include a sump, sump pump or related equipment or a roof drain, gutter, downspout or similar fixtures or equipment.

 HO 00 05 10 00

l. Sudden And Accidental Tearing Apart, Cracking, Burning Or Bulging

This peril means sudden and accidental tearing apart, cracking, burning or bulging of a steam or hot water heating system, an air conditioning or automatic fire protective sprinkler system, or an appliance for heating water.

We do not cover loss caused by or resulting from freezing under this peril.

m. Freezing

(1) This peril means freezing of a plumbing, heating, air conditioning or automatic fire protective sprinkler system or of a household appliance but only if you have used reasonable care to:

(a) Maintain heat in the building; or

(b) Shut off the water supply and drain all systems and appliances of water.

However, if the building is protected by an automatic fire protective sprinkler system, you must use reasonable care to continue the water supply and maintain heat in the building for coverage to apply.

(2) In this peril, a plumbing system or household appliance does not include a sump, sump pump or related equipment or a roof drain, gutter, downspout or similar fixtures or equipment.

n. Sudden And Accidental Damage From Artificially Generated Electrical Current

This peril does not include loss to tubes, transistors, electronic components or circuitry that are a part of appliances, fixtures, computers, home entertainment units or other types of electronic apparatus.

o. Volcanic Eruption

This peril does not include loss caused by earthquake, land shock waves or tremors.

This limit is the most we will pay in any one loss regardless of the number of appliances, carpeting or other household furnishings involved in the loss.

This coverage does not increase the limit of liability applying to the damaged property.

11. Ordinance Or Law

a. You may use up to 10% of the limit of liability that applies to Coverage **A** for the increased costs you incur due to the enforcement of any ordinance or law which requires or regulates:

(1) The construction, demolition, remodeling, renovation or repair of that part of a covered building or other structure damaged by a Peril Insured Against;

(2) The demolition and reconstruction of the undamaged part of a covered building or other structure, when that building or other structure must be totally demolished because of damage by a Peril Insured Against to another part of that covered building or other structure; or

(3) The remodeling, removal or replacement of the portion of the undamaged part of a covered building or other structure necessary to complete the remodeling, repair or replacement of that part of the covered building or other structure damaged by a Peril Insured Against.

b. You may use all or part of this ordinance or law coverage to pay for the increased costs you incur to remove debris resulting from the construction, demolition, remodeling, renovation, repair or replacement of property as stated in **a.** above.

c. We do not cover:

(1) The loss in value to any covered building or other structure due to the requirements of any ordinance or law; or

(2) The costs to comply with any ordinance or law which requires any "insured" or others, to test for, monitor, clean up, remove, contain, treat, detoxify or neutralize, or in any way respond to, or assess the effects of, pollutants in or on any covered building or other structure.

Pollutants means any solid, liquid, gaseous or thermal irritant or contaminant, including smoke, vapor, soot, fumes, acids, alkalis, chemicals and waste. Waste includes materials to be recycled, reconditioned or reclaimed.

This coverage is additional insurance.

12. Grave Markers

We will pay up to $5,000 for grave markers, including mausoleums, on or away from the "residence premises" for loss caused by a Peril Insured Against.

This coverage does not increase the limits of liability that apply to the damaged covered property.

SECTION I – PERILS INSURED AGAINST

We insure against risk of direct physical loss to property described in Coverages **A, B** and **C.**

We do not insure, however, for loss:

A. Under Coverages **A, B** and **C:**

  1. Excluded under Section I – Exclusions;

  2. Caused by:

    a. Freezing of a plumbing, heating, air conditioning or automatic fire protective sprinkler system or of a household appliance, or by discharge, leakage or overflow from within the system or appliance caused by freezing. This provision does not apply if you have used reasonable care to:

      (1) Maintain heat in the building; or

      (2) Shut off the water supply and drain all systems and appliances of water.

    However, if the building is protected by an automatic fire protective sprinkler system, you must use reasonable care to continue the water supply and maintain heat in the building for coverage to apply.

    For purposes of this provision a plumbing system or household appliance does not include a sump, sump pump or related equipment or a roof drain, gutter, downspout or similar fixtures or equipment;

    b. Freezing, thawing, pressure or weight of water or ice, whether driven by wind or not, to a:

      (1) Fence, pavement, patio or swimming pool;

      (2) Footing, foundation, bulkhead, wall, or any other structure or device, that supports all or part of a building or other structure;

      (3) Retaining wall or bulkhead that does not support all or part of a building or other structure; or

      (4) Pier, wharf or dock;

    c. Theft in or to a dwelling under construction, or of materials and supplies for use in the construction until the dwelling is finished and occupied;

    d. Mold, fungus or wet rot. However, we do insure for loss caused by mold, fungus or wet rot that is hidden within the walls or ceilings or beneath the floors or above the ceilings of a structure if such loss results from the accidental discharge or overflow of water or steam from within:

      (1) A plumbing, heating, air conditioning or automatic fire protective sprinkler system, or a household appliance, on the "residence premises"; or

      (2) A storm drain, or water, steam or sewer pipes, off the "residence premises".

    For purposes of this provision, a plumbing system or household appliance does not include a sump, sump pump or related equipment or a roof drain, gutter, downspout or similar fixtures or equipment; or

    e. Any of the following:

      (1) Wear and tear, marring, deterioration;

      (2) Mechanical breakdown, latent defect, inherent vice, or any quality in property that causes it to damage or destroy itself;

      (3) Smog, rust or other corrosion, or dry rot;

      (4) Smoke from agricultural smudging or industrial operations;

      (5) Discharge, dispersal, seepage, migration, release or escape of pollutants unless the discharge, dispersal, seepage, migration, release or escape is itself caused by a Peril Insured Against in **a.** through **o.** as listed in **E.10.** Landlord's Furnishings under Section I – Property Coverages.

      Pollutants means any solid, liquid, gaseous or thermal irritant or contaminant, including smoke, vapor, soot, fumes, acids, alkalis, chemicals and waste. Waste includes materials to be recycled, reconditioned or reclaimed;

      (6) Settling, shrinking, bulging or expansion, including resultant cracking, of bulkheads, pavements, patios, footings, foundations, walls, floors, roofs or ceilings;

      (7) Birds, vermin, rodents, or insects; or

      (8) Animals owned or kept by an "insured".

 HO 00 05 10 00

Exception To 2.e.

Unless the loss is otherwise excluded, we cover loss to property covered under Coverage **A**, **B** or **C** resulting from an accidental discharge or overflow of water or steam from within a:

(i) Storm drain, or water, steam or sewer pipe, off the "residence premises"; or

(ii) Plumbing, heating, air conditioning or automatic fire protective sprinkler system or household appliance on the "residence premises". This includes the cost to tear out and replace any part of a building, or other structure, on the "residence premises", but only when necessary to repair the system or appliance. However, such tear out and replacement coverage only applies to other structures if the water or steam causes actual damage to a building on the "residence premises".

We do not cover loss to the system or appliance from which this water or steam escaped.

For purposes of this provision, a plumbing system or household appliance does not include a sump, sump pump or related equipment or a roof drain, gutter, down spout or similar fixtures or equipment.

Section I – Exclusion **A.3.** Water Damage, Paragraphs **a.** and **c.** that apply to surface water and water below the surface of the ground do not apply to loss by water covered under **d.** and **e.** above.

Under **2.a.** through **e.** above, any ensuing loss to property described in Coverages **A**, **B** and **C** not precluded by any other provision in this policy is covered.

B. Under Coverages **A** and **B**:

1. Caused by vandalism and malicious mischief, and any ensuing loss caused by any intentional and wrongful act committed in the course of the vandalism or malicious mischief, if the dwelling has been vacant for more than 60 consecutive days immediately before the loss. A dwelling being constructed is not considered vacant;

2. Involving collapse, other than as provided in **E.8.** Collapse under Section I – Property Coverages. However, any ensuing loss to property described in Coverages **A** and **B** not precluded by any other provision in this policy is covered.

C. Under Coverage **C** caused by:

1. Breakage of eyeglasses, glassware, statuary, marble, bric-a-brac, porcelains and similar fragile articles other than jewelry, watches bronzes, cameras and photographic lenses.

    However, there is coverage for breakage of the property by or resulting from:

    a. Fire, lightning, windstorm, hail;

    b. Smoke, other than smoke from agricultural smudging or industrial operations;

    c. Explosion, riot, civil commotion;

    d. Aircraft, vehicles, vandalism and malicious mischief;

    e. Collapse of a building or any part of a building;

    f. Water not otherwise excluded;

    g. Theft or attempted theft; or

    h. Sudden and accidental tearing apart, cracking, burning or bulging of:

        (1) A steam or hot water heating system;

        (2) An air conditioning or automatic fire protective sprinkler system; or

        (3) An appliance for heating water;

2. Dampness, of atmosphere or extremes of temperature unless the direct cause of loss is rain, snow, sleet or hail;

3. Refinishing, renovating or repairing property other than watches, jewelry and furs;

4. Collision, other than collision with a land vehicle, sinking, swamping or stranding of watercraft, including their trailers, furnishings equipment and out board engines or motors;

5. Destruction, confiscation or seizure by order of any government or public authority; or

6. Acts or decisions, including the failure to act or decide, of any person, group, organization or governmental body. However, any ensuing loss to property described in Coverage **C** not precluded by any other provision in this policy is covered.

SECTION I – EXCLUSIONS

A. We do not insure for loss caused directly or indirectly by any of the following. Such loss is excluded regardless of any other cause or event contributing concurrently or in any sequence to the loss. These exclusions apply whether or not the loss event results in widespread damage or affects a substantial area.

1. Ordinance Or Law

Ordinance Or Law means any ordinance or law:

a. Requiring or regulating the construction, demolition, remodeling, renovation or repair of property, including removal of any resulting debris. This Exclusion **A.1.a.** does not apply to the amount of coverage that may be provided for in **E.11.** Ordinance Or Law under Section **I** – Property Coverages;

b. The requirements of which result in a loss in value to property; or

c. Requiring any "insured" or others to test for, monitor, clean up, remove, contain, treat, detoxify or neutralize, or in any way respond to, or assess the effects of, pollutants.

Pollutants means any solid, liquid, gaseous or thermal irritant or contaminant, including smoke, vapor, soot, fumes, acids, alkalis, chemicals and waste. Waste includes materials to be recycled, reconditioned or reclaimed.

This Exclusion **A.1.** applies whether or not the property has been physically damaged.

2. Earth Movement

Earth Movement means:

a. Earthquake, including land shock waves or tremors before, during or after a volcanic eruption;

b. Landslide, mudslide or mudflow;

c. Subsidence or sinkhole; or

d. Any other earth movement including earth sinking, rising or shifting;

caused by or resulting from human or animal forces or any act of nature unless direct loss by fire or explosion ensues and then we will pay only for the ensuing loss.

This Exclusion **A.2.** does not apply to loss by theft.

3. Water Damage

Water Damage means:

a. Flood, surface water, waves, tidal water, overflow of a body of water, or spray from any of these, whether or not driven by wind;

b. Water or water-borne material which backs up through sewers or drains or which overflows or is discharged from a sump, sump pump or related equipment; or

c. Water or water-borne material below the surface of the ground, including water which exerts pressure on or seeps or leaks through a building, sidewalk, driveway, foundation, swimming pool or other structure;

caused by or resulting from human or animal forces or any act of nature.

Direct loss by fire, explosion or theft resulting from water damage is covered.

Water damage to property described in Coverage **C** away from a premises or location owned, rented, occupied or controlled by an "insured" is covered.

Water damage to property described in Coverage **C** on a premises or location owned, rented, occupied or controlled by an "insured" is excluded even if weather conditions contribute in any way to produce the loss.

4. Power Failure

Power Failure means the failure of power or other utility service if the failure takes place off the "residence premises". But if the failure results in a loss, from a Peril Insured Against on the "residence premises", we will pay for the loss caused by that peril.

5. Neglect

Neglect means neglect of an "insured" to use all reasonable means to save and preserve property at and after the time of a loss.

6. War

War includes the following and any consequence of any of the following:

a. Undeclared war, civil war, insurrection, rebellion or revolution;

b. Warlike act by a military force or military personnel; or

c. Destruction, seizure or use for a military purpose.

Discharge of a nuclear weapon will be deemed a warlike act even if accidental.

7. Nuclear Hazard

This Exclusion **A.7.** pertains to Nuclear Hazard to the extent set forth in **M.** Nuclear Hazard Clause under Section **I** – Conditions.

8. Intentional Loss

Intentional Loss means any loss arising out of any act an "insured" commits or conspires to commit with the intent to cause a loss.

In the event of such loss, no "insured" is entitled to coverage, even "insureds" who did not commit or conspire to commit the act causing the loss.

9. **Governmental Action**

Governmental Action means the destruction, confiscation or seizure of property described in Coverage **A**, **B** or **C** by order of any governmental or public authority.

This exclusion does not apply to such acts ordered by any governmental or public authority that are taken at the time of a fire to prevent its spread, if the loss caused by fire would be covered under this policy.

B. We do not insure for loss to property described in Coverages **A** and **B** caused by any of the following. However, any ensuing loss to property described in Coverages **A** and **B** not precluded by any other provision in this policy is covered.

1. Weather conditions. However, this exclusion only applies if weather conditions contribute in any way with a cause or event excluded in **A.** above to produce the loss.

2. Acts or decisions, including the failure to act or decide, of any person, group, organization or governmental body.

3. Faulty, inadequate or defective:

   a. Planning, zoning, development, surveying, siting;

   b. Design, specifications, workmanship, repair, construction, renovation, remodeling, grading, compaction;

   c. Materials used in repair, construction, renovation or remodeling; or

   d. Maintenance;

   of part or all of any property whether on or off the "residence premises".

SECTION I – CONDITIONS

A. Insurable Interest And Limit Of Liability

Even if more than one person has an insurable interest in the property covered, we will not be liable in any one loss:

1. To an "insured" for more than the amount of such "insured's" interest at the time of loss; or

2. For more than the applicable limit of liability.

B. Duties After Loss

In case of a loss to covered property, we have no duty to provide coverage under this policy if the failure to comply with the following duties is prejudicial to us. These duties must be performed either by you, or an "insured" seeking coverage, or a representative of either:

1. Give prompt notice to us or our agent;

2. Notify the police in case of loss by theft;

3. Notify the credit card or electronic fund transfer card or access device company in case of loss as provided for in **E.6.** Credit Card, Electronic Fund Transfer Card Or Access Device, Forgery And Counterfeit Money under Section **I** – Property Coverages;

4. Protect the property from further damage. If repairs to the property are required, you must:

   a. Make reasonable and necessary repairs to protect the property; and

   b. Keep an accurate record of repair expenses;

5. Cooperate with us in the investigation of a claim;

6. Prepare an inventory of damaged personal property showing the quantity, description, actual cash value and amount of loss. Attach all bills, receipts and related documents that justify the figures in the inventory;

7. As often as we reasonably require:

   a. Show the damaged property;

   b. Provide us with records and documents we request and permit us to make copies; and

   c. Submit to examination under oath, while not in the presence of another "insured", and sign the same;

8. Send to us, within 60 days after our request, your signed, sworn proof of loss which sets forth, to the best of your knowledge and belief:

   a. The time and cause of loss;

   b. The interests of all "insureds" and all others in the property involved and all liens on the property;

   c. Other insurance which may cover the loss;

   d. Changes in title or occupancy of the property during the term of the policy;

   e. Specifications of damaged buildings and detailed repair estimates;

   f. The inventory of damaged personal property described in **6.** above;

   g. Receipts for additional living expenses incurred and records that support the fair rental value loss; and

   h. Evidence or affidavit that supports a claim under **E.6.** Credit Card, Electronic Fund Transfer Card Or Access Device, Forgery And Counterfeit Money under Section **I** – Property Coverages, stating the amount and cause of loss.

C. Loss Settlement

In this Condition **C.**, the terms "cost to repair or replace" and "replacement cost" do not include the increased costs incurred to comply with the enforcement of any ordinance or law, except to the extent that coverage for these increased costs are provided in **E.11.** Ordinance Or Law under Section **I** – Property Coverages. Covered property losses are settled as follows:

1. Property of the following types:

    a. Personal property;

    b. Awnings, carpeting, household appliances, outdoor antennas and outdoor equipment, whether or not attached to buildings;

    c. Structures that are not buildings; and

    d. Grave markers, including mausoleums;

    at actual cash value at the time of loss but not more than the amount required to repair or replace.

2. Buildings covered under Coverage **A** or **B** at replacement cost without deduction for depreciation, subject to the following:

    a. If, at the time of loss, the amount of insurance in this policy on the damaged building is 80% or more of the full replacement cost of the building immediately before the loss, we will pay the cost to repair or replace, after application of any deductible and without deduction for depreciation, but not more than the least of the following amounts:

    (1) The limit of liability under this policy that applies to the building;

    (2) The replacement cost of that part of the building damaged with material of like kind and quality and for like use; or

    (3) The necessary amount actually spent to repair or replace the damaged building.

    If the building is rebuilt at a new premises, the cost described in **(2)** above is limited to the cost which would have been incurred if the building had been built at the original premises.

    b. If, at the time of loss, the amount of insurance in this policy on the damaged building is less than 80% of the full replacement cost of the building immediately before the loss, we will pay the greater of the following amounts, but not more than the limit of liability under this policy that applies to the building:

    (1) The actual cash value of that part of the building damaged; or

    (2) That proportion of the cost to repair or replace, after application of any deductible and without deduction for depreciation, that part of the building damaged, which the total amount of insurance in this policy on the damaged building bears to 80% of the replacement cost of the building.

    c. To determine the amount of insurance required to equal 80% of the full replacement cost of the building immediately before the loss, do not include the value of:

    (1) Excavations, footings, foundations, piers, or any other structures or devices that support all or part of the building, which are below the undersurface of the lowest basement floor;

    (2) Those supports described in **(1)** above which are below the surface of the ground inside the foundation walls, if there is no basement; and

    (3) Underground flues, pipes, wiring and drains.

    d. We will pay no more than the actual cash value of the damage until actual repair or replacement is complete. Once actual repair or replacement is complete, we will settle the loss as noted in **2.a.** and **b.** above.

    However, if the cost to repair or replace the damage is both:

    (1) Less than 5% of the amount of insurance in this policy on the building; and

    (2) Less than $2,500;

    we will settle the loss as noted in **2.a.** and **b.** above whether or not actual repair or replacement is complete.

    e. You may disregard the replacement cost loss settlement provisions and make claim under this policy for loss to buildings on an actual cash value basis. You may then make claim for any additional liability according to the provisions of this Condition **C.** Loss Settlement, provided you notify us of your intent to do so within 180 days after the date of loss.

D. Loss To A Pair Or Set

In case of loss to a pair or set we may elect to:

1. Repair or replace any part to restore the pair or set to its value before the loss; or

2. Pay the difference between actual cash value of the property before and after the loss.

E. Appraisal

If you and we fail to agree on the amount of loss, either may demand an appraisal of the loss. In this event, each party will choose a competent and impartial appraiser within 20 days after receiving a written request from the other. The two appraisers will choose an umpire. If they cannot agree upon an umpire within 15 days, you or we may request that the choice be made by a judge of a court of record in the state where the "residence premises" is located. The appraisers will separately set the amount of loss. If the appraisers submit a written report of an agreement to us, the amount agreed upon will be the amount of loss. If they fail to agree, they will submit their differences to the umpire. A decision agreed to by any two will set the amount of loss.

Each party will:

1. Pay its own appraiser; and

2. Bear the other expenses of the appraisal and umpire equally.

F. Other Insurance And Service Agreement

If a loss covered by this policy is also covered by:

1. Other insurance, we will pay only the proportion of the loss that the limit of liability that applies under this policy bears to the total amount of insurance covering the loss; or

2. A service agreement, this insurance is excess over any amounts payable under any such agreement. Service agreement means a service plan, property restoration plan, home warranty or other similar service warranty agreement, even if it is characterized as insurance.

G. Suit Against Us

No action can be brought against us unless there has been full compliance with all of the terms under Section I of this policy and the action is started within two years after the date of loss.

H. Our Option

If we give you written notice within 30 days after we receive your signed, sworn proof of loss, we may repair or replace any part of the damaged property with material or property of like kind and quality.

I. Loss Payment

We will adjust all losses with you. We will pay you unless some other person is named in the policy or is legally entitled to receive payment. Loss will be payable 60 days after we receive your proof of loss and:

1. Reach an agreement with you;

2. There is an entry of a final judgment; or

3. There is a filing of an appraisal award with us.

J. Abandonment Of Property

We need not accept any property abandoned by an "insured".

K. Mortgage Clause

1. If a mortgagee is named in this policy, any loss payable under Coverage **A** or **B** will be paid to the mortgagee and you, as interests appear. If more than one mortgagee is named, the order of payment will be the same as the order of precedence of the mortgages.

2. If we deny your claim, that denial will not apply to a valid claim of the mortgagee, if the mortgagee:

   a. Notifies us of any change in ownership, occupancy or substantial change in risk of which the mortgagee is aware;

   b. Pays any premium due under this policy on demand if you have neglected to pay the premium; and

   c. Submits a signed, sworn statement of loss within 60 days after receiving notice from us of your failure to do so. Paragraphs **E.** Appraisal, **G.** Suit Against Us and **I.** Loss Payment under Section I – Conditions also apply to the mortgagee.

3. If we decide to cancel or not to renew this policy, the mortgagee will be notified at least 10 days before the date cancellation or nonrenewal takes effect.

4. If we pay the mortgagee for any loss and deny payment to you:

   a. We are subrogated to all the rights of the mortgagee granted under the mortgage on the property; or

   b. At our option, we may pay to the mortgagee the whole principal on the mortgage plus any accrued interest. In this event, we will receive a full assignment and transfer of the mortgage and all securities held as collateral to the mortgage debt.

5. Subrogation will not impair the right of the mortgagee to recover the full amount of the mortgagee's claim.

L. No Benefit To Bailee

We will not recognize any assignment or grant any coverage that benefits a person or organization holding, storing or moving property for a fee regardless of any other provision of this policy.

M. Nuclear Hazard Clause

1. "Nuclear Hazard" means any nuclear reaction, radiation, or radioactive contamination, all whether controlled or uncontrolled or however caused, or any consequence of any of these.

2. Loss caused by the nuclear hazard will not be considered loss caused by fire, explosion, or smoke, whether these perils are specifically named in or otherwise included within the Perils Insured Against.

3. This policy does not apply under Section **I** to loss caused directly or indirectly by nuclear hazard, except that direct loss by fire resulting from the nuclear hazard is covered.

N. Recovered Property

If you or we recover any property for which we have made payment under this policy, you or we will notify the other of the recovery. At your option, the property will be returned to or retained by you or it will become our property. If the recovered property is returned to or retained by you, the loss payment will be adjusted based on the amount you received for the recovered property.

O. Volcanic Eruption Period

One or more volcanic eruptions that occur within a 72 hour period will be considered as one volcanic eruption.

P. Policy Period

This policy applies only to loss which occurs during the policy period.

Q. Concealment Or Fraud

We provide coverage to no "insureds" under this policy if, whether before or after a loss, an "insured" has:

1. Intentionally concealed or misrepresented any material fact or circumstance;

2. Engaged in fraudulent conduct; or

3. Made false statements;

relating to this insurance.

R. Loss Payable Clause

If the Declarations show a loss payee for certain listed insured personal property, the definition of "insured" is changed to include that loss payee with respect to that property.

If we decide to cancel or not renew this policy, that loss payee will be notified in writing.

SECTION II – LIABILITY COVERAGES

A. Coverage E – Personal Liability

If a claim is made or a suit is brought against an "insured" for damages because of "bodily injury" or "property damage" caused by an "occurrence" to which this coverage applies, we will:

1. Pay up to our limit of liability for the damages for which an "insured" is legally liable. Damages include prejudgment interest awarded against an "insured"; and

2. Provide a defense at our expense by counsel of our choice, even if the suit is groundless, false or fraudulent. We may investigate and settle any claim or suit that we decide is appropriate. Our duty to settle or defend ends when our limit of liability for the "occurrence" has been exhausted by payment of a judgment or settlement.

B. Coverage F – Medical Payments To Others

We will pay the necessary medical expenses that are incurred or medically ascertained within three years from the date of an accident causing "bodily injury". Medical expenses means reasonable charges for medical, surgical, x-ray, dental, ambulance, hospital, professional nursing, prosthetic devices and funeral services. This coverage does not apply to you or regular residents of your household except "residence employees". As to others, this coverage applies only:

1. To a person on the "insured location" with the permission of an "insured"; or

2. To a person off the "insured location", if the "bodily injury":

a. Arises out of a condition on the "insured location" or the ways immediately adjoining;

b. Is caused by the activities of an "insured";

c. Is caused by a "residence employee" in the course of the "residence employee's" employment by an "insured"; or

d. Is caused by an animal owned by or in the care of an "insured".

SECTION II – EXCLUSIONS

A. "Motor Vehicle Liability"

1. Coverages **E** and **F** do not apply to any "motor vehicle liability" if, at the time and place of an "occurrence", the involved "motor vehicle":

a. Is registered for use on public roads or property;

b. Is not registered for use on public roads or property, but such registration is required by a law, or regulation issued by a government agency, for it to be used at the place of the "occurrence"; or

c. Is being:

(1) Operated in, or practicing for, any prearranged or organized race, speed contest or other competition;

(2) Rented to others;

(3) Used to carry persons or cargo for a charge; or

(4) Used for any "business" purpose except for a motorized golf cart while on a golfing facility.

2. If Exclusion **A.1.** does not apply, there is still no coverage for "motor vehicle liability" unless the "motor vehicle" is:

a. In dead storage on an "insured location";

b. Used solely to service an "insured's" residence;

c. Designed to assist the handicapped and, at the time of an "occurrence", it is:

(1) Being used to assist a handicapped person; or

(2) Parked on an "insured location";

d. Designed for recreational use off public roads and:

(1) Not owned by an "insured"; or

(2) Owned by an "insured" provided the "occurrence" takes place on an "insured location" as defined in Definitions **B. 6.a., b., d., e.** or **h.;** or

e. A motorized golf cart that is owned by an "insured", designed to carry up to 4 persons, not built or modified after manufacture to exceed a speed of 25 miles per hour on level ground and, at the time of an "occurrence", is within the legal boundaries of:

(1) A golfing facility and is parked or stored there, or being used by an "insured" to:

(a) Play the game of golf or for other recreational or leisure activity allowed by the facility;

(b) Travel to or from an area where "motor vehicles" or golf carts are parked or stored; or

(c) Cross public roads at designated points to access other parts of the golfing facility; or

(2) A private residential community, including its public roads upon which a motorized golf cart can legally travel, which is subject to the authority of a property owners association and contains an "insured's" residence.

B. "Watercraft Liability"

1. Coverages **E** and **F** do not apply to any "watercraft liability" if, at the time of an "occurrence", the involved watercraft is being:

a. Operated in, or practicing for, any prearranged or organized race, speed contest or other competition. This exclusion does not apply to a sailing vessel or a predicted log cruise;

b. Rented to others;

c. Used to carry persons or cargo for a charge; or

d. Used for any "business" purpose.

2. If Exclusion **B.1.** does not apply, there is still no coverage for "watercraft liability" unless, at the time of the "occurrence", the watercraft:

a. Is stored;

b. Is a sailing vessel, with or without auxiliary power, that is:

(1) Less than 26 feet in overall length; or

(2) 26 feet or more in overall length and not owned by or rented to an "insured"; or

c. Is not a sailing vessel and is powered by:

(1) An inboard or inboard-outdrive engine or motor, including those that power a water jet pump, of:

(a) 50 horsepower or less and not owned by an "insured"; or

(b) More than 50 horsepower and not owned by or rented to an "insured"; or

(2) One or more outboard engines or motors with:

(a) 25 total horsepower or less;

(b) More than 25 horsepower if the outboard engine or motor is not owned by an "insured";

(c) More than 25 horsepower if the outboard engine or motor is owned by an "insured" who acquired it during the policy period; or

(d) More than 25 horsepower if the outboard engine or motor is owned by an "insured" who acquired it before the policy period, but only if:

(i) You declare them at policy inception; or

(ii) Your intent to insure them is reported to us in writing within 45 days after you acquire them.

The coverages in **(c)** and **(d)** above apply for the policy period.

Horsepower means the maximum power rating assigned to the engine or motor by the manufacturer.

C. "Aircraft Liability"

This policy does not cover "aircraft liability".

D. "Hovercraft Liability"

This policy does not cover "hovercraft liability".

E. Coverage E – Personal Liability And Coverage F – Medical Payments To Others

Coverages **E** and **F** do not apply to the following:

1. Expected Or Intended Injury

"Bodily injury" or "property damage" which is expected or intended by an "insured" even if the resulting "bodily injury" or "property damage":

a. Is of a different kind, quality or degree than initially expected or intended; or

b. Is sustained by a different person, entity, real or personal property, than initially expected or intended.

However, this Exclusion **E.1.** does not apply to "bodily injury" resulting from the use of reasonable force by an "insured" to protect persons or property;

2. "Business"

a. "Bodily injury" or "property damage" arising out of or in connection with a "business" conducted from an "insured location" or engaged in by an "insured", whether or not the "business" is owned or operated by an "insured" or employs an "insured".

This Exclusion **E.2.** applies but is not limited to an act or omission, regardless of its nature or circumstance, involving a service or duty rendered, promised, owed, or implied to be provided because of the nature of the "business".

b. This Exclusion **E.2.** does not apply to:

(1) The rental or holding for rental of an "insured location";

(a) On an occasional basis if used only as a residence;

(b) In part for use only as a residence, unless a single family unit is intended for use by the occupying family to lodge more than two roomers or boarders; or

(c) In part, as an office, school, studio or private garage; and

(2) An "insured" under the age of 21 years involved in a part-time or occasional, self-employed "business" with no employees;

3. Professional Services

"Bodily injury" or "property damage" arising out of the rendering of or failure to render professional services;

4. "Insured's" Premises Not An "Insured Location"

"Bodily injury" or "property damage" arising out of a premises:

a. Owned by an "insured";

b. Rented to an "insured"; or

c. Rented to others by an "insured";

that is not an "insured location";

5. War

"Bodily injury" or "property damage" caused directly or indirectly by war, including the following and any consequence of any of the following:

a. Undeclared war, civil war, insurrection, rebellion or revolution;

b. Warlike act by a military force or military personnel; or

c. Destruction, seizure or use for a military purpose.

Discharge of a nuclear weapon will be deemed a warlike act even if accidental;

6. Communicable Disease

"Bodily injury" or "property damage" which arises out of the transmission of a communicable disease by an "insured";

7. Sexual Molestation, Corporal Punishment Or Physical Or Mental Abuse

"Bodily injury" or "property damage" arising out of sexual molestation, corporal punishment or physical or mental abuse; or

8. Controlled Substance

"Bodily injury" or "property damage" arising out of the use, sale, manufacture, delivery, transfer or possession by any person of a Controlled Substance as defined by the Federal Food and Drug Law at 21 U.S.C.A. Sections 811 and 812. Controlled Substances include but are not limited to cocaine, LSD, marijuana and all narcotic drugs. However, this exclusion does not apply to the legitimate use of prescription drugs by a person following the orders of a licensed physician.

Exclusions **A.** "Motor Vehicle Liability", **B.** "Watercraft Liability", **C.** "Aircraft Liability", **D.** "Hovercraft Liability" and **E.4.** "Insured's" Premises Not An "Insured Location" do not apply to "bodily injury" to a "residence employee" arising out of and in the course of the "residence employee's" employment by an "insured".

HO 00 05 10 00

F. Coverage E – Personal Liability

Coverage **E** does not apply to:

1. Liability:

   a. For any loss assessment charged against you as a member of an association, corporation or community of property owners, except as provided in **D. Loss Assessment** under Section **II** – Additional Coverages;

   b. Under any contract or agreement entered into by an "insured". However, this exclusion does not apply to written contracts:

      (1) That directly relate to the ownership, maintenance or use of an "insured location"; or

      (2) Where the liability of others is assumed by you prior to an "occurrence";

      unless excluded in **a.** above or elsewhere in this policy;

2. "Property damage" to property owned by an "insured". This includes costs or expenses incurred by an "insured" or others to repair, replace, enhance, restore or maintain such property to prevent injury to a person or damage to property of others, whether on or away from an "insured location";

3. "Property damage" to property rented to, occupied or used by or in the care of an "insured". This exclusion does not apply to "property damage" caused by fire, smoke or explosion;

4. "Bodily injury" to any person eligible to receive any benefits voluntarily provided or required to be provided by an "insured" under any:

   a. Workers' compensation law;

   b. Non-occupational disability law; or

   c. Occupational disease law;

5. "Bodily injury" or "property damage" for which an "insured" under this policy:

   a. Is also an insured under a nuclear energy liability policy issued by the:

      (1) Nuclear Energy Liability Insurance Association;

      (2) Mutual Atomic Energy Liability Underwriters;

      (3) Nuclear Insurance Association of Canada;

      or any of their successors; or

   b. Would be an insured under such a policy but for the exhaustion of its limit of liability; or

6. "Bodily injury" to you or an "insured" as defined under Definitions **5.a.** or **b.**

This exclusion also applies to any claim made or suit brought against you or an "insured":

   a. To repay; or

   b. Share damages with;

another person who may be obligated to pay damages because of "bodily injury" to an "insured".

G. Coverage F – Medical Payments To Others

Coverage **F** does not apply to "bodily injury":

1. To a "residence employee" if the "bodily injury":

   a. Occurs off the "insured location"; and

   b. Does not arise out of or in the course of the "residence employee's" employment by an "insured";

2. To any person eligible to receive benefits voluntarily provided or required to be provided under any:

   a. Workers' compensation law;

   b. Non-occupational disability law; or

   c. Occupational disease law;

3. From any:

   a. Nuclear reaction;

   b. Nuclear radiation; or

   c. Radioactive contamination;

   all whether controlled or uncontrolled or however caused; or

   d. Any consequence of any of these; or

4. To any person, other than a "residence employee" of an "insured", regularly residing on any part of the "insured location".

SECTION II – ADDITIONAL COVERAGES

We cover the following in addition to the limits of liability:

A. Claim Expenses

We pay:

1. Expenses we incur and costs taxed against an "insured" in any suit we defend;

2. Premiums on bonds required in a suit we defend, but not for bond amounts more than the Coverage **E** limit of liability. We need not apply for or furnish any bond;

3. Reasonable expenses incurred by an "insured" at our request, including actual loss of earnings (but not loss of other income) up to $250 per day, for assisting us in the investigation or defense of a claim or suit; and

4. Interest on the entire judgment which accrues after entry of the judgment and before we pay or tender, or deposit in court that part of the judgment which does not exceed the limit of liability that applies.

B. First Aid Expenses

We will pay expenses for first aid to others incurred by an "insured" for "bodily injury" covered under this policy. We will not pay for first aid to an "insured".

C. Damage To Property Of Others

1. We will pay, at replacement cost, up to $1,000 per "occurrence" for "property damage" to property of others caused by an "insured".

2. We will not pay for "property damage":

    a. To the extent of any amount recoverable under Section I;

    b. Caused intentionally by an "insured" who is 13 years of age or older;

    c. To property owned by an "insured";

    d. To property owned by or rented to a tenant of an "insured" or a resident in your household; or

    e. Arising out of:

        (1) A "business" engaged in by an "insured";

        (2) Any act or omission in connection with a premises owned, rented or controlled by an "insured", other than the "insured location"; or

        (3) The ownership, maintenance, occupancy, operation, use, loading or unloading of aircraft, hovercraft, watercraft or "motor vehicles".

        This exclusion **e.(3)** does not apply to a "motor vehicle" that:

        (a) Is designed for recreational use off public roads;

        (b) Is not owned by an "insured"; and

        (c) At the time of the "occurrence", is not required by law, or regulation issued by a government agency, to have been registered for it to be used on public roads or property.

D. Loss Assessment

1. We will pay up to $1,000 for your share of loss assessment charged against you, as owner or tenant of the "residence premises", during the policy period by a corporation or association of property owners, when the assessment is made as a result of:

    a. "Bodily injury" or "property damage" not excluded from coverage under Section II – Exclusions; or

    b. Liability for an act of a director, officer or trustee in the capacity as a director, officer or trustee, provided such person:

        (1) Is elected by the members of a corporation or association of property owners; and

        (2) Serves without deriving any income from the exercise of duties which are solely on behalf of a corporation or association of property owners.

2. Paragraph **I.** Policy Period under Section II – Conditions does not apply to this Loss Assessment Coverage.

3. Regardless of the number of assessments, the limit of $1,000 is the most we will pay for loss arising out of:

    a. One accident, including continuous or repeated exposure to substantially the same general harmful condition; or

    b. A covered act of a director, officer or trustee. An act involving more than one director, officer or trustee is considered to be a single act.

4. We do not cover assessments charged against you or a corporation or association of property owners by any governmental body.

SECTION II – CONDITIONS

A. Limit Of Liability

Our total liability under Coverage **E** for all damages resulting from any one "occurrence" will not be more than the Coverage **E** limit of liability shown in the Declarations. This limit is the same regardless of the number of "insureds", claims made or persons injured. All "bodily injury" and "property damage" resulting from any one accident or from continuous or repeated exposure to substantially the same general harmful conditions shall be considered to be the result of one "occurrence".

Our total liability under Coverage **F** for all medical expense payable for "bodily injury" to one person as the result of one accident will not be more than the Coverage **F** limit of liability shown in the Declarations.

B. Severability Of Insurance

This insurance applies separately to each "insured". This condition will not increase our limit of liability for any one "occurrence".

 HO 00 05 10 00

C. Duties After "Occurrence"

In case of an "occurrence", you or another "insured" will perform the following duties that apply. We have no duty to provide coverage under this policy if your failure to comply with the following duties is prejudicial to us. You will help us by seeing that these duties are performed:

1. Give written notice to us or our agent as soon as is practical, which sets forth:

   a. The identity of the policy and the "named insured" shown in the Declarations;

   b. Reasonably available information on the time, place and circumstances of the "occurrence"; and

   c. Names and addresses of any claimants and witnesses;

2. Cooperate with us in the investigation, settlement or defense of any claim or suit;

3. Promptly forward to us every notice, demand, summons or other process relating to the "occurrence";

4. At our request, help us:

   a. To make settlement;

   b. To enforce any right of contribution or indemnity against any person or organization who may be liable to an "insured";

   c. With the conduct of suits and attend hearings and trials; and

   d. To secure and give evidence and obtain the attendance of witnesses;

5. With respect to **C.** Damage To Property Of Others under Section **II** – Additional Coverage, submit to us within 60 days after the loss, a sworn statement of loss and show the damaged property, if in an "insured's" control;

6. No "insured" shall, except at such "insured's" own cost, voluntarily make payment, assume obligation or incur expense other than for first aid to others at the time of the "bodily injury".

D. Duties Of An Injured Person – Coverage F – Medical Payments To Others

1. The injured person or someone acting for the injured person will:

   a. Give us written proof of claim, under oath if required, as soon as is practical; and

   b. Authorize us to obtain copies of medical reports and records.

2. The injured person will submit to a physical exam by a doctor of our choice when and as often as we reasonably require.

E. Payment Of Claim – Coverage F – Medical Payments To Others

Payment under this coverage is not an admission of liability by an "insured" or us.

F. Suit Against Us

1. No action can be brought against us unless there has been full compliance with all of the terms under this Section **II**.

2. No one will have the right to join us as a party to any action against an "insured".

3. Also, no action with respect to Coverage **E** can be brought against us until the obligation of such "insured" has been determined by final judgment or agreement signed by us.

G. Bankruptcy Of An "Insured"

Bankruptcy or insolvency of an "insured" will not relieve us of our obligations under this policy.

H. Other Insurance

This insurance is excess over other valid and collectible insurance except insurance written specifically to cover as excess over the limits of liability that apply in this policy.

I. Policy Period

This policy applies only to "bodily injury" or "property damage" which occurs during the policy period.

J. Concealment Or Fraud

We do not provide coverage to an "insured" who, whether before or after a loss, has:

1. Intentionally concealed or misrepresented any material fact or circumstance;

2. Engaged in fraudulent conduct; or

3. Made false statements;

relating to this insurance.

SECTIONS I AND II – CONDITIONS

A. Liberalization Clause

If we make a change which broadens coverage under this edition of our policy without additional premium charge, that change will automatically apply to your insurance as of the date we implement the change in your state, provided that this implementation date falls within 60 days prior to or during the policy period stated in the Declarations.

This Liberalization Clause does not apply to changes implemented with a general program revision that includes both broadenings and restrictions in coverage, whether that general program revision is implemented through introduction of:

1. A subsequent edition of this policy; or

2. An amendatory endorsement.

B. Waiver Or Change Of Policy Provisions

A waiver or change of a provision of this policy must be in writing by us to be valid. Our request for an appraisal or examination will not waive any of our rights.

C. Cancellation

1. You may cancel this policy at any time by returning it to us or by letting us know in writing of the date cancellation is to take effect.

2. We may cancel this policy only for the reasons stated below by letting you know in writing of the date cancellation takes effect. This cancellation notice may be delivered to you, or mailed to you at your mailing address shown in the Declarations. Proof of mailing will be sufficient proof of notice.

   a. When you have not paid the premium, we may cancel at any time by letting you know at least 10 days before the date cancellation takes effect.

   b. When this policy has been in effect for less than 60 days and is not a renewal with us, we may cancel for any reason by letting you know at least 10 days before the date cancellation takes effect.

   c. When this policy has been in effect for 60 days or more, or at any time if it is a renewal with us, we may cancel:

      (1) If there has been a material misrepresentation of fact which if known to us would have caused us not to issue the policy; or

      (2) If the risk has changed substantially since the policy was issued.

      This can be done by letting you know at least 30 days before the date cancellation takes effect.

   d. When this policy is written for a period of more than one year, we may cancel for any reason at anniversary by letting you know at least 30 days before the date cancellation takes effect.

3. When this policy is canceled, the premium for the period from the date of cancellation to the expiration date will be refunded pro rata.

4. If the return premium is not refunded with the notice of cancellation or when this policy is returned to us, we will refund it within a reasonable time after the date cancellation takes effect.

D. Nonrenewal

We may elect not to renew this policy. We may do so by delivering to you, or mailing to you at your mailing address shown in the Declarations, written notice at least 30 days before the expiration date of this policy. Proof of mailing will be sufficient proof of notice.

E. Assignment

Assignment of this policy will not be valid unless we give our written consent.

F. Subrogation

An "insured" may waive in writing before a loss all rights of recovery against any person. If not waived, we may require an assignment of rights of recovery for a loss to the extent that payment is made by us.

If an assignment is sought, an "insured" must sign and deliver all related papers and cooperate with us.

Subrogation does not apply to Coverage **F** or Paragraph **C.** Damage To Property Of Others under Section **II** – Additional Coverages.

G. Death

If any person named in the Declarations or the spouse, if a resident of the same household, dies, the following apply:

1. We insure the legal representative of the deceased but only with respect to the premises and property of the deceased covered under the policy at the time of death; and

2. "Insured" includes:

   a. An "insured" who is a member of your household at the time of your death, but only while a resident of the "residence premises"; and

   b. With respect to your property, the person having proper temporary custody of the property until appointment and qualification of a legal representative.

       HO 00 05 10 00

HOMEOWNERS 6 – UNIT-OWNERS FORM

AGREEMENT

We will provide the insurance described in this policy in return for the premium and compliance with all applicable provisions of this policy.

DEFINITIONS

A. In this policy, "you" and "your" refer to the "named insured" shown in the Declarations and the spouse if a resident of the same household. "We", "us" and "our" refer to the Company providing this insurance.

B. In addition, certain words and phrases are defined as follows:

1. "Aircraft Liability", "Hovercraft Liability", "Motor Vehicle Liability" and "Watercraft Liability", subject to the provisions in **b.** below, mean the following:

   a. Liability for "bodily injury" or "property damage" arising out of the:

      (1) Ownership of such vehicle or craft by an "insured";

      (2) Maintenance, occupancy, operation, use, loading or unloading of such vehicle or craft by any person;

      (3) Entrustment of such vehicle or craft by an "insured" to any person;

      (4) Failure to supervise or negligent supervision of any person involving such vehicle or craft by an "insured"; or

      (5) Vicarious liability, whether or not imposed by law, for the actions of a child or minor involving such vehicle or craft.

   b. For the purpose of this definition:

      (1) Aircraft means any contrivance used or designed for flight except model or hobby aircraft not used or designed to carry people or cargo;

      (2) Hovercraft means a self-propelled motorized ground effect vehicle and includes, but is not limited to, flarecraft and air cushion vehicles;

      (3) Watercraft means a craft principally designed to be propelled on or in water by wind, engine power or electric motor; and

      (4) Motor vehicle means a "motor vehicle" as defined in **7.** below.

2. "Bodily injury" means bodily harm, sickness or disease, including required care, loss of services and death that results.

3. "Business" means:

   a. A trade, profession or occupation engaged in on a full-time, part-time or occasional basis; or

   b. Any other activity engaged in for money or other compensation, except the following:

      (1) One or more activities, not described in **(2)** through **(4)** below, for which no "insured" receives more than $2,000 in total compensation for the 12 months before the beginning of the policy period;

      (2) Volunteer activities for which no money is received other than payment for expenses incurred to perform the activity;

      (3) Providing home day care services for which no compensation is received, other than the mutual exchange of such services; or

      (4) The rendering of home day care services to a relative of an "insured".

4. "Employee" means an employee of an "insured", or an employee leased to an "insured" by a labor leasing firm under an agreement between an "insured" and the labor leasing firm, whose duties are other than those performed by a "residence employee".

5. "Insured" means:

   a. You and residents of your household who are:

      (1) Your relatives; or

      (2) Other persons under the age of 21 and in the care of any person named above;

   b. A student enrolled in school full time, as defined by the school, who was a resident of your household before moving out to attend school, provided the student is under the age of:

      (1) 24 and your relative; or

      (2) 21 and in your care or the care of a person described in **a.(1)** above; or

c. Under Section **II:**

(1) With respect to animals or watercraft to which this policy applies, any person or organization legally responsible for these animals or watercraft which are owned by you or any person included in **a.** or **b.** above. "Insured" does not mean a person or organization using or having custody of these animals or watercraft in the course of any "business" or without consent of the owner; or

(2) With respect to a "motor vehicle" to which this policy applies:

(a) Persons while engaged in your employ or that of any person included in **a.** or **b.** above; or

(b) Other persons using the vehicle on an "insured location" with your consent.

Under both Sections **I** and **II,** when the word an immediately precedes the word "insured", the words an "insured" together mean one or more "insureds".

6. "Insured location" means:

a. The "residence premises";

b. The part of other premises, other structures and grounds used by you as a residence; and

(1) Which is shown in the Declarations; or

(2) Which is acquired by you during the policy period for your use as a residence;

c. Any premises used by you in connection with a premises described in **a.** and **b.** above;

d. Any part of a premises:

(1) Not owned by an "insured"; and

(2) Where an "insured" is temporarily residing;

e. Vacant land, other than farm land, owned by or rented to an "insured";

f. Land owned by or rented to an "insured" on which a one, two, three or four family dwelling is being built as a residence for an "insured";

g. Individual or family cemetery plots or burial vaults of an "insured"; or

h. Any part of a premises occasionally rented to an "insured" for other than "business" use.

7. "Motor vehicle" means:

a. A self-propelled land or amphibious vehicle; or

b. Any trailer or semitrailer which is being carried on, towed by or hitched for towing by a vehicle described in **a.** above.

8. "Occurrence" means an accident, including continuous or repeated exposure to substantially the same general harmful conditions, which results, during the policy period, in:

a. "Bodily injury"; or

b. "Property damage".

9. "Property damage" means physical injury to, destruction of, or loss of use of tangible property.

10. "Residence employee" means:

a. An employee of an "insured", or an employee leased to an "insured" by a labor leasing firm, under an agreement between an "insured" and the labor leasing firm, whose duties are related to the maintenance or use of the "residence premises", including household or domestic services; or

b. One who performs similar duties elsewhere not related to the "business" of an "insured".

A "residence employee" does not include a temporary employee who is furnished to an "insured" to substitute for a permanent "residence employee" on leave or to meet seasonal or short-term workload conditions.

11. "Residence premises" means the unit where you reside shown as the "residence premises" in the Declarations.

DEDUCTIBLE

Unless otherwise noted in this policy, the following deductible provision applies:

Subject to the policy limits that apply, we will pay only that part of the total of all loss payable under Section **I** that exceeds the deductible amount shown in the Declarations.

SECTION I – PROPERTY COVERAGES

A. Coverage A – Dwelling

1. We cover:

a. The alterations, appliances, fixtures and improvements which are part of the building contained within the "residence premises";

Copyright, Insurance Services Office, Inc., 1999 HO 00 06 10 00

b. Items of real property which pertain exclusively to the "residence premises";

c. Property which is your insurance responsibility under a corporation or association of property owners agreement; or

d. Structures owned solely by you, other than the "residence premises", at the location of the "residence premises".

2. We do not cover:

a. Land, including land on which the "residence premises", real property or structures are located;

b. Structures rented or held for rental to any person not a tenant of the dwelling, unless used solely as a private garage;

c. Structures from which any "business" is conducted; or

d. Structures used to store "business" property. However, we do cover a structure that contains "business" property solely owned by an "insured" or a tenant of the dwelling provided that "business" property does not include gaseous or liquid fuel, other than fuel in a permanently installed fuel tank of a vehicle or craft parked or stored in the structure.

B. Coverage C – Personal Property

1. Covered Property

We cover personal property owned or used by an "insured" while it is anywhere in the world. After a loss and at your request, we will cover personal property owned by:

a. Others while the property is on the part of the "residence premises" occupied by an "insured"; or

b. A guest or a "residence employee", while the property is in any residence occupied by an "insured".

2. Limit For Property At Other Residences

Our limit of liability for personal property usually located at an "insured's" residence, other than the "residence premises", is 10% of the limit of liability for Coverage **C,** or $1,000, whichever is greater. However, this limitation does not apply to personal property:

a. Moved from the "residence premises" because it is being repaired, renovated or rebuilt and is not fit to live in or store property in; or

b. In a newly acquired principal residence for 30 days from the time you begin to move the property there.

3. Special Limits Of Liability

The special limit for each category shown below is the total limit for each loss for all property in that category. These special limits do not increase the Coverage **C** limit of liability.

a. $200 on money, bank notes, bullion, gold other than goldware, silver other than silverware, platinum other than platinumware, coins, medals, scrip, stored value cards and smart cards.

b. $1,500 on securities, accounts, deeds, evidences of debt, letters of credit, notes other than bank notes, manuscripts, personal records, passports, tickets and stamps. This dollar limit applies to these categories regardless of the medium (such as paper or computer software) on which the material exists.

This limit includes the cost to research, replace or restore the information from the lost or damaged material.

c. $1,500 on watercraft of all types, including their trailers, furnishings, equipment and outboard engines or motors.

d. $1,500 on trailers or semitrailers not used with watercraft of all types.

e. $1,500 for loss by theft of jewelry, watches, furs, precious and semiprecious stones.

f. $2,500 for loss by theft of firearms and related equipment.

g. $2,500 for loss by theft of silverware, silver-plated ware, goldware, gold-plated ware, platinumware, platinum-plated ware and pewterware. This includes flatware, hollowware, tea sets, trays and trophies made of or including silver, gold or pewter.

h. $2,500 on property, on the "residence premises", used primarily for "business" purposes.

i. $500 on property, away from the "residence premises", used primarily for "business" purposes. However, this limit does not apply to loss to electronic apparatus and other property described in Categories **j.** and **k.** below.

j. $1,500 on electronic apparatus and accessories, while in or upon a "motor vehicle", but only if the apparatus is equipped to be operated by power from the "motor vehicle's" electrical system while still capable of being operated by other power sources.

Accessories include antennas, tapes, wires, records, discs or other media that can be used with any apparatus described in this Category **j.**

k. $1,500 on electronic apparatus and accessories used primarily for "business" while away from the "residence premises" and not in or upon a "motor vehicle". The apparatus must be equipped to be operated by power from the "motor vehicle's" electrical system while still capable of being operated by other power sources.

Accessories include antennas, tapes, wires, records, discs or other media that can be used with any apparatus described in this Category **k.**

4. Property Not Covered

We do not cover:

a. Articles separately described and specifically insured, regardless of the limit for which they are insured, in this or other insurance;

b. Animals, birds or fish;

c. "Motor vehicles".

(1) This includes:

(a) Their accessories, equipment and parts; or

(b) Electronic apparatus and accessories designed to be operated solely by power from the electrical system of the "motor vehicle". Accessories include antennas, tapes, wires, records, discs or other media that can be used with any apparatus described above.

The exclusion of property described in **(a)** and **(b)** above applies only while such property is in or upon the "motor vehicle".

(2) We do cover "motor vehicles" not required to be registered for use on public roads or property which are:

(a) Used solely to service an "insured's" residence; or

(b) Designed to assist the handicapped;

d. Aircraft meaning any contrivance used or designed for flight including any parts whether or not attached to the aircraft.

We do cover model or hobby aircraft not used or designed to carry people or cargo;

e. Hovercraft and parts. Hovercraft means a self-propelled motorized ground effect vehicle and includes, but is not limited to, flarecraft and air cushion vehicles;

f. Property of roomers, boarders and other tenants, except property of roomers and boarders related to an "insured";

g. Property in an apartment regularly rented or held for rental to others by an "insured";

h. Property rented or held for rental to others off the "residence premises";

i. "Business" data, including such data stored in:

(1) Books of account, drawings or other paper records; or

(2) Computers and related equipment.

We do cover the cost of blank recording or storage media, and of prerecorded computer programs available on the retail market;

j. Credit cards, electronic fund transfer cards or access devices used solely for deposit, withdrawal or transfer of funds except as provided in **D.6.** Credit Card, Electronic Fund Transfer Card Or Access Device, Forgery And Counterfeit Money under Section **I** – Property Coverages; or

k. Water or steam.

C. Coverage D – Loss Of Use

The limit of liability for Coverage D is the total limit for the coverages in **1.** Additional Living Expense, **2.** Fair Rental Value and **3.** Civil Authority Prohibits Use below.

1. Additional Living Expense

If a loss by a Peril Insured Against under this policy to covered property or the building containing the property makes the "residence premises" not fit to live in, we cover any necessary increase in living expenses incurred by you so that your household can maintain its normal standard of living.

Payment will be for the shortest time required to repair or replace the damage or, if you permanently relocate, the shortest time required for your household to settle elsewhere.

2. Fair Rental Value

If a loss covered under Section **I** makes that part of the "residence premises" rented to others or held for rental by you not fit to live in, we cover the fair rental value of such premises less any expenses that do not continue while it is not fit to live in.

Payment will be for the shortest time required to repair or replace such premises.

3. Civil Authority Prohibits Use

If a civil authority prohibits you from use of the "residence premises" as a result of direct damage to neighboring premises by a Peril Insured Against, we cover the loss as provided in **1.** Additional Living Expense and **2.** Fair Rental Value above for no more than two weeks.

Copyright, Insurance Services Office, Inc., 1999   HO 00 06 10 00

4. Loss Or Expense Not Covered

We do not cover loss or expense due to cancellation of a lease or agreement.

The periods of time under **1.** Additional Living Expense, **2.** Fair Rental Value and **3.** Civil Authority Prohibits Use above are not limited by expiration of this policy.

D. Additional Coverages

1. Debris Removal

a. We will pay your reasonable expense for the removal of:

(1) Debris of covered property if a Peril Insured Against that applies to the damaged property causes the loss; or

(2) Ash, dust or particles from a volcanic eruption that has caused direct loss to a building or property contained in a building.

This expense is included in the limit of liability that applies to the damaged property. If the amount to be paid for the actual damage to the property plus the debris removal expense is more than the limit of liability for the damaged property, an additional 5% of that limit is available for such expense.

b. We will also pay your reasonable expense, up to $1,000, for the removal from the "residence premises" of:

(1) Tree(s) you solely own felled by the peril of Windstorm or Hail or Weight of Ice, Snow or Sleet; or

(2) A neighbor's tree(s) felled by a Peril Insured Against under Coverage **C;**

provided the tree(s) damage(s) a covered structure.

The $1,000 limit is the most we will pay in any one loss regardless of the number of fallen trees. No more than $500 of this limit will be paid for the removal of any one tree.

This coverage is additional insurance.

2. Reasonable Repairs

a. We will pay the reasonable cost incurred by you for the necessary measures taken solely to protect covered property that is damaged by a Peril Insured Against from further damage.

b. If the measures taken involve repair to other damaged property, we will only pay if that property is covered under this policy and the damage is caused by a Peril Insured Against. This coverage does not:

(1) Increase the limit of liability that applies to the covered property; or

(2) Relieve you of your duties, in case of a loss to covered property, described in **B.4.** under Section **I** – Conditions.

3. Trees, Shrubs And Other Plants

We cover trees, shrubs, plants or lawns, you solely own at the location of the "residence premises", for loss caused by the following Perils Insured Against:

a. Fire or Lightning;

b. Explosion;

c. Riot or Civil Commotion;

d. Aircraft;

e. Vehicles not owned or operated by a resident of the "residence premises";

f. Vandalism or Malicious Mischief; or

g. Theft.

We will pay up to 10% of the limit of liability that applies to Coverage **C** for all trees, shrubs, plants or lawns. No more than $500 of this limit will be paid for any one tree, shrub or plant. We do not cover property grown for "business" purposes.

This coverage is additional insurance.

4. Fire Department Service Charge

We will pay up to $500 for your liability assumed by contract or agreement for fire department charges incurred when the fire department is called to save or protect covered property from a Peril Insured Against. We do not cover fire department service charges if the property is located within the limits of the city, municipality or protection district furnishing the fire department response.

This coverage is additional insurance. No deductible applies to this coverage.

5. Property Removed

We insure covered property against direct loss from any cause while being removed from a premises endangered by a Peril Insured Against and for no more than 30 days while removed.

This coverage does not change the limit of liability that applies to the property being removed.

6. Credit Card, Electronic Fund Transfer Card Or Access Device, Forgery And Counterfeit Money

a. We will pay up to $500 for:

(1) The legal obligation of an "insured" to pay because of the theft or unauthorized use of credit cards issued to or registered in an "insured's" name;

(2) Loss resulting from theft or unauthorized use of an electronic fund transfer card or access device used for deposit, withdrawal or transfer of funds, issued to or registered in an "insured's" name;

(3) Loss to an "insured" caused by forgery or alteration of any check or negotiable instrument; and

(4) Loss to an "insured" through acceptance in good faith of counterfeit United States or Canadian paper currency.

All loss resulting from a series of acts committed by any one person or in which any one person is concerned or implicated is considered to be one loss.

This coverage is additional insurance. No deductible applies to this coverage.

b. We do not cover:

(1) Use of a credit card, electronic fund transfer card or access device:

(a) By a resident of your household;

(b) By a person who has been entrusted with either type of card or access device; or

(c) If an "insured" has not complied with all terms and conditions under which the cards are issued or the devices accessed; or

(2) Loss arising out of "business" use or dishonesty of an "insured".

c. If the coverage in **a.** above applies, the following defense provisions also apply:

(1) We may investigate and settle any claim or suit that we decide is appropriate. Our duty to defend a claim or suit ends when the amount we pay for the loss equals our limit of liability.

(2) If a suit is brought against an "insured" for liability under **a.(1)** or **(2)** above, we will provide a defense at our expense by counsel of our choice.

(3) We have the option to defend at our expense an "insured" or an "insured's" bank against any suit for the enforcement of payment under **a.(3)** above.

7. Loss Assessment

a. We will pay up to $1,000 for your share of loss assessment charged during the policy period against you, as owner or tenant of the "residence premises", by a corporation or association of property owners. The assessment must be made as a result of direct loss to property, owned by all members collectively, of the type that would be covered by this policy if owned by you, caused by a Peril Insured Against under Coverage **A,** other than:

(1) Earthquake; or

(2) Land shock waves or tremors before, during or after a volcanic eruption.

The limit of $1,000 is the most we will pay with respect to any one loss, regardless of the number of assessments. We will only apply one deductible, per unit, to the total amount of any one loss to the property described above, regardless of the number of assessments.

b. We do not cover assessments charged against you or a corporation or association of property owners by any governmental body.

c. Paragraph **P.** Policy Period under Section **I** – Conditions does not apply to this coverage.

This coverage is additional insurance.

8. Collapse

a. With respect to this Additional Coverage:

(1) Collapse means an abrupt falling down or caving in of a building or any part of a building with the result that the building or part of the building cannot be occupied for its current intended purpose.

(2) A building or any part of a building that is in danger of falling down or caving in is not considered to be in a state of collapse.

(3) A part of a building that is standing is not considered to be in a state of collapse even if it has separated from another part of the building.

(4) A building or any part of a building that is standing is not considered to be in a state of collapse even if it shows evidence of cracking, bulging, sagging, bending, leaning, settling, shrinkage or expansion.

HO 00 06 10 00

b. We insure for direct physical loss to covered property involving collapse of a building or any part of a building if the collapse was caused by one or more of the following:

(1) The Perils Insured Against named under Coverage **C;**

(2) Decay that is hidden from view, unless the presence of such decay is known to an "insured" prior to collapse;

(3) Insect or vermin damage that is hidden from view, unless the presence of such damage is known to an "insured" prior to collapse;

(4) Weight of contents, equipment, animals or people;

(5) Weight of rain which collects on a roof; or

(6) Use of defective material or methods in construction, remodeling or renovation if the collapse occurs during the course of the construction, remodeling or renovation.

c. Loss to an awning, fence, patio, deck, pavement, swimming pool, underground pipe, flue, drain, cesspool, septic tank, foundation, retaining wall, bulkhead, pier, wharf or dock is not included under **b.(2)** through **(6)** above, unless the loss is a direct result of the collapse of a building or any part of a building.

d. This coverage does not increase the limit of liability that applies to the damaged covered property.

9. Glass Or Safety Glazing Material

a. We cover:

(1) The breakage of glass or safety glazing material which is part of a building, storm door or storm window and covered under Coverage **A;**

(2) The breakage of glass or safety glazing material which is part of a building, storm door or storm window and covered under Coverage **A** when caused directly by earth movement; and

(3) The direct physical loss to covered property caused solely by the pieces, fragments or splinters of broken glass or safety glazing material which is part of a building, storm door or storm window.

b. This coverage does not include loss:

(1) To covered property which results because the glass or safety glazing material has been broken, except as provided in **a.(3)** above; or

(2) To the "residence premises" if the building containing the "residence premises" has been vacant for more than 60 consecutive days immediately before the loss, except when the breakage results directly from earth movement as provided in **a.(2)** above. A building being constructed is not considered vacant.

c. This coverage does not increase the limit of liability that applies to the damaged property.

10. Ordinance Or Law

a. You may use up to 10% of the limit of liability that applies to Coverage **A** for the increased costs you incur due to the enforcement of any ordinance or law which requires or regulates:

(1) The construction, demolition, remodeling, renovation or repair of that part of property covered under Coverage **A** damaged by a Peril Insured Against;

(2) The demolition and reconstruction of the undamaged part of property covered under Coverage **A,** when that property must be totally demolished because of damage by a Peril Insured Against to another part of that property covered under Coverage **A;** or

(3) The remodeling, removal or replacement of the portion of the undamaged part of property covered under Coverage **A** necessary to complete the remodeling, repair or replacement of that part of the property covered under Coverage **A** damaged by a Peril Insured Against.

b. You may use all or part of this ordinance or law coverage to pay for the increased costs you incur to remove debris resulting from the construction, demolition, remodeling, renovation, repair or replacement of property as stated in **a.** above.

c. We do not cover:

(1) The loss in value to any property covered under Coverage **A** due to the requirements of any ordinance or law; or

(2) The costs to comply with any ordinance or law which requires any "insured" or others, to test for, monitor, clean up, remove, contain, treat, detoxify or neutralize, or in any way respond to, or assess the effects of, pollutants in or on any property covered under Coverage **A.**

Pollutants means any solid, liquid, gaseous or thermal irritant or contaminant, including smoke, vapor, soot, fumes, acids, alkalis, chemicals and waste. Waste includes materials to be recycled, reconditioned or reclaimed.

This coverage is additional insurance.

11. Grave Markers

We will pay up to $5,000 for grave markers, including mausoleums, away from the "residence premises" for loss caused by a Peril Insured Against.

This coverage does not increase the limits of liability that apply to the damaged covered property.

SECTION I — PERILS INSURED AGAINST

We insure for direct physical loss to the property described in Coverages **A** and **C** caused by any of the following perils unless the loss is excluded in Section I — Exclusions.

1. Fire Or Lightning

2. Windstorm Or Hail

This peril includes loss to watercraft of all types and their trailers, furnishings, equipment, and outboard engines or motors, only while inside a fully enclosed building.

This peril does not include loss to the inside of a building or the property contained in a building caused by rain, snow, sleet, sand or dust unless the direct force of wind or hail damages the building causing an opening in a roof or wall and the rain, snow, sleet, sand or dust enters through this opening.

3. Explosion

4. Riot Or Civil Commotion

5. Aircraft

This peril includes self-propelled missiles and spacecraft.

6. Vehicles

This peril does not include loss to a fence, driveway or walk caused by a vehicle owned or operated by a resident of the "residence premises".

7. Smoke

This peril means sudden and accidental damage from smoke, including the emission or puffback of smoke, soot, fumes or vapors from a boiler, furnace or related equipment.

This peril does not include loss caused by smoke from agricultural smudging or industrial operations.

8. Vandalism Or Malicious Mischief

This peril does not include loss to property which pertains to the "residence premises", and any ensuing loss caused by any intentional and wrongful act committed in the course of the vandalism or malicious mischief, if the building containing the "residence premises" has been vacant for more than 60 consecutive days immediately before the loss. A building being constructed is not considered vacant.

9. Theft

a. This peril includes attempted theft and loss of property from a known place when it is likely that the property has been stolen.

b. This peril does not include loss caused by theft:

(1) Committed by an "insured";

(2) In or to a "residence premises" under construction, or of materials and supplies for use in the construction until the "residence premises" is finished and occupied;

(3) From that part of a "residence premises" rented by an "insured" to someone other than another "insured"; or

(4) That occurs away from the "residence premises" or the location of the "residence premises" of:

(a) Trailers, semitrailers and campers;

(b) Watercraft of all types, and their furnishings, equipment and outboard engines or motors; or

(c) Property while at any other residence owned by, rented to, or occupied by an "insured", except while an "insured" is temporarily living there. Property of an "insured" who is a student is covered while at the residence the student occupies to attend school as long as the student has been there at any time during the 60 days immediately before the loss.

10. Falling Objects

This peril does not include loss to the inside of a building or property contained in the building unless the roof or an outside wall of the building is first damaged by a falling object. Damage to the falling object itself is not included.

   HO 00 06 10 00

11. Weight Of Ice, Snow Or Sleet

This peril means weight of ice, snow or sleet which causes damage to a building or property contained in a building.

This peril does not include loss to an awning, fence, patio, pavement, swimming pool, foundation, retaining wall, bulkhead, pier, wharf, or dock.

12. Accidental Discharge Or Overflow Of Water Or Steam

a. This peril means accidental discharge or overflow of water or steam from within a plumbing, heating, air conditioning or automatic fire protective sprinkler system or from within a household appliance. We also pay to tear out and replace any part of a building or other structure owned solely by you which is covered under Coverage **A** and at the location of the "residence premises", but only when necessary to repair the system or appliance from which the water or steam escaped. However, such tear out and replacement coverage only applies to other structures if the water or steam causes actual damage to a building owned solely by you at the location of the "residence premises".

b. This peril does not include loss:

(1) To or within the "residence premises", if the building containing the "residence premises" has been vacant for more than 60 consecutive days immediately before the loss. A building being constructed is not considered vacant;

(2) To the system or appliance from which the water or steam escaped;

(3) Caused by or resulting from freezing except as provided in Peril Insured Against **14.** Freezing;

(4) To or within the "residence premises" caused by accidental discharge or overflow which occurs away from the building where the "residence premises" is located; or

(5) Caused by mold, fungus or wet rot unless hidden within the walls or ceilings or beneath the floors or above the ceilings of a structure.

c. In this peril, a plumbing system or household appliance does not include a sump, sump pump or related equipment or a roof drain, gutter, downspout or similar fixtures or equipment.

d. Section **I** – Exclusion **3.** Water Damage, Paragraphs **a.** and **c.** that apply to surface water and water below the surface of the ground do not apply to loss by water covered under this peril.

13. Sudden And Accidental Tearing Apart, Cracking, Burning Or Bulging

This peril means sudden and accidental tearing apart, cracking, burning or bulging of a steam or hot water heating system, an air conditioning or automatic fire protective sprinkler system, or an appliance for heating water.

This peril does not include loss caused by or resulting from freezing except as provided in Peril Insured Against **14.** Freezing below.

14. Freezing

a. This peril means freezing of a plumbing, heating, air conditioning or automatic fire protective sprinkler system or of a household appliance but only if you have used reasonable care to:

(1) Maintain heat in the building; or

(2) Shut off the water supply and drain all systems and appliances of water.

However, if the building is protected by an automatic fire protective sprinkler system, you must use reasonable care to continue the water supply and maintain heat in the "residence premises" for coverage to apply.

b. In this peril, a plumbing system or household appliance does not include a sump, sump pump or related equipment or a roof drain, gutter, downspout or similar fixtures or equipment.

15. Sudden And Accidental Damage From Artificially Generated Electrical Current

This peril does not include loss to tubes, transistors, electronic components or circuitry that are a part of appliances, fixtures, computers, home entertainment units or other types of electronic apparatus.

16. Volcanic Eruption

This peril does not include loss caused by earthquake, land shock waves or tremors.

SECTION I – EXCLUSIONS

We do not insure for loss caused directly or indirectly by any of the following. Such loss is excluded regardless of any other cause or event contributing concurrently or in any sequence to the loss. These exclusions apply whether or not the loss event results in widespread damage or affects a substantial area.

1. Ordinance Or Law

Ordinance Or Law means any ordinance or law:

a. Requiring or regulating the construction, demolition, remodeling, renovation or repair of property, including removal of any resulting debris. This Exclusion **1.a.** does not apply to the amount of coverage that may be provided for in **D.10.** Ordinance Or Law under Section **I** – Property Coverages;

b. The requirements of which result in a loss in value to property; or

c. Requiring any "insured" or others to test for, monitor, clean up, remove, contain, treat, detoxify or neutralize, or in any way respond to, or assess the effects of, pollutants.

Pollutants means any solid, liquid, gaseous or thermal irritant or contaminant, including smoke, vapor, soot, fumes, acids, alkalis, chemicals and waste. Waste includes materials to be recycled, reconditioned or reclaimed.

This Exclusion **1.** applies whether or not the property has been physically damaged.

2. Earth Movement

Earth Movement means:

a. Earthquake, including land shock waves or tremors before, during or after a volcanic eruption;

b. Landslide, mudslide or mudflow;

c. Subsidence or sinkhole; or

d. Any other earth movement including earth sinking, rising or shifting;

caused by or resulting from human or animal forces or any act of nature unless direct loss by fire or explosion ensues and then we will pay only for the ensuing loss.

This Exclusion **2.** does not apply to loss by theft.

3. Water Damage

Water Damage means:

a. Flood, surface water, waves, tidal water, overflow of a body of water, or spray from any of these, whether or not driven by wind;

b. Water or water-borne material which backs up through sewers or drains or which overflows or is discharged from a sump, sump pump or related equipment; or

c. Water or water-borne material below the surface of the ground, including water which exerts pressure on or seeps or leaks through a building, sidewalk, driveway, foundation, swimming pool or other structure;

caused by or resulting from human or animal forces or any act of nature.

Direct loss by fire, explosion or theft resulting from water damage is covered.

4. Power Failure

Power Failure means the failure of power or other utility service if the failure takes place off the "residence premises". But if the failure results in a loss, from a Peril Insured Against on the "residence premises", we will pay for the loss caused by that peril.

5. Neglect

Neglect means neglect of an "insured" to use all reasonable means to save and preserve property at and after the time of a loss.

6. War

War includes the following and any consequence of any of the following:

a. Undeclared war, civil war, insurrection, rebellion or revolution;

b. Warlike act by a military force or military personnel; or

c. Destruction, seizure or use for a military purpose.

Discharge of a nuclear weapon will be deemed a warlike act even if accidental.

7. Nuclear Hazard

This Exclusion **7.** pertains to Nuclear Hazard to the extent set forth in **M.** Nuclear Hazard Clause under Section **I** – Conditions.

8. Intentional Loss

Intentional Loss means any loss arising out of any act an "insured" commits or conspires to commit with the intent to cause a loss.

In the event of such loss, no "insured" is entitled to coverage, even "insureds" who did not commit or conspire to commit the act causing the loss.

9. Governmental Action

Governmental Action means the destruction, confiscation or seizure of property described in Coverage **A** or **C** by order of any governmental or public authority.

This exclusion does not apply to such acts ordered by any governmental or public authority that are taken at the time of a fire to prevent its spread, if the loss caused by fire would be covered under this policy.

SECTION I – CONDITIONS

A. Insurable Interest And Limit Of Liability

Even if more than one person has an insurable interest in the property covered, we will not be liable in any one loss:

1. To an "insured" for more than the amount of such "insured's" interest at the time of loss; or

2. For more than the applicable limit of liability.

B. Duties After Loss

In case of a loss to covered property, we have no duty to provide coverage under this policy if the failure to comply with the following duties is prejudicial to us. These duties must be performed either by you, an "insured" seeking coverage, or a representative of either:

Copyright, Insurance Services Office, Inc., 1999

HO 00 06 10 00

1. Give prompt notice to us or our agent;

2. Notify the police in case of loss by theft;

3. Notify the credit card or electronic fund transfer card or access device company in case of loss under as provided for in **D.6.** Credit Card, Electronic Fund Transfer Card Or Access Device, Forgery And Counterfeit Money under Section **I** – Property Coverages;

4. Protect the property from further damage. If repairs to the property are required, you must:

   a. Make reasonable and necessary repairs to protect the property; and

   b. Keep an accurate record of repair expenses;

5. Cooperate with us in the investigation of a claim;

6. Prepare an inventory of damaged personal property showing the quantity, description, actual cash value and amount of loss. Attach all bills, receipts and related documents that justify the figures in the inventory;

7. As often as we reasonably require:

   a. Show the damaged property;

   b. Provide us with records and documents we request and permit us to make copies; and

   c. Submit to examination under oath, while not in the presence of another "insured", and sign the same;

8. Send to us, within 60 days after our request, your signed, sworn proof of loss which sets forth, to the best of your knowledge and belief:

   a. The time and cause of loss;

   b. The interests of all "insureds" and all others in the property involved and all liens on the property;

   c. Other insurance which may cover the loss;

   d. Changes in title or occupancy of the property during the term of the policy;

   e. Specifications of damaged buildings and detailed repair estimates;

   f. The inventory of damaged personal property described in **6.** above;

   g. Receipts for additional living expenses incurred and records that support the fair rental value loss; and

   h. Evidence or affidavit that supports a claim under **D.6.** Credit Card, Electronic Fund Transfer Card Or Access Device, Forgery And Counterfeit Money under Section **I** – Property Coverages, stating the amount and cause of loss.

C. Loss Settlement

Covered property losses are settled as follows:

1. Personal property and grave markers, including mausoleums, at actual cash value at the time of loss but not more than the amount required to repair or replace.

2. Coverage **A** – Dwelling:

   a. If the damage is repaired or replaced within a reasonable time, at the actual cost to repair or replace;

   b. If the damage is not repaired or replaced within a reasonable time, at actual cash value but not more than the amount required to repair or replace.

   In this provision, the terms "repaired" or "replaced" do not include the increased costs incurred to comply with the enforcement of any ordinance or law, except to the extent that coverage for these increased costs is provided in **D.10.** Ordinance Or Law under Section **I** – Property Coverages.

D. Loss To A Pair Or Set

In case of loss to a pair or set we may elect to:

1. Repair or replace any part to restore the pair or set to its value before the loss; or

2. Pay the difference between actual cash value of the property before and after the loss.

E. Appraisal

If you and we fail to agree on the amount of loss, either may demand an appraisal of the loss. In this event, each party will choose a competent and impartial appraiser within 20 days after receiving a written request from the other. The two appraisers will choose an umpire. If they cannot agree upon an umpire within 15 days, you or we may request that the choice be made by a judge of a court of record in the state where the "residence premises" is located. The appraisers will separately set the amount of loss. If the appraisers submit a written report of an agreement to us, the amount agreed upon will be the amount of loss. If they fail to agree, they will submit their differences to the umpire. A decision agreed to by any two will set the amount of loss.

Each party will:

1. Pay its own appraiser; and

2. Bear the other expenses of the appraisal and umpire equally.

F. Other Insurance And Service Agreement

1. If a loss covered by this policy is also covered by:

   a. Other insurance, except insurance in the name of a corporation or association of property owners, we will pay only the proportion of the loss that the limit of liability that applies under this policy bears to the total amount of insurance covering the loss; or

   b. A service agreement, except a service agreement in the name of a corporation or association of property owners, this insurance is excess over any amounts payable under any such agreement. Service agreement means a service plan, property restoration plan, home warranty or other similar service warranty agreement, even if it is characterized as insurance.

2. If, at the time of loss, there is other insurance or a service agreement in the name of a corporation or association of property owners covering the same property covered by this policy, this insurance will be excess over the amount recoverable under such other insurance or service agreement.

G. Suit Against Us

No action can be brought against us unless there has been full compliance with all of the terms under Section I of this policy and the action is started within two years after the date of loss.

H. Our Option

If we give you written notice within 30 days after we receive your signed, sworn proof of loss, we may repair or replace any part of the damaged property with material or property of like kind and quality.

I. Loss Payment

We will adjust all losses with you. We will pay you unless some other person is named in the policy or is legally entitled to receive payment. Loss will be payable 60 days after we receive your proof of loss and:

1. Reach an agreement with you;

2. There is an entry of a final judgment; or

3. There is a filing of an appraisal award with us.

J. Abandonment Of Property

We need not accept any property abandoned by an "insured".

K. Mortgage Clause

1. If a mortgagee is named in this policy, any loss payable under Coverage **A** will be paid to the mortgagee and you, as interests appear. If more than one mortgagee is named, the order of payment will be the same as the order of precedence of the mortgages.

2. If we deny your claim, that denial will not apply to a valid claim of the mortgagee, if the mortgagee:

   a. Notifies us of any change in ownership, occupancy or substantial change in risk of which the mortgagee is aware;

   b. Pays any premium due under this policy on demand if you have neglected to pay the premium; and

   c. Submits a signed, sworn statement of loss within 60 days after receiving notice from us of your failure to do so. Paragraphs **E.** Appraisal, **G.** Suit Against Us and **I.** Loss Payment under Section I – Conditions also apply to the mortgagee.

3. If we decide to cancel or not to renew this policy, the mortgagee will be notified at least 10 days before the date cancellation or nonrenewal takes effect.

4. If we pay the mortgagee for any loss and deny payment to you:

   a. We are subrogated to all the rights of the mortgagee granted under the mortgage on the property; or

   b. At our option, we may pay to the mortgagee the whole principal on the mortgage plus any accrued interest. In this event, we will receive a full assignment and transfer of the mortgage and all securities held as collateral to the mortgage debt.

5. Subrogation will not impair the right of the mortgagee to recover the full amount of the mortgagee's claim.

L. No Benefit To Bailee

We will not recognize any assignment or grant any coverage that benefits a person or organization holding, storing or moving property for a fee regardless of any other provision of this policy.

M. Nuclear Hazard Clause

1. "Nuclear Hazard" means any nuclear reaction, radiation, or radioactive contamination, all whether controlled or uncontrolled or however caused, or any consequence of any of these.

2. Loss caused by the nuclear hazard will not be considered loss caused by fire, explosion, or smoke, whether these perils are specifically named in or otherwise included within the Perils Insured Against.

         HO 00 06 10 00

3. This policy does not apply under Section **I** to loss caused directly or indirectly by nuclear hazard, except that direct loss by fire resulting from the nuclear hazard is covered.

N. Recovered Property

If you or we recover any property for which we have made payment under this policy, you or we will notify the other of the recovery. At your option, the property will be returned to or retained by you or it will become our property. If the recovered property is returned to or retained by you, the loss payment will be adjusted based on the amount you received for the recovered property.

O. Volcanic Eruption Period

One or more volcanic eruptions that occur within a 72 hour period will be considered as one volcanic eruption.

P. Policy Period

This policy applies only to loss which occurs during the policy period.

Q. Concealment Or Fraud

We provide coverage to no "insureds" under this policy if, whether before or after a loss, an "insured" has:

1. Intentionally concealed or misrepresented any material fact or circumstance;

2. Engaged in fraudulent conduct; or

3. Made false statements;

relating to this insurance.

R. Loss Payable Clause

If the Declarations show a loss payee for certain listed insured personal property, the definition of "insured" is changed to include that loss payee with respect to that property.

If we decide to cancel or not renew this policy, that loss payee will be notified in writing.

SECTION II – LIABILITY COVERAGES

A. Coverage E – Personal Liability

If a claim is made or a suit is brought against an "insured" for damages because of "bodily injury" or "property damage" caused by an "occurrence" to which this coverage applies, we will:

1. Pay up to our limit of liability for the damages for which an "insured" is legally liable. Damages include prejudgment interest awarded against an "insured"; and

2. Provide a defense at our expense by counsel of our choice, even if the suit is groundless, false or fraudulent. We may investigate and settle any claim or suit that we decide is appropriate. Our duty to settle or defend ends when our limit of liability for the "occurrence" has been exhausted by payment of a judgment or settlement.

B. Coverage F – Medical Payments To Others

We will pay the necessary medical expenses that are incurred or medically ascertained within three years from the date of an accident causing "bodily injury". Medical expenses means reasonable charges for medical, surgical, x-ray, dental, ambulance, hospital, professional nursing, prosthetic devices and funeral services. This coverage does not apply to you or regular residents of your household except "residence employees". As to others, this coverage applies only:

1. To a person on the "insured location" with the permission of an "insured"; or

2. To a person off the "insured location", if the "bodily injury":

a. Arises out of a condition on the "insured location" or the ways immediately adjoining;

b. Is caused by the activities of an "insured";

c. Is caused by a "residence employee" in the course of the "residence employee's" employment by an "insured"; or

d. Is caused by an animal owned by or in the care of an "insured".

SECTION II – EXCLUSIONS

A. "Motor Vehicle Liability"

1. Coverages **E** and **F** do not apply to any "motor vehicle liability" if, at the time and place of an "occurrence", the involved "motor vehicle":

a. Is registered for use on public roads or property;

b. Is not registered for use on public roads or property, but such registration is required by a law, or regulation issued by a government agency, for it to be used at the place of the "occurrence"; or

c. Is being:

(1) Operated in, or practicing for, any prearranged or organized race, speed contest or other competition;

(2) Rented to others;

(3) Used to carry persons or cargo for a charge; or

(4) Used for any "business" purpose except for a motorized golf cart while on a golfing facility.

2. If Exclusion **A.1.** does not apply, there is still no coverage for "motor vehicle liability" unless the "motor vehicle" is:

a. In dead storage on an "insured location";

b. Used solely to service an "insured's" residence;

c. Designed to assist the handicapped and, at the time of an "occurrence", it is:

(1) Being used to assist a handicapped person; or

(2) Parked on an "insured location";

d. Designed for recreational use off public roads and:

(1) Not owned by an "insured"; or

(2) Owned by an "insured" provided the "occurrence" takes place on an "insured location" as defined in Definitions **B.6.a., b., d., e.** or **h.;** or

e. A motorized golf cart that is owned by an "insured", designed to carry up to 4 persons, not built or modified after manufacture to exceed a speed of 25 miles per hour on level ground and, at the time of an "occurrence", is within the legal boundaries of:

(1) A golfing facility and is parked or stored there, or being used by an "insured" to:

(a) Play the game of golf or for other recreational or leisure activity allowed by the facility;

(b) Travel to or from an area where "motor vehicles" or golf carts are parked or stored; or

(c) Cross public roads at designated points to access other parts of the golfing facility; or

(2) A private residential community, including its public roads upon which a motorized golf cart can legally travel, which is subject to the authority of a property owners association and contains an "insured's" residence.

B. "Watercraft Liability"

1. Coverages **E** and **F** do not apply to any "watercraft liability" if, at the time of an "occurrence", the involved watercraft is being:

a. Operated in, or practicing for, any prearranged or organized race, speed contest or other competition. This exclusion does not apply to a sailing vessel or a predicted log cruise;

b. Rented to others;

c. Used to carry persons or cargo for a charge; or

d. Used for any "business" purpose.

2. If Exclusion **B.1.** does not apply, there is still no coverage for "watercraft liability" unless, at the time of the "occurrence", the watercraft:

a. Is stored;

b. Is a sailing vessel, with or without auxiliary power, that is:

(1) Less than 26 feet in overall length; or

(2) 26 feet or more in overall length and not owned by or rented to an "insured"; or

c. Is not a sailing vessel and is powered by:

(1) An inboard or inboard-outdrive engine or motor, including those that power a water jet pump, of:

(a) 50 horsepower or less and not owned by an "insured"; or

(b) More than 50 horsepower and not owned by or rented to an "insured"; or

(2) One or more outboard engines or motors with:

(a) 25 total horsepower or less;

(b) More than 25 horsepower if the outboard engine or motor is not owned by an "insured";

(c) More than 25 horsepower if the outboard engine or motor is owned by an "insured" who acquired it during the policy period; or

(d) More than 25 horsepower if the outboard engine or motor is owned by an "insured" who acquired it before the policy period, but only if:

(i) You declare them at policy inception; or

     HO 00 06 10 00

(ii) Your intent to insure them is reported to us in writing within 45 days after you acquire them.

The coverages in **(c)** and **(d)** above apply for the policy period.

Horsepower means the maximum power rating assigned to the engine or motor by the manufacturer.

C. "Aircraft Liability"

This policy does not cover "aircraft liability".

D. "Hovercraft Liability"

This policy does not cover "hovercraft liability".

E. Coverage E – Personal Liability And Coverage F – Medical Payments To Others

Coverages **E** and **F** do not apply to the following:

1. **Expected Or Intended Injury**

    "Bodily injury" or "property damage" which is expected or intended by an "insured" even if the resulting "bodily injury" or "property damage":

    a. Is of a different kind, quality or degree than initially expected or intended; or

    b. Is sustained by a different person, entity, real or personal property, than initially expected or intended.

    However, this Exclusion **E.1.** does not apply to "bodily injury" resulting from the use of reasonable force by an "insured" to protect persons or property;

2. **"Business"**

    a. "Bodily injury" or "property damage" arising out of or in connection with a "business" conducted from an "insured location" or engaged in by an "insured", whether or not the "business" is owned or operated by an "insured" or employs an "insured".

    This Exclusion **E.2.** applies but is not limited to an act or omission, regardless of its nature or circumstance, involving a service or duty rendered, promised, owed, or implied to be provided because of the nature of the "business".

    b. This Exclusion **E.2.** does not apply to:

    (1) The rental or holding for rental of an "insured location";

       (a) On an occasional basis if used only as a residence;

    (b) In part for use only as a residence, unless a single family unit is intended for use by the occupying family to lodge more than two roomers or boarders; or

    (c) In part, as an office, school, studio or private garage; and

    (2) An "insured" under the age of 21 years involved in a part-time or occasional, self-employed "business" with no employees;

3. **Professional Services**

    "Bodily injury" or "property damage" arising out of the rendering of or failure to render professional services;

4. **"Insured's" Premises Not An "Insured Location"**

    "Bodily injury" or "property damage" arising out of a premises:

    a. Owned by an "insured";

    b. Rented to an "insured"; or

    c. Rented to others by an "insured";

    that is not an "insured location";

5. **War**

    "Bodily injury" or "property damage" caused directly or indirectly by war, including the following and any consequence of any of the following:

    a. Undeclared war, civil war, insurrection, rebellion or revolution;

    b. Warlike act by a military force or military personnel; or

    c. Destruction, seizure or use for a military purpose.

    Discharge of a nuclear weapon will be deemed a warlike act even if accidental;

6. **Communicable Disease**

    "Bodily injury" or "property damage" which arises out of the transmission of a communicable disease by an "insured";

7. **Sexual Molestation, Corporal Punishment Or Physical Or Mental Abuse**

    "Bodily injury" or "property damage" arising out of sexual molestation, corporal punishment or physical or mental abuse; or

8. Controlled Substance

"Bodily injury" or "property damage" arising out of the use, sale, manufacture, delivery, transfer or possession by any person of a Controlled Substance as defined by the Federal Food and Drug Law at 21 U.S.C.A. Sections 811 and 812. Controlled Substances include but are not limited to cocaine, LSD, marijuana and all narcotic drugs. However, this exclusion does not apply to the legitimate use of prescription drugs by a person following the orders of a licensed physician.

Exclusions **A.** "Motor Vehicle Liability", **B.** "Watercraft Liability", **C.** "Aircraft Liability", **D.** "Hovercraft Liability" and **E.4.** "Insured's" Premises Not An "Insured Location" do not apply to "bodily injury" to a "residence employee" arising out of and in the course of the "residence employee's" employment by an "insured".

F. Coverage E – Personal Liability

Coverage **E** does not apply to:

1. Liability:

  a. For any loss assessment charged against you as a member of an association, corporation or community of property owners, except as provided in **D.** Loss Assessment under Section **II** – Additional Coverages;

  b. Under any contract or agreement entered into by an "insured". However, this exclusion does not apply to written contracts:

    (1) That directly relate to the ownership, maintenance or use of an "insured location"; or

    (2) Where the liability of others is assumed by you prior to an "occurrence";

    unless excluded in **a.** above or elsewhere in this policy;

2. "Property damage" to property owned by an "insured". This includes costs or expenses incurred by an "insured" or others to repair, replace, enhance, restore or maintain such property to prevent injury to a person or damage to property of others, whether on or away from an "insured location";

3. "Property damage" to property rented to, occupied or used by or in the care of an "insured". This exclusion does not apply to "property damage" caused by fire, smoke or explosion;

4. "Bodily injury" to any person eligible to receive any benefits voluntarily provided or required to be provided by an "insured" under any:

  a. Workers' compensation law;

  b. Non-occupational disability law; or

  c. Occupational disease law;

5. "Bodily injury" or "property damage" for which an "insured" under this policy:

  a. Is also an insured under a nuclear energy liability policy issued by the:

    (1) Nuclear Energy Liability Insurance Association;

    (2) Mutual Atomic Energy Liability Underwriters;

    (3) Nuclear Insurance Association of Canada;

    or any of their successors; or

  b. Would be an insured under such a policy but for the exhaustion of its limit of liability; or

6. "Bodily injury" to you or an "insured" as defined under Definitions **5.a.** or **b.**

This exclusion also applies to any claim made or suit brought against you or an "insured":

  a. To repay; or

  b. Share damages with;

another person who may be obligated to pay damages because of "bodily injury" to an "insured".

G. Coverage F – Medical Payments To Others

Coverage **F** does not apply to "bodily injury":

1. To a "residence employee" if the "bodily injury":

  a. Occurs off the "insured location"; and

  b. Does not arise out of or in the course of the "residence employee's" employment by an "insured";

2. To any person eligible to receive benefits voluntarily provided or required to be provided under any:

  a. Workers' compensation law;

  b. Non-occupational disability law; or

  c. Occupational disease law;

3. From any:

  a. Nuclear reaction;

  b. Nuclear radiation; or

  c. Radioactive contamination;

  all whether controlled or uncontrolled or however caused; or

  d. Any consequence of any of these; or

4. To any person, other than a "residence employee" of an "insured", regularly residing on any part of the "insured location".

 HO 00 06 10 00

SECTION II – ADDITIONAL COVERAGES

We cover the following in addition to the limits of liability:

A. Claim Expenses

We pay:

1. Expenses we incur and costs taxed against an "insured" in any suit we defend;

2. Premiums on bonds required in a suit we defend, but not for bond amounts more than the Coverage **E** limit of liability. We need not apply for or furnish any bond;

3. Reasonable expenses incurred by an "insured" at our request, including actual loss of earnings (but not loss of other income) up to $250 per day, for assisting us in the investigation or defense of a claim or suit; and

4. Interest on the entire judgment which accrues after entry of the judgment and before we pay or tender, or deposit in court that part of the judgment which does not exceed the limit of liability that applies.

B. First Aid Expenses

We will pay expenses for first aid to others incurred by an "insured" for "bodily injury" covered under this policy. We will not pay for first aid to an "insured".

C. Damage To Property Of Others

1. We will pay, at replacement cost, up to $1,000 per "occurrence" for "property damage" to property of others caused by an "insured".

2. We will not pay for "property damage":

   a. To the extent of any amount recoverable under Section **I**;

   b. Caused intentionally by an "insured" who is 13 years of age or older;

   c. To property owned by an "insured";

   d. To property owned by or rented to a tenant of an "insured" or a resident in your household; or

   e. Arising out of:

      (1) A "business" engaged in by an "insured";

      (2) Any act or omission in connection with a premises owned, rented or controlled by an "insured", other than the "insured location"; or

      (3) The ownership, maintenance, occupancy, operation, use, loading or unloading of aircraft, hovercraft, watercraft or "motor vehicles".

This exclusion **e.(3)** does not apply to a "motor vehicle" that:

(a) Is designed for recreational use off public roads;

(b) Is not owned by an "insured"; and

(c) At the time of the "occurrence", is not required by law, or regulation issued by a government agency, to have been registered for it to be used on public roads or property.

D. Loss Assessment

1. We will pay up to $1,000 for your share of loss assessment charged against you, as owner or tenant of the "residence premises", during the policy period by a corporation or association of property owners, when the assessment is made as a result of:

   a. "Bodily injury" or "property damage" not excluded from coverage under Section **II** – Exclusions; or

   b. Liability for an act of a director, officer or trustee in the capacity as a director, officer or trustee, provided such person:

      (1) Is elected by the members of a corporation or association of property owners; and

      (2) Serves without deriving any income from the exercise of duties which are solely on behalf of a corporation or association of property owners.

2. Paragraph **I.** Policy Period under Section **II** – Conditions does not apply to this Loss Assessment Coverage.

3. Regardless of the number of assessments, the limit of $1,000 is the most we will pay for loss arising out of:

   a. One accident, including continuous or repeated exposure to substantially the same general harmful condition; or

   b. A covered act of a director, officer or trustee. An act involving more than one director, officer or trustee is considered to be a single act.

4. We do not cover assessments charged against you or a corporation or association of property owners by any governmental body.

SECTION II – CONDITIONS

A. Limit Of Liability

Our total liability under Coverage **E** for all damages resulting from any one "occurrence" will not be more than the Coverage **E** limit of liability shown in the Declarations. This limit is the same regardless of the number of "insureds", claims made or persons injured. All "bodily injury" and "property damage" resulting from any one accident or from continuous or repeated exposure to substantially the same general harmful conditions shall be considered to be the result of one "occurrence".

Our total liability under Coverage **F** for all medical expense payable for "bodily injury" to one person as the result of one accident will not be more than the Coverage **F** limit of liability shown in the Declarations.

B. Severability Of Insurance

This insurance applies separately to each "insured". This condition will not increase our limit of liability for any one "occurrence".

C. Duties After "Occurrence"

In case of an "occurrence", you or another "insured" will perform the following duties that apply. We have no duty to provide coverage under this policy if your failure to comply with the following duties is prejudicial to us. You will help us by seeing that these duties are performed:

1. Give written notice to us or our agent as soon as is practical, which sets forth:

    a. The identity of the policy and the "named insured" shown in the Declarations;

    b. Reasonably available information on the time, place and circumstances of the "occurrence"; and

    c. Names and addresses of any claimants and witnesses;

2. Cooperate with us in the investigation, settlement or defense of any claim or suit;

3. Promptly forward to us every notice, demand, summons or other process relating to the "occurrence";

4. At our request, help us:

    a. To make settlement;

    b. To enforce any right of contribution or indemnity against any person or organization who may be liable to an "insured";

    c. With the conduct of suits and attend hearings and trials; and

    d. To secure and give evidence and obtain the attendance of witnesses;

5. With respect to **C.** Damage To Property Of Others under Section **II** – Additional Coverages, submit to us within 60 days after the loss, a sworn statement of loss and show the damaged property, if in an "insured's" control;

6. No "insured" shall, except at such "insured's" own cost, voluntarily make payment, assume obligation or incur expense other than for first aid to others at the time of the "bodily injury".

D. Duties Of An Injured Person – Coverage F – Medical Payments To Others

1. The injured person or someone acting for the injured person will:

    a. Give us written proof of claim, under oath if required, as soon as is practical; and

    b. Authorize us to obtain copies of medical reports and records.

2. The injured person will submit to a physical exam by a doctor of our choice when and as often as we reasonably require.

E. Payment Of Claim – Coverage F – Medical Payments To Others

Payment under this coverage is not an admission of liability by an "insured" or us.

F. Suit Against Us

1. No action can be brought against us unless there has been full compliance with all of the terms under this Section **II**.

2. No one will have the right to join us as a party to any action against an "insured".

3. Also, no action with respect to Coverage **E** can be brought against us until the obligation of such "insured" has been determined by final judgment or agreement signed by us.

G. Bankruptcy Of An "Insured"

Bankruptcy or insolvency of an "insured" will not relieve us of our obligations under this policy.

H. Other Insurance

This insurance is excess over other valid and collectible insurance except insurance written specifically to cover as excess over the limits of liability that apply in this policy.

I. Policy Period

This policy applies only to "bodily injury" or "property damage" which occurs during the policy period.

J. Concealment Or Fraud

We do not provide coverage to an "insured" who, whether before or after a loss, has:

1. Intentionally concealed or misrepresented any material fact or circumstance;

HO 00 06 10 00

2. Engaged in fraudulent conduct; or

3. Made false statements;

relating to this insurance.

SECTIONS I AND II – CONDITIONS

A. Liberalization Clause

If we make a change which broadens coverage under this edition of our policy without additional premium charge, that change will automatically apply to your insurance as of the date we implement the change in your state, provided that this implementation date falls within 60 days prior to or during the policy period stated in the Declarations.

This Liberalization Clause does not apply to changes implemented with a general program revision that includes both broadenings and restrictions in coverage, whether that general program revision is implemented through introduction of:

1. A subsequent edition of this policy; or

2. An amendatory endorsement.

B. Waiver Or Change Of Policy Provisions

A waiver or change of a provision of this policy must be in writing by us to be valid. Our request for an appraisal or examination will not waive any of our rights.

C. Cancellation

1. You may cancel this policy at any time by returning it to us or by letting us know in writing of the date cancellation is to take effect.

2. We may cancel this policy only for the reasons stated below by letting you know in writing of the date cancellation takes effect. This cancellation notice may be delivered to you, or mailed to you at your mailing address shown in the Declarations. Proof of mailing will be sufficient proof of notice.

  a. When you have not paid the premium, we may cancel at any time by letting you know at least 10 days before the date cancellation takes effect.

  b. When this policy has been in effect for less than 60 days and is not a renewal with us, we may cancel for any reason by letting you know at least 10 days before the date cancellation takes effect.

  c. When this policy has been in effect for 60 days or more, or at any time if it is a renewal with us, we may cancel:

   (1) If there has been a material misrepresentation of fact which if known to us would have caused us not to issue the policy; or

   (2) If the risk has changed substantially since the policy was issued.

This can be done by letting you know at least 30 days before the date cancellation takes effect.

  d. When this policy is written for a period of more than one year, we may cancel for any reason at anniversary by letting you know at least 30 days before the date cancellation takes effect.

3. When this policy is canceled, the premium for the period from the date of cancellation to the expiration date will be refunded pro rata.

4. If the return premium is not refunded with the notice of cancellation or when this policy is returned to us, we will refund it within a reasonable time after the date cancellation takes effect.

D. Nonrenewal

We may elect not to renew this policy. We may do so by delivering to you, or mailing to you at your mailing address shown in the Declarations, written notice at least 30 days before the expiration date of this policy. Proof of mailing will be sufficient proof of notice.

E. Assignment

Assignment of this policy will not be valid unless we give our written consent.

F. Subrogation

An "insured" may waive in writing before a loss all rights of recovery against any person. If not waived, we may require an assignment of rights of recovery for a loss to the extent that payment is made by us.

If an assignment is sought, an "insured" must sign and deliver all related papers and cooperate with us.

Subrogation does not apply to Coverage **F** or Paragraph **C.** Damage To Property Of Others under Section **II** – Additional Coverages.

G. Death

If any person named in the Declarations or the spouse, if a resident of the same household, dies, the following apply:

1. We insure the legal representative of the deceased but only with respect to the premises and property of the deceased covered under the policy at the time of death; and

2. "Insured" includes:

  a. An "insured" who is a member of your household at the time of your death, but only while a resident of the "residence premises"; and

  b. With respect to your property, the person having proper temporary custody of the property until appointment and qualification of a legal representative.

HOMEOWNERS 8 – MODIFIED COVERAGE FORM

AGREEMENT

We will provide the insurance described in this policy in return for the premium and compliance with all applicable provisions of this policy.

DEFINITIONS

A. In this policy, "you" and "your" refer to the "named insured" shown in the Declarations and the spouse if a resident of the same household. "We", "us" and "our" refer to the Company providing this insurance.

B. In addition, certain words and phrases are defined as follows:

1. "Aircraft Liability", "Hovercraft Liability", "Motor Vehicle Liability" and "Watercraft Liability", subject to the provisions in **b.** below, mean the following:

    a. Liability for "bodily injury" or "property damage" arising out of the:

    (1) Ownership of such vehicle or craft by an "insured";

    (2) Maintenance, occupancy, operation, use, loading or unloading of such vehicle or craft by any person;

    (3) Entrustment of such vehicle or craft by an "insured" to any person;

    (4) Failure to supervise or negligent supervision of any person involving such vehicle or craft by an "insured"; or

    (5) Vicarious liability, whether or not imposed by law, for the actions of a child or minor involving such vehicle or craft.

    b. For the purpose of this definition:

    (1) Aircraft means any contrivance used or designed for flight except model or hobby aircraft not used or designed to carry people or cargo;

    (2) Hovercraft means a self-propelled motorized ground effect vehicle and includes, but is not limited to, flarecraft and air cushion vehicles;

    (3) Watercraft means a craft principally designed to be propelled on or in water by wind, engine power or electric motor; and

    (4) Motor vehicle means a "motor vehicle" as defined in **7.** below.

2. "Bodily injury" means bodily harm, sickness or disease, including required care, loss of services and death that results.

3. "Business" means:

    a. A trade, profession or occupation engaged in on a full-time, part-time or occasional basis; or

    b. Any other activity engaged in for money or other compensation, except the following:

    (1) One or more activities, not described in (2) through (4) below, for which no "insured" receives more than $2,000 in total compensation for the 12 months before the beginning of the policy period;

    (2) Volunteer activities for which no money is received other than payment for expenses incurred to perform the activity;

    (3) Providing home day care services for which no compensation is received, other than the mutual exchange of such services; or

    (4) The rendering of home day care services to a relative of an "insured".

4. "Employee" means an employee of an "insured", or an employee leased to an "insured" by a labor leasing firm under an agreement between an "insured" and the labor leasing firm, whose duties are other than those performed by a "residence employee".

5. "Insured" means:

    a. You and residents of your household who are:

    (1) Your relatives; or

    (2) Other persons under the age of 21 and in the care of any person named above;

    b. A student enrolled in school full time, as defined by the school, who was a resident of your household before moving out to attend school, provided the student is under the age of:

    (1) 24 and your relative; or

    (2) 21 and in your care or the care of a person described in **a.(1)** above; or

c. Under Section II:

(1) With respect to animals or watercraft to which this policy applies, any person or organization legally responsible for these animals or watercraft which are owned by you or any person included in **a.** or **b.** above. "Insured" does not mean a person or organization using or having custody of these animals or watercraft in the course of any "business" or without consent of the owner; or

(2) With respect to a "motor vehicle" to which this policy applies:

(a) Persons while engaged in your employ or that of any person included in **a.** or **b.** above; or

(b) Other persons using the vehicle on an "insured location" with your consent.

Under both Sections I and II, when the word an immediately precedes the word "insured", the words an "insured" together mean one or more "insureds".

6. "Insured location" means:

a. The "residence premises";

b. The part of other premises, other structures and grounds used by you as a residence; and

(1) Which is shown in the Declarations; or

(2) Which is acquired by you during the policy period for your use as a residence;

c. Any premises used by you in connection with a premises described in **a.** and **b.** above;

d. Any part of a premises:

(1) Not owned by an "insured"; and

(2) Where an "insured" is temporarily residing;

e. Vacant land, other than farm land, owned by or rented to an "insured";

f. Land owned by or rented to an "insured" on which a one, two, three or four family dwelling is being built as a residence for an "insured";

g. Individual or family cemetery plots or burial vaults of an "insured"; or

h. Any part of a premises occasionally rented to an "insured" for other than "business" use.

7. "Motor vehicle" means:

a. A self-propelled land or amphibious vehicle; or

b. Any trailer or semitrailer which is being carried on, towed by or hitched for towing by a vehicle described in **a.** above.

8. "Occurrence" means an accident, including continuous or repeated exposure to substantially the same general harmful conditions, which results, during the policy period, in:

a. "Bodily injury"; or

b. "Property damage".

9. "Property damage" means physical injury to, destruction of, or loss of use of tangible property.

10. "Residence employee" means:

a. An employee of an "insured", or an employee leased to an "insured" by a labor leasing firm, under an agreement between an "insured" and the labor leasing firm, whose duties are related to the maintenance or use of the "residence premises", including household or domestic services; or

b. One who performs similar duties elsewhere not related to the "business" of an "insured".

A "residence employee" does not include a temporary employee who is furnished to an "insured" to substitute for a permanent "residence employee" on leave or to meet seasonal or short-term workload conditions.

11. "Residence premises" means:

a. The one family dwelling where you reside;

b. The two, three or four family dwelling where you reside in at least one of the family units; or

c. That part of any other building where you reside;

and which is shown as the "residence premises" in the Declarations.

"Residence premises" also includes other structures and grounds at that location.

   HO 00 08 10 00

DEDUCTIBLE

Unless otherwise noted in this policy, the following deductible provision applies:

Subject to the policy limits that apply, we will pay only that part of the total of all loss payable under Section **I** that exceeds the deductible amount shown in the Declarations.

SECTION I – PROPERTY COVERAGES

A. Coverage A – Dwelling

1. We cover:

   a. The dwelling on the "residence premises" shown in the Declarations, including structures attached to the dwelling; and

   b. Materials and supplies located on or next to the "residence premises" used to construct, alter or repair the dwelling or other structures on the "residence premises".

2. We do not cover land, including land on which the dwelling is located.

B. Coverage B – Other Structures

1. We cover other structures on the "residence premises" set apart from the dwelling by clear space. This includes structures connected to the dwelling by only a fence, utility line, or similar connection.

2. We do not cover:

   a. Land, including land on which the other structures are located;

   b. Other structures rented or held for rental to any person not a tenant of the dwelling, unless used solely as a private garage;

   c. Other structures from which any "business" is conducted; or

   d. Other structures used to store "business" property. However, we do cover a structure that contains "business" property solely owned by an "insured" or a tenant of the dwelling provided that "business" property does not include gaseous or liquid fuel, other than fuel in a permanently installed fuel tank of a vehicle or craft parked or stored in the structure.

3. The limit of liability for this coverage will not be more than 10% of the limit of liability that applies to Coverage **A**. Use of this coverage does not reduce the Coverage **A** limit of liability.

C. Coverage C – Personal Property

1. **Covered Property**

   We cover personal property owned or used by an "insured" while on the "residence premises". After a loss and at your request, we will cover personal property owned by others while the property is on the part of the "residence premises" occupied by an "insured".

2. **Limit For Property At Other Residences**

   We also cover personal property owned or used by an "insured" while it is anywhere in the world but our limit of liability will not be more than 10% of the limit of liability for Coverage **C** or $1,000, whichever is greater. However, this limitation does not apply to personal property:

   a. Moved from the "residence premises" because it is being repaired, renovated or rebuilt and is not fit to live in or store property in; or

   b. In a newly acquired principal residence for 30 days from the time you begin to move the property there.

3. **Special Limits Of Liability**

   The special limit for each category shown below is the total limit for each loss for all property in that category. These special limits do not increase the Coverage **C** limit of liability.

   a. $200 on money, bank notes, bullion, gold other than goldware, silver other than silverware, platinum other than platinumware, coins, medals, scrip, stored value cards and smart cards.

   b. $1,500 on securities, accounts, deeds, evidences of debt, letters of credit, notes other than bank notes, manuscripts, personal records, passports, tickets and stamps. This dollar limit applies to these categories regardless of the medium (such as paper or computer software) on which the material exists.

   This limit includes the cost to research, replace or restore the information from the lost or damaged material.

   c. $1,500 on watercraft of all types, including their trailers, furnishings, equipment and outboard engines or motors.

   d. $1,500 on trailers or semitrailers not used with watercraft of all types.

e. $2,500 on property, on the "residence premises", used primarily for "business" purposes.

f. $500 on property, away from the "residence premises", used primarily for "business" purposes. However, this limit does not apply to loss to electronic apparatus and other property described in Categories **g.** and **h.** below.

g. $1,500 on electronic apparatus and accessories, while in or upon a "motor vehicle", but only if the apparatus is equipped to be operated by power from the "motor vehicle's" electrical system while still capable of being operated by other power sources.

Accessories include antennas, tapes, wires, records, discs or other media that can be used with any apparatus described in this Category **g.**

h. $1,500 on electronic apparatus and accessories used primarily for "business" while away from the "residence premises" and not in or upon a "motor vehicle". The apparatus must be equipped to be operated by power from the "motor vehicle's" electrical system while still capable of being operated by other power sources.

Accessories include antennas, tapes, wires, records, discs or other media that can be used with any apparatus described in this Category **h.**

4. **Property Not Covered**

We do not cover:

a. Articles separately described and specifically insured, regardless of the limit for which they are insured, in this or other insurance;

b. Animals, birds or fish;

c. "Motor vehicles".

(1) This includes:

(a) Their accessories, equipment and parts; or

(b) Electronic apparatus and accessories designed to be operated solely by power from the electrical system of the "motor vehicle". Accessories include antennas, tapes, wires, records, discs or other media that can be used with any apparatus described above.

The exclusion of property described in **(a)** and **(b)** above applies only while such property is in or upon the "motor vehicle".

(2) We do cover "motor vehicles" not required to be registered for use on public roads or property which are:

(a) Used solely to service an "insured's" residence; or

(b) Designed to assist the handicapped;

d. Aircraft meaning any contrivance used or designed for flight including any parts whether or not attached to the aircraft.

We do cover model or hobby aircraft not used or designed to carry people or cargo;

e. Hovercraft and parts. Hovercraft means a self-propelled motorized ground effect vehicle and includes, but is not limited to, flarecraft and air cushion vehicles;

f. Property of roomers, boarders and other tenants, except property of roomers and boarders related to an "insured";

g. Property in an apartment regularly rented or held for rental to others by an "insured";

h. Property rented or held for rental to others off the "residence premises";

i. "Business" data, including such data stored in:

(1) Books of account, drawings or other paper records; or

(2) Computers and related equipment.

We do cover the cost of blank recording or storage media, and of prerecorded computer programs available on the retail market;

j. Credit cards, electronic fund transfer cards or access devices used solely for deposit, withdrawal or transfer of funds except as provided in **E.6.** Credit Card, Electronic Fund Transfer Card Or Access Device, Forgery And Counterfeit Money under Section **I** – Property Coverages; or

k. Water or steam.

D. **Coverage D – Loss Of Use**

The limit of liability for Coverage **D** is the total limit for the coverages in **1.** Additional Living Expense, **2.** Fair Rental Value and **3.** Civil Authority Prohibits Use below.

1. **Additional Living Expense**

If a loss covered under Section **I** makes that part of the "residence premises" where you reside not fit to live in, we cover any necessary increase in living expenses incurred by you so that your household can maintain its normal standard of living.

HO 00 08 10 00

Payment will be for the shortest time required to repair or replace the damage or, if you permanently relocate, the shortest time required for your household to settle elsewhere.

2. Fair Rental Value

If a loss covered under Section I makes that part of the "residence premises" rented to others or held for rental by you not fit to live in, we cover the fair rental value of such premises less any expenses that do not continue while it is not fit to live in.

Payment will be for the shortest time required to repair or replace such premises.

3. Civil Authority Prohibits Use

If a civil authority prohibits you from use of the "residence premises" as a result of direct damage to neighboring premises by a Peril Insured Against, we cover the loss as provided in **1.** Additional Living Expense and **2.** Fair Rental Value above for no more than two weeks.

4. Loss Or Expense Not Covered

We do not cover loss or expense due to cancellation of a lease or agreement.

The periods of time under **1.** Additional Living Expense, **2.** Fair Rental Value and **3.** Civil Authority Prohibits Use above are not limited by expiration of this policy.

E. Additional Coverages

1. Debris Removal

a. We will pay your reasonable expense for the removal of:

(1) Debris of covered property if a Peril Insured Against that applies to the damaged property causes the loss; or

(2) Ash, dust or particles from a volcanic eruption that has caused direct loss to a building or property contained in a building.

This expense is included in the limit of liability that applies to the damaged property.

b. We will also pay your reasonable expense, up to $1,000, for the removal from the "residence premises" of:

(1) Your tree(s) felled by the peril of Windstorm or Hail; or

(2) A neighbor's tree(s) felled by a Peril Insured Against under Coverage **C**;

provided the tree(s):

(3) Damage(s) a covered structure; or

(4) Does not damage a covered structure, but:

(a) Block(s) a driveway on the "residence premises" which prevent(s) a "motor vehicle", that is registered for use on public roads or property, from entering or leaving the "residence premises"; or

(b) Block(s) a ramp or other fixture designed to assist a handicapped person to enter or leave the dwelling building.

The $1,000 limit is the most we will pay in any one loss regardless of the number of fallen trees. No more than $500 of this limit will be paid for the removal of any one tree.

This coverage is additional insurance.

2. Reasonable Repairs

a. We will pay the reasonable cost incurred by you for the necessary measures taken solely to protect covered property that is damaged by a Peril Insured Against from further damage.

b. If the measures taken involve repair to other damaged property, we will only pay if that property is covered under this policy and the damage is caused by a Peril Insured Against. This coverage does not:

(1) Increase the limit of liability that applies to the covered property; or

(2) Relieve you of your duties, in case of a loss to covered property, described in **B.4.** under Section I – Conditions.

3. Trees, Shrubs And Other Plants

We cover trees, shrubs, plants or lawns, on the "residence premises", for loss caused by the following Perils Insured Against:

a. Fire or Lightning;

b. Explosion;

c. Riot or Civil Commotion;

d. Aircraft;

e. Vehicles not owned or operated by a resident of the "residence premises";

f. Vandalism or Malicious Mischief; or

g. Theft.

We will pay up to 5% of the limit of liability that applies to the dwelling for all trees, shrubs, plants or lawns. No more than $250 of this limit will be paid for any one tree, shrub or plant. We do not cover property grown for "business" purposes.

This coverage is additional insurance.

4. Fire Department Service Charge

We will pay up to $500 for your liability assumed by contract or agreement for fire department charges incurred when the fire department is called to save or protect covered property from a Peril Insured Against. We do not cover fire department service charges if the property is located within the limits of the city, municipality or protection district furnishing the fire department response.

This coverage is additional insurance. No deductible applies to this coverage.

5. Property Removed

We insure covered property against direct loss from any cause while being removed from a premises endangered by a Peril Insured Against and for no more than 30 days while removed.

This coverage does not change the limit of liability that applies to the property being removed.

6. Credit Card, Electronic Fund Transfer Card Or Access Device, Forgery And Counterfeit Money

a. We will pay up to $500 for:

(1) The legal obligation of an "insured" to pay because of the theft or unauthorized use of credit cards issued to or registered in an "insured's" name;

(2) Loss resulting from theft or unauthorized use of an electronic fund transfer card or access device used for deposit, withdrawal or transfer of funds, issued to or registered in an "insured's" name;

(3) Loss to an "insured" caused by forgery or alteration of any check or negotiable instrument; and

(4) Loss to an "insured" through acceptance in good faith of counterfeit United States or Canadian paper currency.

All loss resulting from a series of acts committed by any one person or in which any one person is concerned or implicated is considered to be one loss.

This coverage is additional insurance. No deductible applies to this coverage.

b. We do not cover:

(1) Use of a credit card, electronic fund transfer card or access device:

(a) By a resident of your household;

(b) By a person who has been entrusted with either type of card or access device; or

(c) If an "insured" has not complied with all terms and conditions under which the cards are issued or the devices accessed; or

(2) Loss arising out of "business" use or dishonesty of an "insured".

c. If the coverage in **a.** applies, the following defense provisions also apply:

(1) We may investigate and settle any claim or suit that we decide is appropriate. Our duty to defend a claim or suit ends when the amount we pay for the loss equals our limit of liability.

(2) If a suit is brought against an "insured" for liability under **a.(1)** or **(2)** above, we will provide a defense at our expense by counsel of our choice.

(3) We have the option to defend at our expense an "insured" or an "insured's" bank against any suit for the enforcement of payment under **a.(3)** above.

7. Loss Assessment

a. We will pay up to $1,000 for your share of loss assessment charged during the policy period against you, as owner or tenant of the "residence premises", by a corporation or association of property owners. The assessment must be made as a result of direct loss to property, owned by all members collectively, of the type that would be covered by this policy if owned by you, caused by a Peril Insured Against under Coverage **A**, other than:

(1) Earthquake; or

(2) Land shock waves or tremors before, during or after a volcanic eruption.

The limit of $1,000 is the most we will pay with respect to any one loss, regardless of the number of assessments. We will only apply one deductible, per unit, to the total amount of any one loss to the property described above, regardless of the number of assessments.

b. We do not cover assessments charged against you or a corporation or association of property owners by any governmental body.

c. Paragraph **P.** Policy Period under Section I – Conditions does not apply to this coverage.

This coverage is additional insurance.

 HO 00 08 10 00

8. **Glass Or Safety Glazing Material**

   a. We cover:

      (1) The breakage of glass or safety glazing material which is part of a covered building, storm door or storm window;

      (2) The breakage of glass or safety glazing material which is part of a covered building, storm door or storm window when caused directly by earth movement; and

      (3) The direct physical loss to covered property caused solely by the pieces, fragments or splinters of broken glass or safety glazing material which is part of a building, storm door or storm window.

   b. This coverage does not include loss:

      (1) To covered property which results because the glass or safety glazing material has been broken, except as provided in **a.(3)** above; or

      (2) On the "residence premises" if the dwelling has been vacant for more than 60 consecutive days immediately before the loss, except when the breakage results directly from earth movement as provided in **a.(2)** above. A dwelling being constructed is not considered vacant.

   c. We will pay up to $100 for loss under this coverage.

   d. This coverage does not increase the limit of liability that applies to the damaged property.

SECTION I – PERILS INSURED AGAINST

We insure for direct physical loss to the property described in Coverages **A**, **B** and **C** caused by any of the following perils unless the loss is excluded in Section I – Exclusions.

1. **Fire Or Lightning**

2. **Windstorm Or Hail**

   This peril includes loss to watercraft of all types and their trailers, furnishings, equipment, and outboard engines or motors, only while inside a fully enclosed building.

   This peril does not include loss to the inside of a building or the property contained in a building caused by rain, snow, sleet, sand or dust unless the direct force of wind or hail damages the building causing an opening in a roof or wall and the rain, snow, sleet, sand or dust enters through this opening.

3. **Explosion**

4. **Riot Or Civil Commotion**

5. **Aircraft**

   This peril includes self-propelled missiles and spacecraft.

6. **Vehicles**

   This peril does not include loss caused by a vehicle owned or operated by a resident of the "residence premises".

7. **Smoke**

   This peril means sudden and accidental damage from smoke, including the emission or puffback of smoke, soot, fumes or vapors from a boiler, furnace or related equipment.

   This peril does not include loss caused by smoke from fireplaces or from agricultural smudging or industrial operations.

8. **Vandalism Or Malicious Mischief**

   This peril does not include loss to property on the "residence premises", and any ensuing loss caused by any intentional and wrongful act committed in the course of the vandalism or malicious mischief, if the dwelling has been vacant for more than 60 consecutive days immediately before the loss. A dwelling being constructed is not considered vacant.

9. **Theft**

   a. This peril includes attempted theft and loss of property from a known place on the "residence premises" when it is likely that the property has been stolen.

   b. This peril does not include loss caused by theft:

      (1) Committed by an "insured";

      (2) In or to a dwelling under construction, or of materials and supplies for use in the construction until the dwelling is finished and occupied;

      (3) From that part of a "residence premises" rented by an "insured" to someone other than another "insured"; or

      (4) That occurs off the "residence premises".

   c. Personal property contained in any bank, trust or safe deposit company or public warehouse will be considered on the "residence premises".

   d. Our liability will not be more than $1,000 in any one loss caused by theft.

10. **Volcanic Eruption**

    This peril does not include loss caused by earthquake, land shock waves or tremors.

SECTION I – EXCLUSIONS

We do not insure for loss caused directly or indirectly by any of the following. Such loss is excluded regardless of any other cause or event contributing concurrently or in any sequence to the loss. These exclusions apply whether or not the loss event results in widespread damage or affects a substantial area.

1. **Ordinance Or Law**

   Ordinance Or Law means any ordinance or law:

   a. Requiring or regulating the construction, demolition, remodeling, renovation or repair of property, including removal of any resulting debris;

   b. The requirements of which result in a loss in value to property; or

   c. Requiring any "insured" or others to test for, monitor, clean up, remove, contain, treat, detoxify or neutralize, or in any way respond to, or assess the effects of, pollutants.

      Pollutants means any solid, liquid, gaseous or thermal irritant or contaminant, including smoke, vapor, soot, fumes, acids, alkalis, chemicals and waste. Waste includes materials to be recycled, reconditioned or reclaimed.

   This Exclusion **1.** applies whether or not the property has been physically damaged.

2. **Earth Movement**

   Earth Movement means:

   a. Earthquake, including land shock waves or tremors before, during or after a volcanic eruption;

   b. Landslide, mudslide or mudflow;

   c. Subsidence or sinkhole; or

   d. Any other earth movement including earth sinking, rising or shifting;

   caused by or resulting from human or animal forces or any act of nature unless direct loss by fire or explosion ensues and then we will pay only for the ensuing loss.

   This Exclusion **2.** does not apply to loss by theft.

3. **Water Damage**

   Water Damage means:

   a. Flood, surface water, waves, tidal water, overflow of a body of water, or spray from any of these, whether or not driven by wind;

   b. Water or water-borne material which backs up through sewers or drains or which overflows or is discharged from a sump, sump pump or related equipment; or

   c. Water or water-borne material below the surface of the ground, including water which exerts pressure on or seeps or leaks through a building, sidewalk, driveway, foundation, swimming pool or other structure;

   caused by or resulting from human or animal forces or any act of nature.

   Direct loss by fire, explosion or theft resulting from water damage is covered.

4. **Power Failure**

   Power Failure means the failure of power or other utility service if the failure takes place off the "residence premises". But if the failure results in a loss, from a Peril Insured Against on the "residence premises", we will pay for the loss caused by that peril.

5. **Neglect**

   Neglect means neglect of an "insured" to use all reasonable means to save and preserve property at and after the time of a loss.

6. **War**

   War includes the following and any consequence of any of the following:

   a. Undeclared war, civil war, insurrection, rebellion or revolution;

   b. Warlike act by a military force or military personnel; or

   c. Destruction, seizure or use for a military purpose.

   Discharge of a nuclear weapon will be deemed a warlike act even if accidental.

7. **Nuclear Hazard**

   This Exclusion **7.** pertains to Nuclear Hazard to the extent set forth in **M.** Nuclear Hazard Clause under Section **I** – Conditions.

8. **Intentional Loss**

   Intentional Loss means any loss arising out of any act an "insured" commits or conspires to commit with the intent to cause a loss.

   In the event of such loss, no "insured" is entitled to coverage, even "insureds" who did not commit or conspire to commit the act causing the loss.

9. **Governmental Action**

   Governmental Action means the destruction, confiscation or seizure of property described in Coverage **A, B** or **C** by order of any governmental or public authority.

   This exclusion does not apply to such acts ordered by any governmental or public authority that are taken at the time of a fire to prevent its spread, if the loss caused by fire would be covered under this policy.

SECTION I – CONDITIONS

A. Insurable Interest And Limit Of Liability

Even if more than one person has an insurable interest in the property covered, we will not be liable in any one loss:

1. To an "insured" for more than the amount of such "insured's" interest at the time of loss; or

2. For more than the applicable limit of liability.

B. Duties After Loss

In case of a loss to covered property, we have no duty to provide coverage under this policy if the failure to comply with the following duties is prejudicial to us. These duties must be performed either by you, an "insured" seeking coverage, or a representative of either:

1. Give prompt notice to us or our agent;

2. Notify the police in case of loss by theft;

3. Notify the credit card or electronic fund transfer card or access device company in case of loss as provided for in **E.6.** Credit Card, Electronic Fund Transfer Card Or Access Device, Forgery And Counterfeit Money under Section I – Property Coverages;

4. Protect the property from further damage. If repairs to the property are required, you must:

   a. Make reasonable and necessary repairs to protect the property; and

   b. Keep an accurate record of repair expenses;

5. Cooperate with us in the investigation of a claim;

6. Prepare an inventory of damaged personal property showing the quantity, description, actual cash value and amount of loss. Attach all bills, receipts and related documents that justify the figures in the inventory;

7. As often as we reasonably require:

   a. Show the damaged property;

   b. Provide us with records and documents we request and permit us to make copies; and

   c. Submit to examination under oath, while not in the presence of another "insured", and sign the same;

8. Send to us, within 60 days after our request, your signed, sworn proof of loss which sets forth, to the best of your knowledge and belief:

   a. The time and cause of loss;

   b. The interests of all "insureds" and all others in the property involved and all liens on the property;

   c. Other insurance which may cover the loss;

d. Changes in title or occupancy of the property during the term of the policy;

e. Specifications of damaged buildings and detailed repair estimates;

f. The inventory of damaged personal property described in **6.** above;

g. Receipts for additional living expenses incurred and records that support the fair rental value loss; and

h. Evidence or affidavit that supports a claim under **E.6.** Credit Card, Electronic Fund Transfer Card Or Access Device, Forgery And Counterfeit Money under Section I – Property Coverages, stating the amount and cause of loss.

C. Loss Settlement

Covered property losses are settled as follows:

1. Property of the following types:

   a. Personal property;

   b. Awnings, carpeting, household appliances, outdoor antennas and outdoor equipment, whether or not attached to buildings; and

   c. Structures that are not buildings;

   at actual cash value at the time of loss but not more than the amount required to repair or replace.

2. Buildings under Coverage **A** or **B**:

   a. If you repair or replace the loss to restore the building structure for the same occupancy and use at the same site within 180 days of the date of loss, we will pay the lesser of the following amounts:

   (1) The limit of liability that applies to the damaged or destroyed building structure; or

   (2) The necessary amount actually spent to repair or replace the loss to the building structure but no more than the cost of using common construction materials and methods where functionally equivalent to and less costly than obsolete, antique or custom construction materials and methods.

   b. If you do not make claim under Paragraph **a.** above, we will pay the least of the following amounts:

   (1) The limit of liability that applies to the damaged or destroyed building structure;

   (2) The market value at the time of loss of the damaged or destroyed building structure exclusive of land value; or

(3) The amount which it would cost to repair or replace that part of the building structure damaged or destroyed with material of like kind and quality less allowance for physical deterioration and depreciation.

In this provision, the terms "repair" or "replace" do not include the increased costs incurred to comply with the enforcement of any ordinance or law, except to the extent that coverage for these increased costs is added to this policy.

D. Loss To A Pair Or Set

In case of loss to a pair or set we may elect to:

1. Repair or replace any part to restore the pair or set to its value before the loss; or

2. Pay the difference between actual cash value of the property before and after the loss.

E. Appraisal

If you and we fail to agree on the amount of loss, either may demand an appraisal of the loss. In this event, each party will choose a competent and impartial appraiser within 20 days after receiving a written request from the other. The two appraisers will choose an umpire. If they cannot agree upon an umpire within 15 days, you or we may request that the choice be made by a judge of a court of record in the state where the "residence premises" is located. The appraisers will separately set the amount of loss. If the appraisers submit a written report of an agreement to us, the amount agreed upon will be the amount of loss. If they fail to agree, they will submit their differences to the umpire. A decision agreed to by any two will set the amount of loss.

Each party will:

1. Pay its own appraiser; and

2. Bear the other expenses of the appraisal and umpire equally.

F. Other Insurance And Service Agreement

If a loss covered by this policy is also covered by:

1. Other insurance, we will pay only the proportion of the loss that the limit of liability that applies under this policy bears to the total amount of insurance covering the loss; or

2. A service agreement, this insurance is excess over any amounts payable under any such agreement. Service agreement means a service plan, property restoration plan, home warranty or other similar service warranty agreement, even if it is characterized as insurance.

G. Suit Against Us

No action can be brought against us unless there has been full compliance with all of the terms under Section I of this policy and the action is started within two years after the date of loss.

H. Our Option

If we give you written notice within 30 days after we receive your signed, sworn proof of loss, we may repair or replace any part of the damaged property with material or property of like kind and quality.

I. Loss Payment

We will adjust all losses with you. We will pay you unless some other person is named in the policy or is legally entitled to receive payment. Loss will be payable 60 days after we receive your proof of loss and:

1. Reach an agreement with you;

2. There is an entry of a final judgment; or

3. There is a filing of an appraisal award with us.

J. Abandonment Of Property

We need not accept any property abandoned by an "insured".

K. Mortgage Clause

1. If a mortgagee is named in this policy, any loss payable under Coverage **A** or **B** will be paid to the mortgagee and you, as interests appear. If more than one mortgagee is named, the order of payment will be the same as the order of precedence of the mortgages.

2. If we deny your claim, that denial will not apply to a valid claim of the mortgagee, if the mortgagee:

a. Notifies us of any change in ownership, occupancy or substantial change in risk of which the mortgagee is aware;

b. Pays any premium due under this policy on demand if you have neglected to pay the premium; and

c. Submits a signed, sworn statement of loss within 60 days after receiving notice from us of your failure to do so. Paragraphs **E.** Appraisal, **G.** Suit Against Us and **I.** Loss Payment under Section I – Conditions above also apply to the mortgagee.

3. If we decide to cancel or not to renew this policy, the mortgagee will be notified at least 10 days before the date cancellation or nonrenewal takes effect.

4. If we pay the mortgagee for any loss and deny payment to you:

a. We are subrogated to all the rights of the mortgagee granted under the mortgage on the property; or

Copyright, Insurance Services Office, Inc., 1999

b. At our option, we may pay to the mortgagee the whole principal on the mortgage plus any accrued interest. In this event, we will receive a full assignment and transfer of the mortgage and all securities held as collateral to the mortgage debt.

5. Subrogation will not impair the right of the mortgagee to recover the full amount of the mortgagee's claim.

L. No Benefit To Bailee

We will not recognize any assignment or grant any coverage that benefits a person or organization holding, storing or moving property for a fee regardless of any other provision of this policy.

M. Nuclear Hazard Clause

1. "Nuclear Hazard" means any nuclear reaction, radiation, or radioactive contamination, all whether controlled or uncontrolled or however caused, or any consequence of any of these.

2. Loss caused by the nuclear hazard will not be considered loss caused by fire, explosion, or smoke, whether these perils are specifically named in or otherwise included within the Perils Insured Against.

3. This policy does not apply under Section I to loss caused directly or indirectly by nuclear hazard, except that direct loss by fire resulting from the nuclear hazard is covered.

N. Recovered Property

If you or we recover any property for which we have made payment under this policy, you or we will notify the other of the recovery. At your option, the property will be returned to or retained by you or it will become our property. If the recovered property is returned to or retained by you, the loss payment will be adjusted based on the amount you received for the recovered property.

O. Volcanic Eruption Period

One or more volcanic eruptions that occur within a 72 hour period will be considered as one volcanic eruption.

P. Policy Period

This policy applies only to loss which occurs during the policy period.

Q. Concealment Or Fraud

We provide coverage to no "insureds" under this policy if, whether before or after a loss, an "insured" has:

1. Intentionally concealed or misrepresented any material fact or circumstance;

2. Engaged in fraudulent conduct; or

3. Made false statements;

relating to this insurance.

R. Loss Payable Clause

If the Declarations show a loss payee for certain listed insured personal property, the definition of "insured" is changed to include that loss payee with respect to that property.

If we decide to cancel or not renew this policy, that loss payee will be notified in writing.

SECTION II – LIABILITY COVERAGES

A. Coverage E – Personal Liability

If a claim is made or a suit is brought against an "insured" for damages because of "bodily injury" or "property damage" caused by an "occurrence" to which this coverage applies, we will:

1. Pay up to our limit of liability for the damages for which an "insured" is legally liable. Damages include prejudgment interest awarded against an "insured"; and

2. Provide a defense at our expense by counsel of our choice, even if the suit is groundless, false or fraudulent. We may investigate and settle any claim or suit that we decide is appropriate. Our duty to settle or defend ends when our limit of liability for the "occurrence" has been exhausted by payment of a judgment or settlement.

B. Coverage F – Medical Payments To Others

We will pay the necessary medical expenses that are incurred or medically ascertained within three years from the date of an accident causing "bodily injury". Medical expenses means reasonable charges for medical, surgical, x-ray, dental, ambulance, hospital, professional nursing, prosthetic devices and funeral services. This coverage does not apply to you or regular residents of your household except "residence employees". As to others, this coverage applies only:

1. To a person on the "insured location" with the permission of an "insured"; or

2. To a person off the "insured location", if the "bodily injury":

a. Arises out of a condition on the "insured location" or the ways immediately adjoining;

b. Is caused by the activities of an "insured";

c. Is caused by a "residence employee" in the course of the "residence employee's" employment by an "insured"; or

d. Is caused by an animal owned by or in the care of an "insured".

SECTION II – EXCLUSIONS

A. "Motor Vehicle Liability"

1. Coverages **E** and **F** do not apply to any "motor vehicle liability" if, at the time and place of an "occurrence", the involved "motor vehicle":

   a. Is registered for use on public roads or property;

   b. Is not registered for use on public roads or property, but such registration is required by a law, or regulation issued by a government agency, for it to be used at the place of the "occurrence"; or

   c. Is being:

      (1) Operated in, or practicing for, any prearranged or organized race, speed contest or other competition;

      (2) Rented to others;

      (3) Used to carry persons or cargo for a charge; or

      (4) Used for any "business" purpose except for a motorized golf cart while on a golfing facility.

2. If Exclusion **A.1.** does not apply, there is still no coverage for "motor vehicle liability" unless the "motor vehicle" is:

   a. In dead storage on an "insured location";

   b. Used solely to service an "insured's" residence;

   c. Designed to assist the handicapped and, at the time of an "occurrence", it is:

      (1) Being used to assist a handicapped person; or

      (2) Parked on an "insured location";

   d. Designed for recreational use off public roads and:

      (1) Not owned by an "insured"; or

      (2) Owned by an "insured" provided the "occurrence" takes place on an "insured location" as defined in Definitions **B.6.a., b., d., e.** or **h.;** or

   e. A motorized golf cart that is owned by an "insured", designed to carry up to 4 persons, not built or modified after manufacture to exceed a speed of 25 miles per hour on level ground and, at the time of an "occurrence", is within the legal boundaries of:

      (1) A golfing facility and is parked or stored there, or being used by an "insured" to:

         (a) Play the game of golf or for other recreational or leisure activity allowed by the facility;

         (b) Travel to or from an area where "motor vehicles" or golf carts are parked or stored; or

         (c) Cross public roads at designated points to access other parts of the golfing facility; or

      (2) A private residential community, including its public roads upon which a motorized golf cart can legally travel, which is subject to the authority of a property owners association and contains an "insured's" residence.

B. "Watercraft Liability"

1. Coverages **E** and **F** do not apply to any "watercraft liability" if, at the time of an "occurrence", the involved watercraft is being:

   a. Operated in, or practicing for, any prearranged or organized race, speed contest or other competition. This exclusion does not apply to a sailing vessel or a predicted log cruise;

   b. Rented to others;

   c. Used to carry persons or cargo for a charge; or

   d. Used for any "business" purpose.

2. If Exclusion **B.1.** does not apply, there is still no coverage for "watercraft liability" unless, at the time of the "occurrence", the watercraft:

   a. Is stored;

   b. Is a sailing vessel, with or without auxiliary power, that is:

      (1) Less than 26 feet in overall length; or

      (2) 26 feet or more in overall length and not owned by or rented to an "insured"; or

   c. Is not a sailing vessel and is powered by:

      (1) An inboard or inboard-outdrive engine or motor, including those that power a water jet pump, of:

         (a) 50 horsepower or less and not owned by an "insured"; or

         (b) More than 50 horsepower and not owned by or rented to an "insured"; or

      (2) One or more outboard engines or motors with:

         (a) 25 total horsepower or less;

         (b) More than 25 horsepower if the outboard engine or motor is not owned by an "insured";

         (c) More than 25 horsepower if the outboard engine or motor is owned by an "insured" who acquired it during the policy period; or

Copyright, Insurance Services Office, Inc., 1999

(d) More than 25 horsepower if the outboard engine or motor is owned by an "insured" who acquired it before the policy period, but only if:

(i) You declare them at policy inception; or

(ii) Your intent to insure them is reported to us in writing within 45 days after you acquire them.

The coverages in **(c)** and **(d)** above apply for the policy period.

Horsepower means the maximum power rating assigned to the engine or motor by the manufacturer.

C. "Aircraft Liability"

This policy does not cover "aircraft liability".

D. "Hovercraft Liability"

This policy does not cover "hovercraft liability".

E. Coverage E – Personal Liability And Coverage F – Medical Payments To Others

Coverages **E** and **F** do not apply to the following:

1. Expected Or Intended Injury

"Bodily injury" or "property damage" which is expected or intended by an "insured" even if the resulting "bodily injury" or "property damage":

a. Is of a different kind, quality or degree than initially expected or intended; or

b. Is sustained by a different person, entity, real or personal property, than initially expected or intended.

However, this Exclusion **E.1.** does not apply to "bodily injury" resulting from the use of reasonable force by an "insured" to protect persons or property;

2. "Business"

a. "Bodily injury" or "property damage" arising out of or in connection with a "business" conducted from an "insured location" or engaged in by an "insured", whether or not the "business" is owned or operated by an "insured" or employs an "insured".

This Exclusion **E.2.** applies but is not limited to an act or omission, regardless of its nature or circumstance, involving a service or duty rendered, promised, owed, or implied to be provided because of the nature of the "business".

b. This Exclusion **E.2.** does not apply to:

(1) The rental or holding for rental of an "insured location";

(a) On an occasional basis if used only as a residence;

(b) In part for use only as a residence, unless a single family unit is intended for use by the occupying family to lodge more than two roomers or boarders; or

(c) In part, as an office, school, studio or private garage; and

(2) An "insured" under the age of 21 years involved in a part-time or occasional, self-employed "business" with no employees;

3. Professional Services

"Bodily injury" or "property damage" arising out of the rendering of or failure to render professional services;

4. "Insured's" Premises Not An "Insured Location"

"Bodily injury" or "property damage" arising out of a premises:

a. Owned by an "insured";

b. Rented to an "insured"; or

c. Rented to others by an "insured";

that is not an "insured location";

5. War

"Bodily injury" or "property damage" caused directly or indirectly by war, including the following and any consequence of any of the following:

a. Undeclared war, civil war, insurrection, rebellion or revolution;

b. Warlike act by a military force or military personnel; or

c. Destruction, seizure or use for a military purpose.

Discharge of a nuclear weapon will be deemed a warlike act even if accidental;

6. Communicable Disease

"Bodily injury" or "property damage" which arises out of the transmission of a communicable disease by an "insured";

7. Sexual Molestation, Corporal Punishment Or Physical Or Mental Abuse

"Bodily injury" or "property damage" arising out of sexual molestation, corporal punishment or physical or mental abuse; or

8. Controlled Substance

"Bodily injury" or "property damage" arising out of the use, sale, manufacture, delivery, transfer or possession by any person of a Controlled Substance as defined by the Federal Food and Drug Law at 21 U.S.C.A. Sections 811 and 812. Controlled Substances include but are not limited to cocaine, LSD, marijuana and all narcotic drugs. However, this exclusion does not apply to the legitimate use of prescription drugs by a person following the orders of a licensed physician.

Exclusions **A.** "Motor Vehicle Liability", **B.** "Watercraft Liability", **C.** "Aircraft Liability", **D.** "Hovercraft Liability" and **E.4.** "Insured's" Premises Not An "Insured Location" do not apply to "bodily injury" to a "residence employee" arising out of and in the course of the "residence employee's" employment by an "insured".

F. Coverage E – Personal Liability

Coverage **E** does not apply to:

1. Liability:

   a. For any loss assessment charged against you as a member of an association, corporation or community of property owners, except as provided in **D.** Loss Assessment under Section **II** – Additional Coverages;

   b. Under any contract or agreement entered into by an "insured". However, this exclusion does not apply to written contracts:

      (1) That directly relate to the ownership, maintenance or use of an "insured location"; or

      (2) Where the liability of others is assumed by you prior to an "occurrence";

      unless excluded in **a.** above or elsewhere in this policy;

2. "Property damage" to property owned by an "insured". This includes costs or expenses incurred by an "insured" or others to repair, replace, enhance, restore or maintain such property to prevent injury to a person or damage to property of others, whether on or away from an "insured location";

3. "Property damage" to property rented to, occupied or used by or in the care of an "insured". This exclusion does not apply to "property damage" caused by fire, smoke or explosion;

4. "Bodily injury" to any person eligible to receive any benefits voluntarily provided or required to be provided by an "insured" under any:

   a. Workers' compensation law;

b. Non-occupational disability law; or

c. Occupational disease law;

5. "Bodily injury" or "property damage" for which an "insured" under this policy:

   a. Is also an insured under a nuclear energy liability policy issued by the:

      (1) Nuclear Energy Liability Insurance Association;

      (2) Mutual Atomic Energy Liability Underwriters;

      (3) Nuclear Insurance Association of Canada;

      or any of their successors; or

   b. Would be an insured under such a policy but for the exhaustion of its limit of liability; or

6. "Bodily injury" to you or an "insured" as defined under Definitions **5.a.** or **b.**

This exclusion also applies to any claim made or suit brought against you or an "insured":

a. To repay; or

b. Share damages with;

another person who may be obligated to pay damages because of "bodily injury" to an "insured".

G. Coverage F – Medical Payments To Others

Coverage **F** does not apply to "bodily injury":

1. To a "residence employee" if the "bodily injury":

   a. Occurs off the "insured location"; and

   b. Does not arise out of or in the course of the "residence employee's" employment by an "insured";

2. To any person eligible to receive benefits voluntarily provided or required to be provided under any:

   a. Workers' compensation law;

   b. Non-occupational disability law; or

   c. Occupational disease law;

3. From any:

   a. Nuclear reaction;

   b. Nuclear radiation; or

   c. Radioactive contamination;

   all whether controlled or uncontrolled or however caused; or

   d. Any consequence of any of these; or

4. To any person, other than a "residence employee" of an "insured", regularly residing on any part of the "insured location".

SECTION II – ADDITIONAL COVERAGES

We cover the following in addition to the limits of liability:

A. Claim Expenses

We pay:

1. Expenses we incur and costs taxed against an "insured" in any suit we defend;

2. Premiums on bonds required in a suit we defend, but not for bond amounts more than the Coverage **E** limit of liability. We need not apply for or furnish any bond;

3. Reasonable expenses incurred by an "insured" at our request, including actual loss of earnings (but not loss of other income) up to $250 per day, for assisting us in the investigation or defense of a claim or suit; and

4. Interest on the entire judgment which accrues after entry of the judgment and before we pay or tender, or deposit in court that part of the judgment which does not exceed the limit of liability that applies.

B. First Aid Expenses

We will pay expenses for first aid to others incurred by an "insured" for "bodily injury" covered under this policy. We will not pay for first aid to an "insured".

C. Damage To Property Of Others

1. We will pay, at replacement cost, up to $1,000 per "occurrence" for "property damage" to property of others caused by an "insured".

2. We will not pay for "property damage":

a. To the extent of any amount recoverable under Section **I**;

b. Caused intentionally by an "insured" who is 13 years of age or older;

c. To property owned by an "insured";

d. To property owned by or rented to a tenant of an "insured" or a resident in your household; or

e. Arising out of:

(1) A "business" engaged in by an "insured";

(2) Any act or omission in connection with a premises owned, rented or controlled by an "insured", other than the "insured location"; or

(3) The ownership, maintenance, occupancy, operation, use, loading or unloading of aircraft, hovercraft, watercraft or "motor vehicles".

This exclusion **e.(3)** does not apply to a "motor vehicle" that:

(a) Is designed for recreational use off public roads;

(b) Is not owned by an "insured"; and

(c) At the time of the "occurrence", is not required by law, or regulation issued by a government agency, to have been registered for it to be used on public roads or property.

D. Loss Assessment

1. We will pay up to $1,000 for your share of loss assessment charged against you, as owner or tenant of the "residence premises", during the policy period by a corporation or association of property owners, when the assessment is made as a result of:

a. "Bodily injury" or "property damage" not excluded from coverage under Section **II** – Exclusions; or

b. Liability for an act of a director, officer or trustee in the capacity as a director, officer or trustee, provided such person:

(1) Is elected by the members of a corporation or association of property owners; and

(2) Serves without deriving any income from the exercise of duties which are solely on behalf of a corporation or association of property owners.

2. Paragraph **I.** Policy Period under Section **II** – Conditions does not apply to this Loss Assessment Coverage.

3. Regardless of the number of assessments, the limit of $1,000 is the most we will pay for loss arising out of:

a. One accident, including continuous or repeated exposure to substantially the same general harmful condition; or

b. A covered act of a director, officer or trustee. An act involving more than one director, officer or trustee is considered to be a single act.

4. We do not cover assessments charged against you or a corporation or association of property owners by any governmental body.

SECTION II – CONDITIONS

A. Limit Of Liability

Our total liability under Coverage **E** for all damages resulting from any one "occurrence" will not be more than the Coverage **E** limit of liability shown in the Declarations. This limit is the same regardless of the number of "insureds", claims made or persons injured. All "bodily injury" and "property damage" resulting from any one accident or from continuous or repeated exposure to substantially the same general harmful conditions shall be considered to be the result of one "occurrence".

Our total liability under Coverage **F** for all medical expense payable for "bodily injury" to one person as the result of one accident will not be more than the Coverage **F** limit of liability shown in the Declarations.

B. Severability Of Insurance

This insurance applies separately to each "insured". This condition will not increase our limit of liability for any one "occurrence".

C. Duties After "Occurrence"

In case of an "occurrence", you or another "insured" will perform the following duties that apply. We have no duty to provide coverage under this policy if your failure to comply with the following duties is prejudicial to us. You will help us by seeing that these duties are performed:

1. Give written notice to us or our agent as soon as is practical, which sets forth:

   a. The identity of the policy and the "named insured" shown in the Declarations;

   b. Reasonably available information on the time, place and circumstances of the "occurrence"; and

   c. Names and addresses of any claimants and witnesses;

2. Cooperate with us in the investigation, settlement or defense of any claim or suit;

3. Promptly forward to us every notice, demand, summons or other process relating to the "occurrence";

4. At our request, help us:

   a. To make settlement;

   b. To enforce any right of contribution or indemnity against any person or organization who may be liable to an "insured";

   c. With the conduct of suits and attend hearings and trials; and

   d. To secure and give evidence and obtain the attendance of witnesses;

5. With respect to **C.** Damage To Property Of Others under Section **II** – Additional Coverages, submit to us within 60 days after the loss, a sworn statement of loss and show the damaged property, if in an "insured's" control;

6. No "insured" shall, except at such "insured's" own cost, voluntarily make payment, assume obligation or incur expense other than for first aid to others at the time of the "bodily injury".

D. Duties Of An Injured Person – Coverage F – Medical Payments To Others

1. The injured person or someone acting for the injured person will:

   a. Give us written proof of claim, under oath if required, as soon as is practical; and

   b. Authorize us to obtain copies of medical reports and records.

2. The injured person will submit to a physical exam by a doctor of our choice when and as often as we reasonably require.

E. Payment Of Claim – Coverage F – Medical Payments To Others

Payment under this coverage is not an admission of liability by an "insured" or us.

F. Suit Against Us

1. No action can be brought against us unless there has been full compliance with all of the terms under this Section **II**.

2. No one will have the right to join us as a party to any action against an "insured".

3. Also, no action with respect to Coverage **E** can be brought against us until the obligation of such "insured" has been determined by final judgment or agreement signed by us.

G. Bankruptcy Of An "Insured"

Bankruptcy or insolvency of an "insured" will not relieve us of our obligations under this policy.

H. Other Insurance

This insurance is excess over other valid and collectible insurance except insurance written specifically to cover as excess over the limits of liability that apply in this policy.

I. Policy Period

This policy applies only to "bodily injury" or "property damage" which occurs during the policy period.

J. Concealment Or Fraud

We do not provide coverage to an "insured" who, whether before or after a loss, has:

1. Intentionally concealed or misrepresented any material fact or circumstance;

2. Engaged in fraudulent conduct; or

 HO 00 08 10 00

3. Made false statements;

relating to this insurance.

SECTIONS I AND II – CONDITIONS

A. Liberalization Clause

If we make a change which broadens coverage under this edition of our policy without additional premium charge, that change will automatically apply to your insurance as of the date we implement the change in your state, provided that this implementation date falls within 60 days prior to or during the policy period stated in the Declarations.

This Liberalization Clause does not apply to changes implemented with a general program revision that includes both broadenings and restrictions in coverage, whether that general program revision is implemented through introduction of:

1. A subsequent edition of this policy; or

2. An amendatory endorsement.

B. Waiver Or Change Of Policy Provisions

A waiver or change of a provision of this policy must be in writing by us to be valid. Our request for an appraisal or examination will not waive any of our rights.

C. Cancellation

1. You may cancel this policy at any time by returning it to us or by letting us know in writing of the date cancellation is to take effect.

2. We may cancel this policy only for the reasons stated below by letting you know in writing of the date cancellation takes effect. This cancellation notice may be delivered to you, or mailed to you at your mailing address shown in the Declarations. Proof of mailing will be sufficient proof of notice.

   a. When you have not paid the premium, we may cancel at any time by letting you know at least 10 days before the date cancellation takes effect.

   b. When this policy has been in effect for less than 60 days and is not a renewal with us, we may cancel for any reason by letting you know at least 10 days before the date cancellation takes effect.

   c. When this policy has been in effect for 60 days or more, or at any time if it is a renewal with us, we may cancel:

     (1) If there has been a material misrepresentation of fact which if known to us would have caused us not to issue the policy; or

     (2) If the risk has changed substantially since the policy was issued.

This can be done by letting you know at least 30 days before the date cancellation takes effect.

   d. When this policy is written for a period of more than one year, we may cancel for any reason at anniversary by letting you know at least 30 days before the date cancellation takes effect.

3. When this policy is canceled, the premium for the period from the date of cancellation to the expiration date will be refunded pro rata.

4. If the return premium is not refunded with the notice of cancellation or when this policy is returned to us, we will refund it within a reasonable time after the date cancellation takes effect.

D. Nonrenewal

We may elect not to renew this policy. We may do so by delivering to you, or mailing to you at your mailing address shown in the Declarations, written notice at least 30 days before the expiration date of this policy. Proof of mailing will be sufficient proof of notice.

E. Assignment

Assignment of this policy will not be valid unless we give our written consent.

F. Subrogation

An "insured" may waive in writing before a loss all rights of recovery against any person. If not waived, we may require an assignment of rights of recovery for a loss to the extent that payment is made by us.

If an assignment is sought, an "insured" must sign and deliver all related papers and cooperate with us.

Subrogation does not apply to Coverage **F** or Paragraph **C.** Damage To Property Of Others under Section **II** – Additional Coverages.

G. Death

If any person named in the Declarations or the spouse, if a resident of the same household, dies, the following apply:

1. We insure the legal representative of the deceased but only with respect to the premises and property of the deceased covered under the policy at the time of death; and

2. "Insured" includes:

   a. An "insured" who is a member of your household at the time of your death, but only while a resident of the "residence premises"; and

   b. With respect to your property, the person having proper temporary custody of the property until appointment and qualification of a legal representative.

POLICY NUMBER:

HOMEOWNERS
HO 04 41 10 00

THIS ENDORSEMENT CHANGES THE POLICY. PLEASE READ IT CAREFULLY.

ADDITIONAL INSURED
RESIDENCE PREMISES

SCHEDULE*

Name And Address Of Person Or Organization
Interest

*Entries may be left blank if shown elsewhere in this policy for this coverage.

DEFINITIONS

Definition **5.** which defines "insured" is extended to include the person or organization named in the Schedule above, but only with respect to:

1. Coverage **A** – Dwelling and Coverage **B** – Other Structures; and

2. Coverage **E** – Personal Liability and Coverage **F** – Medical Payments To Others but only with respect to "bodily injury" or "property damage" arising out of the ownership, maintenance or use of the "residence premises".

SECTION II – EXCLUSIONS

This coverage does not apply to "bodily injury" to an "employee", "residence employee" or a temporary employee furnished to the "insured" to substitute for a permanent "residence employee" arising out of or in the course of the employee's employment by the person or organization.

CANCELLATION AND NONRENEWAL NOTIFICATION

If we decide to cancel or not to renew this policy, the person or organization named in the Schedule will be notified in writing.

All other provisions of this policy apply.

POLICY NUMBER:

HOMEOWNERS
HO 04 51 10 00

THIS ENDORSEMENT CHANGES THE POLICY. PLEASE READ IT CAREFULLY.

BUILDING ADDITIONS AND ALTERATIONS
INCREASED LIMIT
FORM HO 00 04

SCHEDULE*

SECTION I – PROPERTY COVERAGES

C. Additional Coverages

    10. Building Additions And Alterations

       The limit of liability for this Building Additions And Alterations coverage is increased as noted below.

Increase In Limit Of Liability	**Total Limit Of Liability**

All other provisions of this policy apply.

*Entries may be left blank if shown elsewhere in this policy for this coverage.

HOMEOWNERS
HO 04 91 10 00

THIS ENDORSEMENT CHANGES THE POLICY. PLEASE READ IT CAREFULLY.

COVERAGE B – OTHER STRUCTURES AWAY FROM THE RESIDENCE PREMISES
FORMS HO 00 02, HO 00 03 AND HO 00 05 ONLY

SECTION I – PROPERTY COVERAGES

B. Coverage B – Other Structures

The following is added to Paragraph **1.**:

We also cover other structures which are owned by you and located away from the "residence premises", if used by you in connection with the "residence premises".

The following is added to Paragraph **2.**:

e. With respect to other structures away from the "residence premises", other structures:

(1) Being used as a dwelling;

(2) Capable of being used as a dwelling;

(3) From which any "business" is conducted;

(4) Used to store "business" property; or

(5) Rented or held for rental to any person not a tenant of the dwelling.

Paragraph **3.** is deleted and replaced by the following:

3. The limit of liability for other structures on or away from the "residence premises" will not be more than 10% of the limit of liability that applies to Coverage **A**. Use of this limit does not reduce the Coverage **A** limit of liability.

SECTION I – CONDITIONS

C. Loss Settlement

With respect to structures covered under this endorsement, Condition **C.** Loss Settlement is deleted and replaced by the following:

Covered losses will be settled at actual cash value at the time of loss, but not more than the amount required to repair or replace.

All other provisions of this policy apply.

POLICY NUMBER:

HOMEOWNERS
HO 04 65 10 00

THIS ENDORSEMENT CHANGES THE POLICY. PLEASE READ IT CAREFULLY.

COVERAGE C INCREASED SPECIAL LIMITS OF LIABILITY

SCHEDULE*

SECTION I – PROPERTY COVERAGES

COVERAGE C – PERSONAL PROPERTY

3. Special Limits Of Liability

The special limits of liability are increased as noted below:

Property	Increase In Limit Of Liability	Total Limit Of Liability
a. Money, bank notes, bullion, gold other than goldware, silver other than silverware, platinum other than platinumware, coins, medals, scrip, stored value cards and smart cards.		
b. Securities, accounts, deeds, evidences of debt, letters of credit, notes other than bank notes, manuscripts, personal records, passports, tickets and stamps.		
e. Jewelry, watches, furs, precious and semiprecious stones for loss by theft, but not more than $1,000 for any one article.		
f. Firearms and related equipment for loss by theft.		
g. Silverware, silver-plated ware, goldware, gold-plated ware, platinumware, platinum-plated ware and pewterware for loss by theft.		
j. Electronic apparatus and accessories, while in or upon a "motor vehicle", but only if the apparatus is equipped to be operated by power from the "motor vehicle's" electrical system while still capable of being operated by other power sources.		
k. Electronic apparatus and accessories used primarily for "business" while away from the "residence premises" and not in or upon a "motor vehicle". The apparatus must be equipped to be operated by power from the "motor vehicle's" electrical system while still capable of being operated by other power sources.		

All other provisions of this policy apply.

*Entries may be left blank if shown elsewhere in this policy for this coverage.

HO 04 65 10 00   Copyright, Insurance Services Office, Inc., 1999   Page 1 of 1

POLICY NUMBER:

HOMEOWNERS
HO 04 53 10 00

THIS ENDORSEMENT CHANGES THE POLICY. PLEASE READ IT CAREFULLY.

CREDIT CARD, ELECTRONIC FUND TRANSFER CARD OR ACCESS DEVICE, FORGERY AND COUNTERFEIT MONEY COVERAGE
INCREASED LIMIT

SCHEDULE*

SECTION I – PROPERTY COVERAGES

   ADDITIONAL COVERAGES

  6. **Credit Card, Electronic Fund Transfer Card Or Access Device, Forgery And Counterfeit Money**

     The limit of liability for this coverage is increased as noted below.

     Increase In Limit Of Liability   **Total Limit Of Liability**

All other provisions of this policy apply.

*Entries may be left blank if shown elsewhere in this policy for this coverage.

HO 04 53 10 00   Copyright, Insurance Services Office, Inc., 1999   **Page 1 of 1**

POLICY NUMBER:

HOMEOWNERS
HO 04 54 10 00

THIS ENDORSEMENT CHANGES THE POLICY. PLEASE READ IT CAREFULLY.

EARTHQUAKE

SCHEDULE*

Earthquake Deductible Percentage Amount:

Exterior Masonry Veneer Exclusion **1.**
    Check here only if this exclusion does not apply.

---

*Entries may be left blank if shown elsewhere in this policy for this coverage.

A. Coverage

1. We insure for direct physical loss to property covered under Section I caused by earthquake, including land shock waves or tremors before, during or after a volcanic eruption.

   One or more earthquake shocks that occur within a seventy-two hour period constitute a single earthquake.

2. This coverage does not increase the limits of liability stated in this policy.

B. Special Deductible

The following replaces any other deductible provision in this policy with respect to loss covered under this endorsement:

We will pay only that part of the total of all loss payable under Section I, except:

1. Coverage **D;** and

2. The Additional Coverages;

that exceeds the earthquake deductible.

The dollar amount of the earthquake deductible is determined by multiplying either the:

Coverage **A;** or

Coverage **C;**

limit of liability shown in the Declarations, whichever is greater, by the deductible percentage amount shown in the Schedule above.

The total deductible amount will not be less than $250.

C. Special Exclusions

1. **Exterior Masonry Veneer**

   We do not cover loss to exterior masonry veneer caused by earthquake. The value of exterior masonry veneer will be deducted before applying the earthquake deductible described above. For the purpose of this exclusion, stucco is not considered masonry veneer.

2. **Flood**

   We do not cover loss resulting directly or indirectly from flood of any nature or tidal wave, whether:

   a. Caused by;

   b. Resulting from;

   c. Contributed to by; or

   d. Aggravated by;

   earthquake.

3. **Filling Land**

   This coverage does not include the cost of filling land.

D. Exception To The Earth Movement Exclusion

The Section I — Earth Movement Exclusion does not apply to loss caused by earthquake, including land shock waves or tremors before, during or after a volcanic eruption.

All other provisions of this policy apply.

POLICY NUMBER:

HOMEOWNERS
HO 04 46 10 00

THIS ENDORSEMENT CHANGES THE POLICY. PLEASE READ IT CAREFULLY.

INFLATION GUARD

SCHEDULE*

Percentage Amount:

*Entry may be left blank if shown elsewhere in this policy for this coverage.

The limits of liability for Coverages **A, B, C** and **D** will be increased annually by the percentage amount that is:

1. Shown in the Schedule above; and

2. Applied pro rata during the policy period.

POLICY NUMBER:

THIS ENDORSEMENT CHANGES THE POLICY. PLEASE READ IT CAREFULLY.

HOME DAY CARE COVERAGE ENDORSEMENT

SCHEDULE*

We cover the home day care "business" described in this Schedule, provided such "business" is conducted by an "insured" on the "residence premises", subject to the provisions of this endorsement.

SECTION I – PROPERTY

Number Of Persons Receiving Day Care Services:

Business Location (Check **1.** and/or **2.** that follows):

1. In the dwelling building or unit in which the "insured" resides and shown as "residence premises"

2. In an other structure on or at the location of the "residence premises"
(Enter the Limit of Liability and Description of the Structure(s) below.)

Limit Of Liability   **Description Of Other Structure(s)**

*Entries may be left blank if shown elsewhere in this policy for this coverage.

SECTION I – PROPERTY COVERAGES

1. We cover the other structure described in the Schedule for direct physical loss by a Peril Insured Against for not more than the limit shown in the Schedule.

   For such structures, Coverage **B** in Forms **HO 00 02, HO** 00 **03** and **HO 00 05** and Coverage A in Form HO 00 06 do not apply.

2. Coverage **C – Personal Property,** Special Limit of Liability **3.h.** is deleted and replaced by the following:

   h. $2,500 on property, on the "residence premises", used primarily for "business" purposes, other than furnishings, supplies and equipment of the "business" described in the Schedule.

The Coverage **C** limit of liability applies to property of the "business" described in the Schedule.

SECTION II – LIABILITY COVERAGES

Coverages **E –** Personal Liability and **F –** Medical Payments To Others apply to "bodily injury" and "property damage" arising out of home day care services regularly provided by an "insured" and for which an "insured" receives money or other compensation.

SECTION II – EXCLUSIONS

Section **II** Exclusion **E.2.** "Business" does not apply to the coverage provided under this endorsement. However, the coverage provided under this endorsement does not apply:

1. To "bodily injury" or "property damage" arising out of the:

   a. Ownership,

   b. Maintenance, occupancy, operation, use, loading or unloading of;

   c. Entrustment by an "insured" to any person of; or

   d. Negligent supervision of or failure to supervise any person involving:

      (1) Draft or saddle animals or vehicles for use therewith;

      (2) "Motor vehicles";

      (3) Aircraft or hovercraft; or

      (4) Watercraft;

      owned or operated, or hired by or for an "insured" or "employee" or used by an "insured" for the purpose of instruction in the use thereof; or

2. To "bodily injury" to any "employee" arising out of the "business" described above.

SECTION II – CONDITIONS

With respect to the coverage provided by this endorsement, Section **II – Conditions, A. Limit Of Liability** and **B. Severability Of Insurance** are deleted and replaced by the following:

A. Limit Of Liability

Aggregate Limit of Liability: Our total limit of liability in an annual policy period for the sum of damages payable under Coverage **E** and medical expense payable under Coverage **F** will be an annual aggregate limit of liability that corresponds to the dollar amount shown in the Declarations for Coverage **E.** This is the most we will pay regardless of the number of "occurrences", "insureds", claims made or persons injured.

Sub-Limit of Liability: Subject to the annual aggregate limit of liability described above, our total liability under Coverage **F** for all medical expense payable for "bodily injury" to one person as the result of one accident will not be more than the dollar amount shown in the Declarations for Coverage **F.** This Sub-Limit of Liability does not increase the Aggregate Limit of Liability.

The limits described above apply regardless of any provision to the contrary contained in this policy, including the policy Declarations.

B. Severability Of Insurance

This insurance applies separately to each "insured" except with respect to the Limit of Liability. Therefore, this condition will not increase the Annual Aggregate Limit of Liability regardless of the number of "insureds".

All other provisions of this policy apply.

 HO 04 97 10 00

THIS ENDORSEMENT CHANGES THE POLICY. PLEASE READ IT CAREFULLY.

MOBILEHOME ENDORSEMENT

This insurance is subject to all provisions of the Homeowners form and endorsements attached to this policy except as revised in the following areas:

DEFINITIONS

11. "Residence premises" is deleted and replaced by the following:

11. "Residence premises" means the mobilehome and other structures located on land:

   a. Owned or leased by you where you reside; and

   b. Which is shown as the "residence premises" in the Declarations.

SECTION I – PROPERTY COVERAGES

A. Coverage A – Dwelling

Paragraph **1.** is deleted and replaced by the following:

1. We cover:

   a. The mobilehome on the "residence premises":

      (1) Shown in the Declarations.

      (2) Used principally as a private residence.

   b. Structures and utility tanks attached to the mobilehome and the following and similar type items installed on a permanent basis:

      (1) Floor coverings;

      (2) Appliances; and

      (3) Dressers and cabinets.

   c. Materials and supplies located on or next to the "residence premises" used to:

      (1) Construct;

      (2) Alter; or

      (3) Repair;

      the mobilehome or other structures on the "residence premises".

B. Coverage B – Other Structures

Paragraph **3.** is deleted and replaced by the following:

3. The limit of liability for this coverage will not be more than 10% of the limit that applies to Coverage **A**. However, if 10% of the Coverage **A** limit of liability is less than $2000, we will provide a minimum limit of $2000 for this coverage. Use of this coverage does not reduce the Coverage **A** limit of liability.

E. Additional Coverages

5. Property Removed

The following paragraph is added:

At any time, if:

   a. The mobilehome is endangered by a Peril Insured Against; and

   b. Removal is necessary to avoid damage,

we will pay the reasonable expense you incur, not to exceed $500, for its removal and return. No deductible applies to this expense.

11. Ordinance Or Law

This Additional Coverage does not apply.

SECTION I – CONDITIONS

C. Loss Settlement

Paragraph **1.b.** is deleted and replaced by the following:

   b. Awnings, outdoor antennas and outdoor equipment, whether or not attached to buildings; and

D. Loss To A Pair Or Set

The following paragraph is added:

Pay in any loss involving part of a series of pieces or panels, the reasonable cost to:

   a. Repair or replace the damaged part to match the remainder as closely as possible; or

b. Provide an acceptable decorative effect or use as conditions warrant. However, we:

(1) Do not guarantee the availability of replacements; and

(2) We will not be liable, in the event of:

(a) Damage to; or

(b) Loss of;

a part, for the value, repair or replacement of the entire series of pieces or panels.

K. Mortgage Clause

The following paragraph is added:

6. The word "mortgagee" includes lienholder.

All other provisions of this policy apply.

 MH 04 01 10 00

POLICY NUMBER:

HOMEOWNERS
HO 04 77 10 00

THIS ENDORSEMENT CHANGES THE POLICY. PLEASE READ IT CAREFULLY.

ORDINANCE OR LAW
INCREASED AMOUNT OF COVERAGE

SCHEDULE*

New Total Percentage Amount:

*Entry may be left blank if shown elsewhere in this policy for this coverage.

SECTION I – PROPERTY COVERAGES

ADDITIONAL COVERAGES

11. Ordinance Or Law

The total limit of liability that applies:

a. To Coverage **A**, or

b. For Form **HO 00 04**, to Building Additions And Alterations;

is increased from 10% to the percentage amount shown in the Schedule above.

This is Additional Coverage **10.** in Form **HO 00 06.**

All other provisions of this policy apply.

POLICY NUMBER:

HOMEOWNERS
HO 04 48 10 00

THIS ENDORSEMENT CHANGES THE POLICY. PLEASE READ IT CAREFULLY.

OTHER STRUCTURES ON THE RESIDENCE PREMISES
INCREASED LIMITS

SCHEDULE*

Description Of Structure And Additional Limit Of Liability

*Entries may be left blank if shown elsewhere in this policy for this coverage.

SECTION I – PROPERTY COVERAGES

COVERAGE B – OTHER STRUCTURES

We cover each structure that is:

1. On the "residence premises"; and
2. Described in the Schedule above;

for the additional limit of liability shown in the Schedule for that structure.

The limit shown is in addition to the Coverage **B** limit of liability.

Each additional limit of liability shown applies only to that described structure.

All other provisions of this policy apply.

HOMEOWNERS
HO 04 90 10 00

THIS ENDORSEMENT CHANGES THE POLICY. PLEASE READ IT CAREFULLY.

PERSONAL PROPERTY REPLACEMENT COST LOSS SETTLEMENT

A. Eligible Property

1. Covered losses to the following property are settled at replacement cost at the time of the loss:

   a. Coverage **C**; and

   b. If covered in this policy:

      (1) Awnings, outdoor antennas and outdoor equipment; and

      (2) Carpeting and household appliances;

      whether or not attached to buildings.

2. This method of loss settlement will also apply to the following articles or classes of property if they are separately described and specifically insured in this policy and not subject to agreed value loss settlement:

   a. Jewelry;

   b. Furs and garments:

      (1) Trimmed with fur; or

      (2) Consisting principally of fur;

   c. Cameras, projection machines, films and related articles of equipment;

   d. Musical equipment and related articles of equipment;

   e. Silverware, silver-plated ware, goldware, gold-plated ware and pewterware, but excluding:

      (1) Pens or pencils;

      (2) Flasks;

      (2) Smoking implements; or

      (3) Jewelry; and

   f. Golfer's equipment meaning golf clubs, golf clothing and golf equipment.

   Personal Property Replacement Cost loss settlement will not apply to other classes of property separately described and specifically insured.

B. Ineligible Property

Property listed below is not eligible for replacement cost loss settlement. Any loss will be settled at actual cash value at the time of loss but not more than the amount required to repair or replace.

1. Antiques, fine arts, paintings and similar articles of rarity or antiquity which cannot be replaced.

2. Memorabilia, souvenirs, collectors items and similar articles whose age or history contribute to their value.

3. Articles not maintained in good or workable condition.

4. Articles that are outdated or obsolete and are stored or not being used.

C. Replacement Cost Loss Settlement Condition

The following loss settlement condition applies to all property described in **A.** above:

1. We will pay no more than the least of the following amounts:

   a. Replacement cost at the time of loss without deduction for depreciation;

   b. The full cost of repair at the time of loss;

   c. The limit of liability that applies to Coverage **C,** if applicable;

   d. Any applicable special limits of liability stated in this policy; or

   e. For loss to any item described in **A.2.a. - f.** above, the limit of liability that applies to the item.

2. If the cost to repair or replace the property described in **A.** above is more than $500, we will pay no more than the actual cash value for the loss until the actual repair or replacement is complete.

3. You may make a claim for loss on an actual cash value basis and then make claim for any additional liability in accordance with this endorsement provided you notify us of your intent to do so within 180 days after the date of loss.

All other provisions of this policy apply.

HOMEOWNERS
HO 04 95 10 00

THIS ENDORSEMENT CHANGES THE POLICY. PLEASE READ IT CAREFULLY.

WATER BACK UP AND SUMP DISCHARGE OR OVERFLOW

A. Coverage

We insure, up to $5,000, for direct physical loss, not caused by the negligence of an "insured", to property covered under Section I caused by water, or water-borne material, which:

1. Backs up through sewers or drains; or

2. Overflows or is discharged from a:

    a. Sump, sump pump; or

    b. Related equipment;

    even if such overflow or discharge results from mechanical breakdown. This coverage does not apply to direct physical loss of the sump pump, or related equipment, which is caused by mechanical breakdown.

This coverage does not increase the limits of liability for Coverages **A, B, C** or **D** stated in the Declarations.

B. Section I – Perils Insured Against

With respect to the coverage described in **A.** above, Paragraph:

A.2.c.(6)(b) in Form **HO 00 03;**

A.2.e.(2) in Form **HO 00 05;**

2.j.(2) in Endorsement **HO 05 24;**

3.j.(2) in Endorsement **HO 17 31;** and

2.c.(6)(b) in Endorsement **HO 17 32;**

is deleted and replaced by the following:

Latent defect, inherent vice, or any quality in property that causes it to damage or destroy itself;

C. Special Deductible

The following replaces any other deductible provision in this policy with respect to loss covered under this endorsement.

We will pay only that part of the total of all loss payable under Section **I** that exceeds $250. No other deductible applies to this coverage. This deductible does not apply with respect to Coverage **D** – Loss of Use.

D. Exclusion

The Water Damage exclusion is deleted and replaced by the following:

Water Damage, meaning:

a. Flood, surface water, waves, tidal water, overflow of a body of water, or spray from any of these, whether or not driven by wind;

b. Water, or water-borne material, which:

    (1) Backs up through sewers or drains; or

    (2) Overflows or is discharged from a sump, sump pump or related equipment;

    as a direct or indirect result of flood; or

c. Water, or water-borne material, below the surface of the ground, including water which:

    (1) Exerts pressure on; or

    (2) Seeps or leaks through;

    a building, sidewalk, driveway, foundation, swimming pool or other structure;

caused by or resulting from human or animal forces or any act of nature.

Direct loss by fire or explosion resulting from water damage is covered.

All other provisions of this policy apply.

HOMEOWNERS
HO 04 98 10 00

THIS ENDORSEMENT CHANGES THE POLICY. PLEASE READ IT CAREFULLY.

REFRIGERATED PROPERTY COVERAGE

A. Definitions

The following definition is added:

"Loss of power" means the complete or partial interruption of electric power due to conditions beyond an "insured's" control.

B. Coverage

1. We insure, for up to $500, covered property stored in freezers or refrigerators on the "residence premises" for direct loss caused by:

   a. "Loss of power" to the refrigeration unit. "Loss of power" must be caused by damage to:

      (1) Generating equipment; or

      (2) Transmitting equipment; or

   b. Mechanical failure of the unit which stores the property.

2. Coverage will apply only if you have maintained the refrigeration unit in proper working condition immediately prior to the loss.

3. This endorsement does not increase the limit of liability for Coverage **C.**

C. Special Deductible

The following will replace any other deductible provision in this policy with respect to loss covered under this endorsement:

We will pay only that part of the total of all loss payable that exceeds $100. No other deductible applies to this coverage.

D. Exception To Power Failure Exclusion

The Power Failure exclusion does not apply to this coverage.

All other provisions of this policy apply.

POLICY NUMBER:

HOMEOWNERS
HO 04 61 10 00

THIS ENDORSEMENT CHANGES THE POLICY. PLEASE READ IT CAREFULLY.

SCHEDULED PERSONAL PROPERTY ENDORSEMENT

SCHEDULE*

	Class Of Personal Property	Amount Of Insurance	Premium
1.	**Jewelry,** as scheduled below.	$	$
2.	**Furs** and garments trimmed with fur or consisting principally of fur, as scheduled below.		
3.	**Cameras,** projection machines, films and related articles of equipment, as listed below.		
4.	**Musical instruments** and related articles of equipment, as listed below. You agree not to perform with these instruments for pay unless specifically provided under this policy.		
5.	**Silverware,** silver-plated ware, goldware, gold-plated ware and pewterware, but excluding pens, pencils, flasks, smoking implements or jewelry.		
6.	**Golfer's equipment** meaning golf clubs, golf clothing and golf equipment.		
7.a.	**Fine Arts,** as scheduled below. This premium is based on your statement that the property insured is located at the following address: at at	Total Fine Arts Amount $	
7.b.	For an additional premium, Paragraph **5.b.** under **C.** Perils Insured Against is deleted only for the articles marked with a double asterisk (**) in the schedule below.	Amount of **7.b.** only $	
8.	**Postage Stamps**		
9.	**Rare and Current Coins**		

Article Or Property	Description	Amount Of Insurance

THE AMOUNTS SHOWN FOR EACH ITEM IN THIS SCHEDULE ARE LIMITED BY THE LOSS SETTLEMENT CONDITION IN PARAGRAPH F.2.

*Entries may be left blank if shown elsewhere in this policy for this coverage.

We cover the classes of personal property which are indicated in the Schedule above by an amount of insurance.

This coverage is subject to the:

1. Definitions;

2. Section I – Conditions; and

3. Sections I and II – Conditions;

in the policy and all provisions of this endorsement.

Any deductible stated in this policy does not apply to this coverage.

A. Newly Acquired Property – Jewelry, Furs, Cameras And Musical Instruments Only

1. We cover newly acquired property of a class of property already insured. The lesser of the following limits applies:

   a. 25% of the amount of insurance for that class of property; or

   b. $10,000.

2. When you acquire new property you must:

   a. Report these objects to us within 30 days; and

   b. Pay the additional premium from the date acquired.

B. Newly Acquired Fine Arts

When Fine Arts are scheduled, we cover objects of art acquired during the policy period for their actual cash value. However, we will pay no more than 25% of the amount of insurance for fine arts scheduled. For coverage to apply for newly acquired fine arts you must:

1. Report these objects to us within 90 days; and

2. Pay the additional premium from the date acquired.

C. Perils Insured Against

We insure against risks of direct loss to property described only if that loss is a physical loss to property; however, we do not insure loss caused by any of the following:

1. Wear and tear, gradual deterioration or inherent vice.

2. Insects or vermin.

3. War, including the following and any consequence of any of the following:

   a. Undeclared war, civil war, insurrection, rebellion or revolution;

   b. Warlike act by a military force or military personnel; or

   c. Destruction, seizure or use for a military purpose.

   Discharge of a nuclear weapon will be deemed a warlike act even if accidental.

4. Nuclear Hazard, to the extent set forth in the Nuclear Hazard Clause of Section I – Conditions.

5. If Fine Arts are covered:

   a. Repairing, restoration or retouching process;

   b. Breakage of art glass windows, glassware, statuary, marble, bric-a-brac, porcelains and similar fragile articles. We cover loss by breakage if caused by:

      (1) Fire or lightning;

      (2) Explosion, aircraft or collision;

      (3) Windstorm, earthquake or flood;

      (4) Malicious damage or theft;

      (5) Derailment or overturn of a conveyance.

   We do not insure loss, from any cause, to property on exhibition at fair grounds or premises of national or international expositions unless the premises are covered by this policy.

6. If Postage Stamps or Rare and Current Coins collections are covered:

   a. Fading, creasing, denting, scratching, tearing or thinning;

   b. Transfer of colors, inherent defect, dampness, extremes of temperature, or depreciation;

   c. Being handled or worked on;

   d. The disappearance of individual stamps, coins or other articles unless the item is:

      (1) Described and scheduled with a specific amount of insurance; or

      (2) Mounted in a volume and the page it is attached to is also lost; or

   e. Shipping by mail other than registered mail.

   However, we do not insure loss, from any cause, to property in the custody of transportation companies or not part of a stamp or coin collection.

D. Territorial Limits

We cover the property described worldwide.

E. Special Provisions

1. Fine Arts: You agree that the covered property will be handled by competent packers.

2. Golfer's Equipment includes your other clothing while contained in a locker when you are playing golf. We cover golf balls for loss by fire or burglary provided there are visible marks of forcible entry into the building, room or locker.

HO 04 61 10 00

3. Postage Stamps includes the following owned by or in the custody or control of the "insured":

a. Due, envelope, official, revenue, match and medicine stamps;

b. Covers, locals, reprints, essays, proofs and other philatelic property; or

c. Books, pages and mounting of items in **a.** and **b.**

4. Rare and Current Coins includes the following owned by or in custody or control of the "insured":

a. Medals, paper money, bank notes;

b. Tokens of money and other numismatic property; or

c. Coin albums, containers, frames, cards and display cabinets in use with such collection.

F. Conditions

1. Loss Clause

The amount of insurance under this endorsement will not be reduced except for a total loss of a scheduled article. We will refund the unearned premium applicable to such article after the loss or you may apply it to the premium due for the replacement of the scheduled article.

2. Loss Settlement

Covered property losses are settled as follows:

a. Fine Arts

(1) We will pay, for each article designated in the Schedule, the full amount shown in the Schedule which is agreed to be the value of that article or property. At our request, you will surrender that article or property to us if not lost or stolen.

(2) If the scheduled article or property is a pair or set, or consists of several parts when complete, we will pay the full amount shown in the Schedule for that pair, set or complete article. At our request, you will surrender that article or property to us if not lost or stolen.

(3) In the event lost or stolen property is recovered and we have paid you the full amount shown in the Schedule for that property, you will surrender that property to us.

(4) We will, at your request, sell back to you, at a price you and we agree upon, any class of property or scheduled article you surrendered to us to comply with the terms in (1), (2) or (3) above.

b. POSTAGE STAMPS OR RARE AND CURRENT COIN COLLECTION

IN CASE OF LOSS TO ANY SCHEDULED ITEM, THE AMOUNT TO BE PAID WILL BE DETERMINED IN ACCORDANCE WITH PARAGRAPH 2.c. OTHER PROPERTY.

WHEN COINS OR STAMPS ARE COVERED ON A BLANKET BASIS, WE WILL PAY THE CASH MARKET VALUE AT TIME OF LOSS BUT NOT MORE THAN $1,000 ON ANY UNSCHEDULED COIN COLLECTION NOR MORE THAN $250 FOR ANY ONE STAMP, COIN OR INDIVIDUAL ARTICLE OR ANY ONE PAIR, STRIP, BLOCK, SERIES SHEET, COVER, FRAME OR CARD.

WE WILL NOT PAY A GREATER PROPORTION OF ANY LOSS ON BLANKET PROPERTY THAN THE AMOUNT INSURED ON BLANKET PROPERTY BEARS TO THE CASH MARKET VALUE AT TIME OF LOSS.

c. OTHER PROPERTY

(1) THE VALUE OF THE PROPERTY INSURED IS NOT AGREED UPON BUT WILL BE ASCERTAINED AT THE TIME OF LOSS OR DAMAGE. WE WILL NOT PAY MORE THAN THE LEAST OF THE FOLLOWING AMOUNTS:

(a) THE ACTUAL CASH VALUE OF THE PROPERTY AT THE TIME OF LOSS OR DAMAGE;

(b) THE AMOUNT FOR WHICH THE PROPERTY COULD REASONABLY BE EXPECTED TO BE REPAIRED TO ITS CONDITION IMMEDIATELY PRIOR TO LOSS;

(c) THE AMOUNT FOR WHICH THE ARTICLE COULD REASONABLY BE EXPECTED TO BE REPLACED WITH ONE SUBSTANTIALLY IDENTICAL TO THE ARTICLE LOST OR DAMAGED; OR

(d) THE AMOUNT OF INSURANCE.

(2) THE ACTUAL CASH VALUE CONDITION IN PARAGRAPH (1)(a) ABOVE DOES NOT APPLY IF, AT THE TIME OF LOSS, COVERAGE C – PERSONAL PROPERTY COVERED IN THE POLICY TO WHICH THIS ENDORSEMENT IS ATTACHED IS SUBJECT TO REPLACEMENT COST LOSS SETTLEMENT.

3. PAIR, SET OR PARTS OTHER THAN FINE ARTS

a. LOSS TO A PAIR OR SET

IN CASE OF A LOSS TO A PAIR OR SET WE MAY ELECT TO:

(1) REPAIR OR REPLACE ANY PART TO RESTORE THE PAIR OR SET TO ITS VALUE BEFORE THE LOSS; OR

(2) PAY THE DIFFERENCE BETWEEN ACTUAL CASH VALUE OF THE PROPERTY BEFORE AND AFTER THE LOSS.

b. PARTS

IN CASE OF A LOSS TO ANY PART OF COVERED PROPERTY, CONSISTING OF SEVERAL PARTS WHEN COMPLETE, WE WILL PAY FOR THE VALUE OF THE PART LOST OR DAMAGED.

 HO 04 61 10 00

HOMEOWNERS
HO 04 99 10 00

THIS ENDORSEMENT CHANGES THE POLICY. PLEASE READ IT CAREFULLY.

SINKHOLE COLLAPSE

A. Definitions

The following definition is added:

"Sinkhole collapse" means actual physical damage:

1. Arising out of; or

2. Caused by;

sudden settlement or collapse of the earth supporting such property. The settlement or collapse must result from subterranean voids created by the action of water on limestone or similar rock formations.

B. Coverage

We insure for direct physical loss to property covered under Section I caused by "sinkhole collapse".

C. Exception To The Earth Movement Exclusion

The Earth Movement Exclusion does not apply to "sinkhole collapse".

All other provisions of this policy apply.

HOMEOWNERS
HO 04 56 10 00

THIS ENDORSEMENT CHANGES THE POLICY. PLEASE READ IT CAREFULLY.

SPECIAL LOSS SETTLEMENT
FORMS HO 00 02, HO 00 03 AND HO 00 05 ONLY

SCHEDULE*

Percentage Amount Of Full Replacement Cost:

*Entry may be left blank if shown elsewhere in this policy for this coverage.

SECTION I – CONDITIONS

Paragraph **C. Loss Settlement** is deleted and replaced by the following:

C. Loss Settlement

In this Condition **C.**, the terms "cost to repair or replace" and "replacement cost" do not include the increased costs incurred to comply with the enforcement of any ordinance or law, except to the extent that coverage for these increased costs is provided in Additional Coverage **E.11.** Ordinance Or Law. Covered property losses are settled as follows:

1. Property of the following type:

   a. Personal property;

   b. Awnings, carpeting, household appliances, outdoor antennas and outdoor equipment, whether or not attached to buildings;

   c. Structures that are not buildings; and

   d. Grave markers, including mausoleums;

   at actual cash value at the time of loss but not more than the amount required to repair or replace.

2. Buildings covered under Coverage **A** or **B** at replacement cost without deduction for depreciation, subject to the following:

   a. If, at the time of loss, the amount of insurance in this policy on the damaged building is equal to or more than the percentage amount of the full replacement cost of the building immediately before the loss, shown in the Schedule above, we will pay the cost to repair or replace, after application of any deductible and without deduction for depreciation, but not more than the least of the following amounts:

   (1) The limit of liability under this policy that applies to the building;

   (2) The replacement cost of that part of the building damaged with material of like kind and quality and for like use; or

   (3) The necessary amount actually spent to repair or replace the damaged building.

   If the building is rebuilt at a new premises, the cost described in **(2)** above is limited to the cost which would have been incurred if the building had been built at the original premises.

   b. If, at the time of loss, the amount of insurance in this policy on the damaged building is less than the percentage amount of the full replacement cost of the building immediately before the loss, shown in the Schedule, we will pay the greater of the following amounts, but not more than the limit of liability under this policy that applies to the building:

   (1) The actual cash value of that part of the building damaged; or

   (2) That proportion of the cost to repair or replace, after application of any deductible and without deduction for depreciation, that part of the building damaged, which the total amount of insurance in this policy on the damaged building bears to the percentage of the full replacement cost of the building shown in the Schedule.

c. To determine the amount of insurance required to equal the percentage amount of the full replacement cost of the building immediately before the loss, shown in the Schedule, do not include the value of:

(1) Excavations, footings, foundations, piers, or any other structures or devices that support all or part of the building, which are below the undersurface of the lowest basement floor; or

(2) Those supports in (1) above which are below the surface of the ground inside the foundation walls, if there is no basement; and

(3) Underground flues, pipes, wiring and drains.

d. We will pay no more than the actual cash value of the damage until actual repair or replacement is complete. Once actual repair or replacement is complete, we will settle the loss according to the provisions of **2.a.** and **b.** above.

However, if the cost to repair or replace the damage is both:

(1) Less than 5% of the amount of insurance in this policy on the building; and

(2) Less than $2,500;

we will settle the loss according to the provisions of **2.a.** and **b.** above whether or not actual repair or replacement is complete.

e. You may disregard the replacement cost loss settlement provisions and make claim under this policy for loss to buildings on an actual cash value basis. You may then make claim for any additional liability according to the provisions of this Condition **C.** Loss Settlement, provided you notify us of your intent to do so within 180 days after the date of loss.

All other provisions on this policy apply.

 HO 04 56 10 00

HOMEOWNERS
HO 05 24 10 00

THIS ENDORSEMENT CHANGES THE POLICY. PLEASE READ IT CAREFULLY.

SPECIAL PERSONAL PROPERTY COVERAGE
FORM HO 00 04 ONLY

AGREEMENT

We agree to provide the special personal property coverage in this endorsement with the understanding that:

1. You occupy the "residence premises" which contains the covered property; and

2. Such residence is not rented or sublet to another.

SECTION I – PROPERTY COVERAGES

A. Coverage C – Personal Property

  3. Special Limits Of Liability

    Categories **e.**, **f.**, and **g.** are deleted and replaced by the following:

    e. $1,500 for loss by theft, misplacing or losing of jewelry, watches, furs, precious and semiprecious stones.

    f. $2,500 for loss by theft, misplacing or losing of firearms and related equipment.

    g. $2,500 for loss by theft, misplacing or losing of silverware, silver-plated ware, goldware, gold-plated ware, platinumware, platinum-plated ware and pewterware. This includes flatware, hollowware, tea sets, trays and trophies made of or including silver, gold or pewter.

C. Additional Coverages

  With respect to Coverage **C**, Paragraph **8.** Collapse is deleted.

SECTION I – PERILS INSURED AGAINST

This section is deleted and replaced by the following:

We insure against risk of direct physical loss to property described in Coverage **C**.

We do not insure, however, for loss:

1. Excluded under Section I – Exclusions;

2. Caused by:

  a. Freezing of a plumbing, heating, air conditioning or automatic fire protective sprinkler system or of a household appliance, or by discharge, leakage or overflow from within the system or appliance caused by freezing. This provision does not apply if you have used reasonable care to:

    (1) Maintain heat in the building; or

    (2) Shut off the water supply and drain all systems and appliances of water;

    However, if the building is protected by an automatic fire protective sprinkler system, you must use reasonable care to continue the water supply and maintain heat in the building for coverage to apply.

    For purposes of this provision a plumbing system or household appliance does not include a sump, sump pump or related equipment or a roof drain, gutter, downspout or similar fixtures or equipment;

  b. Freezing, thawing, pressure or weight of water or ice, whether driven by wind or not, to a:

    (1) Fence, pavement, patio or swimming pool;

    (2) Footing, foundation, bulkhead, wall or any other structure or device that supports all or part of a building or other structure; or

    (3) Retaining wall or bulkhead that does not support all or part of a building or other structure; or

    (4) Pier, wharf or dock;

  c. Theft in or to a dwelling under construction, or of materials and supplies for use in the construction until the dwelling is finished and occupied;

  d. Mold, fungus or wet rot. However, we do insure for loss caused by mold, fungus or wet rot that is hidden within the walls or ceilings or beneath the floors or above the ceilings of a structure if such loss results from the accidental discharge or overflow of water or steam from within:

    (1) A plumbing, heating, air conditioning or automatic fire protective sprinkler system, or a household appliance, on the "residence premises" or

    (2) A storm drain, or water, steam or sewer pipes, off the "residence premises".

    For the purposes of this provision, a plumbing system or household appliance does not include a sump, sump pump or related equipment or a roof drain, gutter, downspout or similar fixtures or equipment;

e. Breakage of eyeglasses, glassware, statuary, marble, bric-a-brac, porcelains and similar fragile articles other than jewelry, watches, bronzes, cameras and photographic lenses.

There is coverage for breakage of the property by or resulting from:

(1) Fire, lightning, windstorm, hail;

(2) Smoke, other than smoke from agricultural smudging or industrial operations;

(3) Explosion, riot, civil commotion;

(4) Aircraft, vehicles, vandalism and malicious mischief;

(5) Collapse of a building or any part of a building;

(6) Water not otherwise excluded;

(7) Theft or attempted theft; or

(8) Sudden and accidental tearing apart, cracking, burning or bulging of:

(a) A steam or hot water heating system;

(b) An air conditioning or automatic fire protective sprinkler system; or

(c) An appliance for heating water;

f. Dampness of atmosphere or extremes of temperature unless the direct cause of loss is rain, snow, sleet or hail;

g. Refinishing, renovating or repairing property other than watches, jewelry and furs;

h. Collision, other than collision with a land vehicle, sinking, swamping or stranding of watercraft, including their trailers, furnishings, equipment and outboard engines or motors;

i. Acts or decisions, including the failure to act or decide, of any person, group, organization or governmental body; or

j. Any of the following:

(1) Wear and tear, marring, deterioration;

(2) Mechanical breakdown, latent defect, inherent vice, or any quality in property that causes it to damage or destroy itself;

(3) Smog, rust or other corrosion, or dry rot;

(4) Smoke from agricultural smudging or industrial operations;

(5) Discharge, dispersal, seepage, migration, release or escape of pollutants unless the discharge, dispersal, seepage, migration, release or escape is itself caused by one or more of the Perils Insured Against that would apply under Coverage **C** of the policy form if this endorsement were not attached to the policy form.

Pollutants means any solid, liquid, gaseous or thermal irritant or contaminant, including smoke, vapor, soot, fumes, acids, alkalis, chemicals and waste. Waste includes materials to be recycled, reconditioned or reclaimed;

(6) Settling, shrinking, bulging or expansion, including resultant cracking, of bulkheads, pavements, patios, footings, foundations, walls, floors, roofs or ceilings;

(7) Birds, vermin, rodents or insects; or

(8) Animals owned or kept by an "insured".

Exception To 3.j.

Unless the loss is otherwise excluded, we cover loss to property covered under Coverage **C** resulting from an accidental discharge or overflow of water or steam from within a:

(a) Storm drain, or water, steam or sewer pipe, off the "residence premises"; or

(b) Plumbing, heating, air conditioning or automatic fire protective sprinkler system or household appliance on the "residence premises".

We do not cover loss to the system or appliance from which this water or steam escaped.

For the purposes of this provision, a plumbing system or household appliance does not include a sump, sump pump or related equipment or a roof drain, gutter, down spout or similar fixtures or equipment.

Section I – Exclusion 3. Water Damage, Paragraphs **a.** and **c.** that apply to surface water and water below the surface of the ground, do not apply to loss by water covered under Paragraphs **2.d.** and **j.** above.

Under Paragraphs **2.a.** through **d.**, **i.** and **j.** above, any ensuing loss to property described in Coverage **C** not precluded by any other provision in this policy is covered.

SECTION I – EXCLUSIONS

3. Water Damage

The following paragraphs are added:

This exclusion does not apply to property described in Coverage **C** that is away from a premises or location owned, rented, occupied or controlled by an "insured".

This exclusion applies to property described in Coverage **C** that is on a premises or location owned, rented, occupied or controlled by an "insured" even if weather conditions contribute in any way to produce the loss.

All other provisions of this policy apply.

 HO 05 24 10 00

HOMEOWNERS
HO 04 14 10 00

THIS ENDORSEMENT CHANGES THE POLICY. PLEASE READ IT CAREFULLY.

SPECIAL COMPUTER COVERAGE
ALL FORMS EXCEPT HO 00 05, HO 00 04 WITH HO 05 24 AND HO 00 06 WITH HO 17 31

DEFINITIONS

With respect to the coverage provided by this endorsement, "computer equipment" means:

1. Computer hardware, software, operating systems or networks; and

2. Other electronic parts, equipment or systems solely designed for use with or connected to equipment in **1.** above

SECTION I – PERILS INSURED AGAINST

With respect to "computer equipment" defined above, the Perils Insured Against which apply to **Coverage C – Personal Property** are deleted and replaced by the following:

1. We cover an "insured's" "computer equipment", as defined in this endorsement, against risk of direct physical loss.

2. We do not insure, however, for loss:

  a. Excluded under Section I – Exclusions.

  b. Caused by:

    (1) Freezing of a plumbing, heating, air conditioning or automatic fire protective sprinkler system or of a household appliance, or by discharge, leakage or overflow from within the system or appliance caused by freezing. This provision does not apply if you have used reasonable care to:

      (a) Maintain heat in the building; or

      (b) Shut off the water supply and drain all systems and appliances of water;

    However, if the building is protected by an automatic fire protective sprinkler system, you must use reasonable care to continue the water supply and maintain heat in the building for coverage to apply.

    For purposes of this provision a plumbing system or household appliance does not include a sump, sump pump or related equipment or a roof drain, gutter, downspout or similar fixtures or equipment.

    (2) Theft in or to a dwelling under construction, until the dwelling is finished and occupied;

    (3) Mold, fungus or wet rot;

    (4) Vandalism and malicious mischief, and any ensuing loss caused by any intentional and wrongful act committed in the course of the vandalism or malicious mischief, if the dwelling has been vacant for more than 60 consecutive days immediately before the loss. A dwelling being constructed is not considered vacant;

    (5) Dampness of atmosphere or extremes of temperature unless the direct cause of loss is rain, snow, sleet or hail;

    (6) Refinishing, renovating or repairing property;

    (7) Collision, other than collision with a land vehicle, sinking, swamping or stranding of watercraft of all types, including their trailers, furnishings, equipment and outboard engines or motors;

    (8) Acts or decisions, including the failure to act or decide, of any person, group, organization or governmental body. However, any ensuing loss not excluded or excepted in this policy is covered; or

    (9) Any of the following:

      (a) Wear and tear, marring, deterioration;

      (b) Mechanical breakdown, latent defect, inherent vice, or any quality in property that causes it to damage or destroy itself;

      (c) Smog, rust or other corrosion or dry rot;

      (d) Smoke from agricultural smudging or industrial operations;

      (e) Discharge, dispersal, seepage, migration, release or escape of pollutants unless the discharge, dispersal, seepage, migration, release or escape is itself caused by one or more of the Perils Insured Against that would apply under Coverage **C** of the policy form if this endorsement were not attached to the policy form.

      Pollutants means any solid, liquid, gaseous or thermal irritant or contaminant, including smoke, vapor, soot, fumes, acids, alkalis, chemicals and waste. Waste includes materials to be recycled, reconditioned or reclaimed;

(f) Settling, shrinking, bulging or expansion, including resultant cracking, of bulkheads, pavements, patios, footings, foundations, walls, floors, roofs or ceilings;

(g) Birds, vermin, rodents or insects; or

(h) Animals owned or kept by an "insured".

Exception To b.(9)

Unless the loss is otherwise excluded, we cover loss to "computer equipment" resulting from an accidental discharge or overflow of water or steam from within a:

(i) Storm drain or water, steam or sewer pipe off the "residence premises"; or

(ii) Plumbing, heating, air conditioning or automatic fire protective sprinkler system or household appliance on the "residence premises".

We do not cover loss to the system or appliance from which this water or steam escaped.

For the purposes of this provision, a plumbing system or household appliance does not include a sump, sump pump or related equipment or a roof drain, gutter, down spout or similar fixtures or equipment.

Section I – Water Damage Exclusion Paragraphs **a.** and **c.**, that apply to surface water and water below the surface of the ground, do not apply to loss by water covered under **b.(9)** above.

With respect to the precluded perils in **2.b.(1)** through **(3)** and **b.(9)**, any ensuing loss not precluded by any other provision in this policy is covered.

SPECIAL CONDITIONS

The coverage provided by this endorsement does not:

1. Increase the Coverage **C** limit of liability;

2. Modify the Coverage **C** Special Limits of Liability; or

3. Modify any provision that applies to Coverage **C** Property Not Covered.

All other provisions of this policy apply.

HO 04 14 10 00

HOMEOWNERS
HO 04 94 10 00

THIS ENDORSEMENT CHANGES THE POLICY. PLEASE READ IT CAREFULLY.

WINDSTORM OR HAIL EXCLUSION

SECTION I – PERILS INSURED AGAINST

In all forms, coverage for the peril of windstorm or hail is deleted. However, we do cover for loss of use under Coverage **D.**

SECTION I – EXCLUSIONS

The following exclusion is added. In Forms **HO 00 03** and **HO 00 05,** it is added to Paragraph **A:**

WINDSTORM OR HAIL

However, this exclusion does not apply to direct loss by fire or explosion resulting from windstorm or hail.

All other provisions of this policy apply.

POLICY NUMBER:

HOMEOWNERS
HO 04 12 10 00

THIS ENDORSEMENT CHANGES THE POLICY. PLEASE READ IT CAREFULLY.

INCREASED LIMITS ON BUSINESS PROPERTY

SCHEDULE*

Increase In Limit Of Liability	Total Limit Of Liability

* Entries may be left blank if shown elsewhere in this policy for this coverage.

SECTION I – PROPERTY COVERAGES

Coverage C – Personal Property

3. Special Limits Of Liability

  a. The Special Limit Of Liability in Category **3.h.** that applies to "business" property on the "residence premises" is increased by the Increase In Limit Of Liability shown in the Schedule above.

  This Increase In Limit Of Liability does not apply to "business" property:

  (1) In storage or held:

   a. As a sample; or

   b. For sale or delivery after sale; or

  (2) That pertains to a "business" actually conducted on the "residence premises".

  b. The Special Limit Of Liability in Category **3.i.** that applies to "business" property away from the "residence premises" is increased to an amount that is 20 percent of the Total Limit Of Liability shown in the Schedule.

  The Special Limit Of Liability in Category **3.i.** does not apply to electronic apparatus as described in Categories **3.j.** and **k.**

  This endorsement does not increase the limit of liability for Coverage **C.**

  All other provisions of this policy apply.

HO 04 12 10 00   Copyright, Insurance Services Office, Inc., 1999   **Page 1 of 1**

HOMEOWNERS
HO 17 32 10 00

THIS ENDORSEMENT CHANGES THE POLICY. PLEASE READ IT CAREFULLY.

UNIT-OWNERS COVERAGE A
SPECIAL COVERAGE
FORM HO 00 06 ONLY

SECTION I – PERILS INSURED AGAINST

For Coverage **A**, the Perils Insured Against are deleted and replaced by the following:

PERILS INSURED AGAINST

1. We insure against risk of direct physical loss to property described in Coverage **A**.

2. We do not insure, however, for loss:

   a. Excluded under Section I – Exclusions;

   b. Involving collapse, except as provided in **D.8.** Collapse under Section I – Property Coverages.

   c. Caused by:

   (1) Freezing of a plumbing, heating, air conditioning or automatic fire protective sprinkler system or of a household appliance, or by discharge, leakage or overflow from within the system or appliance caused by freezing. This provision does not apply if you have used reasonable care to:

   (a) Maintain heat in the building; or

   (b) Shut off the water supply and drain all systems and appliances of water.

   However, if the building is protected by an automatic fire protective sprinkler system, you must use reasonable care to continue the water supply and maintain heat in the building for coverage to apply.

   For purposes of this provision a plumbing system or household appliance does not include a sump, sump pump or related equipment or a roof drain, gutter, downspout or similar fixtures or equipment;

   (2) Freezing, thawing, pressure or weight of water or ice, whether driven by wind or not, to a:

   (a) Fence, pavement, patio or swimming pool;

   (b) Footing, foundation, bulkhead, wall, or any other structure or device, that supports all or part of a building or other structure;

   (c) Retaining wall or bulkhead that does not support all or part of a building or other structure; or

   (d) Pier, wharf or dock;

   (3) Theft in or to a unit under construction, or of materials and supplies for use in the construction until the unit is finished and occupied;

   (4) Vandalism and malicious mischief, and any ensuing loss caused by any intentional and wrongful act committed in the course of the vandalism or malicious mischief, if the building containing the "residence premises" has been vacant for more than 60 consecutive days immediately before the loss. A building being constructed is not considered vacant;

   (5) Mold, fungus or wet rot. However, we do insure for loss caused by mold, fungus or wet rot that is hidden within the walls or ceilings or beneath the floors or above the ceilings of a structure if such loss results from the accidental discharge or overflow of water or steam from within:

   (a) A plumbing, heating, air conditioning or automatic fire protective sprinkler system, or a household appliance, on the "residence premises"; or

   (b) A storm drain, or water, steam or sewer pipes, off the "residence premises".

   For the purpose of this provision, a plumbing system or household appliance does not include a sump, sump pump or related equipment or a roof drain, gutter, downspout or similar fixtures or equipment; or

   (6) Any of the following:

   (a) Wear and tear, marring, deterioration;

   (b) Mechanical breakdown, latent defect, inherent vice, or any quality in property that causes it to damage or destroy itself;

(c) Smog, rust or other corrosion or dry rot;

(d) Smoke from agricultural smudging or industrial operations;

(e) Discharge, dispersal, seepage, migration, release or escape of pollutants unless the discharge, dispersal, seepage, migration, release or escape is itself caused by a Peril Insured Against named under Coverage **C** of this policy.

Pollutants means any solid, liquid, gaseous or thermal irritant or contaminant, including smoke, vapor, soot, fumes, acids, alkalis, chemicals and waste. Waste includes materials to be recycled, reconditioned or reclaimed;

(f) Settling, shrinking, bulging or expansion, including resultant cracking, of bulkheads, pavements, patios, footings, foundations, walls, floors, roofs or ceilings;

(g) Birds, vermin, rodents, or insects; or

(h) Animals owned or kept by an "insured".

Exception To c.(6)

Unless the loss is otherwise excluded, we cover loss to property covered under Coverage **A** resulting from an accidental discharge or overflow of water or steam from within a:

(i) Storm drain, or water, steam or sewer pipe, off the "residence premises"; or

(ii) Plumbing, heating, air conditioning or automatic fire protective sprinkler system or household appliance on the "residence premises". This includes the cost to tear out and replace any part of a building, or other structure owned solely by you, at the location of the "residence premises", but only when necessary to repair the system or appliance. However, such tear out and replacement coverage only applies to other structures if the water or steam causes actual damage to a building owned solely by you at the location of the "residence premises".

We do not cover loss to the system or appliance from which this water or steam escaped.

For the purposes of this provision, a plumbing system or household appliance does not include a sump, sump pump or related equipment or a roof drain, gutter, down spout or similar fixtures or equipment.

Section I – Exclusion **3.** Water Damage, Paragraphs **a.** and **c.** that apply to surface water and water below the surface of the ground, do not apply to loss by water covered under **c.(5)** and **(6)** above.

Under **2.b.** and **c.** above, any ensuing loss to property described in Coverage **A** not precluded by any other provision in this policy is covered.

SECTION I – EXCLUSIONS

The following exclusions are added:

We do not insure for loss to property described in Coverage **A** caused by any of the following. However, any ensuing loss to property described in Coverage **A** not precluded by any other provision in this policy is covered.

1. Weather conditions. However, this exclusion only applies if weather conditions contribute in any way with a cause or event excluded in Section I – Exclusions, other than Exclusions **2.** and **3.** below, to produce the loss;

2. Acts or decisions, including the failure to act or decide, of any person, group, organization or governmental body; or

3. Faulty, inadequate or defective:

a. Planning, zoning, development, surveying, siting;

b. Design, specifications, workmanship, repair, construction, renovation, remodeling, grading, compaction;

c. Materials used in repair, construction, renovation or remodeling; or

d. Maintenance;

of part or all of any property whether on or off the "residence premises".

All other provisions of this policy apply.

 HO 17 32 10 00

HOMEOWNERS
HO 17 31 10 00

THIS ENDORSEMENT CHANGES THE POLICY. PLEASE READ IT CAREFULLY.

UNIT-OWNERS COVERAGE C
SPECIAL COVERAGE
FORM HO 00 06 ONLY

AGREEMENT

We agree to provide the Special Coverage in this endorsement with the understanding that you occupy the unit in which the property covered under Coverage **C** is located.

SECTION I – PROPERTY COVERAGES

B. Coverage C – Personal Property

   3. Special Limits Of Liability

   Categories **e.**, **f.** and **g.** are deleted and replaced by the following:

   e. $1,500 for loss by theft, misplacing or losing of jewelry, watches, furs, precious and semiprecious stones.

   f. $2,500 for loss by theft, misplacing or losing of firearms and related equipment.

   g. $2,500 for loss by theft, misplacing or losing of silverware, silver-plated ware, goldware, gold-plated ware, platinumware, platinum-plated ware and pewterware. This includes flatware, hollowware, tea sets, trays and trophies made of or including silver, gold or pewter.

D. Additional Coverages

   8. Collapse

   Paragraph **b.(1)** is deleted and replaced by the following:

   (1) The Perils Insured Against under Coverage **A;**

   With respect to Coverage **C**, Paragraph **8. Collapse** is deleted.

SECTION I – PERILS INSURED AGAINST

For Coverage **C**, the Perils Insured Against are deleted and replaced by the following:

We insure against risk of direct physical loss to property described in Coverage **C.**

We do not insure, however, for loss:

1. Excluded under Section I – Exclusions;

2. To property in a unit regularly rented or held for rental to others by you;

3. Caused by:

   a. Freezing of a plumbing, heating, air conditioning or automatic fire protective sprinkler system or of a household appliance, or by discharge, leakage or overflow from within the system or appliance caused by freezing. This provision does not apply if you have used reasonable care to:

   (1) Maintain heat in the building; or

   (2) Shut off the water supply and drain all systems and appliances of water.

   However, if the building is protected by an automatic fire protective sprinkler system, you must use reasonable care to continue the water supply and maintain heat in the building for coverage to apply.

   For purposes of this provision a plumbing system or household appliance does not include a sump, sump pump or related equipment or a roof drain, gutter, downspout or similar fixtures or equipment;

   b. Freezing, thawing, pressure or weight of water or ice, whether driven by wind or not, to a:

   (1) Fence, pavement, patio or swimming pool;

   (2) Footing, foundation, bulkhead, wall, or any other structure or device, that supports all or part of a building or other structure;

   (3) Retaining wall or bulkhead that does not support all or part of a building or other structure; or

   (4) Pier, wharf or dock;

   c. Theft in or to a dwelling under construction, or of materials and supplies for use in the construction until the dwelling is finished and occupied;

HO 17 31 10 00   Copyright, Insurance Services Office, Inc., 1999   **Page 1 of 3**

d. Mold, fungus or wet rot. However, we do insure for loss caused by mold, fungus or wet rot that is hidden within the walls or ceilings or beneath the floors or above the ceilings of a structure if such loss results from the accidental discharge or overflow of water or steam from within:

(1) A plumbing, heating, air conditioning or automatic fire protective sprinkler system, or a household appliance, on the "residence premises"; or

(2) A storm drain, or water, steam or sewer pipes, off the "residence premises".

For the purpose of this provision, a plumbing system or household appliance does not include a sump, sump pump or related equipment or a roof drain, gutter, downspout or similar fixtures or equipment;

e. Breakage of eyeglasses, glassware, statuary, marble, bric-a-brac, porcelains and similar fragile articles other than jewelry, watches, bronzes, cameras and photographic lenses.

There is coverage for breakage of the property by or resulting from:

(1) Fire, lightning, windstorm, hail;

(2) Smoke, other than smoke from agricultural smudging or industrial operations;

(3) Explosion, riot, civil commotion;

(4) Aircraft, vehicles, vandalism and malicious mischief;

(5) Collapse of a building or any part of a building;

(6) Water not otherwise excluded;

(7) Theft or attempted theft; or

(8) Sudden and accidental tearing apart, cracking, burning or bulging of:

(a) A steam or hot water heating system;

(b) An air conditioning or automatic fire protective sprinkler system; or

(c) An appliance for heating water;

f. Dampness of atmosphere or extremes of temperature unless the direct cause of loss is rain, snow, sleet or hail;

g. Refinishing, renovating or repairing property other than watches, jewelry and furs;

h. Collision, other than collision with a land vehicle, sinking, swamping or stranding of watercraft, including their trailers, furnishings, equipment and outboard engines or motors; or

i. Acts or decisions, including the failure to act or decide, of any person, group, organization or governmental body; or

j. Any of the following:

(1) Wear and tear, marring, deterioration;

(2) Mechanical breakdown, latent defect, inherent vice, or any quality in property that causes it to damage or destroy itself;

(3) Smog, rust or other corrosion or dry rot;

(4) Smoke from agricultural smudging or industrial operations;

(5) Discharge, dispersal, seepage, migration, release or escape of pollutants unless the discharge, dispersal, seepage, migration, release or escape is itself caused by one or more of the Perils Insured Against that would apply under Coverage **C** of the policy form if this endorsement were not attached to the policy form.

Pollutants means any solid, liquid, gaseous or thermal irritant or contaminant, including smoke, vapor, soot, fumes, acids, alkalis, chemicals and waste. Waste includes materials to be recycled, reconditioned or reclaimed;

(6) Settling, shrinking, bulging or expansion, including resultant cracking, of bulkheads, pavements, patios, footings, foundations, walls, floors, roofs or ceilings;

(7) Birds, vermin, rodents or insects; or

(8) Animals owned or kept by an "insured".

Exception To 3.j.

Unless the loss is otherwise excluded, we cover loss to property covered under Coverage C resulting from an accidental discharge or overflow of water or steam from within a:

(a) Storm drain, or water, steam or sewer pipe, off the "residence premises"; or

(b) Plumbing, heating, air conditioning or automatic fire protective sprinkler system or household appliance on the "residence premises".

We do not cover loss to the system or appliance from which this water or steam escaped.

For the purposes of this provision, a plumbing system or household appliance does not include a sump, sump pump or related equipment or a roof drain, gutter, down spout or similar fixtures or equipment.

Section **I** – Exclusion **3.** Water Damage, Paragraphs **a.** and **c.** that apply to surface water and water below the surface of the ground, do not apply to loss by water covered under Paragraphs **3.d.** and **j.** above.

     HO 17 31 10 00

Under Paragraphs **3.a.** through **e.**, **i.** and **j.**, any ensuing loss to property described in Coverage **C** not precluded by any other provision in this policy is covered.

SECTION I – EXCLUSIONS

3. Water Damage

The following paragraphs are added:

This exclusion does not apply to property described in Coverage **C** that is away from a premises or location owned, rented, occupied or controlled by an "insured".

This exclusion applies to property described in Coverage **C** that is on a premises or location owned, rented, occupied or controlled by an "insured" even if weather conditions contribute in any way to produce the loss.

All other provisions of this policy apply.

**HOMEOWNERS
HO 17 33 10 00**

THIS ENDORSEMENT CHANGES THE POLICY. PLEASE READ IT CAREFULLY.

UNIT-OWNERS RENTAL TO OTHERS
FORM HO 00 06 ONLY

Coverage provided by this policy is extended to apply while the "residence premises" is regularly rented or held for rental to others.

SECTION I – PROPERTY COVERAGES

B. Coverage C – Personal Property

    4. Property Not Covered

        Paragraph **g.** is deleted and replaced by the following:

        g. Property in an apartment, other than the "residence premises", regularly rented or held for rental to others by an "insured";

SECTION I – PERILS INSURED AGAINST

Under Peril **9.** Theft, Paragraph **b.(3)** is deleted.

SECTION I – EXCLUSIONS

The following exclusion is added:

Theft, from the "residence premises" of:

a. Money, bank notes, bullion, gold, goldware, gold-plated ware, silver, silverware, silver-plated ware, pewterware, platinum, platinumware, platinum-plated ware, coins, medals, scrip, stored value cards and smart cards;

b. Securities, accounts, deeds, evidences of debt, letters of credit, notes other than bank notes, manuscripts, personal records, passports, tickets and stamps regardless of the medium (such as paper or computer software) on which the material exists; or

c. Jewelry, watches, furs, precious and semiprecious stones.

SECTION II – EXCLUSIONS

Exclusion **E.2.** "Business" is deleted and replaced by the following:

2. "Business"

a. "Bodily injury" or "property damage" arising out of or in connection with a "business" conducted from an "insured location" or engaged in by an "insured", whether or not the "business" is owned or operated by an "insured" or employs an "insured".

b. This Exclusion **E.2.** applies but is not limited to an act or omission, regardless of its nature or circumstance, involving a service or duty rendered, promised, owed, or implied to be provided because of the nature of the "business".

This Exclusion **E.2.** does not apply to the rental or holding for rental of the "residence premises".

All other provisions of this policy apply.